T0288134

SIXTEENTH PRESIDENT-IN-WAITING

SIXTEENTH
PRESIDENT-IN-WAITING

ABRAHAM LINCOLN
AND THE
SPRINGFIELD DISPATCHES
OF HENRY VILLARD,
1860–1861

Edited by Michael Burlingame

Southern Illinois University Press
Carbondale

Southern Illinois University Press
www.siupress.com

21   20   19   18   4   3   2   1

Jacket illustrations: Abraham Lincoln (Library of Congress) and
Henry Villard (Wikimedia Commons).

Library of Congress Cataloging-in-Publication Data
Names: Villard, Henry, 1835–1900, author. | Burlingame, Michael,
  1941– editor.
Title: Sixteenth president-in-waiting : Abraham Lincoln and the
  Springfield dispatches of Henry Villard, 1860–1861 / edited by
  Michael Burlingame.
Description: Carbondale : Southern Illinois University Press, 2018.
  | Includes bibliographical references and index.
Identifiers: LCCN 2017029784 | ISBN 9780809336432 (hardback)
  | ISBN 9780809336449 (ebook)
Subjects: LCSH: Lincoln, Abraham, 1809–1865—Political career
  before 1861—Press coverage. | Presidents—United States—
  Election—1860—Press coverage. | Political campaigns—
  United States—History—19th century—Press coverage. | United
  States—Politics and government—1857–1861—Press coverage.
  | BISAC: HISTORY / United States / 19th Century. | HISTORY /
  United States / Civil War Period (1850–1877). | HISTORY / United
  States / State & Local / Midwest (IA, IL, IN, KS, MI, MN, MO,
  ND, NE, OH, SD, WI). | BIOGRAPHY & AUTOBIOGRAPHY /
  Presidents & Heads of State.
Classification: LCC E457 .V656 2018 | DDC 973.5—dc23 LC record
  available at https://lccn.loc.gov/2017029784

Printed on recycled paper. ♻

This paper meets the requirements of ANSI/NISO Z39.48-1992
(Permanence of Paper) ∞

For Lois, beloved wife-in-waiting

CONTENTS

ACKNOWLEDGMENTS

I AM GRATEFUL to Sheila Sullivan, who heroically and scrupulously typed the manuscript from photocopies of microfilmed newspapers. Many images were difficult to decipher, for the microfilms were not of the highest quality. Thanks to the generosity of Val E. Vaden, the venture capitalist and philanthropist who handsomely endowed the Chancellor Naomi B. Lynn Distinguished Chair in Lincoln Studies at the University of Illinois Springfield (which I hold), I was able not only to hire Sheila but also to help defray the cost of publishing this volume.

The kind editors at Southern Illinois University Press, most notably Sylvia Frank Rodrigue, have supported this project with the same professionalism and encouragement that marked their earlier support of the press's publication of several other Lincoln-related primary source collections that I have edited. All students, scholars, and admirers of Lincoln owe the press a debt of gratitude for publishing so many important books about the sixteenth president, not only documentary editions like this one but also monographs, essay collections, and the extensive Concise Lincoln Library.

The staff of libraries throughout the country—especially at Harvard University's Houghton Library, the New York Public Library, the Connecticut College Library, the Abraham Lincoln Presidential Library, the Brookens Library at the University of Illinois Springfield, and the Library of Congress—have been unfailingly helpful as I worked on this volume and the others.

Finally, I owe more than I can say to the patience, love, and forbearance of the lovely and long-suffering Lois McDonald, my fiancée of thirty years' standing.

SIXTEENTH PRESIDENT-IN-WAITING

INTRODUCTION

BEST KNOWN AS a successful nineteenth-century railroad promoter and financier, German-born Henry Villard (1835–1900) was also "one of the ablest and most conscientious reporters" of the 1860s, as a leading historian of Civil War journalism observed.[1] His most noteworthy reportage dates from late 1860 and early 1861, when he was embedded in Springfield for the three months following Lincoln's election. The scores of dispatches gathered in this volume constitute the most intensive journalistic coverage that Lincoln ever experienced, for Villard filed stories from the Illinois capital almost daily to the New York *Herald,* slightly less often to the Cincinnati *Commercial,* and occasionally to the San Francisco *Bulletin.* Many historians have consulted excerpts of Villard's New York *Herald* dispatches contained in a brief, pamphlet-like 1941 edition compiled by his sons.[2] That slender volume omits much valuable information about Lincoln during the secession winter that appears not only in the complete run of the *Herald* dispatches but also in dozens of others published in the *Commercial* and the *Bulletin.* Articles from those two papers are virtually unknown to historians.[3] Recognizing that their edition of excerpts from the *Herald* was inadequate, Villard's sons intended to issue a complete edition, but their plan fell through.

Villard's dispatches are not only informative but also highly readable; his editor at the Cincinnati *Commercial,* Murat Halstead, noted that Villard's work "had the merits of terse statement, evident sincerity, and reliability. The style was not ambitious and the meaning not obscure. He had a keen eye for essential points of a complex state of facts."[4] The dispatches constitute high-grade ore for the historian's smelter, offering descriptions of Lincoln's appearance, his daily routine, his visitors, and his views, as well as of the Illinois capital. Anyone interested in Lincoln, or the secession crisis, or Springfield will find them highly informative.

VILLARD AND THE LINCOLN-DOUGLAS CAMPAIGN OF 1858

Born Ferdinand Heinrich Gustav Hilgard in Germany in 1835, Villard as an adolescent immigrated to the United States, where he changed his name and worked at various jobs, including journalist.[5] He first encountered Lincoln in 1858, when he covered the Illinois senatorial campaign for a New York paper. Early that year, the twenty-three-year-old Villard left Pennsylvania, where he had been toiling as schoolteacher, and set out for New York. There he called at the office of a large, prosperous Democratic German paper, the *Staats-Zeitung,* for which he had earlier written some freelance pieces. Brimming with self-confidence and eager to become a full-time journalist, he persuaded the editor, Oswald Ottendorfer, to hire him as a special agent to canvass the Midwest, drumming up business for the weekly edition of the paper, collecting overdue bills, and reporting his observations. Frustrated by his lack of success after working a month as a canvasser, he asked to be reassigned as a reporter covering the Lincoln-Douglas campaign in Illinois. Ottendorfer agreed, and Villard promptly went to Chicago.[6]

Because he admired Senator Stephen A. Douglas's opposition to President Buchanan's support for the proslavery Lecompton constitution in Kansas, Villard also offered to submit articles gratis to the pro-Douglas Philadelphia *Press.*[7]

Villard arrived in the Windy City just in time to observe Douglas's tumultuous reception on July 9. The following day he obtained the senator's permission to accompany him during the campaign. (Villard had met briefly with Douglas two years earlier as Villard vainly sought support for a plan to settle young German men in Kansas.) Villard covered the first three debates, held in Ottawa, Freeport, and Jonesboro. At Freeport, he met Lincoln for the first time, and as the campaign wore on, he heard him and Douglas on several other occasions.

In his memoirs, Villard described a memorable encounter he had with Lincoln in late October: He and I met accidentally, about nine o'clock on a hot, sultry evening, at a flag railroad station about twenty miles west of Springfield, on my return from a great meeting at Petersburg in Menard County. He had been driven to the station in a buggy and left there alone. I was already there. The train that we intended to take for Springfield was about due. After vainly waiting for half an hour for its arrival, a thunderstorm compelled us to take refuge in an empty freight-car standing on a side track, there being no buildings of any sort at the station. We squatted down on the floor of the car and fell to talking on all sorts of subjects. It was then and there he told me that, when he was clerking in a country store, his highest political ambition was to be a member of the State Legislature. "Since then, of course," he said laughingly, "I have grown some, but my friends got me into this business [the canvass]. I did not consider myself qualified for the United States Senate, and it took me a long time to persuade myself that I was. Now, to be sure," he continued, with another of his peculiar laughs, "I am convinced that I am good enough for it; but, in spite of it all, I am saying to myself every day: 'It is too big a thing for you; you will never get it.' Mary

[Lincoln's wife] insists, however, that I am going to be Senator and President of the United States, too." These last words he followed with a roar of laughter, with his arms around his knees, and shaking all over with mirth at his wife's ambition. "Just think," he exclaimed, "of such a sucker as me as President!" He then fell to asking questions regarding my antecedents, and expressed some surprise at my fluent use of English after so short a residence in the United States. Next he wanted to know whether it was true that most of the educated people in Germany were "infidels." I answered that they were not openly professed infidels, but such a conclusion might be drawn from the fact that most of them were not church-goers. "I do not wonder at that," he rejoined; "my own inclination is that way." I ventured to give expression to my own disbelief in the doctrine of the Christian church relative to the existence of God, the divinity of Christ, and immortality. This led him to put other questions to me to draw me out. He did not commit himself, but I received the impression that he was of my own way of thinking. . . . Our talk continued till half-past ten, when the belated train arrived. I cherish this accidental rencontre as one of my most precious recollections, since my companion of that night has become one of the greatest figures in history.[8]

But in 1858, Villard described Lincoln far less positively, in part because he had joined Douglas's campaign as a speaker and organizer (roles that Villard did not reveal either in his dispatches or his memoirs). On August 24, he wrote to the senator, deeming himself "as enthusiastic and faithful a supporter of your political claims as any can be found anywhere in the state of Illinois." He reminded the Little Giant that in late July he had gone to Monticello, Illinois (where the campaign officially began), "to receive instructions from you as to the best mode of conducting my part of the canvass." There, he said, he "was received somewhat slightingly" and so "in order to be noticed, I had to urge myself into notice." Despite the cool reception, he obtained Douglas's approval of his scheme to promote the senator's candidacy. Villard then proceeded to Springfield, where he consulted with members of the Illinois Democratic Central Committee, among them Charles Lanphier, editor of the *Illinois State Register* and Douglas's de facto campaign manager. Villard claimed that he soon "went to work, delivered speeches in thirteen different localities; organized clubs, etc."[9]

As a Democratic activist, he delivered pro-Douglas speeches in Peru, Bloomington, Alton, Joliet, Quincy, and elsewhere.[10] At Joliet, he reportedly

surveyed the whole ground occupied by the democratic party at the present time. He took special pains to explain the true position in reference to the slavery question, by a full illustration of the doctrine of

Popular Sovereignty. He also took occasion to reduce the imaginary terrors of the Dred Scott decision, and to show its merits in the true light. He then proceeded to pay a glowing tribute to the talents and achievements of Senator Douglas; to exhort his hearers to exert every nerve to bring about the victory of Democratic principles, the election of democratic candidates, and the return of the great anti-Lecompton champion of the United States Senate, and concluded by denouncing in the strongest terms, the treason and defection of the so called Nationals [i.e., pro-Buchanan, anti-Douglas Democrats].[11]

In August and early September, Villard spent much time in Quincy, giving speeches and reportedly offering to pay anyone who would sign an affidavit alleging that Lincoln had been a member of a Know-Nothing lodge there.[12] (Villard vehemently denied the charge, insisting that he was merely investigating rumors about Lincoln's membership in a Know-Nothing lodge. If they were true, he planned to obtain corroborating affidavits.[13])

Villard left Douglas's employ sometime after the September 15 debate at Jonesboro. In his memoirs, he explained that he had grown so tired of hearing the same speeches over and over again that he returned to Chicago for the duration of the campaign. But in his August 24 letter to Douglas, he said that he intended to quit because he had not been paid: "The only remuneration I have received, is that in a few of the visited places, the Democrats paid my hotel bill. Seeing my services unappreciated, I now propose to let my remaining appointments to go by default & return to the East."[14]

But in fact Villard remained on the campaign trail, submitting reports to the New York *Staats-Zeitung* in early and mid-September. The following month, he became editor of the *Beobachter*, a weekly German paper published in Alton. There he delivered a pro-Douglas speech on October 23.[15] A few days later he covered Lincoln's appearance in Petersburg.

In his memoirs, Villard explained why he was less than enthusiastic about Lincoln: "I believed, with many prominent leaders of the Republican party, that, with regard to separating more effectively the antislavery Northern from the proslavery Southern wing of the Democracy, it would have been better if the reëlection of Douglas had not been opposed." He added that "if Stephen A. Douglas had lived, he would have had a brilliant national career. Freed by the Southern rebellion from all identification with pro-slavery interests, the road would have been open to the highest fame and position for which his unusual talents qualified him."[16]

In reflecting on the 1858 election, he wrote that he was "struck with the efficient party organizations, the skilful tactics of the managers, the remarkable feats of popular oratory, and the earnestness and enthusiasm of the audiences I witnessed. It was a most instructive object-lesson in practical party politics, and filled me with admiration for the Anglo-American method of working out popular destiny" (Memoirs 1:94).

Upon leaving Illinois, Villard was not filled with admiration for Lincoln, however. As he explained in his memoirs:

> Although I found him most approachable, good-natured, and full of wit and humor, I could not take a real personal liking to the man, owing to an inborn weakness for which he was even then notorious and so remained during his great public career. He was inordinately fond of jokes, anecdotes, and stories. He loved to hear them, and still more to tell them himself out of the inexhaustible supply provided by his good memory and his fertile fancy. There would have been no harm in this but for the fact that, the coarser the joke, the lower the anecdote, and the more risky the story, the more he enjoyed them, especially when they were of his own invention. He possessed, moreover, a singular ingenuity in bringing about occasions in conversation for indulgences of this kind. (1:93–94)

Villard added that Lincoln

> often allowed himself altogether too much license in the concoction of the stories. He seemed to be bent upon making his hit by fair means or foul. In other words, he never hesitated to tell a coarse or even outright nasty story, if it served his purpose. All his personal friends could bear testimony on this point. It was a notorious fact that this fondness for low talk clung to him even in the White House. More than once I heard him "with malice aforethought" get off purposely some repulsive fiction in order to rid himself of an uncomfortable caller. Again and again I felt disgust and humiliation that such a person should have been called upon to direct the destinies of a great nation in the direst period of its history. Yet his achievements during the next few years proved him to be one of the great leaders of mankind in adversity, in whom low leanings only set off more strikingly his better qualities. At the time of which I speak, I could not have persuaded myself that the man might possibly possess true greatness of mind and nobility of heart. (1:93–94)

But, he added, "I do not wish to convey the idea . . . that he was mainly given to trivialities and vulgarities in his conversation; for, in spite of his frequent outbreaks of low humor, his was really a very sober and serious nature, and even inclined to gloominess" (1:143–144).

Villard's 1858 dispatches from Illinois are included as an appendix to this volume.

VILLARD IN SPRINGFIELD

In 1859, Villard covered the Pike's Peak gold rush for the San Francisco *Bulletin,* the St. Louis *Missouri Republican,* and the Cincinnati *Commercial.*[17] While returning east from that assignment, he by chance in Missouri encountered Lincoln, who was en route home from a political stumping tour in Kansas. In his memoirs, Villard described their meeting:

> About thirty miles from St. Joseph an extraordinary incident occurred. A buggy with two occupants was coming towards us over the open prairie. As it approached, I thought I recognized one of them, and, sure enough, it turned out to be no less a person than Abraham Lincoln! I stopped the wagon, called him by name, and jumped off to shake hands. He did not recognize me with my full beard and pioneer's costume. When I said, "Don't you know me?" and gave my name, he looked at me, most amazed, and then burst out laughing. "Why, good gracious! You look like a real Pike's-Peaker." His surprise at this unexpected meeting was as great as mine. He was on a lecturing tour [actually campaigning for Republican candidates] through Kansas. It was a cold morning, and the wind blew cuttingly from the northwest. He was shivering in the open buggy without even a roof over it, in a short overcoat, and without any covering for his legs. I offered him one of my buffalo robes, which he gratefully accepted. He undertook, of course, to return it to me, but I never saw it again. After ten minutes' chat, we separated. The next time I saw him he was the Republican candidate for the Presidency.[18]

As a strong admirer of William Henry Seward, Villard was disappointed in Lincoln's nomination: "I had not got over the prejudice against Lincoln with which my personal contact with him in 1858 imbued me. It seemed to me incomprehensible and outrageous that the uncouth, common Illinois politician, whose only experience in public life had been service as a member of the State legislature and in Congress for one term, should carry the day over the eminent and tried statesman, the foremost figure, indeed, in the country" (1:137–38). Nonetheless, he rejoiced when Lincoln won in November: "Though no great admirer of the Republican standard-bearer, I desired, of course, his success, and felt greatly gratified by it" (1:138).

Just after the election, Villard submitted an article on western mining to the managing editor of the New York *Herald,* Frederic Hudson, whom he called "a fine-looking man, and one of the most courteous and obliging I ever met, with extraordinary qualifications for newspaper management" (1:163).[19] Hudson bought the piece and, upon learning that Villard had reported the 1858 Lincoln-Douglas debates, asked him to cover the president-elect in Springfield during the coming months (1:140 n2).[20] After obtaining authorization to write for western papers as well as the *Herald*, Villard accepted the proposal to embed himself in Springfield. (As mentioned above, two of the western papers for which he submitted articles were the Cincinnati *Commercial* and the San Francisco *Bulletin*.) In addition, some of his dispatches for the *Herald* appeared in the New York *Tribune* and the Boston *Daily Advertiser*.

Upon arriving in the Illinois capital a few days after the election, Villard told Lincoln of his assignment. As the journalist recorded in his memoirs, the president-elect "gave me a very friendly welcome, and authorized me to come to him at any time for any information I needed."[21] Villard often availed himself of that generous offer (1:144). He explained how he gathered news from other sources: "I was present almost daily for more or less time during his morning receptions. I generally remained a silent listener, as I could get at him at other hours when I was in need of information" (1:142). Villard also derived information from others. In all likelihood, he enjoyed a close rapport with another young German immigrant, John G. Nicolay, Lincoln's private secretary, who was only three years his senior. In his dispatches, Villard often describes Lincoln's incoming mail, which Nicolay opened, sorted, and sometimes answered.

Another source of information, aside from Nicolay and Lincoln, may well have been the president-elect's good friend and near neighbor, Jesse K. Dubois. During an 1890 visit to Springfield, Villard told a reporter: "I used to live here you know." Based evidently on what Villard told him, the journalist wrote that the visitor "was also at one time on the staff of one of the local papers in this city and was a clerk in the auditor's office, together with E. F. Leonard, now president of the Toledo, Peoria and Western Railway, when Jesse Dubois was the auditor."[22] Other possible sources included friends that he had made during his 1858 sojourn and in the 1860 campaign: Stephen T. Logan, Lincoln's second law partner and close friend; Governor Richard Yates; and journalists William M. Springer, John Hay, and Robert R. Hitt.[23]

The *Herald*, the Cincinnati *Commercial*, and the San Francisco *Bulletin* were the only out-of-town papers to deploy a full-time correspondent to Springfield during the period between Lincoln's election in November 1860 and his departure for Washington the following February. (His connections with the *Commercial* and the *Bulletin* are explored below.) During that span, other newspapers occasionally ran stories datelined Springfield. The *Herald* was proud of its journalistic coup, though the editors evidently disliked paying for Villard's lengthy submissions. Less than two weeks after he began filing reports, an editorial note in the *Herald* informed readers: "We are receiving every day telegraphic despatches, and pretty expensive ones, too, from Springfield."[24] Despite their expense, Villard recalled, the *Herald* published his dispatches "without change or omission."[25]

In those early dispatches, Villard occasionally criticized Lincoln. On November 19, for example, he called the president-elect a "man of good heart and good intentions" who unfortunately was "not firm. The times demand a [President Andrew] Jackson." But after a brief while he grew to admire the president-elect.

Villard boasted that he did Lincoln a service by scaring off would-be office-seekers who, fearing to see their names published in newspapers, gave up plans to visit the Illinois capital to badger the president-elect. As Villard wrote in late December 1860:

> Although your correspondent has no desire to claim any undue importance, he yet flatters himself that he has rendered, and is rendering, pre-eminent services to the President elect. The Herald's faithful chronicles of whatever transpires in this region has saved many an hour of annoyance and perplexity to the "powers that are to be." It is solely owing, indeed, to the untiring vigilance with which he watches, and the regardless mercilessness with which he brings to publicity, the movements of place-seekers and tuft-hunters, that Abraham has not suffered any overwhelming attacks from the rapacious expectants among his supporters. No more efficient means of keeping the eager host at a safe distance could have been adopted than that which is now daily exercised to his benefit in the columns of the Herald. The regular advertising of all political characters that venture hitherward in search of something in the way of Presidential favor is a most powerful scourge, that strikes terror to the hearts of all of them, and restrains them more than any apprehension of cold comforts at the hands of the Presidential elect. Several times your correspondent has already been besought with solicitations of mercy in the shape of silence as to the arrivals and manoeuvres in this locality of certain personages. But he is determined to do his duty without fear or favor, and protect "Old Abe" from the "black plague" of American politics.[26]

In late January, Villard again described his efforts to protect Lincoln:

For this welcome relief [from the pressure of office-seekers] the President elect is certainly indebted to a great extent to the disinterested vigor with which the Herald's correspondent has labored during the last few days towards the dispersion of the hungry, howling crowd of solicitors for themselves and friends, that have plagued Abraham so remorselessly these many weeks. It is true Abraham's gain will prove his [i.e., Villard's] own loss, the impudence of place seekers having furnished almost exclusively his stock in trade since the holidays. But our humane instincts of the pitiful sight of Abraham's sufferings did not allow us to act otherwise.[27]

Villard may have done an even greater service by indirectly publicizing Lincoln's views on the secession crisis. Formally, the president-elect refused to comment on the seven Southern states that had withdrawn from the Union between December 20 and February 1. But informally over the years Lincoln had regularly used newspapers to voice his opinion, often in the form of anonymous and pseudonymous articles from his own pen. In addition, he had journalists float trial balloons on his behalf. Among them were two young men (John Hay and John G. Nicolay) whom he hired in 1860 as private secretaries. During the fall and winter they contributed anonymous articles to newspapers describing events and opinion in Springfield. (Hay and Nicolay served a similar function during the Civil War, writing articles that explained and defended the administration's policies.[28])

In 1859, Lincoln surreptitiously bought a German-language newspaper in Springfield to promote the Republican cause and, with other party leaders, planned to take over a St. Louis paper that circulated widely in southern Illinois. During the Civil War, Lincoln asked influential journalists such as John W. Forney to prepare public opinion for the announcement of actions that might not prove immediately popular.

Lincoln may have been using Villard for similar purposes. In these dispatches, the president-elect is seldom quoted directly, though his remarks are sometimes paraphrased. Moreover, the views of Springfielders in general and the opinions of denizens of the State House are often described. Readers may well have inferred that those views and opinions were shared by Lincoln. Most notably, Lincoln seemed to hint that, although he generally took a hard line against secessionists, he just might accept some compromise proposals for solving the sectional crisis. (In his memoirs, however, Villard denied that Lincoln would discuss such matters: "There was . . . one limitation to the freedom of his talks with his visitors. A great many of them naturally tried to draw him out as to his future policy as President regarding the secession movement in the South, but he would not commit himself."[29]) Such dispatches made him appear more flexible than he was generally thought to be.

For example, on January 12, 1861, Villard reported that although Lincoln was "entirely loath to see slavery spread over another inch of ground, he would yet affix his signature to a Congressional enactment embodying . . . the restoration and extension to the Pacific coast of the Missouri compromise line, provided he could be satisfied that it was demanded by the bulk of the nation, and the only means of saving the Union."[30] Similarly, he reported nine days later: "One of the most prominent Republican politicians of this State addressed a direct inquiry to the President elect within the last forty-eight hours as to his views on the Border State [compromise] propositions. His frank reply was *that they would only be worth noticing in case a proposition for a Constitutional amendment, requiring the consent of two-thirds of all the States to any additional acquisition of territory, should be incorporated.* This is authentic."[31]

VILLARD AND THE CINCINNATI *COMMERCIAL*

In his memoirs, Villard explained how he first began to write for the Cincinnati *Commercial* in 1859:

> During my sojourn in Ohio [in 1858 as a canvasser for the New York *Staats-Zeitung*], I had daily read the Cincinnati *Daily Commercial* and noticed the ability and enterprise displayed in its columns. At a venture I went to Cincinnati and offered my services to the publisher of the *Commercial*, M. D. Potter. He referred me to the news-editor, Murat Halstead, afterwards the principal proprietor and editor-in-chief of the paper. After a few talks with him, we agreed that I should report the important proceedings at the impending sessions of the Illinois and Indiana Legislatures for the *Commercial*. In the former, I was to look after the reelection of Douglas. In Indiana, I was to watch the legislative complications that were expected to arise in connection with the claim of each of the two political parties to the rightful control of the majority of the Legislature, which resulted eventually in the election of two sets of United States Senators, by the Republicans and the Democrats respectively.[32]

Later that year he covered the Colorado gold rush for the *Commercial*.

During the 1860 campaign, Villard continued to write for the *Commercial* as well as the New York *Tribune* and the St. Louis *Missouri Democrat*.[33]

The many Springfield dispatches appearing in the *Commercial* between November 1860 and February 1861 are clearly by Villard, for some of them appeared verbatim in the *Herald,* one was signed VILLARD,[34] and another was signed *V,* the letter that also appeared beneath one of his 1858 articles for the Philadelphia *Press.*[35] Occasionally the *Herald* ran Springfield dispatches that had first appeared in the *Commercial.*

Almost all of the Springfield dispatches in the *Commercial* between November 1860 and February 1861 are included in this volume; when an identical dispatch appears in both papers, only one is reproduced here. The many dispatches containing similar information are included, however, for the tone sometimes varies, perhaps indicating subtle variations in meaning.

VILLARD AND THE SAN FRANCISCO *BULLETIN*

The editors of the *Bulletin* inserted the following comments in an 1888 article titled "A Sketch of Henry Villard": "Mr. Villard acted as a special correspondent of this journal" in 1859 when he covered the Pike's Peak gold rush. "After Lincoln's election and prior to his inauguration Mr. Villard placed himself in close relations with the President [elect], at Springfield. His letters to this journal in the winter of 1861 fairly outlined the policy which the great President afterward adopted in dealing with the rebellious States."[36]

*

The dispatches included here are divided into chronological chapters, one each for November, December, January, and February. In February 1861, Villard accompanied Lincoln on his train journey to Washington. Because his dispatches filed en route reveal little that is not covered in the many reports of the other journalists aboard, they are not included in this volume.[37]

CHAPTER ONE

———

NOVEMBER 1860

November 10, 1860

Springfield, 10 November 1860
[New York *Herald*, 11 November 1860]

Mr. Lincoln's advices from Southern States look like anything but secession. He is stormed with applications for office.[1] When asked what he will do about the attempt to break up the Union, he replies that he is only a citizen; that Mr. Buchanan is President; that it will be time enough to announce his intention after the 4th of March next. He remarked, in conversation with a gentleman a day or two since, that he should carefully guard against infringing upon the constitutional rights of any section of the country, and should take the same precaution to see that each section was equally loyal.

Telegraphic correspondents here sent to the country yesterday a Cabinet cooked up by a paper not in Mr. Lincoln's confidence. The main object of that Cabinet was, undoubtedly, to bring Judge Logan before the public.[2] He resides here, and is said to have been one of the ablest judges that ever wore the judicial ermine in Illinois; but I believe it is considered settled among the advisers of Mr. Lincoln that neither Illinois nor Maine is entitled to a Cabinet officer. They have not forgotten the howl that was made because Mr. Buchanan selected his law officer of the Cabinet (Mr. Black) from Pennsylvania,[3] the President's own State. Mr. Lincoln will profit by the lesson. This Cabinet, which the political enemies of Mr. Lincoln have made for him, throws out H. Winter Davis, of Maryland,[4] as Attorney General, and names him as Secretary of the Navy, in order to get Judge Logan in as Attorney General. It is a fact that Mr. Davis has been named, very generally, by the leading republicans of the country, as a suitable man for Attorney General, and if he don't get that he won't have any place in the Cabinet, as it is the only one he is fit for, and it is stretching the mark somewhat to suppose him equal to the duties of Attorney General. Mr. Davis is popular among the republicans, more in consequence of his active opposition to the [Buchanan] administration, as a politician in Baltimore, and his boldness in voting for Mr. Pennington for Speaker,[5] than because of any extraordinary legal acquirements he ever manifested.

The same Cabinet names Mr. Seward for Secretary of State.[6] Mr. Seward will not be in the Cabinet.[7] If he accepts any place under Mr. Lincoln, he will go Minister to England; otherwise he will remain in the Senate. Weed[8] still insists that he shall remain in the country, and control the distribution of the spoils in New York. Mr. Lincoln is very cautious about entering into conversation relative to the subject of a Cabinet, but it is not difficult to understand the drift of his mind by his bestowal of compliments. From this standpoint, the intimation of his immediate confidential friends, and the popular current in the minds of the leading republicans, I venture to predict that Mr. Lincoln's Cabinet will be nearly as follows:

Secretary of State .... Judge McLean, of Ohio.[9]

Secretary of Treasury .... Wm. L. Dayton, of N.J.[10]

Postmaster General .... Fitz Henry Warren, of Iowa.[11]

Secretary of War .... Cassius M. Clay, of Ky.[12]

Secretary of the Navy .... Emerson Etheridge, of Tenn.[13]

Secretary of the Interior .... Galusha A. Grow, of Pa.[14]

Attorney General .... H. Winter Davis, of Md.

The country may rest assured that the Cabinet will be of the type indicated above, if not exactly the same. It will not be less conservative, but more so, if anything.

Mr. Grow is the youngest and most radical man in the above named list, and he is of the Banks school of politics,[15] an old Pennsylvania democrat and supporter of [President James K.] Polk and [Vice-President George M.] Dallas, and probably no man knows more about the public land question, in all its details, than he, which fact makes him the more valuable for the post of Secretary of the Interior.

An able artist has been here for several days doing pictures of Mr. Lincoln's reception room at the State House; the interior of his private residence; Mrs. Lincoln, the future queen of the White House, who, I am happy to say, possesses the peculiar qualifications for that distinguished and difficult position. These pictures will soon grace the pages of one of your illustrated papers.[16]

November 11, 1860

Springfield, 11 November 1860

[New York *Herald*, 12 November 1860]

The republican Mecca is comparatively quiet to-day. Mr. Lincoln is getting some repose. His mail is immense. Most of his letters are from impolitic men, who have thrust themselves forward in the campaign in order to become prominent, in hope thereby to induce Mr. Lincoln to believe that they had done him immense service, and consequently that he was under great obligations to them. He would have been better off without them. Among the letters he has received since his election are two or three from prominent republican politicians in the country who [in 1858] did all they could to defeat his election for the Senate and secure that of [Stephen A.] Douglas. These demagogues have the audacity to suppose that Mr. Lincoln has forgotten their treachery to him and their party and that he will now accept them as his advisers, they will find themselves mistaken. Greeley[17] can hardly be counted in this boat, as he more than compensated for the political sin he committed in fighting against Lincoln for the Senate [in 1858], by his efforts to secure his nomination against Seward at [the] Chicago [convention last May]. Not so with others, some of whom, like Wilson,[18] of Massachusetts, secretly whisper in the ear of [abolitionist William Lloyd] Garrison sentiments that he dare not utter to the public. Mr. Lincoln has been cheated by them once and will never trust them again.

A gentleman who had a private interview with Mr. Lincoln last evening, says he conversed with the President elect about the secession movement [in the] South, and the latter expressed his regret that the South, having always been so loyal to the Union, should be the first to manifest a disposition to break it up, and especially under a democratic administration, and before the policy of the new (Lincoln) administration is thoroughly tested.

Advices here indicate that the present excited state of feeling in the South will soon give place to [a] more politic movement, perhaps a national Convention, to be composed of the best minds of all the States, to consider and settle peacefully the question of Union and disunion. The conduct of the present administration is closely watched with reference to the existing state of affairs in the South, and by no one with more interest than Mr. Lincoln himself. Springfield still continues to be crowded with people, and the inferior hotels here do not half accommodate them.

November 15, 1860

Springfield, 15 November 1860
[New York *Herald*, 16 November 1860]

The republican Mecca is at present one of the most attractive places on the globe. Mr. Lincoln is burdened with an immense correspondence.[19] About fifty of his letters today solicited autographs.

Mr. Lincoln talks freely with every one who calls, having something pleasant to say to each. He has been urged to announce his policy in advance of his inauguration. He, however, positively declines, as he also declines indicating to any one who will compose his Cabinet. He said today that some of the politicians of the South had falsely announced, during the recent campaign, that if he (Mr. Lincoln) was elected armed bands were formed in the North to go down there and liberate the slaves, and the most that he feared was, that an insurrectionary movement among the slaves would result from their own teachings.

It is settled that no Cabinet officer will be taken from this State, as in that event many of the lesser lights could not consistently be rewarded. It is understood that Mr. Lincoln will acquiesce in this policy, as I indicated in my dispatch in Sunday's HERALD.

The most amazing thing to the republicans of Illinois is the worse than Garrisonian radicalism of John Wentworth, who daily insists upon burdening Mr. Lincoln with his intemperate and impolitic notions about slavery.[20] They do not reflect the conservative ideas of the republicans of the State, and greatly anger Mr. Lincoln, who does not hesitate to express his disapprobation of them.

Mr. Lincoln has so many callers that he continues to receive them in the Executive Chamber of the State House; and in order to obtain time to attend to his correspondence he has been obliged to fix the hours of from ten to twelve A.M. and from two to four P.M. for his receptions.[21]

Mrs. Lincoln, also, has many callers. She does not appear to realize that she has been elected to preside at the White House the next four years; but by the easy grace and dignity with which she receives those who call upon her daily, she shows that she possesses the necessary qualifications to assume the higher duties of the President's wife at Washington.[22] Her sister, Mrs. Ninian Edwards,[23] of this city, an educated and accomplished lady, and a niece [Mary Wallace],[24] a beautiful young lady of eighteen, will accompany Mrs. Lincoln to the White House, and assist her in doing the honors at the President's levees.

November 16, 1860

Springfield, 16 November 1860
[New York *Herald*, 22 November 1860]
The bluntest of observers cannot fail to notice that this provincial city does not bear the aspect one looks for in the biding place of the chieftain of a powerful party, just emerged victorious from a fierce and protracted contest. A new sun has risen on the political horizon, but the satellites are still wanting. The battle is won, but the general is not yet surrounded by the rank and file of his army, with a view to the division of the spoils. Abe Lincoln is elected President, but the tide of those who expect to share both the honors and profits of his triumph has yet to roll into this, his abode.

Whatever sensation writers may impose upon distant readers to the contrary, a short sojourn in this town of negative attractions will convince any one that the crowd of Presidential electors, campaign speakers, members of State and national conventions, defeated candidates, free soil martyrs from the border slave States [Kentucky, Maryland, Missouri, and Delaware] and Kansas, &c., &c., that is sure to appear in this latitude to bow to the powers that are to be, and ask substantial recognition of their services and federal plasters for their wounds, is not to be found in this burg at this moment. It is not, of course, to be believed that the expectant host will stay back altogether. Their apparent abstinence is only temporary, and that from various causes.

It is evident, in the first place, that the silence and reservedness with which Mr. Lincoln met the forerunners produced a certain hesitation to press forward at this hour. Fear of present rebuke and consequent absolute denial has doubtless stemmed the current. Again, the threatening attitude of some of the Southern States has much to do with the seeming modesty of the many that think to have well deserved of Mr. Lincoln. They want to await the denouement of these unlooked for complications. They are anxious to learn something further as to the force of the impending storm, before running the risk of being called upon to break it. Many also propose to await a formal announcement of Mr. Lincoln's policy, in order to be better able to divine the prospect of his administration and the mode of successfully pushing their own claims.

Many republican journals have been in the habit of pointing jeeringly at the alleged frequency of written and personal Southern applications for office to Mr. Lincoln.[25] The truth with regard to this matter is, however, that very few Southerners of distinction have, up to date, importuned Mr. Lincoln, either by letter or in person, with similar requests. Their number, indeed appears insignificant, when compared with that of Northern applicants.

Letters of congratulation and advice have been received by Mr. Lincoln from nearly all the prominent citizens of the border slave States, that have heretofore openly espoused the republican cause. But prayers for office come only from the less discreet and lower stratum of Southern sympathizers, and hence are totally ignored. From the cotton States letters and visits have been very scanty until now.

No one that knows Mr. Lincoln will suppose him to be wanting so much common sense as to proclaim, either by word or in writing, his executive intentions at the present time, when he is really not yet elected President of the United States by the vote of the electors from the several republican States. Present appearances even justify the belief that the act of casting the electoral vote will not be immediately followed by the publication of an official programme. Among Mr. Lincoln's most intimate supporters, at least, the opinion appears to prevail that the part of a mere looker on will best suit him as to the Souther[n] imbroglio until his formal inauguration.

The republican glorification in honor of Lincoln's election that is to come off in this place on Tuesday next [November 20], after several postponements, does not promise to turn out anything like an imposing demonstration. People about here seem to be surfeited with such empty exhibitions, and furthermore, not especially disposed to be hilarious over the Southern news. A few thousand visiters from adjoining counties and towns may attend, but other States will hardly be represented.

Mr. Wm. H. Herndon, the law partner of Mr. Lincoln, became involved a few days since in a quarrel that attracts much attention.[26] The [Stephen A.] Douglas State organ, the [Springfield] *Daily [Illinois State] Register*, brought the charge against him that he knew of and approved the use of republican money in sustaining the Breckinridge[27] faction of the democracy [i.e., Democratic Party]. Mr. Herndon denounced the charge as a base fabrication, without the least foundation in fact, and published cards to that effect in the [Springfield] *Daily [Illinois State] Journal* and [St. Louis] *Missouri Republican. The Register*, however, insists upon it, and claims more veracity for its witnesses, &c, than, it asserts, is given in this community to Mr. Herndon. But the latter is pronounced free from blame in the matter, even by democrats of high standing.

Springfield, 16 November 1860
[New York *Herald*, 17 November 1860]

Mr. Healy left here yesterday, having completed a fine portrait of the President elect.[28]

Mr. Lincoln continues to have applications for office from the South. He was delayed at the State House to-day with visiters until after dark.

Mr. Jno. G. Nicolay,[29] the private secretary of Mr. Lincoln, is constantly employed answering letters.

Senator Trumbull arrived here to-day,[30] and had a private interview with Mr. Lincoln. The former leaves here to-morrow for Washington.

The prevailing opinion here is, that although Mr. [James] Buchanan would undoubtedly like to turn the government over to Mr. Lincoln as much confused as possible, he will not care to have secession occur during his administration. It is difficult to make the republicans believe Mr. Buchanan is not in complicity with the South Carolina secessionists, and the fact that he has left the United States arms unguarded by federal troops, and put them in possession of a volunteer company of secessionists, is quoted as evidence thereof.

The celebration here on Tuesday next [November 20], will be confined chiefly to this place and vicinity, and a State demonstration will be made the day the electoral votes are counted. Numerous applications are already made for the New York Post Office and Custom House.

Springfield, 16 November 1860
[New York *Herald*, 17 November 1860]

The republican jubilee on Tuesday, the 20th, in this place, Mr. Lincoln's home, is likely to be but a local affair. Visiters from the neighboring counties and St. Louis and Chicago are expected, but none from other States. The Southern news prevent[s] exuberant enthusiasm.

The total arrivals at the three leading hotels during the last twenty-four hours are but eighty, and none of them of prominence.

It is untrue that many Southerners personally apply for office, and urge upon Mr. Lincoln a public expression of his policy. But two notables from border Slave States thus far have appeared.[31] Written advice is freely received from Southern sympathizers of distinction, but the applications for office from the South are only by obscure personages.

November 17, 1860

Springfield, 17 November 1860
[New York *Herald*, 18 November 1860]

John Covode, of Pennsylvania,[32] arrived here this morning and had a private interview with Mr. Lincoln, and left in the return train. There is evidently trouble about who shall represent Pennsylvania in the Cabinet.

Tom Corwin,[33] of Ohio, will make a strong effort for the Treasury Department, but will be terribly assailed, as unfit to manage the finances of the nation. The Secretary of the Treasury will be more likely to come from New York, and Moses Grinnell's chances will be good.[34]

I learn from high authority that Mr. Seward will not accept any place in the Cabinet, and in that event he will be tendered the mission to England, which he will also decline, with the intention, at the close of next session of Congress, to resume his travels abroad.

Michigan will urge Senator Chandler,[35] and Indiana press Schuyler Colfax,[36] for Postmaster General.

There is a strong public sentiment all over the West, and represented here, in favor of Cassius M. Clay, of Kentucky,[37] or Frank P. Blair, Jr., of Missouri,[38] for Secretary of War, and Galusha A. Grow, of Pennsylvania, for Secretary of the Interior.

Candidates accumulate for the Attorney Generalship, and Wm. L. Dayton, of New Jersey, is quite strong.

Edward Bates, of Missouri,[39] may be tendered a place in the Cabinet, and if so he will decline it. His friends say authoritatively that he does not wish to exchange, at his age, his present domestic quiet for severe Cabinet duties.

The gossip about calling John Bell, of Tennessee, to the Cabinet, is received here as absurd.[40]

The [Springfield *Illinois*] *State Register* (Douglas' organ), of to-day, volunteers a Cabinet for Lincoln too nonsensical for comment.

Springfield, 17 November 1860
[New York *Herald*, 18 November 1860]
Mr. Lincoln remarked today to a visiter, in regard to an expected public definition of his policy in advance of his inaugural, as follows: *"During the last six years I have placed my views on all public questions so fully and frequently on record, that all those desiring can learn them by simply referring to it. If my past assertions obtain no credit, present ones will be treated no better."*

Springfield, 17 November 1860
[New York *Herald*, 18 November 1860]
Senator Douglas' letter to the New Orleans merchants, received in St. Louis papers this morning, produces quite a sensation in republican circles.[41]

Mr. Lincoln smiles, and his friends are indignant at its bitter and insulting reference to the President elect. They think it a graceless performance on the part of a defeated rival.

John Covode, of the Covode Committee, arrived early this morning, but stayed only a few hours. He was closeted with the President elect for an hour, supposedly as to the attitude of the republicans in Congress towards secession, and supposedly, also, in reference to the Cabinet and other spoils—the two great troubles of the incoming chief magistrate.[42]

Springfield, 17 November 1860
[New York *Herald*, 22 November 1860]
One momentous question is constantly asked by the political quidnuncs [busybodies], Bonifaces [innkeepers] and rumsellers of this Western burg. An anxious "Where are [Thurlow] Weed, Webb,[43] Raymond,[44] King,[45] Draper,[46] Grinnell, Nye,[47] Evarts?"[48] &c., &c., meets me at every street crossing. It will be remembered that most of these republican *Marechals de Camp* [field marshals], the overthrow of their own idol [William Henry Seward] to the contrary notwithstanding, made *"bonne mine a mauvais jeu"* [put a good

face on a bad bargain], visited this place after the breaking up of the Chicago Convention [in May] to make a loyal bow to the newly nominated chieftain. During their brief sojourn they produced quite a favorable impression.[49] They were thought to be clever, to have plenty of the needful [i.e., money], and a disposition to spend it freely. Hence the aforesaid anxiety for their return.

Eager as this craving to see their cheerful countenances and plethoric purses once more has proved, it has thus far remained entirely unsatisfied.

Not the shadow of a single one of them has as yet flitted before the "powers that are to be." This absentation was entirely unlooked for, and various are the surmises as to its causes.

Some contend that the fear of a cool reception delays their advent. Others claim that they are determined to stand on their dignity and await advances on the part of the President elect towards the disappointed choice of the Empire State. Again, it is argued that the [Horace] Greeley wing of the party has the inside track hereabouts. An intimate friend of Mr. Lincoln expressed another reason within the last twenty-four hours. He said: "They want to wait a little while longer, so as to let us forget that they did not quite roll up the eighty thousand majority promised by Mr. Seward."[50]

But New York is not the only State unrepresented here. New England is equally tardy in rendering homage to the now mighty Illinoisian. The same can be said of nearly all other Eastern States. The West alone has sent its representatives—whether from a greater longing for the spoils or truer loyalty I will not venture to say.

Small as the number of attendants has been for some days—not over 150 per day—the receptions of the President are nevertheless highly interesting and worthy of detailed notice. They are held daily from ten A.M. to twelve M., and from three P.M. to half past five P.M., in the Governor's room at the State House, which has been for some time given up to the wants of Mr. Lincoln.

On entering the State House the visiter will see groups of quietly conversing individuals, occupying various portions of the spacious hall of the first story. Their conversation, of course, turns about "Old Abe." Some he will find "wondering how he looks;" others, "whether he puts on airs," and how he treats callers. Excessively bashful personages, who are altogether afraid to venture into the Presidential presence, are also never wanting.

An exceedingly loquacious old man, who claims to be four score and three years of age, daily bores [i.e., pesters] his old friend "Abe," usually entertaining the intended visiters with Lincoln anecdotes, most of which are so evidently drawn from imagination as to excite the scorn rather than the laughter of the hearers.

The appointed hour having arrived, the crowd moves upstairs into the second story, in the southeast corner of which the reception room is located. Passing through a rather dark sort of a doorway, the clear voice and often ringing laughter of the President [elect] usually guide them to the right door. The boldest of the party having knocked, a ready "Come in" invites [them] to enter. On opening the door, the tall, lean form of "Old Abe" directly confronts the leader of the party. Seizing the latter's hand with a hearty shake, he leads him in, and bids the rest to follow suit by an encouraging "Get in, all of you." The whole party being in, he will ask for their names, and then immediately start a running conversation. In this respect he displays more than ordinary talent and practice. Although he is naturally more listened than talked to, he does not allow a pause to become protracted. He is never at a loss as to the subjects that please the different classes of visiters, and there is a certain quaintness and originality about all he has to say, so that one cannot help feeling interested. His "talk" is not brilliant. His phrases are not ceremoniously set, but pervaded with a humorousness, and, at times, a grotesque joviality, that will always please. I think it would be hard to find one who tells better jokes, enjoys them better and laughs oftener, than Abraham Lincoln.

The room of the Governor of the State of Illinois can not be said to indicate the vast territorial extent of that Commonwealth. It is altogether inadequate for the accommodation of Mr. Lincoln's visiters. Twenty persons will not find standing room in it, and the simultaneous presence of a dozen only will cause inconvenience.

The room is furnished with a sofa, half a dozen arm chairs, a table and a desk, the latter being assigned to the private secretary [John G. Nicolay], who is always present during visiting hours. These, together with countless letters and files of newspapers, and quite an assortment of odd presents, constitute the only adornments of the apartment.

No restrictions whatever being exercised as to visiters, the crowd that daily waits on the President is always of a motley description. Everybody that lives in this vicinity or passes through this place goes to take a look at "Old Abe." Muddy boots and hickory shirts are just as frequent as broadcloth, fine linen, &c. The ladies, however, are usually dressed up in their very best, although they cannot possibly hope to make an impression on old married Lincoln.

Offensively democratic exhibitions of free manners occur every once in a while. Churlish fellows will obtrude themselves with their hats on, lighted segars and their pantaloons tucked into their boots. Dropping into chairs, they will sit puffing away and trying to gorgonize the President with their silent stares, until their boorish curiosity is fully satisfied.

Formal presentations are dispensed with in most cases. Nearly everybody finds his own way in and introduces himself. Sometimes half a dozen rustics rush in, break their way through other visiters up to the object of their search, and, after calling their names and touching the Presidential fingers, back out again without delay.

Springfield, 17 November 1860

[New York *Herald*, 17 November 1860]

We have the cheering news from Springfield, Illinois, that "Honest Abe Lincoln" becomes angry when Long John Wentworth's violent abolition outpourings through the Chicago *Democrat* are referred to as representing among some credulous men the views of the President elect. This is a good sign. It is but a straw, but it shows the drift of the wind. Let the conservative men of the republican camp, acting upon this hint, lay before "Old Abe" the issue upon which John Sherman was defeated as the republican candidate for Speaker of the present Congress, and read to him also the black list of the [Hinton Rowan] Helper book; for this kindness may save Mr. Lincoln a world of trouble.[51]

November 18, 1860

Springfield, 18 November 1860

[New York *Herald*, 22 November 1860]

The happiest man at the present moment in this latitude is not the President elect, but Senator Trumbull. A constant smile illuminates his face. The light of perfect inner satisfaction and complacency beams from his eyes. His hand is ever ready for a friendly grasp. His constituents never appeared dearer to him. And why all this?

His political future was at stake in the late canvass in this State. His Senatorial term expires on the 4th of March next, and hence the triumph or defeat of his party also implied a personal one. Among his republican confederates his claims to a re-election were universally recognized. But the followers of Senator Douglas strained every nerve to defeat him by returning the wanted democratic majority to the State Legislature. They hated him far more intensely than [they hated] Lincoln. They feared his shrewd tactics more than the honest frankness of the latter's opposition. They knew that, as long as Trumbull lived, their own chieftain would enjoy no power, and hence they were bent on his political death with a desperation. But the gods willed it otherwise. They visited a most signal discomfiture upon the Douglasites. Instead of the majority of five on [the] joint ballot in the last Legislature that re-elected Douglas [in 1859], they came out of the battle with one [i.e., a majority] of seven for his bitterest foe. Thus Trumbull may well feel at ease, carry his head erect, and think this world a nice place to live in.

Mr. Trumbull appears to be—to use a popular Western phrase—the right bower [i.e., a close friend or partner] of the President elect. Although residing at Alton, in the southern part of the State, he spends most of his time here. His intercourse with Mr. Lincoln is continued and most intimate, and present appearances justify the belief that he will be a "power in the land" during the next four years.

The history of these two republican leaders contains another chapter, in which both were also equally interested, but in a less harmonious way. Five years ago Trumbull succeeded in overleaping Lincoln and securing a seat in the United States Senate. It was then commonly thought that Lincoln was properly entitled to the seat, and that Trumbull got it by outmanoeuvring him in the Legislature. Everybody considered it a fatal blow to Lincoln's political aspiration. How little did the sequence prove the correctness of this supposition. At the same time that Trumbull had to struggle with might and main to retain the advantage gained over Lincoln, his unsuccessful rival of 1855 was being quietly lifted into the Presidential chair without any effort of his own.[52] A more singular turn of political fortune it would be hard to find in the political annals of this country.

The St. Louis papers of yesterday contained a lengthy letter, written by Senator Douglas to a committee of New Orleans business men, in reply to an invitation to speak. It produced quite a storm of indignation among Mr. Lincoln's adherents, owing to several extremely bitter and insulting passages in reference to the probable position of the President elect. The latter's only comment was a smile. His friends, however, denounce the epistolary effusion a "graceless exhibition of morbid jealousy," in unmeasured terms. Several quoted from a speech made by Lincoln at Freeport, in 1858, in refutation of certain charges also emanating from Senator Douglas. In the passage L. remarks, that "being charitably disposed, he was ready to accept the only supposition that furnished a key to Judge Douglas' unwarranted allegations, viz: 'That he was crazy.'"[53]

It may be safely asserted that a definition of Mr. Lincoln's policy need not be looked for previous to the 4th of March. His declarations on this subject are so frequent and decided in their tenor that there can be no longer any doubt as to his determination to remain silent. Only in the course of yesterday he remarked, to an inquisitive visiter, that his opinions on all public matters had been so unequivocally and comprehensively expressed since 1854 that he considered further explanations quite superfluous.

The exciting news from the South does not appear to disturb Mr. Lincoln's equanimity. Without underrating its bearing, he still adheres to the opinion that actual secession will not be attempted. He avoids discussing this delicate question in the presence of visiters, but when referring to it his words are said to indicate a firm and settled opinion against the right to secede.

The decline of the Southern State stocks has already had a visible effect upon this section of the country. Under the laws of this State the Bank Commissioners are bound to require all banks of issue to make up immediately whatever depreciation the securities deposited with the Auditor of the State may experience by the fluctuations of the stock market. Owing to the recent fall of Southern bonds, on which most of the currency of this State is based, the securities of a large number of banks have become insufficient. To meet this emergency, a meeting of the Bank Commissioners took place in this city yesterday. A large number of bankers were also in town from all parts of the State. It is rumored that many will refuse to make up the deficiency. If this should be true their banks will have to go at once into liquidation, and a crisis will then ensue, compared with which that of 1857 will prove insignificant.

Springfield, 18 November, via Chicago, 19 November 1860
[New York *Herald*, 20 November 1860]
Mr. Lincoln received a special despatch last evening from W. B. Farwell,[54] one of the editors of the *Alta California*, dated San Francisco, November 8, via Fort Kearney, announcing that Lincoln leads in California [by] several thousand, as far as heard from, and would carry the State if no frauds were perpetrated in the interior counties. There is great rejoicing among the Lincolnites at this news, while the Douglasites swear not a little.

An attempt has been made to get up a bank panic in this State. An examination of the Bank Commissioners shows that out of one hundred banks in Illinois, representing eleven million dollars circulation, only twenty-two are deficit to the amount of two hundred and ninety-six thousand three hundred and eighty five dollars, upon which a call has been made to-day, and it is believed all will respond. The eleven millions represented is secured by upwards of thirteen millions of State and United States stocks, only about two millions of which is Missouri.

November 19, 1860

Springfield, 19 November 1860
[New York *Herald*, 20 November 1860]
Mr. Lincoln will leave here for Chicago on Wednesday [November 21], in the morning train, accompanied by Mrs. Lincoln and Senator Trumbull. He

will decline all ovations, and make no speeches, as the object of his visit is to attend to private matters before entering upon his public duties, which already crowd upon him in the form of an immense correspondence.

Mr. Hamlin,[55] the Vice President elect, will meet Mr. Lincoln at Chicago on Wednesday. They will then see each other for the first time.

The indications about who will go into the Cabinet, as reflected in the editorial in Friday's HERALD, are wide of the mark. The name of Mr. [Massachusetts Senator Henry] Wilson is especially obnoxious—excuse the undignified remark. The Cabinet announced in the dispatch in the HERALD of the 10th inst. is nearer the mark than anything yet published. It is as follows:

Secretary of State	Judge McLean, of Ohio.
Secretary of Treasury	Wm. L. Dayton, of N. J.
Postmaster General	Fitz Henry Warren, of Iowa.
Secretary of War	Cassius M. Clay, of Ky.
Secretary of the Navy	Emerson Etheridge, of Tenn.
Secretary of the Interior	Galusha A. Grow, of Pa.
Attorney General	H. Winter Davis, of Md.

A large number of people have called upon the President elect to-day from Kentucky, Virginia, South Carolina, Massachusetts, New York and Pennsylvania.

Mr. Lincoln continues to receive applications for office in the South.

Of all the callers Mr. Lincoln had to-day not one was after office. Office seekers write letters, and would stand a better chance if they did not write any. The stampede for the important offices in the country has not commenced. The applicants so far are mostly for Post Offices.

The republican jubilee to-morrow night promises to be a brilliant affair. Mr. Lincoln will be called upon at his residence. He will present himself, but make no speech. Senator Trumbull, Don[n] Piatt of Cincinnati[56]; Mr. Yates,[57] Governor elect of Illinois, will speak at the Wigwam.[58] It is understood Mr. Trumbull will represent the views of Mr. Lincoln.

Mr. Lincoln received a despatch to-day from the Secretary of the Republican State Committee of California, stating that he has probably carried that State. It says the total vote heard from is ninety thousand, and that Lincoln leads Douglas [by] 2,500, while Breckinridge is far behind Douglas.

Springfield, 19 November 1860
[New York *Herald*, 20 November 1860]

Mr. Lincoln received the California election news by special despatch yesterday afternoon. Himself and friends are elated, but think Douglas will carry the State by a small plurality.

There were no place seekers here to-day.

Mr. Lincoln entertained himself and a few visiters by reading aloud articles from the [New York] *Independent*. He takes the Southern news calmly, and says: "My time not having arrived, I am content to receive all possible light on the subject, and glad to be out of the ring."

Senator Trumbull speaks at the republican jubilee to-morrow. He is expected to indicate Lincoln's policy, without claiming to speak authoritatively.

Springfield, 19 November 1860

[New York *Herald*, 24 November 1860]

Whatever the sensation[al]ists may say to the contrary, our little city wears a very quiet aspect. Business is very dull; and as for the "Southerners begging for office," we do not see them. No men of reputation in politics at the South have yet been here, and the two or three who do arrive daily are not certainly known to be "begging for office;" but it is probable that the Southerners who will take office under Mr. Lincoln will be of the class of village politicians which abounds especially there—thus laying "upon the shelf" even a larger number of mummies than did the death of the old whig party. The scramble for office among the republicans, however, is terrible. There are a hundred active, clamorous applicants for every office within the gift of the President elect.

To-morrow night a grand congratulatory torchlight demonstration is to take place. The "note of preparation," however, does not argue a very enthusiastic affair. The effort will be a partial failure, I think, for the three-fold reason that the republicans are "hurrahed out," have spent all their "spare change," and now see a financial storm coming that seems to be their own unwitting work. It has been supposed by many that Mr. Lincoln would take this occasion to pour oil upon the troubled waters of secession. His own feelings prompt him to conservatism and conciliation; but he is overruled in this by his friends, who argue that if he attempts to conciliate the South he will exasperate the more ultra of the Eastern electors, and thus fall between two stools, even before he reaches the Presidency. Now that the contest is over, the feeling of conservatism is reasserting itself among the Western republicans, while the East is thought to be more radical than ever in freesoilism. Under this view of the case, his most discreet advisers counsel silence, under the excusatory declaration that Mr. Lincoln is merely a citizen, and has no right to speak as Chief Magistrate. The speciousness of this dodge is self-evident, but it is, perhaps, the best solution for the two-horse act it obviates.

Mr. Lincoln's personal appearance is the subject of daily remark among those who have known him formerly. Always cadaverous, his aspect is now almost ghostly. His position is wearing him terribly. Letters threatening his life are daily received from the South—occasionally, also, a note of warning from some Southerner who does not like his principles, but would regret violence. But these trouble him little compared with the apprehended difficulty of conciliating the South without destroying the integrity of his own party. The present aspect of the country, I think, augurs one of the most difficult terms which any President has yet been called to weather; and I doubt Mr. Lincoln's capacity for the task of bringing light and peace out of the chaos that will surround him. A man of good heart and good intentions, he is not firm. The times demand a [President Andrew] Jackson.

The waves from Wall street have reached us. For several days past exchange could only be had at three per cent, and that only for [the] best customers. On Saturday the Bank Commissioners made a "call" on the banks for about $300,000, to make up the depreciation of the stocks deposited as bases of their circulation, giving only thirty-five days instead of sixty, as heretofore. Gov. Matteson's[59] share of this is $46,000, and though he will meet the call, it makes him groan "some." I hardly think any of our banks will go into liquidation on this call. However, were depreciation to continue much longer, ruin and disaster must follow. Our banks rest so largely on Southern stocks—especially Missouri's—that the secession of even the Gulf States would immensely injure if not ruin our banks. I understand that one large pork packing establishment here, which has heretofore drawn on a New York house for means, has been notified not to draw this fall. I heard one republican say that this would affect him to the extent of $300 on his pork operations; and he is not the only man that is now on the stool of repentance for his vote for Old Abe. The reaction has already begun.

In the ensuing session of Congress the action of the Western members will be looked to with some interest. One member—Col. John A. McClernand[60]—entertains very proper views in relation to the secession movement, as affecting the West, and will doubtless seek an early occasion to present them to the country. The ultraism of the East and of the South finds no echo among us. We are attached to the Union from feelings of patriotism as well as from ties of interest; and if those sections are irreconcileably hostile, we shall not, in the event of separation, become the tail of either. The Mississippi Valley is an empire of itself, and has all the elements of greatness within itself—regions of eternal snow, alluvial gardens and evergreen savannahs. We shall cleave to the Union "as it is," but will never consent to a Union as sectionalism makes it.

Turning over a volume of the old [Springfield *Illinois*] *State Register* for 1839, '40 and '41, I frequently came across the names of E. D. Baker, Senator elect from Oregon[61]; Abe Lincoln, President elect; John Calhoun, of Kansas notoriety[62]; Judge Douglas, late a candidate for President; Peter Cartwright, the pioneer preacher[63]; Professor Bledsoe, now of the University of Virginia,[64] and others. These men were then our "village politicians," whose ambition gratified itself in gaining seats in the church used for a Legislative Hall.[65] There were other young men here then of bright promise, but who "by the wayside fell and perished."[66] But those I mention all reached distinction. Calhoun hardly reached fame—notoriety were the better word—but he is dead; and let candle boxes be forgotten. Col. Baker's career among us would form an interesting biography. Brilliant, eloquent, disinterested and unselfish, he was very profound and very poor. But he has found the theatre of a higher ambition, and I doubt not that he will reflect honor on the choice of the Oregonese. His old friends hope to see him soon. It is thought that he will take a more conservative and patriotic ground than will the majority of his party. Uncle Peter Cartwright was somewhat taken aback by the defeat of his old friend Douglas, but hopes to see him in the right place in 1864.

The weather has been remarkably fine up to this writing. Flowers are yet blooming in our gardens, and so pleasant is it that I can hardly believe we have seen "the last rose of summer."

Springfield, 19 November 1860

[New York *Herald*, 24 November 1860]

If any reader of the HERALD should expect to be informed in the following [dispatch] whether the President elect takes beefsteak or mutton chops at breakfast; whether he prefers his roast beef rare or well done at dinner, and whether he furthers his digestion with 'lager' or stronger stimulants, he will find himself doomed to disappointment. Although well aware of the intimate reciprocal relations between the body and mind, our insight into the Presidential existence has as yet failed to cover the above momentous phases. Our disquisition will relate only to the routine of the public life of its distinguished subject.

Mr. Lincoln makes his appearance in the State House regularly before eight o'clock A.M. He is often found there earlier than the State officers, and sometimes is even sooner ready for work than his private secretary [John G. Nicolay], who sleeps in the building.

The first thing done in the morning is the opening and reading of his daily increasing mail matter.[67] When visiters of distinction are in town who are entitled to more attention than the ordinary crowd of callers, they usually seek his presence at an early hour, and their hearings then take place under lock. At ten A.M. the door of the reception room is opened, and the general levees commence, and continue until noon. At one P.M. Mr. Lincoln repairs to dinner, after which he allows himself to rest until three P.M., when he again receives calls until half past five, at which time he retires from the public gaze.

After supper he engages either in consultations with intimate political friends, or works with his secretary, sifting his correspondence, inditing replies, &c, &c. Light is seen in his room very late every evening, and he hardly ever allows anything to lay over unattended until the next day.

Altogether, he cannot be said to rest on a "bed of roses," although the real duties of his position do not yet weigh upon him. The most laborious part of his present daily task is the entertainment of his numerous callers. As everybody is more anxious to hear than to be heard, (place seekers excepted), he is obliged to do nearly all the talking himself. His extreme fondness of and great practice in the light tone of social chat enables him to carry this heavy burthen with comparative ease.

His professional business is, of course, neglected. Mr. Wm. H. Herndon, his partner in the practice of the law, has now sole charge of it.

Persons who had intercourse with Mr. Lincoln before and after his election contend that he has lately assumed a very careworn look. That this should be so is not to be wondered at, in view of the quiet and retired life he was theretofore accustomed to live. This very change in his appearance, however, indicates and speaks well for the earnestness with which he realizes the responsibilities of his newly attained office.

His old friends, who have been used to a great indifference as to the "outer man," on his part, say that "Abe is putting on airs." By this they refer to the fact that he is now wearing a bran[d] new hat and suit, and that he has commenced cultivating the—with him—unusual adornment of whiskers. One of his adherents jocularly remarked the other day, on noticing these various improvements, that "he is trying to disguise himself so as to get unrecognized through Maryland to Washington."

But, these late outward embellishments to the contrary notwithstanding, a Broadway tailor would probably feel no more tempted to consider Lincoln as coming up to his artistic requirements of a model man than Peter Cooper.[68] The angularity of the Presidential form, and its habitual *laissez aller*, preclude a like possibility. We venture to say that Fifth avenue snobs, if unaware who he was, would be horrified at the idea of walking across the street with him. And yet there is something about the man that makes one at once forget these exterior shortcomings and feel attracted towards him.

More well meaning than discreet visiters have succeeded at various times during the last few days in eliciting from Mr. Lincoln more or less significant expressions of opinion as to the course he intends to pursue in reference to appointments to office. From their tenor it may be safely asserted that honesty and capability, and not party affiliations, are the main qualifications in his eyes. It is indeed the prevalent opinion, even among his political opponents hereabouts, that he will continue worthy present incumbents. Those republicans who expect him to adopt [former New York Governor William] Marcy's maxim, that "to the victors belong the spoils," are not unlikely to find themselves sadly disappointed, and democratic officials, with clean records, may take heart, and no longer tremble in their boots at [in anticipation of] a supposed inevitable decapitation after the 4th of March next.

The President elect being the very embodiment of good humor, it seems as though, from this fact, much that happens about him partakes of a comical character. Funny incidents occur so frequently that the enumeration of them all would fill a book. For the sake of illustration, a few are subjoined:

Some days ago a tall Missourian marched into the reception room. Seeing the tall form of the President [elect] rise before him, and not knowing what else to say, he ejaculated, "I reckon one is about as big as the other." "Let us measure," was the instantaneous reply; and the Missourian was actually placed against the wall, told "to be honest, and stand flat on his heels," and his height ascertained with a stick.

On Saturday last [November 17], while Mr. Covode was calling on Mr. Lincoln, an old man, on hearing the former's name, walked up to him, and scanning his face closely, exclaimed, "You don't look like the man that scented 'Old Buck' [President James Buchanan] so well."[69]

On the same day, one of a party that waited in the ante rooms asked another how high Lincoln was. "Well," was the reply, "as he carries himself ordinarily (referring to his habit of stooping), he stands about six feet four inches in his boots; but when he stretches himself up to his full height, the Lord only knows how tall he grows."

On going to the State House on Friday last [November 16] Mr. L. was stopped by a man that had fish for sale, and requested to accept one. "Thank you," replied he, "I hardly think I can carry it along now; but if you will take it up to my house, I reckon we will keep it."

Springfield, 19 November 1860
[Cincinnati *Commercial*, 21 November 1860]

Hardly any social barrier being interposed in this country between the highest official and the lowest citizen, it is but natural that not only the public but also the more private relations of the President-elect should be objects of anxious curiosity. It may be of little consequence to the people at large to know when Mr. Lincoln rises, at what hour his levees commence, how he receives his visitors, &c., &c. But the interest in these minor incidents of his daily life nevertheless exists, and it being the province of a live newspaper to attend to *all* wants of information, the readers of the [Cincinnati] Commercial may not feel ungrateful for the subjoined details as to the present doings of Mr. Lincoln.

Mr. L. is a very early riser. He is always found astir long before sun up. His morning meal is regularly taken shortly after seven o'clock, and at a quarter of eight he repairs to the State house, where, for want of room in his private dwelling, he has been for some time in the habit of receiving all visitors. From eight to ten he employs himself in reading his steadily increasing correspondence and giving private interviews. Visiting politicians of note usually seek the Presidential presence in the course of these two hours. The door of the Executive department, which has been given up to him, is kept locked during the same time. At ten o'clock the levee for the general public opens and is continued until twelve. From that hour until three the President occupies himself privately. At the last mentioned hour his room is again thrown open to all that choose to call, and the reception continues until half past five, when he retires. These four hours and a half of his now valuable time, are daily yielded to the curiosity of the public.

The most interesting features of this daily routine are, of course, the general receptions. They take place in a room not over ten feet wide and fourteen feet long, so that a "jam" does not unfrequently occur. It is very pleasantly furnished with two tables, half a dozen chairs and a sofa. The only "ornaments" are the various presents sent by enthusiastic or speculative admirers. One of the tables is occupied by Mr. Nicholls [Nicolay], Mr. L.'s private secretary, and always groaning under a huge pile of letters and newspapers.

The President [elect] does not remain in any particular spot, awaiting the approach of visitors, but generally moves about and walks towards visitors as soon as they enter. His greeting is always of the most cordial character. When the callers prove to be old acquaintances, it is accompanied by loud exclamations of delight. The heartiness of Mr. Lincoln's shake of the hand is altogether western. He usually opens his conversation with some familiar questions in the most unaffected manner, thereby making people at once feel at their ease. Once agoing, he stops talking only when interrupted by the remarks of visitors. He is really an exceedingly agreeable conversationalist. His fluent chat is always flavored with humor. Attic salt [i.e., wit, humor] in the shape of [witty?] sayings and funny personal reminiscences is untiringly served up by him. Altogether, he succeeds without making an extra effort, in entertaining all that come, and producing a favorable impression on everybody.

The character of his visitors is greatly variegated. Up to this time the visitors from curiosity outnumbered those "on business."—To the honor of the Republican party it may be said that the number of place-seekers has been unexpectedly small. Whether they are holding back only until they can learn something of Mr. Lincoln's manner of receiving such interested patriots, or whether real shame is the cause of their backwardness, remains, of course, to be seen. Calls from professional politicians have been remarkably few, newspaper reports to the contrary notwithstanding. They comprised all but exclusively representatives of various sections of this State. From abroad, the only visitor of note has been [Congressman] John Covode, of Pa., who spent a few hours here on Saturday [November 17]. From the South, no one worth mentioning has appeared. Crowds of Southern applicants for office exist in the imagination of brainless correspondents only. During the last three days of the week just closed, the average number of visitors was not over one hundred and fifty per day.

Rustics largely predominated among them. Fustian and buckram outshone broadcloth. A primitiveness of manners was often exhibited, and hats were not always removed, and anything but aromatic cigars kept lighted. The price of corn and wheat was frequently discussed, to the exclusion of "secession." On Saturday last [November 17] the influx of the Sangamon County peasantry was especially voluminous. A refreshing contrast to them formed, however, many angels in expanded silk and velvet.

Mr. Lincoln's correspondence is not by far as large as it is represented abroad for the sake of sensation. It averages from fifty to sixty letters per day. They mostly contain congratulations. The number of direct applications for office has also been exaggerated. In many letters reference is made to the services of the writers during the campaign, and occasionally a hint at substantial recognition. But few, only, are, however, impertinent enough to ask directly for rewards.

Of presents, scarcely any have been received by Mr. L. since election. During the canvass, however, a large number, of which an ox chain, carved out of a rail, a box of cigars, and a *bottle of brandy*, (Mr. L. uses neither article,)[70] were the most noteworthy. Newspapers, sent free by adoring editors, are now almost the only gratuities forced upon the "powers that are to be."

I should be lo[a]th to know any reader of the Commercial possessed of so little sense as to believe the senseless stories already started as to the probable composition of Lincoln's cabinet. He has not given the matter a serious thought,[71] and will not until he is actually made President by the electors from the several States. No one laughs more at the absurd newspaper combinations than himself. A settled idea appears, however, to prevail among many of Mr. L.'s friends that Tom Corwin will be a leading member of the cabinet.

I am able to state positively that Mr. Lincoln has no idea of making any public announcement of his executive intentions previous to the 4th of March. He is often questioned by visitors on this point, but uniformly states that his record contains all his views, and is open to all. Some expect that he will be induced to say something further on the occasion of the Republican jollification in this city on Tuesday next. I learn, however, from the most direct sources, that a few words of acknowledgment will be at most elicited from him.

The threatened secession is frequently discussed in Presidential circles. Mr. L. takes matters very calmly. He deplores the infatuation of the cotton States, but, being unconscious of any wrong on his part, does not dream of making any concessions to the spirit of rebellion. He will not be frightened by the hurly-burly of the fire-eaters; and while he does not possess an aggressive disposition, he has a sufficiency of nerve to see the laws of the country respected, after being called upon to administer them.

November 20, 1860

Springfield, 20 November 1860
[New York *Herald*, 21 November 1860]

Springfield is in a blaze of glory to-night. Although the celebration was intended to be strictly local, people have been pouring in in all sorts of conveyances the whole day. The city is splendidly illuminated, mostly with Chinese lanterns. The State House, a large square building, in the centre of a square in the middle of the city, has the appearance of four walls of fire. The Wide Awake torchlight procession was quite large.[72] It halted in front of Mr. Lincoln's home, and cheered for Lincoln until he appeared and spoke as follows:

FRIENDS AND FELLOW CITIZENS—Please excuse me on this occasion from making a speech. I thank you, in common with all those who have thought fit by their votes to endorse the republican cause. [*Applause*] I rejoice with you in the success which has so far attended that cause. [*Applause*] Yet in all our rejoicings let us neither express nor cherish any hard feelings towards any citizen who by his vote has differed with us. (Loud cheering) Let us at all times remember that all American citizens are brothers of a common country, and should dwell together in the bonds of fraternal feeling. (Immense applause) Let me again beg you to accept my thanks, and to excuse me from further speaking at this time.

The speech called forth most unbounded enthusiasm and numerous cries of "Go on," "That's right," &c. At the conclusion cheers were given for Mr. Lincoln, Mrs. Lincoln, Governor Yates, &c. The crowd then adjourned to the Wigwam.

The Wigwam was thronged the whole evening. After the procession terminated its march, speeches were made by R. Yates (Governor elect), Senator Trumbull, and others.

Mr. Trumbull's speech, in view of his high position and well known relations to the President elect, is taken as a reflex of the views of Mr. Lincoln. Hence it is the more important. The immense applause with which Mr. Trumbull was received having subsided, he said: "It is meet that republicans should make merry and be glad, for the spirit of liberty, which with our rulers was dead, is alive again, and the constitution ordained to secure its blessings, which was lost sight of, is found.["] Mr. Trumbull then branched off into a vein of State glorification, the republicans of Illinois having not only elevated one of their citizens to the Presidency, but have elected an entire State government, and secured thereby a United States Senator—the re-election of Mr. Trumbull.

Upon national topics Senator Trumbull discountenanced the idea of triumphing over political opponents, accepting all, by whatever name called, as brethren of a common country. He said Mr. Lincoln, although the candidate of the republican party, as Chief Magistrate will neither belong to that or any other party when inaugurated. He will be the President of the country, and of the whole country; and I doubt not will be as ready to defend and protect the State in which he has not received a solitary vote against any encroachment upon its constitutional rights, as the one in which he has received the largest majority. While they by whose votes he has been designated as Chief Magistrate of the people will expect him to maintain and carry forward the principles on which he was elected, they know that in doing so no encroachments will be made on the reserved rights of any of the States. They know that the federal government is one of delegated powers; that it can do nothing except the authority for the act can be found in the instrument which created it; that all powers not conferred are reserved to the States or the people of the States. Hence when their political opponents have charged them with abolitionism, or attributed to them a desire to interfere with slavery in the States, or some fanatic has insisted they ought to do so, the reply has invariably been that the people who made the federal government, did not think proper to confer on it such authority; and *it has, therefore, no more right to meddle with slavery in a State than it has to interfere with serfdom in Russia.* Nor are the people of the non slaveholding States in any way responsible for slavery in the States which tolerate it, because as to that question they are as foreign from each other as independent governments. I have labored in and for the republican organization with entire confidence, that whenever it should be in power each and all of the States would be left in as complete control of their own affairs respectively, and at as perfect liberty to choose and employ their own means of protecting property and preserving peace and order within their respective limits, as they have ever been under any administration. Those who have voted for Mr. Lincoln have expected and still expect this. They would not have voted for him had they expected otherwise. I regard it as extremely fortunate for the peace of the whole country that this point, upon which the republicans have been so long and so persistently misrepresented, is now to be brought to a practical test and placed beyond the possibility of doubt. It should be a matter of rejoicing to all true republicans that they will now have an opportunity of demonstrating to their political adversaries and to the world that they *are not for interfering with the domestic institutions of any of the States, nor the advocates of negro equality,* or of amalgamation, with which political demagogues have so often charged them. When this is shown, a reaction will assuredly take place in favor of republicanism. The Southern mind, even, will be satisfied; the rights of Northern men will be respected, and the fraternal feeling existing in olden times, when men from all parts of the country went forth together to battle for a common cause against a common enemy, will be restored. Disunionists, *per se,* of whom unfortunately there has been a few in the country for some years, understand this, and are now in hot haste to get out of the Union, precisely because they perceive they cannot much longer maintain an apprehension among the Southern people that their homes, and firesides, and lives, are to be endangered by the action of the federal government. With such "now or never" is the maxim; hence they seek to inflame the public mind by misrepresenting the objects and purposes of the republican party, with the hope of precipitating some of the Southern States into positions from which they cannot without dishonor afterwards recede, well knowing if they delay till after the new administration is inaugurated and tested it will furnish no cause for their complaints. *Secession is an impracticability, or rather an impossibility. The constitution provides no way by which a State may withdraw from the Union—no way for the dissolution for the government.* It creates the general good, interferes but little with the individual rights of the citizen, except for protection. It is chiefly felt in its benefits and its blessings—not its exactions. If every federal officer in South Carolina were to resign, their offices remain vacant, and its Legislature declare the State out of the Union, it would all amount to little except to inconvenience the citizens of the State. So long as the State did not interfere with the collection of the revenue on the seaboard, the people in other portions of the Union would not be in the least incommoded. What is the South Carolina army to do when raised? Whom is it to fight? Manifestly, if it commences a war on the United States officers engaged in collecting the revenues, it becomes the aggressor. This would be revolution, and making war without a cause, for South Carolina makes no complaint again the present revenue laws. Is she prepared for this—to become the aggressor? The only use I can see for her Minute Men is that they will enable the people the more readily to suppress any uprisings in their midst which their misrepresentations of purposes may have encouraged. She complains that the Fugitive Slave law is not executed in some of the States. This, if true, the whole country knows to be a sham. So far as South Carolina is concerned, she is so situated that no slave can escape from her limits into free States. However much cause the border slave States may have to complain of the escape of their negroes into the free States, it is clear South Carolina can have no such complaint. In her resolves she professes to be preparing to defend herself against encroachments on her rights. Let her adhere to this policy and not attempt to dictate to other States what they shall do, and no collision will occur, for no encroachments will be made. The disunion feeling in the South is doubtless greatly exaggerated. A sort of terrorism seems to prevail in some places, which for the time appears to have crushed out any manifestation of Union sentiment; but as the causes for this excitement are all imaginary, the election of a republican President in the constitutional mode certainly affording no excuse for it, it is reasonable to suppose that a reaction will soon take place among the Southern people themselves, which will overthrow the disunionists at home.

It is a great mistake to class the supporters of Mr. [John C.] Breckinridge as disunionists. Some few of them may be, but Mr. Breckinridge himself, and his supporters as a class, are, I doubt not, as sincerely attached to the Union as many of those who for political purposes during the recent excited contest sought to fasten upon them the stigma of disunion. Should the conservative and Union men in any particular locality be unable to cope with their adversaries, and South Carolina or any other State under the lead of nullifiers and disunionists, who have for years been seeking a pretext for breaking up the government, plunge into rebellion, and without cause assail by force of arms the constituted authorities of the Union, there will be but one sentiment among the great mass of the people of all parties and in all parts of the country, and that will be that "the Union, it must and shall be preserved;" and woe to the traitors who are marshaled against it.

Mr. Trumbull concluded his speech with a rehearsal of the points which he conceived to be gained by the election of Lincoln, and retired amidst the most enthusiastic applause.[73]

ELEVEN O'CLOCK.

The Wigwam is still crowded, and Don[n] Piatt, of Ohio, is speaking.

Mrs. Lincoln gave a reception this evening, and was visited by an immense number of people.

Mr. Lincoln leaves here at eleven o'clock to-morrow, and will arrive in Chicago at seven in the evening, when there will undoubtedly be a demonstration of people to see him, notwithstanding he wishes to travel quietly.

The statement of several Western papers, that Mr. Lincoln constantly receives large numbers of threatening letters from the South, is unfounded. Some indiscreet epistles have reached him, but outright blackguardism and threats of violence are indulged in only in a few instances, and these bear evidence of originating in the lowest sources on their face.[74] Verbal and written requests to resign for the sake of the country have been made by well meaning men anxious for the preservation of the Union, which were kindly received, but produced no effect.

Springfield, 20 November 1860
[Cincinnati *Commercial*, 21 November 1860]

Senator Trumbull, after congratulating the assembled Republicans on their victory, and eulogizing Mr. Lincoln, said: [Trumbull's speech, given in the above dispatch, is omitted here.]

Hamlin will meet Lincoln in Chicago, where a grand conclave of Republican leaders of the Northwest will be held. Lincoln goes to Chicago to-morrow. Trumbull's speech was inspired by him, and expresses his views in full.

V[illard]

Springfield, 20 November 1860, 10 P.M.
[Cincinnati *Commercial*, 24 November 1860]

The President elect was nearly killed with kindness to-day, on the occasion of the Republican jubilee. That to be President is not altogether like resting on roses, was demonstrated to him in the most palpable manner. From eight o'clock this morning until after five this evening he submitted, with the exception of an hour's respite at dinner, to a never-lessening crowd of visitors.

His reception room was so jammed all day that he could hardly find standing room. At one time he was fairly forced out of the apartment by the human pressure, and he struggled hard all the afternoon in retaining a position in a corner, close to the door.

The callers were mostly from the rural districts, immediately adjoining. At times the throng had a very rough aspect. The peculiar odor, that emanates from individuals in daily bovine and equine intercourse, was disagreeably intense. Few of the visitors took the trouble of removing their hats on getting into the Presidential presence. They seemed to look upon the reception as a sort of public show, to which they were fully entitled, having paid their admission by voting the Republican ticket. Little was spoken, both by the President [elect] and callers, beyond the ordinary exchange of salutations. In two minutes I counted at one time, no less than nineteen squeezes of the Presidential fingers, and that the latter were not benumbed before night relieved them from their functions, is indeed miraculous.

The number of representatives of the better sex was unusually great. As it is their wont, they generally claimed the privilege of staying longer than the male lookers-on, and gazing at the wonder of the day to their hearts' content.

THE REPUBLICAN JUBILEE.

This much vaunted occasion proved a rather slim affair. It showed poor judgment to expect that a general demonstration could be gotten up two weeks after the Presidential election. People were surfeited with parades, meetings, speeches, etc., etc., during the campaign, and were satisfied to be done with them for some time. But the reason of the postponement—the slow coming in of the returns from Egypt [i.e., southern Illinois], and the consequent uncertainty of the actual result of the election—will explain the delay.

Not two thousand participants in the jollification were from abroad; they hailed almost exclusively from the neighboring counties and towns. Hardly any body was here from St. Louis or Chicago. From the other States, Donn Piatt was the only one of note.

Of Wide Awakes, not over five hundred joined in the torchlight procession. Being mostly young yeomen, it could not be said that their appearance was of a dashing brilliancy. They marched badly, kept no order in the ranks, and altogether produced an unfavorable impression.

The most interesting incident of the procession, was the short address made by Lincoln, while the torch bearers were drawn up in front of his house. He came out, on hearing a sonorous voice exclaim from amongst the crowd: "Come out, old Abe, and show your honest face." Lincoln's remarks were listened to with the utmost respect and silence.

As large a party of ladies and gentlemen as the limited space would admit, were assembled in Mr. Lincoln's dwelling, while the procession passed. A rush was also made by outsiders into Lincoln's parlor, and the flowing amplitudes of the hooped angels were greatly reduced by pressure.

Mrs. Lincoln was, as usual, the object of as general attention as her husband.

THE PRESIDENT ELECT ABOUT TRAVELING

Mr. Lincoln will start on a short visit to Chicago this morning. He will be accompanied by Senator Trumbull, Governors Wood[75] and Yates, and other Republican notables. At Chicago he is expected to meet the Vice President elect [Hannibal Hamlin], and the Republican leaders of the Northwest.

CONDITION OF ILLINOIS BANKS.

The call for additional security made upon twenty-two banks of issue by the Bank Commissioners of this State, is about six per cent. of their circulation. [Former] Governor [Joel] Matteson's banks are assessed to the amount of about $50,000.00. It is thought that all will respond.

Springfield, 20 November 1860
[New York *Herald*, 4 December 1860]

To-day's work was the hardest "Old Abe" did since his election. He had hardly appeared at the State House when he was beset by an eager crowd that had been on the lookout for him ever since daylight. They gave him no time to occupy himself the usual two hours previous to the morning receptions with his private Secretary, but clung to his coat tail with an obstinacy worthy of a better cause. He had to admit them at once into his apartment, and then submit for nearly ten long, weary hours to the importunities of a steady tide of callers. Limited as the space required by the lean proportions of the President [elect] is, he found it a most difficult task to find sufficient standing room. By constant entreaties to make room only he maintained himself in close proximity to the door, which position he had chosen with a view to facilitating the inevitable hand shakings. But he found to his intense bodily inconvenience that this deference to the comfort of the callers was not the most practical plan he might have adopted. The curious defiled past him, after squeezing the Presidential fingers, into the room, and settled either on the sofa or chairs or remained standing for protracted observation. Only after having stared with open mouths to their heart's content—many employed hours in that agreeable pastime—they would move out of the room and enable others to gain admittance. A tight jam prevailed, therefore, all

39

day around the President, who found himself frequently "driven to the wall."

Beyond the customary exchange of salutations and some commonplace remarks, little was spoken. The monotony was varied at times only by some intended compliment of doubtful politeness and propriety from the lips of some unsophisticated yeoman.

The reception was anything but ceremonious. Few only took the trouble of removing their hats and segars, and the affair looked, indeed, more like the trial before a country squire than a Presidential levee.

Many Sangamon county youths brought their sweethearts along and presented them to "Old Abe," who was at times wholly surrounded by robust beauty.

Place seekers were in despair all day. In vain they tried to gain the Presidential ear. It was monopolized from early in the morning until late in the evening by the "people."

As predicted by me some days ago, the republican jollification of to-day was, as to display of enthusiasm and number of attendance, a comparative failure, although held at the capital of the State and the home of the President elect. The American people are known not to be able to foster a protracted excitement on one particular subject. Having been treated *ad nauseum* to Wide Awake processions, meetings, speeches, fireworks, &c., during the campaign, they are now sick of all such empty demonstrations, and wish to see no more of them for some time. The aggregate number of attendants from abroad did not exceed two thousand, and that of actual participants well below five hundred.

The Wide Awakes that joined in the torchlight procession were a sorry looking body, hailing, as they did, mostly from country towns. They revealed all the clumsiness, slowness of movement and lack of general vivacity that distinguishes rural from city bred youths.

The illumination was fine but not general. The State House presented a brilliant appearance, every window being lighted up from the cupola to the basement.

A lot of distinguished Illinoisians were in town, but, with the exception of Don[n] Piatt, from Ohio, and John Covode, of Pennsylvania, no one of note from abroad.

Although "Old Abe" had been nearly tortured to death during the daytime, the people gave him no rest after dark, even at his private residence. At half-past six he was once more crowded upon in his parlor, and had to undergo another agony of presentations. The whole lower story of the building was filled all the evening with well dressed ladies and gentlemen, whose comfort was, however, greatly diminished by the constant influx of an ill-mannered populace. Mrs. Lincoln had to endure as many importunities as the head of the family. She often had to hear callers ask each other, "Is that the old woman?" The President's offspring, however, seemed to enjoy the fuss hugely. The cheering outside was always responded to by their juvenile yells.

Mr. Lincoln repaired in front of the house, while the Wide Awake procession was drawn up, in response to a call made by an especially enthusiastic admirer, whose stentorian voice, rising far above the clamor of the multitude, enjoined upon "Old Abe to come out and show his honest face." What little was said by the President was spoken with great deliberation, emphasis and distinctness.

The most momentous event of the day was, of course, Mr. Trumbull's speech. It was prepared under Mr. Lincoln's direct supervision, and already in type on Monday evening. Coming as a clear and full definition of Lincoln's policy, after the latter's many seeming refusals to indicate his administrative plans previous to the 4th of March, it created great surprise.

That such a pronunciamento was desired even by a majority of the republicans is plainly shown by the universal satisfaction it produced. Its conservative tone is but an echo of the conservative views of this part of the country. It is believed by all that it will go a great ways in clearing the Southern sky of the clouds of disunion.

November 22, 1860

Springfield, 22 November 1860
[New York *Herald*, 26 November 1860]

In view of Mr. Lincoln's frequent and unmistakeable declarations to visiters as to his unwillingness to define his executive intentions in some official manner, previous to the 4th of March, the Eastern public was doubtlessly somewhat surprised at the explicit proclamation of his programme through the medium of Senator Trumbull's speech, on Tuesday evening last [November 20]. It is true the manifesto did not imply a formal contradiction and inconsistency on the part of the President elect, as it did not directly emanate from himself. But even the use of another party as a spokesman, could not have been determined upon without feelings of reluctance, in the face of former refusals to speak out, and it is but reasonable to suppose that causes of more than ordinary moment only brought about this change of purpose.

This was indeed the case. Stubborn facts of the most fearful portent were daily developed since the eventful sixth day of the month. They stared at the newly made President [elect] with all their ill-boding earnestness. He could not possibly shut his eyes to their growing gravity. He could not block

41

his mind to their serious logic. Every newspaper he opened was filled with glaring indications of an impending national catastrophe. Every mail brought him written, and every hour verbal entreaties to abandon his perilous silence, repress untimely feelings of delicacy, and pour the oil of conciliatory, conservative assurances upon the turbulent waves of Southern excitement. Even among his own political adherents many Union loving men exhorted him to yield. But a few steps from his reception room, the leading financiers of the State were assembled for many days to counsel and devise the best means of averting the commercial crisis threatened by the unexampled decline of the various State stocks, on which the paper currency—the vital foundation of Western commerce—was based. Telegraphic despatches, conveying the troubles and anxieties of Eastern financial commercial centres, constantly flashed upon him. Would it have been possible for any man in whose breast even but a solitary spark of patriotism glimmered, to remain unmoved and withhold the relief asked of him, when appealed to so continuously and urgently?

Whatever the political inclinations of the President elect may be, he is fortunately possessed of a large heart, and hence could not, at the sight of the ruin and misery already and about being engendered, fail to respond in the desired manner.

Sufficient time having elapsed for the proper digestion of Trumbull's speech, the impression that it will produce dissatisfaction in the extreme wing of the party that elected Lincoln is gaining ground both among the republicans and democrats of this section of the country. In the various offices at the State House, the usual places of rendezvous for the republicans of Springfield; in hotel parlors and barrooms, and everywhere on the streets, its probable effect North and South was the universal theme of animated discussion on yesterday. The republicans all look thoughtful, while the gloom spread over democratic countenances, ever since their overwhelming discomfiture, is somewhat lessened in intensity by the prospect of internal dissension among the victors. The flourish of partisan phrases in the exordium and peroration of Trumbull's effort is not deemed sufficient, among many of the former, to paralyze the anti-radicalism of the intervening portions, and a growl of disappointment is expected from New England, Northwestern New York, the "Western Reserve" [area of northeastern Ohio] and the radical States of the Northwest. It is apprehended that its conservatism will impart a fear of an abandonment of the Chicago platform in a backward direction, and bring the incoming administration between two fires, that may result in its utter humiliation and failure.

It is claimed by many well informed politicians of this latitude that Lincoln's trip to Chicago originated in a similar apprehension. His object is believed to be to impress the members of Congress from the Northwest, most of whom will meet him, with the absolute necessity of moderation during the next session, and of preventing angry outbursts of discontent among their extreme constituencies.

Leading Douglas men of this vicinity have been crowing for some days over the daily widening split between John Wentworth and the more moderate Lincoln faction. They express confidence in the ability of that great political tactician to prevent Trumbull's coalition, in the hatred of whom they hardly excel John Elongatus ["Long John"]. They expect to see this accomplished by a reelection of the democratic members of the Legislature with a few republicans, who will dance to the tune of Wentworth's dollars.

Springfield, like most State capitals, is ordinarily as dull as a New England village on Sunday. Its wonted lack of vivacity was interrupted heretofore only by the biennial sessions of the Legislature, but the unexpected windfall in the shape of the election of one of its citizens to the Presidency proved, however, a source of vitality altogether unparalleled in its annals. It will be the fortune of its hotel keepers and rumsellers. How great the influence of the fact of its being the residence of the President elect is upon the status of the town, is plainly shown by the now demonstrated effect of Lincoln's temporary absence. The relapse into the old monotony was instantaneous and complete.

A ludicrous scene was enacted to-day by half a dozen place seekers from Ohio and Indiana that arrived from the East on the early morning train with a view to presenting their claims to substantial rewards for services in the campaign to "Old Abe." Having heard on the way of his intended excursion, they rushed frantically out of the omnibus into the hotel office, and pantingly asked the clerk whether the rumor of his absentation was well founded. The elongation of their faces on being answered in the affirmative was marvelous. After giving full vent to their anger and disappointment, in language more forcible than refined, they concluded to extend their pilgrimage to the City of the Lakes [Chicago], in search of the departed idol.

On Tuesday evening [November 20] more business was transacted in the telegraph office of this place than on the 6th inst. Trumbull's speech was telegraphed to six different papers in full, and the number of special despatches was prodigious. The office was crowded until after midnight with special correspondents waiting for their turn. The operating force was hardly adequate to the emergency. The HERALD's ample despatches alone occupied one [operator] nearly all evening.

Springfield, 22 November 1860
[New York *Herald*, 23 November 1860]

The [Springfield] *Daily [Illinois State] Register*, the central organ of the Douglas democracy in this State, expresses satisfaction, in an elaborate editorial in today's issue, at Mr. Lincoln's conservative intentions, as reflected in Senator Trumbull's speech, but predicts the disintegration of the republican party in case they should be carried out.

It is currently asserted that Mr. Lincoln's visit to Chicago is intended to counteract the dissatisfaction expected to arise among the radical republicans of the Northwest at the conservatism of Senator Trumbull's speech, and to impress the Congressmen from the same section with the necessity of moderation during the next session of Congress.

It is stated on good authority that a confidential agent of Mr. Lincoln started South last night to prove Mr. [John] Bell's willingness to accept a seat in the Cabinet.

The Douglas leaders express confidence that the present feud between the almighty John Wentworth and Lincoln's followers will result in supplanting Senator Trumbull, whom "Long John" hates intensely, with another republican.

A violent snow storm prevails here to-day, and the town looks gloomy and deserted since the temporary removal of the centre of attraction.

Several expectants arrived this morning from Ohio and Indiana, and felt sorely vexed on finding Mr. Lincoln gone.

November 24, 1860

Springfield, 24 November 1860
[San Francisco *Bulletin*, 22 December 1860]

THE MAGNETISM OF POLITICAL POWER

The axiom that "success makes the man" holds good in politics, more than any other sphere of human aspirations. If anyone doubts this, let him come to this place and behold the eager crowds that, ever since the result of the late contest for the Presidential succession became known, have invaded this middle-sized western city, to humble themselves at the feet of the victorious Republican standard-bearer. Let him see the respectful anxiety with which his every word is caught up, and his every motion watched. Let him witness the reverential acquiescence in all the sentiments he is pleased to express. Let him laugh at the frantic efforts to discover and admire beauty in his unusually plain features; and be disgusted at a disgraceful persistency in attempting to discover heretofore-hidden merits in his moral and intellectual composition.

The most marked illustration of the aforesaid truism lies in the enlivened aspect of this western burg, in consequence of the steady attraction of luminous and illuminous political characters from all parts of the Union, by the accidental circumstance of its being the present seat of the powers that are to be. Springfield, like most State capitals, was distinguished for an unmitigated dullness only. Its unpaved streets—fathomless in muddy weather; the unartistic style and irregular combination of its business and other edifices; the want of sociability among its inhabitants; the meanness of its hotel accommodations, rather deterred than attracted visitors.[76] But now all these negative characteristics appear to be forgotten. Congressmen, governors, judges, editors, etc., wend their way to this newly-risen Mecca simultaneously with a countless host of [the] curious—and expectants. To the West, and no longer to the East, the country looks for political light.

So much of the intelligence, wisdom, celebrity, wealth, selfishness and patriotism of the land being now represented here, it is no wonder that the capital of the Prairie State has suddenly got to be one of the most interesting spots in the Union. Already a sort of court surrounds the President elect. Gossip on his internal and foreign policy; on the probable character of his Cabinet; on his intentions as to appointments to office, etc., fills hotel parlors and bar-rooms. Experienced tide waiters commence intrigues of every description for the realization of their plans. And all this fawning, talking and conspiracy being performed on so narrow a stage, it excites one's attention more readily.

HOW "OLD ABE" BEARS HIS DIGNITY

Sudden and unexpected as his elevation to the highest office in the land must have been to Mr. Lincoln, and dazzling as the great change of his social position must have proved to him, who had spent all his life amidst humble surroundings, be it said to his credit, that the acquisition of Presidential honors has not affected him in any way that might estrange or lessen the respect of his old friends. He has remained the same frank, open-hearted, good-natured, well-meaning, plain-spoken and mannered western man, that through his many qualities of the head and of the heart, is endeared both politically and privately to so many of the people of this State. There is not a shadow of presumption or vain-gloriousness perceptible. One feels still more inclined to bestow his well-known nickname upon him than his high-sounding title. He still communicates with everybody in his old familiar way. He still loves to tell funny stories and play off jokes on his acquaintances.[77] Nor is it likely that the air of Washington will make him abandon his wonted ways. I predict that he will horrify many of the fashionables, who will flock around him at the Federal Capital, by his persistency in frankness of thought and speech, simplicity of manners and habits.

HOW HE SPENDS HIS TIME

Ever since the day after the election, the demands of the public upon Mr. Lincoln's time have been so numerous and constant that he was soon obliged to divide it so as to enable him to do justice to all. His habit to rise early assists him greatly in this respect. Daybreak always finds him astir. His morning meal is taken at 7 o'clock, and after spending half an hour with his family, he repairs to the State House, where the Governor's room was given up in view of the limitedness of space in his own private residence. From 8 until 10, he busies himself in examining his mail matter, in which he is assisted by the Private Secretary [John G. Nicolay] he has been obliged to engage from the pressure of his correspondence, or receive visitors of distinction who are entitled to private interviews. At 10 o'clock the doors of his apartment are thrown open, and the general receptions begin. Everybody is admitted after that hour until noon without any further formality. Regular presentations are not made in the majority of cases. People walk in, mention their names themselves, and are allowed a shake of the Presidential hand without being backed up by someone personally known to the President [elect].

At noon, the latter retires from the public gaze, and spends his time at home until 3 o'clock, when he returns to the State House, to reopen the levees, which are then continued until half-past 5. At that hour he again seeks relief at his private dwelling until 7 P.M., when he resumes his labors with his Secretary. The daily increasing number of letters he is now receiving, renders it altogether impossible to answer them all himself. Only those from persons of distinction elicit personal replies, which the bulk of his correspondence—mostly from petty aspirants to office, and disinterested, but indiscreet, patriots, who offer gratuitously advice—is either left unnoticed or attended to by his amanuensis. Light is hardly ever extinguished in his room before 10 o'clock.[78]

WHAT HE THINKS OF THE QUESTIONS OF THE DAY

No discrimination whatever being made in the numerous callers that daily ask a sight at the President elect, it is but natural that he should be frequently approached by parties, of whose nature discretion is not the better part. Interrogatories on the most delicate and embarrassing questions of the day are constantly addressed to him with a perfect looseness by the unsophisticated sovereigns, who, in consequence of having contributed their elective mite to his success, presume to have as good a right to cross-examine him as any of the candidates for local offices in their own county. But very pertinent, and at times even impertinent, as some of their "pumping" attempts are, Mr. Lincoln but rarely tries to evade a response. He converses with the utmost freedom on current topics during his public receptions, and hence his opinions may be reiterated without incurring the risk of undue revelations of private matters.

The secession movement in the South pre-occupies, of course, his mind. Although far from acknowledging the right of the Cotton States to sever the ties that attach them to the confederacy, he yet thinks that any attempt at coercing them to remain in the Union, would but increase the calamities likely to arise from a separation. While he believes that it will be his duty as Chief Magistrate to uphold the Federal laws with all constitutional means, and hence to protect the United States' property, and secure the collection of customs in the rebellious States, he is yet disinclined to interfere in any other way. He is confident that the disunion epidemic carries its remedy in itself, and that the violent flames that now blaze, whereof cotton is king, will soon subside if unfed by aggressive demonstrations. Conscious of being elected in strict conformity to the Constitution, having committed no wrong, and determined to do justice to all sections of the country, he hopefully faces the future.

As to his views on the Slavery question, I feel warranted to say that Mr. Lincoln, as President of the United States, will never allow his private opinions to weaken his sense of duty and render him slow in executing the mandates of the Constitution. As it was stated by Senator Trumbull, in his short but pregnant speech, delivered in this city on the evening of the 20th inst., on the occasion of the Republican jubilee, "Mr. Lincoln, although the candidate of the Republican party, as Chief Magistrate will neither belong to that nor any other party. When inaugurated he will be the President of the country and the whole country, and I doubt not will be as ready to defend and protect the State in which he has not received a solitary vote against any encroachment upon its constitutional rights, as the one in which he has received the largest majority."

Senator Trumbull's effort, the whole of which was doubtlessly received by you ere this through the Pony Express, is a more comprehensive reflection of the President's executive intentions than any verbal statement yet made by himself since the election. It will be remembered that so soon as the triumph of the Republicans was a settled fact, many urgent calls were made upon Mr. Lincoln through public journals and otherwise for a public definition of his policy. For many days they were uniformly responded to by a simple reference to his published speeches. It was thought by the President [elect] himself, and most of his friends, that the demanded special *pronunciamento* would receive no credit, unaccompanied by acts, as its assertions would have to remain until 4th of March next, and would but be construed into a quailing before the threatening Southern storm. This opinion was frequently expressed to visitors by Mr. Lincoln. But the panic that suddenly rose in commercial circles in consequence of the Southern uproar and the apparent imminence of a general crash, induced many of his most ardent supporters to change their minds on this subject and recommend a declaration of policy in advance of the inaugural address. Such a one was embodied in the speech of Mr. Trumbull, who was selected as spokesman in order to avoid the charge of inconsistency on account of former refusals to speak out. The manifesto was prepared under Mr. Lincoln's direct supervision and in type long before its delivery. Its effect upon commercial matters proved that it was universally received as the President [elect]'s programme. Nearly all the drooping State stocks and many railroad securities rose immediately after its tenor was known in Wall street. It was telegraphed in full from here to all the leading journals.

Its conservative tone has produced the apprehension in the minds of many leading adherents of Mr. Lincoln, that disaffection will soon manifest itself among the ultras of the party. A suppressed growl of disappointment is already heard in many quarters.

THE RUSH OF PLACE-HUNTERS—HOW THEY ARE RECEIVED

That the "lust of spoils" is already drawing many Republican tuft-hunters[79] near him, upon whom the distribution of the fruits of victory devolves, is but natural. Predilections for an easy living at the public expense are among the attributes of all American politicians. A large number of aspirants are already nosing about the President [elect] with all the keenness of scent of the professional place-seekers. They urge themselves upon his attention in various ways. Some indulge in broad hints as to distinguished services in the late campaign. Others, especially the many free-soil martyrs from Kansas and Missouri, point to unhealed wounds. Again, not a few try stintless wheedling and unctuous flattery to secure favorable consideration. But all their devices rebound ineffectively from the object of their importunities. Mr. Lincoln will listen to their stories, but never gives them any encouragement. When urged too much he sometimes gives utterance to general reflections as to his intentions with regard to appointments, salted with some indirect allusions to the impropriety of office-seeking obtrusions, that prevent any closer approach. He has not received and will not receive any direct applications for office until after the 4th of March.

His most intimate friends express the belief, that "woe to the vanquished" will not be his standard of action, as to appointments. He is expected to retain the honest and capable of the present incumbents, and select new ones from among all parties. He has himself, indeed, already intimated as much on many occasions.

All the speculations, as to Mr. Lincoln's Cabinet—with which newspapers have amused themselves at the present moment—are preposterous. Although Mr. Lincoln has probably given this matter many thoughts, he knows too much to be guilty of the impropriety of acting in the premises before being formally made President by the Electoral College.

November 26

Springfield, 26 November 1860
[New York *Herald*, 1 December 1860]

Just about two years ago the writer was accidentally obliged to stop a day in this city.[80] Partly from curiosity and partly from a natural sympathy with misfortune, he felt induced to pay a visit to old Abe Lincoln. He found him sitting solitary and alone in his dingy, dusty law office. He had been baffled but a short [while] before in his powerful and protracted struggle with the "Little Giant" for the latter's seat in the United States Senate. The only spoils he had carried off in that momentous contest were a pile of campaign documents, rising to his right. But loss of time and labor, disappointed hopes and thwarted aspirations did not seem to grate upon his mind. He was resigned. He knew that he had made a good fight—no matter what the result. His talk was cheerful. His wit and humor had not deserted him. Altogether, he was a striking variation from the picture usually presented by unsuccessful aspirants to office.

At the same time a different scene was enacted not over a hundred yards from his office. In a spacious room in the second story of a three story brick building on the east side of the public square, a hilarious, exulting company was assembled. They were the sachems of the Illinois democracy [i.e., Democratic Party], who had assembled in their time honored Wigwam—the Tammany Hall of the Prairie State—to rejoice over the triumph of their chieftain [Stephen A. Douglas]. The flash of victory gleamed from their eyes. Party zeal, intensified by free indulgence in things spirituous, animated their countenances. Eloquent words of congratulation flowed from their lips. And well enough it was for them to be jubilant. The political world looked like their own. An unobstructed path to the Presidency appeared to be open to their leader. He seemed the man of the day. His prospect of being elevated to the highest office in the land was evidently certain. No wonder, then, that they were brim-full of hopeful expectations and elated at the coming "good time."

But times change, and so do men and matters. The other day I repeated my visit to the same locality. Alas! as with your own [New York City] Tammany, its glory had departed. The jubilant crowd of yore was wanting. A table, a few armchairs, a collection of empty bottles and a bust of the vanquished champion of popular sovereignty [Douglas]—not veiled in mourning but thick layers of dust—were now the only occupants of the hallowed spot. And all that at a time when he, whose defeat once caused it to resound with lusty cheers, was receiving directly opposite the homage of those that had placed him at the head of the nation, and disowned the victor of '58.

One of the numerous drawbacks to political prominence in this country is the persistency with which conceited, ignorant and boorish personages constantly thrust epistolary effusions upon men of distinction. In spite of all the dictates of common sense, courtesy and propriety to the contrary, they will make persons of mark the repositories of all their ideas, schemes, hopes and wishes. The fact that they have contributed their mite, by vote or otherwise, to the success of public characters, seems to be sufficient justification in their eyes to entrust all that occupies their thoughts, strikes their fancy and excites their cupidity, to paper, and obtrude it thus embalmed upon the unwilling objects of their epistolary mania.

Few persons of political renown but suffer from these letter writing bores—especially those upon whom the public attention is concentrated for the time being are visited with these vehicles of morbid curiosity, unmanly adulation, indiscreet solicitation and outright impertinence. That [the] present centre of the political gravitation—the President elect—should become a regular from this cause, is of course to be expected.

Mr. Lincoln's correspondence would offer a most abundant source of knowledge to the student of human nature. It emanates from representatives of all grades of society. The grave effusions of statesmen; the disinterested advice of patriots reach him simultaneously with the well calculated, wheedling praises of the expectant politician and the meaningless commonplaces of scribblers from mere curiosity. Female forwardness and inquisitiveness are frequently brought to his notice. Exuberant wide awake enthusiasm, with difficulty pressed into the narrow forms of a letter, is lavished upon him. Poets hasten to tax their muse in his glorification. A perfect shower of "able editorials" is clipped out and enclosed. Artists express their happiness in supplying him with wretched wood-cut representations of his surround-ings. Authors and speculative booksellers freely send their congratulations, accompanied by complimentary volumes. Inventors are exceedingly liberal with circulars and samples. More impulsive than [they are] well mannered[,] Southrons indulge in occasional missives conveying senseless fulminations and, in a few instances, disgraceful threats and indecent drawings. A goodly number of seditious pamphlets and manifestos has also arrived—in fine, all the "light and shadow" of Anglo-American political humanity is reflected by the hundreds of letters daily received by the President elect.

Mr. Lincoln returned this evening from Chicago with his family. He looks rather the worse for wear, but has preserved the even tenor of his temper, the incessant importunities of place seekers in the North to the contrary notwithstanding. If he expects relief here he will be disappointed. A number of expectants have been lying in wait for him during the last twenty-four hours, who will swoop upon him in the morning with an eagerness doubled by the delay.

Springfield, 26 November 1860
[New York *Herald* and New York *Tribune*, 27 November 1860]
Mr. Lincoln arrived here at 6:30 P.M. from Chicago, to the delight of the reporters and a number of office-seekers, who have been lying in wait for him since Saturday.

The President [elect] and party travelled in separate cars. No ovations were received on the way on account of the rainy weather.

A. H. Connor, Chairman of the Indiana Central Committee, was awaiting his arrival.[81]

Judge Arny, [general agent] of the Kansas Relief Committee,[82] was here to-day, and denies emphatically the report that Montgomery[83] received any countenance from the committee. He collected a large quantity of provisions in Central Illinois.

November 27, 1860

Springfield, 27 November 1860
[New York *Herald*, New York *Tribune*, 28 November 1860]
Mr. Lincoln occupied himself to-day principally with reading several hun-dred letters, accumulated during his absence.

Mr. Lincoln is in possession of reliable private information from Kansas, showing the published accounts of the Montgomery affair to be greatly ex-aggerated, and no attack on the border slave States intended.[84]

Mr. [Edward] Bates, of Missouri, is strongly urged by Western politicians.

The town is oppressively dull, and office seekers command a premium with hotel keepers.

_____

November 28, 1860

Springfield, 28 November 1860

[New York *Herald*, 2 December 1860]

Immediately after his arrival from Chicago on Monday evening last, the President elect repaired to his reception room to open and digest his accumulated correspondence. A pile of letters greeted him before which a less determined soul might well have quailed. Until late last night and all day yesterday did it absorb his attention. With a creditable patience he waded through the contents of several hundred letters, the perusal of which made him no wiser. Even his keen sense of the ludicrous begins to be bloated by the frequency of its imitation. Bad grammar and worse penmanship, stylistic originality, frankness of thought and pertinence of expression, vainglorious assurance, and impudent attempts at exaction may do well enough for the temporary excitement of humor. But this daily affliction must soon prove a source of weariness and annoyance.

But few visitors diverted Mr. Lincoln's attention from his correspondence yesterday. Some old acquaintances, of twenty and more years standing, called on him in the morning, and engaged in a lively discussion of the past and the present. He led them back to the period of his first public services in the Legislature of this State, in the years of 1837 and 1838 [Lincoln had served in the Illinois General Assembly from 1834 to 1841], and dwelt with evident satisfaction on the time when he and eight other six-footers—universally known in those days as the "long nine"—represented this section [i.e., Sangamon County] in that body.

In the course of the day "Old Abe" was induced to give an account of the sights he had seen in Chicago. He did it with his usual grotesque *bon homie*. His sketch of the dinner and other parties, and the Sunday school meetings he had to attend—of the crowds of curious that importuned him at all hours of the day, of the public levees he was obliged to hold, &c, &c., was graphic. It seems that instead of enjoying rest and relief, as expected, he was even more molested than in this place. If people only knew his holy horror of public ovations, they would probably treat him more sparingly.

To be lugged around from place to place to satisfy the curiosity of the populace, is a doubtful mode of bestowing honor and rendering homage, &c. Mr. Lincoln's experience at Chicago in this respect will probably deter him from undertaking another journey previous to his final departure for Washington City.

Since his return he has openly avowed that the principal object of his trip was to meet the Vice President elect. The position of the New England members of Congress during the next session, and the distribution of the federal offices in Yankeedom, was doubtless the main motive of the interview. All applications for office, from Maine down to Rhode Island, will probably be referred to Mr. Hamlin. Such an arrangement would certainly prove convenient to place seeking New Englanders, who would be enabled to save the heavy expenses of a personal pilgrimage to this place.

During the public reception of yesterday a visiter expressed his regret that the vexatious slavery question should be the first matter of public policy the new administration would have to deal with. The remark elicited an illustrative story from the President [elect] it will be well to repeat. He said that many years ago an unsophisticated farmer—more honest than learned—commonly known as "Old Zach"—undertook to run for the office of Justice of the Peace in Kentucky. Being successful, the first case he was called upon to adjudicate was a criminal prosecution for the abuse of negro slaves. Its merits being somewhat beyond his comprehension, he sought enlightenment (after hearing the evidence) in the statutes of the Commonwealth and various "handbooks for Justices of the Peace," he had provided himself with on assuming the ermine. But his search for precedents proved in vain, and growing still more puzzled, he exclaimed at last, angrily, "I will be damned if I don't feel almost sorry for being elected, when the niggers is the first thing I have to attend to." The story was, of course, intended more as a humorous reply, than an indication of Mr. Lincoln's own sentiments.

Considerable surprise has been expressed in republican circles hereabouts at the silence observed by the [New York] *Daily Tribune* with regard to the late semi-official exposition of Mr. Lincoln's policy through the medium of Trumbull's speech. The manifesto is said to have been telegraphed in full to that paper, at the editor's own request; and in view of this fact, the friends of Mr. Lincoln have been earnestly looking for some editorial comments from that source upon the effort in question. But thus far their expectations have been disappointed. Some begin to suspect that its conservative tone did not exactly suit your neighbor [Horace Greeley] and that between words of disapprobation and silence, he chose the latter. Senator Trumbull's visit to New York is reported to have something to do with this matter.

During the last few days the name of Edward Bates has been brought in various ways to the notice of the President elect, in connection with a seat in the Cabinet. It seems that the advocates of the claims of the distinguished

Missourian have become frightened at the urgent demonstrations of rival aspirants in Chicago, and hence endeavor to paralyze their possible unfavorable effect upon the future "giver of all good things" in the shape of offices. The [St. Louis] *Daily Missouri Democrat*, the organ of the Missouri freesoilers, has indulged in some strong hints at the propriety of Mr. Bates' appointment, and among the republicans of whig antecedents who figure in Presidential circles, these advances are well countenanced.

An Ohio farmer arrived here on Friday last, with two turnips of immense size, which he intended to present in person to Mr. Lincoln. He waited until Sunday evening for his return, but was finally compelled to leave without having the great satisfaction. The turnips, however, he left behind, and they were yesterday duly transferred to the President [elect].

Springfield is indescribably dull just now. A few obscure Western village politicians are the only place seekers in town. Will not [Thurlow] Weed, Gen. [James W.] Nye or other distinguished New Yorkers come to the rescue of despairing correspondents?

Springfield, 28 November 1860
[Cincinnati *Commercial*, 1 December 1860]

The President elect returned from his trip to Chicago on Monday evening last. Your correspondent was delighted to behold once more his angular form. His occupation was absolutely gone as soon as it had been removed beyond sight. The relapse of Springfield into its wonted dullness was instantaneous. This Capital of the Prairie State without Lincoln was worse than Washington without Congress. It struck the listless sojourner like one grand Quaker meeting house. Hotel parlors were deserted; book-keepers enjoyed an uninterrupted leisure; billiard tables stood unoccupied; the capitol looked like a dead-house—in fine, many a distressing place your special correspondent has visited in his time, he feels constrained to pronounce Springfield the most distressing of all.

Lincoln was glad to get back. They had worried him nearly to death with dinners, parties, Sunday-school meetings, church visits, levees, etc. etc. The Scylla of Springfield was nothing compared with the Charybdis of Chicago. The bores here were mostly villagers, and made no other pretensions than to take a good look at "Old Abe." In the Garden City they claimed him body and soul. They hauled him all over that city of respectable distances. They surfeited him, who yearned for his plain roast beef, with French dinners. They annoyed him with parties, "attended by the beauty and fashion." Expectants of distinction, from all parts of the Northwest, were clung to him like burs. What wonder, then, that he felt his heart gladdened, on reaching once more the comparative quiet of his old home?

Human nature is capable of many eccentricities. Negative and positive traits are frequently combined in one and the same character. Mr. Lincoln's experience since his election, at least, goes to show this. Just think of men, claiming the full possession of their mental equilibrium, and yet addressing him with the modest request to resign, "for the sake of our common country." It may sound incredible, that such odd human compositions should have any claims to the existence of reasonable beings. But the fact of such patriotic demands having been made, is undeniable. Men came here in person from distant portions of the State, to urge the propriety of a like step upon Mr. Lincoln. Letters conveying similar appeals, reached him frequently. That opposition papers should importune the Republican nominee, during the campaign, with impudent suggestions to resign, was not surprising. But that men, pretending to be of sound mind, and even such as supported Mr. Lincoln's Presidential aspirations, should walk up to him after the hard-fought battle was won, and ask him to sacrifice himself and his party, in order to restrain Southern rebels from attempts at secession, truly surpasses all comprehension.

As fruitless as the labors of those weak-kneed patriots [were?] the powerless means of intimidation employed by unscrupulous political opponents. Flaming printed manifestoes, with the most threatening passages underscored, were mailed to him by so-called theater men. Some scurrilous letters replete with coarse denunciation and vindictiveness were also received by him. Vile drawings and obscure caricatures were likewise forwarded to him. But all this exquisite mode of vengeance will avail them nothing. Mr. Lincoln reads and beholds everything philosophically, and preserves the most valuable literary and artistic gems, and consigns the balance to the stove or paper basket.

The scheme of the Washington Republicans in regard to the starting of an "organ" receives no countenance hereabouts. Mr. Lincoln's independence and self-reliance precludes the idea of his consenting to wear the contemplated journalistic fetters.

It seems that some of your contemporaries in the sourness of their temper at being somewhat behind time in the publication of the exposition of Mr. Lincoln's intended policy through the medium of Senator Trumbull, question the authoritativeness of the effort. Let them be assured that the speech was prepared under Mr. Lincoln's supervision, and that it was in type long before its delivery. There is not a person in Mr. Lincoln's confidence in this place, that has ever attempted to deny or conceal the fact of its being an exact reflection of the executive plans of the President elect. The attempts of these journalistic slow coaches to doubt its official character remind one very decidedly of the fox and the sour grapes.

As many a reader of the [Cincinnati] Commercial is doubtlessly itching to make his bow to the powers that are to be, with a view to a slice of the spoils, it will perhaps do to relate for their special benefit what happened on yesterday to a gentleman from Iowa, supposed to have come on a similar errand. He came into Mr. Lincoln's reception room—introduced himself— talked pleasantly for a long time, and after doing his utmost to produce a favorable impression on the President [elect], retired. He had hardly closed the door, when the latter asked: "What name did that man give?" No one could remember. Thus, if you come at all, be sure to not let your name slip out of the President [elect]'s mind before you turn your back on him.

On Saturday last, the morning train from the East, landed an Ohio yeoman, who had traveled all the way from the Scioto Valley for the purpose of seeing "Honest Abe Lincoln," and presenting him with two immense turnips he had brought along. Lincoln being gone, he waited patiently for him until Monday. Not being able to lose any more time, he departed, with sorrow in his heart. The turnips, however, he left with a friend of Mr. Lincoln, who presented them formally, and they were gratefully received, and will probably elicit a written acknowledgment for the disappointed Buckeye.

Springfield, 28 November 1860
[San Francisco *Bulletin*, 24 December 1860]

HOW "OLD ABE" RECEIVED THE ELECTION
NEWS FROM THE PACIFIC

The first inkling which the President elect received of the November election, in the Golden State [California], was, through a telegram from Fort Kearny, dated San Francisco, November 9th, and brought from the western to the eastern telegraphic terminus, by the Pony Express. It was sent by Dr. Hathaway, the Chairman of the Republican Central Committee,[85] and reached Mr. Lincoln in the afternoon of the 18th. Although fully aware of the confidence of his supporters on the Pacific Coast, in carrying the most Democratic of Free States for him, he had yet doubted their ability to achieve this political miracle, and hence was agreeably disappointed by the unexpectedly favorable first returns. But, although these figures augured well for the possibility of his carrying the State by a plurality, he yet thought it would be too much good luck, and with his wonted generosity, conceded it to his unfortunate rival, the "Little Giant" [Stephen A. Douglas]. A second despatch with still more encouraging news, reached him a few days later, during his short visit to Chicago in the course of last week. On his return from the "City of the Lakes" [Chicago] last evening, he found a third one, giving him strong assurance that California was good for him by several hundred votes.[86] Many times has he expressed his admiration of the bold fight made by his friends in your State [California]. He thinks, that having had to contend with fearful odds, they should receive the more credit for it. He holds that the unrivalled stump-speaking attainments of Col. [Edward] Baker, contributed largely to their success. Baker, by the way, is an old and intimate acquaintance of Mr. Lincoln, and although he once [in 1843] outmaneuvered "Old Abe," who relied more on his merits than tactics, in a race after a nomination for Congress, is held in kind remembrance. I should not wonder if Mr. Baker should turn out a "power in the land" during the next four years.

As to Oregon, Mr. Lincoln's friends had strong hopes of the electoral vote of that State ever since the election of Mr. Baker to the United States Senate. They calculated that the result of the October elections in Pennsylvania, Ohio and Indiana would satisfy the Douglas Democrats that there was no chance for their favorite, and hence would freely vote the Lincoln ticket for the sake of defeating the Lane[87] faction.

THE EXCURSION TO CHICAGO

The political quid-nuncs of this latitude were rather surprised by Mr. Lincoln's sudden determination to make a trip to Chicago. The close retirement he had adhered to throughout the entire campaign had impressed them with the belief that his dislike of public orations would induce him to remain quietly in his western home until the assumption of his official station. This was indeed his original intention; but circumstances arose that rendered a change of resolution advisable. In the first place, Mr. Lincoln desired to make the personal acquaintance of Mr. Hamlin, whom he had never met, although a member of the House at the time the Vice-President [elect] first appeared in the Senate. Not thinking it proper to ask him to come all the way from Maine to Springfield, he proposed Chicago as a place of meeting, to which the Vice-President [elect] at once acceded. Again, Mr. Lincoln was anxious to exchange opinions with the Republican leaders of the northwest, as to the course best to be pursued by the Republican members of Congress during the coming session, and to urge circumspection and moderation, in view of the Southern imbroglio. Ultra anti-slavery demonstration[s]—oratorical, legislative and otherwise—being deemed both uncalled for and likely to have no other effect than to increase the sectional complications that appeared to greet the new Administration on the threshold of power—a defensive posture was recommended as best suited to the occasion. From the result of the Chicago conference, I feel warranted in making the prediction that no measure of an anti-slavery or anti-Southern bearing will be urged by the Congressional friends of Mr. Lincoln this winter. The protective tariff question, the Central Pacific Railroad, the proposed organization of new territories, and all other issues that are likely to prove a source of irritation to the slave States, will be avoided until the incoming Administration will have gained a secure footing, and appeased the unfounded Southern apprehensions of aggressive executive steps.

Mr. Lincoln was accompanied to Chicago by his wife and his niece, Miss [Mary] Wallace. He had flattered himself with the hope of finding in the North a temporary relief from the importunities of the incessant stream of visitors from curiosity and otherwise, that had beset him in this place ever since the day after [the] election. But in this he was doomed to disappointment. On the journey, as well as during his stay in Chicago, the kindness shown to him nearly "killed him," to use an expression of his own. He kept the few callers who made their appearance this morning at his first public reception since his return for nearly an hour in a side-splitting roar by a humorous description of his adoration. His account of the parties and dinners he had to attend, the Sunday School visits he had to make,[88] and the rush of callers during the levees, he was obliged to hold, his pleas for mercy to the contrary notwithstanding, was unique. "Just think of it," exclaimed he, in the course of his witty narratives, "order-loving, sedate, quiet and well-behaved citizen that I am, they never allowed me to retire until 2 o'clock in the morning!"

MR. LINCOLN'S CORRESPONDENCE

From the day of his nomination at Chicago until the present hour, a perfect flood of letters has been daily poured upon Mr. Lincoln. As many as 150 letters have reached him in 24 hours. He found it indeed a matter of absolute impossibility to wade through all of it himself, and here he secured the services of John J. [G.] Nicolay, formerly a clerk in one of the State offices in this city, as his Private Secretary.[89] Mr. Nicolay opens all the correspondence, sifts it from trash unworthy of notice, and then submits it to the President elect, who makes known his pleasure as to replies after reading these several letters. Only such as come from eminent sources receive personal replies. All others are attended to by his secretary. Applications for office wandered all into the stove with a very few exceptions up to this time. No notice will be taken of any such until the formal indorsement of the popular vote by the majority of the Electoral College.

Every Pony Express and Overland Mail brings numerous letters of congratulation, in a goodly number of which strong hints at distinguished campaign services and expected adequate remuneration are indulged in. Let me say to those patrons of the [San Francisco] *Bulletin* who feel "hit" on reading this, that this expenditure of money and epistolary labor was altogether fruitless. They will have to try it again, and use that much labor, and in an entirely different way, if they desire any notice to be taken of their yearnings for office. Some unsophisticated individuals on the Pacific coast, I understand, have even carried their modesty so far as to ask Mr. Lincoln to "reply at once by Pony Express!" To these it will be well to suggest, that the President elect is a poor lawyer, and that he has no loose five-dollar pieces to invest in replies to his impatient California correspondents.

One is loath to believe human nature capable of such degrading adulation, incredible indiscretion, elaborate discourtesy, unblushing impertinence and relentless spite and vindictiveness, as is known to be daily revealed in Mr. Lincoln's correspondence. Sheets of intense personal admiration, whole pages of enumerations of services to the "cause," long chapters of distant county and township politics, windy dissertations on the "perils of the land of our birth," modest requests to resign "for the sake of the Union," denunciatory epistles from Southern blackguards, insulting caricatures from both Northern and Southern poltroons, are steadily obtruded upon him. What an interesting and instructive contribution to political literature these epistolary inflictions would make, if published in book form!

PRESENTS RECEIVED BY LINCOLN

Not so abundantly as letters, but sufficiently frequent to become uncomfortable, are Mr. Lincoln's receipts of presents from both disinterested or speculative admirers. His reception-room is crowded with them. There are hickory chairs; a wooden ox-chain, cut out of a single rail; any number of axes and mauls; brooms of stupendous size; a barrel overfilled with apples; boxes of segars; complimentary volumes from authors and publishers; piles of pamphlets and newspapers—the latter usually containing marked "leaders" from the pen of some expectant country editor—and many other articles, "too numerous to mention." Even a bottle of brandy was sent to the Presidential teetotaler the other day. Its contents and those of the segar-boxes were freely appropriated by visitors. An Ohio farmer arrived here on Friday last with two mighty turnips, which he desired to present in person to "Old Abe." Having in vain waited two days for his return from Chicago, he was reluctantly obliged to depart without having seen the object of his anxiety.

The turnips, however, he left behind, and they were duly transferred to the possession of the President [elect] this morning.

November 29, 1860

Springfield, 29 November 1860

[New York *Herald*, 4 December 1860]

This being Thanksgiving day, quite a large number of country people came into town to eat the customary turkeys with their city friends and pay their respects to the President elect. At the hotel of your correspondent, [there was] an old couple put up in the course of the forenoon, that from the moment of their arrival would talk of nothing but "Old Abe." They were exceedingly communicative, and hearing from the landlord that they were among the oldest settlers in the county, and had known Lincoln many years, I made it an object to get into conversation with them. The garrulous old lady soon delivered a highly interesting stock of Lincoln reminiscences. She said that she had been acquainted with the new President [elect] of the United States when people didn't call him "Old" Abe, but simply, "Abe;" in fact, that she well remembered him when still a boy in his old home in Kentucky, near which she had also been raised. She expressed great astonishment at his elevation to the highest office in the land. "Why," she said, "he was the gawkiest, dullest looking boy you ever saw." "But," she added, "there was one thing remarkable about him. He could always remember things better than any other boy in the neighborhood."

The best evidence of Mr. Lincoln's personal popularity in this vicinity, where he has lived for nearly thirty years, is furnished by the fact that it is altogether impossible to converse with any old resident about him without eliciting one or more stories illustrative of his ever ready wit, inexhaustible humor, quick repartee, honest frankness and good understanding with everybody. One could with ease collect a volume of personal anecdotes by a week's canvass of the lawyers' offices, court rooms, State and county offices, barrooms, &c, in search of similar information. Only last night a democrat of twenty years' standing treated me to an incident of this kind. Some twenty-three years ago, when Lincoln was doing this State his first service, in the capacity of a member of the lower branch of the General Assembly, the legislators saw fit to raise their per diem from two to four dollars. The passage of this measure excited a good deal of feeling in those poor times. It was thought entirely uncalled for, extravagant, and an outrage upon the taxpayers of the State. Lincoln had to endure a good deal of denunciation upon that score after his return. One day an old acquaintance, in the shape of a blunt, hard-working yeoman, met him and also commenced remonstrating about the same matter. He could and would not understand why men should be paid four dollars per day for "doing nothing but talking and sitting on benches," while he averaged only about one [dollar] for the hardest kind of work. Having fully given vent to his feelings, he wound up at last with an angry, "Now, Abe, I want to know what in the world made you do it." Nothing daunted by the dissatisfaction of his constituent, "Abe" replied instanter, "I reckon the only reason was that we wanted the money."

During the last two days the President [elect]'s correspondence experienced a remarkable increase. The number of applications for office was prodigious. From "away down East" [i.e., Maine] especially the supplications were frequent. The epistolary avalanche from that section probably originates in the supposition that since his meeting with Mr. Hamlin, as the representative of New England, the President [elect] is more favorably inclined towards Yankeedom than before. All the aspirants in that latitude will, however, do well to procure the Vice President [elect]'s endorsement before addressing themselves directly to the dispensing power.

Judging from the heavy newspaper mail Mr. Lincoln is daily receiving, he must be well posted as to current events. The leading dailies from the East, North, West and South will be found on his tables. Every editorial and item of news bearing upon the questions of the day is faithfully perused. Of the New York dailies he reads the HERALD, *Tribune*, *Times*, *Courier and Enquirer*, *Post* and *Express* regularly. Of weeklies, a large number is sent to him, but with the exception of the [New York] *Independent* and one or two others, hardly any are ever opened by him. Country editors, who have endeavored to ingratiate themselves by supplying their respective sheets gratuitously, will please take notice. I do not think that Mr. Lincoln reads the [New York] *Ledger.*

The more peaceful character of the latest news from the South produced a feeling of relief in Presidential circles. Although the probability of a secession of two or three of the cotton States is no longer questioned, it is not believed that any of the sugar growing and border States will be drawn into the disunion vortex. Mr. Lincoln watches every manifestation of Union sentiments in the South with intense interest. The great and patriotic effort of Mr. Alexander H. Stephens was fully appreciated by him, and formed the subject of protracted conversation.[90] Highly beneficial results are expected from the restraining influence of the distinguished Georgian in the coming State Convention.

Mr. George G. Fogg, of Concord, N.H., the secretary of the National Republican Committee,[91] arrived here from the East on the early morning train. He had a long private interview with Mr. Lincoln in the course of the forenoon. It is rumored that his visit is connected with the intended issue of a manifesto by the body he represents.

November 30, 1860

Springfield, 30 November 1860

[New York *Herald*, 1 December 1860[92]]

Yesterday being Thanksgiving Day, quite a number of country people were in town and paid their respects to the President elect. Mr. Lincoln, like the rest of Anglo-American mankind, feasted on a roast turkey, and, having special cause to thank his Maker, attended Divine service.

The President elect feels greatly relieved by the prospect of a peaceable solution of the Kansas troubles.

Mr. Stephens' Union speech was read by Mr. Lincoln with great satisfaction. He is reported to have said that the best item of news he had received since the 6th of November was that of Mr. Stephens' election as delegate to the Georgia State Convention.

George G. Fogg, secretary of the National Republican Executive Committee, was here yesterday, and had a long private interview with Mr. Lincoln.

At last a New Yorker has arrived, in the person of Hon. Hugh White, ex-member of Congress from Saratoga district,[93] who reached here this morning. White, having served simultaneously with Lincoln, was heartily received as an old acquaintance.

CHAPTER TWO

DECEMBER 1860

December 1, 1860

Springfield, 1 December 1860

[New York *Herald*, 6 December 1860]

Alas, the prince of the New York lobbyists. Poor [Thurlow] Weed.[1] His glory has departed—his metal is broken—his pride is humbled—his self reliance is gone—the air of conscious superiority no longer graces him—he crouches for want of back bone—his knees are shaky—he halts—he moves backward—he demands and defies no more, but supplicates and conciliates—he confesses to wrongs—he is weak and penitent. The metamorphosis is unexpected; it borders on the marvelous, but it is nevertheless real and complete.

Such is the gist and drift of the current talk in and about the State House during the last few days. From the highest to the lowest occupant all kinds of surmises, speculations, inferences and conclusions were indulged in on this exciting subject. Weed, Seward's henchman, faltering. He receding that was expected to "set his foot as far as the farthest." And that now, when the prospect of a share in the federal spoils should brace his nerves and cheer his temper.

All acknowledge that, strange things as had happened in our eventful days, this was yet the strangest of all. It was an absolute puzzle to [the] uninitiated. Some ascribed it to old age, others to fright. But the knowing ones had no trouble in solving the mystery. They easily traced the wonder to Wall street. They found in the condition of the stock market a perfect means of explanation.

Would that the transfigured and deposed king of the Albany lobby was possessed of the ring of Gyges,[2] so as to be able to hear unseen the remarks, comments, utterances of dissatisfaction, denunciations, &c, &c., daily made hereabouts in reference to his back-sliding. Would that he could see the negative interest with which his [Albany *Evening*] *Journal* is daily read by the future dispenser of what he yearns for most. He would then learn some bitter truths. He would then be taught that inconsistency is considered a poor peace offering; that although conservative feelings prevail in Presidential circles, the motives of his sudden retrogression are duly appreciated, and that "compromise for the sake of the spoils" is not the watchword of the powers that are to be.

The question whether the views put forth and the measures advocated of late by Weed are inspirations of Senator Seward is frequently discussed in the State House.[3] But although the Chicago record is not yet forgotten, there seems to be a unanimous opinion that the former is backing down from his "irrepressible conflict" position[4] of his own accord, and without the approbation of the latter.

Many of Mr. Lincoln's whig friends flattered themselves that the semi-official exposition of the internal policy of the incoming administration in Senator Trumbull's [November 20] speech would go a great ways towards allaying the secession furor now sweeping over the cotton States, but their expectations in this respect have as yet failed to be realized.

The Southern press, as well as Southern politicians, seem to have hardly noticed it. This wanton disregard of conservative assurances of the manifesto in question, is to them (Mr. Lincoln's supporters) conclusive evidence that disunion has been determined upon, and that it will be accomplished at all hazards. They nearly all have made up their minds to the certainty of the secession of South Carolina, and their apprehensions now centre in the question whether she will be followed by any other of the restive States.

The ineffectiveness of Trumbull's effort precludes the probability of another definition of Mr. Lincoln's executive intentions in advance of the inaugural. A repetition of the attempt to pacify the South by mere words, without the additional guarantee of official acts, it is believed would prove equally fruitless, and perhaps be construed into a sign of fear and weakness.

The story first published in the Chattanooga (Tenn.) *Gazette*, and now making the rounds, about the interview of a Mississippi planter with Mr. Lincoln, rests on an actual occurrence, and hence is well deserving general notice, as the replies of the President elect to the comprehensive questions of his Southern visiter are unusually explicit and cover all the points at issue.[5] The declaration that "no coercion will be used in case of secession, unless required by special act of Congress," was repeated to several callers within the last few days. It appears rather strange, in view of the unreserved and full answers given to all interrogatories made in relation to matters of public policy by visiters during reception hours, misconception should exist in some quarters as to the character of Mr. Lincoln's administration, as each of these answers is made with a special regard to their expected publicity.

The Hon. Hugh White, ex-member of Congress from the Saratoga district of New York, whose arrival I noticed in my last, is still tarrying here, and is said to spend most of his time in company with the President elect. Mr. White is known to represent the [Horace] Greeley wing of Empire State republicanism, and his protracted presence warrants the inference that it is in the ascendency in the State House.

Several Kentuckians of standing visited Mr. Lincoln in the course of yesterday. His conversational powers appeared to impress them quite favorably.

The only distinguished arrival on yesterday was John C. Heenan, who gave a pugilistic exhibition in the evening, in conjunction with several other champions of the ring.[6] The "Hero of Farnborough" did not condescend to visit Mr. Lincoln—a slight which did not seem to shock the latter in the least.

December 2, 1860

Springfield, 2 December 1860
[New York *Herald*, 6 December 1860]

Questions, it is well known, are more easily asked than answered. While they always produce a feeling of relief in those from whom they emanate, they often prove a source of pain and perplexity to those who are expected to respond to them. Such has been the case with the multifarious interrogations daily and hourly put to the President elect. It is true, those who elevated him to the highest office within their gift, have an abstract right to know his opinion relative to all matters of public policy. But some delicacy might nevertheless be observed in the mode of asserting it. People should understand that the rapid transfiguration [that] the condition of political affairs is undergoing at the present moment, renders prudent reserve and cautious expression advisable on the part of one whose every publicly-spoken word is forthwith clothed with an official interest, and heralded all over the land. Again, it should be remembered, that the uncertainty as to the denouement of the present complications, may make a mere opinion, that appears right to-day, wrong on the morrow, and furthermore, that as yet Mr. Lincoln considers himself a private citizen, and converses as such, and that many of his acts as President of the United States, may not conform to the views he now expresses, as the former will be dictated by his constitutional obligations, while the latter are given without being under any restraint whatever.

All these reasons for abstaining from "pumping" the President elect, are, however, not acted upon by only few of his various visitors. Most thrust the most pertinent questions upon him with a vengeance, and never allow any evasions or circumscriptions. They question and cross-question, worthy of a criminal lawyer. Fortunately, Mr. Lincoln is nearly always ready with a frank, comprehensive answer. But the questions often range beyond public affairs. Indiscreet persons suppose that not only public matter, but also public men are objects on which they are entitled to obtain Mr. Lincoln's views. Every day during reception hours some visiting scold will hold forth against some one prominent man, and after discharging his tirade, will call upon the President for a critical opinion of the same personage. This places the latter, of course, uniformly in a disagreeable dilemma, as a disapprobation of the expressed views will excite on the one hand the displeasure of the visitor and their indorsement on the other [hand] involves the risk of making personal enemies, owing to the constant presence of eaves-droppers and tell-tales. But a day or two ago, an Eastern gentleman, of distinction,[7] who should have known much better, perplexed Mr. Lincoln in the same way, within the hearing of the writer. He was very anxious to get the President's opinion of some well known New York politicians and kept insisting, although the latter's unwillingness to speak out before half a dozen visitors was very obvious, until a mark of displeasure caused him to recover his sense of propriety.

No President ever occupied a position more delicate than that in which Mr. Lincoln is likely to find himself on the fourth of March. Every day additional difficulties seem to arise. By every move on the political chess boards new issues are sprung upon him. The confusion on the public stage grows greater as the beginning of his term approaches. Nor is it probable, that his predecessor will do aught to bring order into the chaos before resigning his place at the helm of the ship of state. He himself bids fair to be called upon to bear the brunt of the present imbroglio. He will be elected either to settle the surging breakers of rebellion and disunion with the oil of passive forbearance and conciliatory measures, or to whip them into subsidence, while executing the Federal laws. He will doubtlessly be given an opportunity to exercise a decisive influence upon one of the most momentous phases of human history, and if he [should] prove equal to the occasion, engraft his name in immortal characters on the political records of his country.

In view of the heavy responsibilities likely to be loaded upon his shoulders, it is gratifying to know, that he will be prepared for the emergency. The clearness and decision, with which he points out to his visitors the causes of the present crisis, and the efficiency of the remedies he proposes to apply, warrant the supposition that events will not get the better of him. His free exchange of thoughts during reception hours renders it comparatively easy to compare his ideas on all points of public interest, especially as he does not obscure them with verbose argumentation, but defines them perspicuously in the least possible words. From these occasional declarations it appears:

1. That his last assurances through Senator Trumbull's speech having been intentionally disregarded by the South, he will

not repeat the public exposition of his policy before his inauguration; that he will continue a quiet looker on until his time
shall have arrived.

2. That he will endeavor to unite in his Cabinet representatives
of all sections of the country.

3. That he will not act upon the "maxim," "to the victors belong
the spoils," but will retain in office, and appoint honest and
capable men of all parties.

4. That he will strictly fulfill all his constitutional obligations, and
before doing so will not consider whether his acts may prove
obnoxious to a portion of the party that elected him.

5. That, although he does not acknowledge the right to secede,
he thinks it both would be unwise, impracticable and fruitless
to prevent its exercise by force, and hence he will not employ
such, unless compelled to do so by special act of Congress.

This is the sum and substance of what he is daily revealing in his intercourse
with callers, and although your correspondent does not claim to speak by
"express authority," your readers may yet consider the above reflection of
the view of the President elect, reliable.

As Congress has met at the hour of this writing, and the public attention
will be concentrated with more than ordinary steadiness on the proceedings
of [that] body, it may be well to state, that the general impression about here is
that Messrs. Trumbull and Cameron will indicate Mr. Lincoln's policy in the
Senate, and Messrs. Corwin and Covode will be his exponents in the House.

A rumor is circulating to-day in this place, that Mr. Lincoln will announce
his policy immediately after the meeting of the Electoral College. I doubt
its having any foundation. In fact the unsettled condition of the country
and Mr. Lincoln's well-known prudence and dislike of precipitation, render
it altogether impossible.

Many of Mr. Lincoln's friends assert, with a good deal of positiveness,
that the leading seats in the Cabinet will be filled with men of decided
conservatism from the Western and Southern States; and I expect to see
all New England in an uproar upon the announcement of Mr. Lincoln's
choice. The [Charles] Sumner, [Henry] Wilson, [William Henry] Seward,
etc., etc., wing, it is believed, will be ignored, in view of the irritation in
the South.[8]

John C. Heenan was here on Saturday last, but thought it incompatible
with his pugilism laurels, and Democratic predilections, to attend the receptions.

Joshua R. Giddings[9] arrived here this evening. He had a long talk with Mr. Lincoln, but I fear he did not set very sympathetic chords in vibration in the latter's bosom.

The other arrivals from Ohio at the three leading hotels are: D. H. Mead, Dayton; D. W. Corwin, Cincinnati[10]; F. Guiterman,[11] &c; D. W. Beall, &c.

Springfield, 2 December 1860
[San Francisco *Bulletin*, 27 December 1860]

MR. LINCOLN'S ANXIETY ABOUT THE SECESSION MOVEMENT

The impending secession catastrophe in the Cotton States continues to absorb the attention of the President elect. The idea that without cause he is made the pretext for breaking up the Union is, of course, mortifying to him, and greatly exercises his mind. It is true, he is unconscious of being moved with any aggressive spirit toward and of having inflicted any wrong upon the South, and hence he may well feel assured of the approbation and support of all well-meaning, reflecting, Union-loving citizens, and confident of a historical verdict in his favor. But the certainty of being elevated to the highest office in the land, only to see the country pass through its most trying hours since the days of the Revolution, and of being perhaps prevented, by the force of circumstances, from demonstrating his profound sense of the duties and restrictions imposed upon the Chief Magistrate by the Federal Constitution, to the different sections of the Union, proves, nevertheless, an abundant source of annoyance and anxiety to him.

The probability of becoming the reluctant inheritor of the fruits of all the missteps, derelictions and short-comings of the two preceding Administrations [of Presidents Franklin Pierce and James Buchanan], is likewise little apt to leave his equanimity undisturbed. He inclines, indeed, to the belief that, owing to the partiality shown by Mr. Buchanan to the South, the explosion will be put off until after the 4th of March, in order to devolve the whole burden of dealing with open rebellion upon his own Administration.

COMPOSITION OF HIS CABINET

This apprehension renders the selection of the constitutional advisers of the President elect a most delicate and difficult task. To make a choice now from among the many prominent public characters sympathizing with the Republican cause, when the morrow may impart a complexion to public affairs entirely at variance with the political predilections of the persons in question, would be both unwise and hazardous. Nor is Mr. Lincoln unaware of the inexpediency and risk of a premature decision in reference to this grave subject. He is satisfied for the present with making himself more fully acquainted with the merits of the prominent men [whom] his thoughts have connected with positions in his Cabinet, deferring a definite indication of preferences to a later day, when the aspect of public matters will be less confused.

But, although his disinclination to countenance any direct advocacy of the claims of aspirants to seats in the Cabinet is obvious, demonstrations have nevertheless been made and brought to bear upon him, in favor of several distinguished Western personages. Edward Bates of Missouri has been vigorously pressed within the past few days for the Secretaryship of the Interior. Judge [Stephen T.] Logan of this place, perhaps the oldest and most devoted friend Mr. Lincoln ever had, (he is said, indeed, to have made the latter what he is,) is strongly urged for the Attorney Generalship. Schuyler Colfax of Indiana, who rendered good service, as a stump speaker, to Mr. Lincoln, in the memorable Anti-Douglas State canvass,[12] (and he is pre-eminently qualified for the post, from his intimate acquaintance with the routines of the Department,) is eagerly pushed for the office of Postmaster-General. The President being a warm personal friend of all these gentlemen, and fully cognizant of their worthiness and fitness, I would not be surprised if their claims were ultimately endorsed.

HIS GRATIFICATION AT THE UNION
DEMONSTRATIONS IN THE SOUTH

It is with an eager watchfulness that Mr. Lincoln observes the progress of events in the Slave States, and with an unmistakable delight that he receives the views of the Union-demonstrations made here and there in that section during the last week. He was especially gratified by the tenor of the bold and patriotic speech of Alexander H. Stephens, which has probably reached you ere this. He flatters himself that men of like soberness of thought, and energy of action, will yet rise in larger numbers, so soon as the first gust of momentary irritation, in consequence of the result of the Presidential election, will have passed away, and check the reckless plans of the Seceders. Yet, although he entertains the belief that his unsuccessful rival for the Presidency [Stephen A. Douglas] might do a great deal towards allaying the Southern excitement by taking a bold public stand for the Union, he fears that the "pangs of jealousy" will prevent like patriotic acts on his part.[13]

EFFORTS FOR APPOINTMENTS IN CALIFORNIA

Since Mr. Lincoln's return from Chicago, he has been greatly annoyed by a number of parties, who, on the strength of alleged valuable service during the campaign, claim substantial rewards, not for themselves, but for brothers and other near relations residing in California. These magnanimous applicants on behalf of their friends all hail from this State, and some have had friendly relations with Mr. Lincoln for many years, so that they were at least sure of a kind reception of their representations. But the President [elect] did make neither promises nor assurances. He remained altogether non-committal, and the parties had to abandon their hopes for the present. It was remarkable that the efforts of all of them was aimed at the United States Marshalship of your State [California]—probably on account of its being the best paying Federal office on the Pacific coast; one of the "California brothers" was a delegate to the Chicago Convention.

LINCOLN AND THE REPUBLICAN PRESS OF THE EAST

Those of your readers who are *au courant* with the tone of the Republican press of the Atlantic States, with regard to the secession plans of the Cotton States, are doubtlessly aware of the wide difference in the various attitudes severally recommended by them to the Republican party in reference to this issue. While the more conservative organs, and even those that were heretofore looked upon as the most advanced, advise the taking of conciliatory steps by Congress, State Legislatures, and the party they represent. The most influential journals urge absolute passiveness, both as to the concessions demanded from the North by the South, and the contemplated actual secession. The former desire to see preventives employed; the latter pronounce all such undignified and useless, as the Cotton States were bound to go out of the Union at all hazards. Strange as it may sound, such papers as the Albany *Evening Journal* and the Springfield (Mass.) *Republican*, are found to advocate the first mentioned programme. Without pretending to speak by authority, I venture to say, that Mr. Lincoln, although conservative in his intentions, does not agree with the proposed attempts at pacification and reconciliation—not from any feeling of defiance, but from a conviction that they will be scorned by the Southern ultraists, who are bent on severing the ties of their several States to the "accursed Union," notwithstanding all offers of concessions, compromises, etc. In this respect, he comes very near the views of the New York *Tribune.* The motives of Thurlow Weed in shooting off from his customary position of the head of progressive political journalism, are well understood here, as well as the fact that in this matter he is not the exponent of Mr. Seward's ideas.

The above-mentioned divergences in the Republican press have excited the fear of imminent disruption of their party in many of Mr. Lincoln's most intelligent and reflecting friends.

LINCOLN ON SOUTHERN SECESSION

Much anxiety is naturally felt in all parts of the Union as to the convictions of the President elect in relation to the secession issue which he will be, in all likelihood, called upon to face; and hence it will be well to state, in addition to what I have said on this subject in a former letter, a reply he recently made to an interrogatory put to him by a Mississippi planter, who made the journey to this place for the express purpose of satisfying himself as to the position that Mr. Lincoln's Administration was likely to assume towards the South. He intended to invest a large amount of money in the purchase of Virginia negroes, but did not wish to risk his means without being assured of a non-intervention programme on the part of the powers that are to be. After having elicited the positive declaration from the President elect that his Administration would protect the slave property of the South with all constitutional means, that it would not try to meddle with slavery in the District of Columbia, and that it would see the Fugitive Slave law enforced, he wound up his questions by asking whether Mr. Lincoln recognized the right of the Southern States to secede, and if not, what he would do in case of secession. To the first question Mr. Lincoln answered, that he *did not recognize the right to secede*; to the second, *that he would not use coercion unless compelled to do so by the passage of a Force bill by Congress.* It will be seen that this view of secession is identical with that taken by the New York *Tribune's* most Republican leaders [i.e., leading editorials].

SCARCITY OF VISITORS AND OFFICE-SEEKERS

The smallness of the number of visitors to this place from other States is really remarkable. Of callers from curiosity, not over a hundred paid their respects to the President elect during the week just ended, and of office-seekers, hardly a dozen appeared in the same period. It is evident that the expectants are holding back in view of the troubled state of the country. That the crowd of Presidential electors, campaign speakers, members of State and National Conventions, Congressmen, etc., will absent themselves altogether, is not very probable. But that many think it prudent to await the denouement of the present complications and the assumption of well-defined positions on the secession question by the different parties, before identifying themselves too closely with the incoming Administration, is also certain. The only noteworthy visitors since Mr. Lincoln's return from the North, were George G. Fogg of Concord, N. H., Secretary of the National Republican Committee, and Hugh White, ex-Member of Congress from the Saratoga District, N.Y. The last mentioned gentleman served in Washington simultaneously with

Mr. Lincoln, and as an old acquaintance, was quite intimate with his former colleague. *He was the first New Yorker of distinction, that came to see Mr. Lincoln since his election.* More about this strange phenomenon in my next.

December 3, 1860

Springfield, 3 December 1860

[New York *Herald*, 9 December 1860]

As the electoral colleges are about to meet in the Northern States, and by their votes to make Lincoln the *bona fide* President of the United States, after which event the pangs of office seekers may be supposed to commence in good earnest, your correspondent has compiled a sort of directory for the benefit of such of that hungry kidney as hail from the Western States. It will tell them where to procure the necessary certificate, showing the time served in the ranks, the zeal manifested and the money spent for the cause, &c., &c., before setting out on the pilgrimage to the biding place of the republican Allah. By availing themselves of the information contained in the subjoined reliable list of political characters that will control the distribution of the federal patronage in the several States, they are likely to save much unnecessary trouble and anxiety:

OHIO—Tom Corwin, Senator Wade, Robert D. [C.] Schenck, Judge Ewing.[14]

INDIANA—Henry S. Lane,[15] John D. Defrees,[16] Schuyler Colfax, Col. Thompson.[17]

ILLINOIS—N[orman] B. Judd,[18] Senator Trumbull, Wm. B. Ogden,[19] Judge [Stephen T.] Logan, J. Gillespie,[20] E. Peck.[21]

WISCONSIN—Senator [James R.] Doolittle,[22] Gov. Randall,[23] Karl Schurz,[24] and members of Congress generally.

IOWA—Members of Congress.

MISSOURI—F. P. Blair[25] and Edward Bates.

KANSAS—Mark W. Delahay,[26] Tom Ewing, Jr.,[27] M. J. Parrot, M. C.[28]; C. A. Wilder,[29] Judge Johnston.[30]

It is believed that Kansas and Missouri will send a comparatively more numerous host of expectants than any other section of the Union. The number of free soil martyrs, both bogus and otherwise, that will present themselves for consideration from these two regions, will be prodigious. The Kansas delegation will be headed by Mark W. Delahay, an empty-headed, self puffing, vainglorious strut, who bases his pretensions on unsolicited campaign services of doubtful efficacy in Illinois and Indiana. The Missourians that will before long beset the President elect, under the leadership of F. P. Blair, are likely to fare relatively better than the applicants from any other State, as their slice will be unusually large, in view of the fact that the largest republican vote cast in a slave State was given in Missouri, and that the bulk of the free soil party of Missouri is made of Germans, who have never been in the habit of running after offices, but content themselves with voting, and leave the division of the spoils to the comparatively few natives that figure as their leaders.

A rumor has been afloat to-day that the President elect contemplates a selection of his constitutional advisors immediately after the meeting of the electoral colleges, and making his choice known to the country at large in order to allay the Southern excitement. Having been unable to trace it to any authoritative source, I place no credence in it. It must appear evident to every intelligent mind that the present political aspect of the country renders the composition of the Cabinet a most difficult task, hardly admitting of a hasty discharge.

The name of Robert E. Scott, of Fauquier County, Virginia,[31] has been freely mentioned of late in connection with the Secretaryship of the Interior. He is pressed principally by Indiana and Pennsylvania influences. Botts is nowhere.[32] His name has not been presented by any one. I think his Union speeches will prove ineffectual bids for office. He seems to be pretty well appreciated in Presidential circles.

Mr. Lincoln keeps himself fully posted as to the condition of the money market. Mr. Dubois, the State Auditor,[33] who is in daily and intimate telegraphic and epistolary intercourse with many leading Wall street operators, furnishes him constantly such information as enables him to understand the strange capers of your bulls and bears.

Joshua R. Giddings, the renowned prophet of Ashtabula [Ohio], arrived here this morning to fill an oratorical engagement. He called upon the President elect, and was privately engaged with him for some time. Although cordially received, I doubt that he succeeded in eliciting an expression of sentiments on the issues of the day in harmony with his own.

Hon. Hugh White left for New York early this morning.

None of the electors have arrived as yet. A heavy fall of snow occurred during the last two days throughout the State, which may delay their movements.

December 4, 1860

Springfield, 4 December 1860
[New York *Herald*, 9 December 1860]

That foreign elements prevail much more extensively in the Northwestern than in the Eastern States is a fact that cannot fail to be noticed by even the most cursory traveller. That of the heterogeneous mosaic of nationalities that constitutes the population of the former, the German is, next to the native, the most numerous component part, will also be learned by a short acquaintance with the respective localities. Ever since the reaction upon the revolutionary era of 1848 and 1849 began to swell the numbers of those that annually sought the hospitable shores of this republic to theretofore unknown proportions, nine out of every ten of the newcomers crossed the Alleghenies in search of a cheap home in the broad free West, and hence the increase of the German settlers in all the States west of the aforesaid mountain barrier and north of the Ohio river has been prodigious during the last ten years. Sameness of language, habits and tendencies made them a compact body, whose influence was from year to year more decidedly felt in the political scales, as the number of voters among them was augmented by steady naturalization. In 1856 their numerical strength asserted itself far less strikingly than during the Presidential campaign just ended, and that owing to the fact that the immigration of 1854 and 1855 (the most voluminous ever landed in this country in a like space of time) had not been naturalized in the former year. But in the late contest it may be well said that the voters of German extraction held the balance of power in Ohio, Indiana, Illinois, Wisconsin, Minnesota and Iowa. In each of these States they numbered tens of thousands, and on whatever side they were to throw the whole weight of their vote was sure to be the winning one.

There was not an intelligent politician in the Northwest that was ignorant of the importance of his "German friends." Hence all possible appliances were brought to bear upon them by each of the contending parties with equal vigor, but different success.

The majority of the Germans of the Northwest, unlike that of their countrymen in the Atlantic cities, contributed to the success of the republican party. Nor is this stubborn fact to be wondered at. Their ablest journals, their best speakers, their most prominent and popular men, reflected republican views. They worked with the peculiar zeal, earnestness and indefatigableness with which the German mind is wont to make propaganda for its convictions; and hence the result—namely, an overwhelming majority among their compatriots for Lincoln and Hamlin.

In Ohio, Illinois, Indiana, Iowa and Wisconsin, native republicans now openly acknowledge that their victory was, if not wholly, at least to a great extent, due to the large accessions they received in the most hotly contested sections from the German ranks. Whether their share of the fruits of the triumph, in accomplishing which they assisted all but decisively, will be commensurate to the aid they furnished, remains to be seen.

That the Germans, as a rule, run less after office than the natives, no candid overseer of political life will deny. But that all those among them that made themselves conspicuous by their efforts, both on the stump and otherwise, in behalf of Lincoln, are disinterested patriots, free from all yearning for office, can hardly be supposed.

It is well known, on the contrary, that quite a number are ready to serve their country. Of these Teutonic expectants the most prominent are:

George Schneider, editor *State Gazette*, Chicago, Ill.[34]
H. Bornstein, editor *Advertiser*, St. Louis, Mo.[35]
B. Dromshke, editor *Atlas*, Milwaukee.[36]
J. F. Mansfield, Indiana Elector at Large.[37]
F. Hassaurek, Ohio Elector at Large.[38]
Gustavus Koerner, ex-Lieutenant Governor of Illinois.[39]
[Nicholas J.] Rusch, ex-Lieutenant Governor of Iowa.[40]
S. Kaufmann, New York District Elector.[41]

Karl Schurz, whose claims are the strongest, in consideration of his having delivered over a hundred campaign speeches and spent a small fortune for the cause, expects to be United States Senator, and hence will keep out of the ring.

The ambition of all of the above aspirants is a mission in one of the German courts. But as all cannot be gratified in this way, some will have to content themselves with something else. I would not be surprised, however, if ex-Governor Koerner should be sent to Berlin.[42]

The greatest drawback the German candidates for federal appointments will experience in pushing their claim, will be the difficulty of making Mr. Lincoln acquainted with the drift of the German wishes as reflected in their press; and hence, I trust, they will feel grateful to your correspondent for the publication of the above details, which were furnished to him by one of the most eminent German citizens of this State. Mr. Lincoln is disposed to be just to his German friends, and will doubtless act upon the hints herein thrown out.

The approaching meeting of the electoral college has greatly enlivened Springfield. All the electors have already arrived. Each one brought a whole suite of expectant friends along, and the hotels and barrooms are once more well filled.

Mr. Lincoln's room was crowded all day during reception hours, and there was no end of introductions, salutations, congratulations, compliments, &c., &c.

The attention of the President elect is now fixed on Congress. He awaits the appearance of his predecessor's [annual] Message [to Congress] with the greatest anxiety. The attitudes likely to be assumed by Northern and Southern Congressmen are also a frequent theme of conversation with him.

Father [Joshua R.] Giddings departed early this morning for the East.

George G. Fogg, the Secretary of the National Republican Executive Committee, is again in town, and figures prominently about the President [elect].

Some wags are daily entering the names of distinguished Eastern politicians on the registers of the leading hotels. Each such bogus arrival works the political gossipers of this city into a considerable excitement, until the "sell" is discovered by attempted calls upon the hotel strangers.

December 5, 1860

Springfield, 5 December 1860
[San Francisco *Bulletin*, 2 January 1861]

BACKWARDNESS OF NEW YORK POLITICIANS

It will be remembered that a good deal of ill feeling was produced by the result of the Chicago Convention, among the New York delegation—the very flower of the Empire State—who had staked their political fortunes on the success of William H. Seward. It is true, they displayed a creditable resignation, and, their foiled hopes to the contrary notwithstanding, did not swerve from their party obligations during the campaign. But that the pangs of disappointment are still rankling in their bosoms, is most plainly indicated by the distance at which they have remained—since the election—from the foot-stool of power. While representations from all the States that gave majorities for the Republican candidate have already paid their personal respects to the President elect, the Seward wing of New York Republicanism, has up to this day kept "afar off." It is evident, indeed, at the present moment, that they intend to continue aloof, unless advances be made to them in return for their generosity towards the successful rival of their favorite. [James Watson] Webb, [Henry J.] Raymond, [William] Evarts, [James W.] Nye, [Moses] Grinnell, [Simeon] Draper, etc., have all resolved upon this conditional abstinence from participation in the enjoyment of the spoils. Weed alone is shaking, and his last compromise and concession gyrations show that he is bound to have his [share?] at all hazards.

The tardiness of the New-Yorkers in rendering homage to the "fountain-head of power," is the subject of general remark in Presidential circles. Their seeming determination to persist in a dignified repose, and quietly await the pleasure of the powers that are to be, is, however, anything but a source of grief in view of the present complicated condition of public affairs. It promises, on the contrary, to remove the most dangerous stumbling block, viz., a close identification with the Seward faction, out of the way of the new administration. Although the thought of ignoring them altogether in the division of the Federal patronage is far from being entertained, the odium attached to the propounder of the "irrepressible conflict" doctrine [William Henry Seward] in Southern eyes is so deep and universal, that the less the President elect will, at least for the time being, appear to have to do with him, the smoother his administration is likely to be. Whatever admiration and sympathy he may in reality entertain towards his unlucky competitor, he cannot be ignorant of the fact, that the offer of a seat in his Cabinet to the distinguished Senator from New York would kindle a dissension blaze not only in South Carolina, but from Baltimore to Galveston, from Charleston to Fort Smith, and from Louisville to Mobile.

THE LINCOLN CABINET

A strong rumor has had currency during the last three days, that Mr. Lincoln intends proclaiming the names of his constitutional advisers immediately after the meeting of the Electoral Colleges, to-morrow. There is not the slightest probability of the existence of any such programme. Events crowd each other so rapidly just now, that the complexion of public affairs to-morrow may be so greatly different from that of to-day, as to render a modification of the choice of the President elect likewise necessary, and hence precipitation might only increase the present perplexities of his position. Furthermore, the intended effect of such a step, viz: the pacification of the South, is at best doubtful, and it would most certainly estrange the party that elected him, just as much as it would possibly bring the restive Southrons nearer. The utter disregard of the conciliatory assurances of Senator Trumbull's speech [given in Springfield on November 20] by the Cotton States renders it more than probable that they would treat the announcement of a Cabinet, no matter how conservative, no better, while the North might well look upon it as a sign of fright and weakness. Again, Mr. Lincoln has knocked the bottom out of this absurd street-tale by a direct declaration to the contrary in the course of yesterday afternoon. He expressed himself distinctly that he had no concessions, advances or peace-offerings to make, as such would be an indirect recognition of the justness of the complaints and presumptions of the seditious States. There is certainly no cow[er]ing, crouching or temporizing to be expected from Mr. Lincoln.

It is now understood that Henry S. Love [Lane], John D. Defrees, and other Indiana politicians, have made a strong epistolary demonstration in favor of Robert E. Scott, of Fauquier county, Va., for the Secretaryship of the Interior. [John Minor] Botts has very little show, as an intimate friend of Mr. Lincoln remarked to me the other day: "he has been too long after the Presidency to make a good Secretary." The general impression here is that three members of the Cabinet will be taken from the South, if a satisfactory selection can be made in that quarter.

CONGRESS AND THE PRESIDENT ELECT

The fate of Mr. Lincoln's administration will depend, to a great extent, on the result of the present session of Congress, and hence all eyes are now turned in the State House in the direction of Washington City. The appearance of President Buchanan's [annual] Message [to Congress] is awaited with the greatest anxiety, as the character of the inheritance likely to be left by him to Mr. Lincoln is presumed to be foreshadowed in it. Much trouble is apprehended from the violent outbursts of partisan feeling that both Northern and Southern ultraists are expected to indulge in. The opinion, however, predominates that the Southern fire-eaters will be more aggressive than the Northern radicals, as the former are supposed to have determined upon secession at all hazards.

Special telegrams from Washington to-day constantly flashed into the President's room. They proved anything but sedatives.

LINCOLN'S CONGRESSIONAL EXPONENTS

As many of the readers of the [San Francisco] *Bulletin* are perhaps anxious to know who are to reflect Mr. Lincoln's views in the upper and lower branch of Congress, I will state that they will not go much out of the way, by looking to Messrs. Trumbull and Cameron of the Senate, and Messrs. Covode and Corwin in the House, for light as to the wishes and intentions of the President elect. Mr. Trumbull, especially, will speak "by authority." Mr. Hamlin's position [as vice-president-elect] would render it somewhat improper for him to become Mr. Lincoln's mouth-piece.

MEETING OF THE ELECTORAL COLLEGE OF ILLINOIS

This is the day on which the electors of the several Republican States meet in accordance with the constitutional provision, to cast their votes in favor of Lincoln and Hamlin. A heavy fall of snow having occurred on Sunday and Monday last throughout Illinois, the electors of the Prairie State all set out early on their journey to the capital, for fear of detention on the road, and hence all arrived here yesterday afternoon. They met Mr. Lincoln by candle-light, and spent the greater part of the evening in his company. Judging from the frequency with which his visitors availed themselves of the things spirituous that were dispensed in an adjoining room, they must have had a rather jolly time of it. It was even asserted this morning, that after the retirement of the President elect, they adjourned to the Chenery House (the leading hotel of the place), and made sad havoc among the stores of sparkling wines of that establishment until the small hours of the night.

Precisely at 12 M. the Electors assembled in the Senate-chamber at the State House, and after organizing themselves, successively proceeded to ballot for Lincoln and Hamlin. The voting occupied but a few minutes, and took place without any special ceremonies. Only about fifty outsiders witnessed the momentous occasion. . . .

Leonard Swett was appointed to carry the vote of the State to Washington. Having discharged their duties, the Electors repaired to Mr. Lincoln's reception-room, and informally congratulated him on his election. No speeches, however, were delivered.

All the State officers were present in the Senate Chamber.

At 3 P.M., the President elect and all the electors assembled in the house of one of their number, James C. Conkling, who is a resident of this place, and partook of a splendid dinner. Toasts in honor of Mr. Lincoln, the Republican party, the Union, etc. were brought out, and enthusiastically responded to.

A simultaneous salute of forty-four guns—thirty-three for the Union, and eleven for the electoral vote of the State—was fired in front of the State House.

In the course of the afternoon special despatches, announcing the results of the meeting of the Electoral Colleges in the several State capitals, reached Mr. Lincoln from nearly every Northern State. Congratulations from Washington city were also received in abundance.

VISITORS

The assembling of the Electors, each of whom was accompanied by some expectant friends, brought a large number of strangers to this place. They were, however, mostly from different sections of this State. From abroad, Joshua R. Giddings was the only one of distinction. He had a long talk with Mr. Lincoln, but the extreme position he advised him to take found little favor. Justice to Mr. Giddings requires a statement of the fact that his visit was merely accidental, he having a lecture engagement to fulfill.

Springfield, 5 December 1860
[New York *Herald*, 10 December 1860]

The synopsis of the President's [Annual] Message sent to the press was read by Mr. Lincoln this morning. He very freely gave vent to his surprise at its tenor, as it plainly revealed, in his opinion, Mr. Buchanan's desire to rest the whole responsibility of the secession movement on the free States. He expressed himself likewise in strong language on that part that refers to himself, as he says it entirely misrepresents his view.[43]

The deed begun on the 6th of November was accomplished to-day. The Electoral Colleges of the free States have met. They have to-day made Abraham Lincoln and Hannibal Hamlin President and Vice President of these United States.

The meeting of the electors of this State passed off with little pomp and less circumstance. A heavy fall of snow having occurred throughout the State on Saturday and Sunday last [December 1 and 2], they had all taken care to start early upon their important journey to the capital, so as to be in time for the discharge of their duties, even if unexpected delays should happen, and hence were all in town yesterday morning. The afternoon as well as the evening they whiled away, partly in Mr. Lincoln's reception room, and partly in a cosy, comfortable apartment, closely adjoining the former, and well supplied with segars and things spirituous by some of the occupants of the State House, who thus demonstrated their *savoir vivre* in a most acceptable manner.

At ten o'clock this morning the electors had a sort of caucus, in which their *modus operandi*, the propriety of a formal congratulatory demonstration after the voting was over, and the candidates for the office of "messenger," were discussed.

At twelve M. precisely the eleven members of the Electoral College made their appearance in the Senate chamber, which had been especially prepared for the occasion. There were the electors at large, viz:—Leonard Swett[44] and John M. Palmer,[45] and the nine district electors, viz:—Allen C. Fuller,[46] W. B. Plato,[47] Lawrence Weldon,[48] Wm. P. Kellogg,[49] James Stark,[50] James C. Conkling,[51] H. P. H. Bromwell,[52] Thos. G. Allen[53] and John Olney.[54] They formed a most respectable and intelligent looking body. Mr. John M. Palmer called the assemblage to order, and nominated W. B. Plato as president, and Thos. G. Allen as secretary of the College. Both being elected, the casting of the ballots was proceeded with without any further ceremony. The chairman first called them up by name, one after the other, to deposit their ballots for President in a hat that stood before them on a small table. This being done, the majority of the electors seemed to suppose the affair all over, and the secretary was doing up the votes in an envelope, when their attention was called to the fact they were about forgetting to vote for Hamlin. The discovery caused a good deal of merriment. The mistake being corrected, a motion for adjournment until after dinner was immediately made and carried.

The voting was witnessed by about one hundred persons, among whom were all the State officers, the newly elected Governor, R. Yates, and many other notables of the Prairie State. From abroad, no one of distinction was in attendance.

At two o'clock in the afternoon, the electors again met, and chose Leonard Swett, one of their number, as messenger. Swett had been a prominent candidate for Governor, and feeling somewhat chagrined at his failure to get the nomination, received the appointment with a view to its operation as a restorative of his former evenness of temper.

Their duties being all discharged, the electors all repaired to Mr. Lincoln's reception rooms, and formally congratulated him upon his election. No set speeches were delivered on the occasion.

At four o'clock the President elect, his lady and the electors, assembled at the house of Mr. [James C.] Conkling, the elector for this district, to partake of a dinner. The President and lady, the republican party, the Union, &c., were duly toasted, the best feeling prevailed, and the convivialities were prolonged to a late hour.

In the course of the afternoon a salute of forty-four guns—thirty-three for the Union and eleven for the electoral vote of the State—was fired in front of the State House, and a rather tattered specimen of the "stars and stripes" hoisted on the cupola.

The presence of the Electoral College attracted a good many visiters from the interior of the State to the capital, and Mr. Lincoln's receptions were more numerously attended to-day than at any previous time since his return from Chicago.

The electors will all leave for their several homes to-morrow morning.

December 6, 1860

Springfield, 6 December 1860
[New York *Herald*, 11 December 1860]

In the course of last evening I sent you a special despatch reflecting the views of Mr. Lincoln on the last annual Message of his predecessor. They were the result, I understand, of the perusal of the unsatisfactory synopsis sent out by the Washington agent of the Associated Press on Tuesday afternoon. The second, more complete and correct condensation, disseminated late in the evening of the same day, showed the passages relating to Mr. Lincoln's position to be much milder and less personal than they were inferred to be from the first. I have reason, indeed, to believe that after the proper digestion of the Message *in toto*, in the course of to-day, the opinions of Mr. Lincoln and his friends were somewhat modified as to the bearing of the document upon the President elect. It is true the same severity of comments are still applied to that portion of it that charges the republicans with having been the main agents in entailing the present political crisis upon the country. But this alleged indulgence in misrepresenting insinuations as to the antecedents of Mr. Lincoln is no longer insisted upon.

The attitude assumed by Mr. Buchanan towards the secession movement is much bolder than it was supposed to be by Mr. Lincoln's intimate friends. Several among them have already given expression to the belief that the practical test of secession, viz: resistance to encroachments on the part of the restive States upon federal authority, may after all devolve upon the outgoing administration. This desire to see the explosion—if one is to occur at all—take place under the latter, is of course natural with the friends of the successor.

As the session advances the intensity of the feelings with which the doings of Congress are watched in the State House appears to increase. The appearance of the South Carolina members in their seats was not looked upon as indicative of that delicate sense of honor and propriety that is usually claimed by the Southern chivalry. The resolution offered by Mr. Morris, of Illinois,[55] was construed into a sign that the so-called anti-Lecompton democrats would co-operate with the republicans in offering a strong Union front to the seditious predilections of the majority of the Southern members. It is, however, known here, that Morris is, and always was, somewhat of a Douglasite in regard to the slavery question. [Villard later explained that the final portion of this sentence should have read: "somewhat ahead of Douglas on the slavery question."]

In a former letter I ventured the prediction that republicans would content themselves with the defensive, and rather avoid than push the "all-absorbing topic of the day." The proceedings of the first three days prove its correctness. The programme now carried out, it is said, was agreed upon in Chicago.

Not a little excitement was produced last night by the advent of ex-Gov. Reeder,[56] of Pennsylvania. The tongues of political gossipers were at once set in full motion, and before he had retired he was already connected with a seat in the Cabinet, a foreign mission and a United States Judgeship. Some pretended to know him to be bearer of despatches from Simon Cameron. Others said that he had journeyed hither for the purpose of procuring Mr. Lincoln's endorsement of his claims to the United States Senatorship about to be vacated in his State. But I give both the President elect and the ex-Governor too much credit for good sense to believe them to have anything to do with any such transaction. Mr. Reeder, I understand on the contrary, is on his way to Kansas, and simply stopped over a day to pay his respects to Mr. Lincoln.

Since the meeting of Congress Mr. Lincoln's correspondence has undergone a very gratifying decrease. It is evident that the attention of politicians is monopolized for the time being by the events at Washington.

Hon. Leonard Swett, the bearer of the electoral vote of this State, will start for Washington to-morrow morning.

Senator Trumbull is expected to return here in a few days to attend to his re-election.

Senator E. D. Baker is said to have written a letter of congratulation to the President elect, since his arrival in New York.

December 7, 1860

Springfield, 7 December 1860
[New York *Herald*, 15 December 1860]

However prejudiced by partisan bias the daily observer of Mr. Lincoln's doings might be, he could not resist the impression that all he does and thinks bears the stamp of conscientious earnestness and solicitous dutifulness. It would be sheer falsification, indeed, to deny that he entertains a sincere anxiety, not so much as to the special interests of the party that elected him and the furtherance of his own political fortunes, as with regard to his duties to the country at large and the means of discharging them to the best of his power and ability. It is evident, beyond all refutation, that he draws a distinct line between his private opinions and convictions and the public obligations he will be called upon to fulfill, no matter whether they are consonant with his inward impulses or not. All his utterances, since and before his election, go to confirm this fact. Were not such his settled purpose and firm resolution, it would have been absolutely impossible for him, with his habitual frankness of expression, not to reveal secret intentions to the contrary in his replies to the innumerable pointed and searching interrogatories put to him daily by visitors representing every section and political persuasion of the land, on the issues of the day. I venture to say that not one of these passed out of his reception room without being firmly convinced that he honestly means to sink the man in the public officer, the partisan in the patriot, the republican in the faithful executor and protector of the federal laws in every State of the republic.

This being the case, it only remains to be seen whether circumstances will not prove too strong for him—whether he will simply float on the current of events or prove able to direct their course, as far as his official power goes.

Giving him credit for honesty of purpose, we only know Mr. Lincoln in addition to be a strong debater, a good dialectician, a well informed politician and a sound lawyer. What his executive abilities are we still have to learn. These are great and perilous times, and great must be the man for them. The stuff of which he is made must be as stern as the aspect of our days. Mediocrity will no longer do. The innermost resources of the highest statesmanship will be required. Illusion will be no more in place. Difficulties will have to be looked boldly and squarely in the face. Irresoluteness will be dangerous. Incompetence will prove pregnant with mischief. Both together must be fatal. To believe, then, as I do, that Mr. Lincoln will be found but little wanting in these several respects, is certainly no mean source of gratification. Having closely observed him since the election, and well noted the impressions made upon him by the secession [successive] phases of the present imbroglio, I dare say that there are dormant qualities in "Old Abe" which occasion will draw forth, develope and remind people to a certain degree of the characteristics of "Old Hickory" [Andrew Jackson].

Whether the sequence bear[s] out my judgment or not, an earnest of his high sense of the requirements of his position at least will be found in the fact that he is indefatigable in his efforts to arrive at the fullest comprehension of the present situation of public affairs and the most proper conclusions as to its probable consequences. He never contents himself with a superficial opinion based on newspaper accounts and arguments, but always fortifies his position by faithful researches for precedents, analogies, authorities, &c. He is at all times surrounded by piles of standard works, to which constant reference is made. His strong desire for full and reliable information on all current topics renders it especially regretful to him that circumstances debar him from obtaining anything but ex parte statements as to the progress of events in the South.

As the 4th of March is drawing nearer, the impending removal to the federal capital becomes more and more the subject of discussion and preparation with the President elect and his family. It is true his worldly goods are so few that their disposition will hardly cause him any great embarrassment. It is, however, but natural that the prospective exodus from the town with which his life has been identified for over a quarter of a century should produce some mental tribulation. Mr. Lincoln himself as yet devotes only thoughts to this matter; but the lady members of his family are said to be already busily engaged in preparing for a becoming entrance into the White House. That present haunt of a lonely bachelor [James Buchanan] promises to be greatly enlivened after the inauguration of the new administration. Mr. Lincoln's youthfulness alone will bring about a revolution.

It is stated that the President elect intends to make his departure from Springfield about the middle of February. He will travel slowly, and probably visit some of the Atlantic cities before directing his course toward Washington city.

On the first Monday of the coming month the Legislature of this State will meet here for a session of forty days. Their biennial advent inaugurates the harvest home of hotel keepers, rumsellers, &c., &c.; hence great preparations are already made for the reception and depletion [sic] of the members and their enormous tail of lobbyists and other hangers on; they always drag along simultaneously. The usual scantiness of accommodations in the way of board and lodging will doubtless be greatly increased by the voluminous influx of applicants for office under Mr. Lincoln, who will improve the presence of legislative friends for pressing their claims.

The following "Lincoln" item appeared in the local column of this morning's [*Illinois State*] *Journal:*

COAT FOR THE PRESIDENT ELECT—We yesterday were shown, at the clothing store of Messrs. Wood & Henkle, a very handsome and elegantly made dress coat, gotten up at that establishment as a present to the President elect. The stitching upon it is very elaborate, and ornamented with a great deal of extra work.

December 8, 1860

Springfield, 8 December 1860
[New York *Herald*, 15 December 1860]

A few days ago an intimate friend of Mr. Lincoln, while animadverting upon a certain reference in Mr. Buchanan's Message to the antecedents of the President elect, took occasion to speak of a bill bearing upon the abolition of the slave trade [actually slavery itself] between the District of Columbia and the slave States, unsuccessfully urged upon Congress by Mr. Lincoln in the course of the single term he served in that body. He remarked, at the time, that it was a striking illustration of the conservatism and the deep sense of justice and equity that pervades the President elect. My curiosity being excited, I hunted up an old file of one of the dailies of this place, and after diligent search succeeded in finding the bill alluded to in full. This Congressional relic having never been published entire, within my knowledge, in either the numerous campaign liars [sic] or any of the Eastern journals, I thought it well enough, in view of the present complications, to transmit a copy to you for publication. Section five of the bill deserves especial attention, from the fact that it was intended to provide a sort of limited Fugitive

Slave law several years [actually one year] before the general act to the same effect, for the country at large, was passed by Congress.

This history of the bill in question is: On the 21st of December, 1848, Mr. [Daniel] Gott, of New York, offered a resolution in the House, instructing the Committee on the District of Columbia to report a bill for the abolition of the slave trade in the District. As soon as the resolution was read, a motion was made to lay it on the table, but lost by a vote of 81 to 85. A hot struggle ensued, but after a good deal of parliamentary skirmishing the resolution was adopted. An immediate attempt to reconsider was made, but proved ineffectual. The action upon the motion to reconsider was postponed from day to day until the 10th of January following, when Mr. Lincoln proposed an amendment in the shape of the following bill:

Be it enacted, &c., &c., That no person not now within the District of Columbia, nor now owned by any person or persons now resident within it, nor hereafter born within it, shall be held in slavery within said district.

Sec. 2 That no person now within said district, or now owned by any person or persons now resident within the same, or hereafter born within it, shall ever be held in slavery without the limits of said district; provided, that officers of the government of the United States, being citizens of the slaveholding States, coming into said district on public business and remaining only so long as may be reasonably necessary for that object, may be attended into and out of said district and while there, by the necessary servants of themselves and their families, without their right to hold such servants in service being thereby impaired.

Sec. 3. That all children born of slave mothers within said district on or after the 1st day of January, A.D. 1850, shall be free, but shall be reasonably supported and educated by the respective owners of their mothers or by their heirs or representatives, and shall owe reasonable services as apprentices to such owners, heirs and representatives, till they respectively arrive at the age of —— years, when they shall be entirely free, and the municipal authorities of Washington and Georgetown, within their respective jurisdictional limits, are hereby empowered and required to make all suitable and necessary provisions for enforcing obedience to this section on the part of both master and apprentices.

Sec. 4. That all persons now within said district lawfully held as slaves, or now owned by any person or persons now resident within said district, shall remain such as the will of their respective owners, their heirs and legal representatives, provided that any such owner or their legal representatives may at any time receive from the treasury of the United States the full value of his or her slave of the class in the section mentioned, upon which said such slave shall be forthwith and forever free. And provided further, that the President of the United States, the Secretary of State and the Secretary of the Treasury shall be a Board for determining the value of such slaves as their owners may desire to emancipate under this section, and whose duty it shall be to hold a session for the purpose on the first Monday of each calendar month to receive all applications, and on satisfactory evidence in each case that the person presented for valuation is a slave, and of the class in this section mentioned, and is owned by the applicant, shall value such slave at his or her full cash value, and give to the applicant an order on the treasury for the amount, and also such slave a certificate of freedom.

Sec. 5.—That the municipal authorities of Washington and Georgetown, within their respective jurisdictional limits, are hereby empowered and required to provide active and efficient means to arrest and deliver up to their owners all slaves escaping into said district.

Sec. 6.—That the elective officers within said District of Columbia, are hereby empowered and requested to open polls at all the usual places of holding elections on the first Monday of April next, and receive the vote of every white male citizen above the age of twenty one, having resided within said district for the period of one year or more, next preceding the time of such voting for or against this act; to proceed in taking said votes, in all respects not herein specified, as at elections under the municipal laws, and with as little delay as possible to transmit correct statements of the votes so cast to the President of the United States; and it shall be the duty of the President to canvass said votes immediately, and if a majority of them be found to be for this act, to forthwith issue his proclamation giving notice of the fact, and this act shall only be in full force and effect on and after the day of such proclamation.

In order to give an opportunity to compare the views of the President elect on one and the same subject at different periods, ('49 and '58,) I subjoin also a series of replies made by him in '58 at Freeport and Charleston to a corresponding number of interrogatories emanating from Senator Douglas:

1. I do not now, nor ever did, stand in favor of the unconditional repeal of the Fugitive Slave law.
2. I do not now, nor ever did, stand pledged against the admission of any more slave States into the Union.
3. I do not stand pledged against the admission of a new State into the Union with such a constitution as the people of that State may see fit to make.
4. I do not stand pledged to the abolition of slavery in the District of Columbia.

5. I do not stand pledged to the prohibition of the slave trade between the different States.
6. I am not in favor of negro citizenship.

The assurance with which some Western papers presume to speak of Mr. Lincoln's intentions as to appointments is truly refreshing. The idea that the President elect takes all visiting scribblers of more or less obscurity into his heart, and makes them the repositories of the innermost resolves of his mind, is so preposterous that none but the greenest of their readers should be taken in with it. Yet every mail brings dailies and weeklies from various sections of the West containing leaded leaders, in which the imaginative theories of the several "able editors," with regard to the distribution of patronage by the new administration, are elaborately set forth with an impudent air of authority. The anxiety of some of this gentry to have their respective sheets looked upon as "organs" is especially ludicrous. The price of that glory being low impudence, mendacity and strong faith in the credulity of their readers—all that is wanted to constitute a modern organ grinder—and the occupation being comparatively harmless, they might well be allowed its undisturbed enjoyment, were it not for the wrong impressions their fabrications sometimes produce upon the public.

The truth is that Mr. Lincoln has not talked, and will not talk for some time to come, with any one on the subject of appointments. In fact, his most intimate friends give us to understand that beyond the composition of his Cabinet he has not given the matter a thought, not to speak of signalizing his preferences of certain persons for certain offices of minor importance. Even as to his immediate constitutional advisers no definite selection has as yet been made. The course, indeed, [that] events in the South have taken, and the uncertainty of the ultimate fruits of the present agitation in that section, render delay desirable, as the character of the Cabinet will have to be made up, under the present circumstances, to wait the political condition of the country. The examination only of the merits of the different persons upon whom a *portefeuille* [cabinet portfolio] might be fitly bestowed occupies, therefore, the mind of the President elect, and a choice is not thought of at the present time. Hence I wish the reader to understand that in mentioning prominent political characters, in connection with offices under Mr. Lincoln's administration, I merely reflect the current of outside influences hereabouts. The friends of several parties are busily at work in creating a public opinion of more or less strength for the benefit of their favorites, and may ultimately succeed in producing an impression on the President. But thus far they have not been able to elicit either promises or even an encouraging word.

Among many republicans of this city that have cultivated close relations with Mr. Lincoln for years, the propriety of presenting their townsman, Judge [Stephen T.] Logan, as a proper occupant for a seat in the Cabinet is very strongly urged. The department he is recommended for is the Attorney Generalship. The onerous duties of that office would, however, be almost too much for a person so far advanced in age as [the sixty-year-old] Mr. Logan. A quiet federal judgeship would be much more adapted to that venerable gentleman, and I think his own predilections go that way.

Should Mr. Logan desire an appointment, Mr. Lincoln would hardly refuse it. The old Judge and the President elect have been on the most intimate terms for nearly a quarter of a century. The latter is, indeed, indebted to the former to a large extent for what he is. He pursued his law studies under Mr. Logan's tutorship, and he always found him an ardent friend and active promoter of his political fortunes. When he was a candidate for United States Senatorship, in 1855, Mr. Logan worked for him day and night, and when Senator Trumbull succeeded in outmanoeuvring him, the Judge shed tears of anguish over the defeat of his friend, and gave vent to his feelings in a public speech which caused quite a sensation at the time. In view of all this it may be presumed that Mr. Logan can have what he wants for the mere asking.

It seems that the West is pretty nearly unanimous in the advocacy of the claims of Mr. Schuyler Colfax to the Postmaster Generalship. That Mr. Colfax would make a faithful, intelligent and efficient officer, even his political opponents will acknowledge. Like Mr. Logan, he has rendered some personal services to Mr. Lincoln. In the memorable campaign of '58, for the Senatorial succession, he came over from Indiana and stumped the central portion of this State for Mr. Lincoln. His voluntary efforts in those hours of need are not forgotten by the latter, and render a compliance with the wishes of Mr. C.'s friends more than probable.

In the last few days Mr. Lincoln was annoyed by hints at a new kind of nepotism. Several parties from different sections of this State, who claimed to have done some service in the canvass, called upon him and intimated their readiness to relinquish their own title to substantial rewards in favor of their brothers, who reside in California, and would like to share the spoils in the Golden State; with a singular uniformity of wishes they all had the United States Marshalship in view.

It is, probably, not universally known that Col. Baker, the newly elected United States Senator from Oregon, once proved, like Trumbull, a stumbling block in the political career of Mr. Lincoln by dint of superior tactics. They were both members of the whig party, and rival aspirants to the nomination for Congress. The county in which they both resided having been accorded the privilege to name the candidate for the district, and no one else disputing their claims to the nomination, they agreed to let a meeting of delegates from the various precincts pass upon their merits, and abide by their decision. Lincoln, by his confidence in being the choice of the county—which he really was—thought any extra exertions to secure a majority in the convention superfluous. Baker, however, worked like a beaver at the preliminary meetings throughout the county, and played his game so well that his friends were in the ascendency in the county convention, and that, to the utter astonishment of the unsuspecting Lincoln, he succeeded in getting the nomination, which was equivalent to an election.

The awful revelations of your Washington correspondent, in relation to an alleged grand land speculating scheme of republican leaders, caused more merriment than terror in the State House. Any one who, like the writer, knows the utter flatness of the real estate market in the States west of the Mississippi, and the absolute worthlessness of all speculative town property in distant Territories, cannot help joining in the laugh.

The partisan war waged during the past summer and fall in the Union at large, raged with extraordinary fury in this State. It was a renewal, with doubled vigor on both sides, of the hot fight of 1858. The opposite forces being arrayed against each other under the same leaders, since chosen national standard bearers, the ancient feud broke out with a fury unequalled in any former encounters. The prospect of a prevailing influence in national affairs, in case of the triumph of their champion, animated the republican host with unusual ardor and determination. The democratic ranks, on the other hand, entered upon the struggle from the very start with feelings of diffidence, in view of the disruption of their party into several factions in every State of the Union. They were discouraged by the belief that they would have to fight for principles only, the spoils being altogether beyond their reach, owing to the disaffection among themselves. They perceived an ill omen in the forced sale in the very outset of the campaign of their Chicago organ [the Chicago *Times*], and the involuntary withdrawal from the field of its editor, James Sheahan, the most devoted friend of their choice for the Presidency.[57] Their movements were furthermore embarrassed to a considerable degree by the lately discovered tampering with State funds, traced to former democratic State officers. In short, they began the strife without the hope of victory, and hence defeat could not be well averted.

The rout entailed upon them on the 6th of November was complete. The State gave the cold shoulder to the Presidential aspirations of the "Little Giant" in a rather signal manner. Their every candidate on the State ticket was overwhelmingly defeated. They lost their former majority in both houses of the Legislature—the most dreaded stab yet, from its securing the re-election of their mortal foe, Trumbull. Many local disappointments were also added to these general disasters. Among these, the most painful in this particular section of the State is the unexpected defeat in a race for a county office of Charles Lanphear [Lanphier],[58] the editor of the *Daily [State] Register*, the central organ of the Douglas democracy.

Alas for the vanquished! Scorn, derision, humiliation "stabs while down," and, what is still more bitter, oblivion is their lot. Feelings of mercy and compassion seldom move the victors in the political contests of this country. Unlike those that fight with swords and bullets, they recognize no virtues in their enemies. They have no commendation of their valor, but live by triumph and exultations and tangible demonstrations of their loss of power to increase the pangs of prostrate adversaries.

Such is the disposition of the successful republicans in this State towards the overpowered Douglas party. They feel not content with the glory of victory and the sole possession of the spoils. They are determined to crush their opponents out, and render another dispute of the political ascendency in the Prairie State all but impossible. For their antagonism does not flow from mere variations of opinion only. They are spurred on to attempts at annihilation by more relentless motives. They not only do not love, but hate, the adherents of Douglas with a more than ordinary fervor. It would be difficult to find a State in which the party animosity is more acrimonious than in Illinois, and that principally from the fact that the respective leaders have always been rival aspirants to office. The republicans, indeed, will give themselves no rest until they have tied their now helpless foes in a manner that will prevent them from doing any further harm for all time to come.

To bring this about, the first thing their majority in the Legislature is likely to do will be to repeal the law under which the present apportionment of the State into legislative districts was effected. They claim that the unfair preponderance it gave to the democratic Southern portion of the State alone enabled their opponents to re-elect Douglas [in 1858]. They contend that the republican North, being much more populous than the democratic "Egypt," an equal representation of the two sections in the upper and lower houses will place the recurrence of a like emergency beyond all possibility.

Their next step is expected to revive the investigation into the notorious canal scrip operations, with which the late democratic Governor, Joel A. Matteson, is somewhat mysteriously connected.[59] They hope to succeed in making revelations that will fix a fatal odium on the shattered remains of the popular sovereignty democracy.

In addition to all this, they flatter themselves that the new allotment of members of Congress under the recent census will change the present democratic majority of the delegation from this State into a republican one, so that the last vestige of democratic preponderance will be wiped out. This change of the political fortunes is a most glaring illustration of the fickleness of popular favor. But two years ago the followers of Douglas had it all their own way. The "Little Giant" was able to ride back to his seat in the Senate on a legislative majority, in bold defiance of the "powers that be," that had thrown all their influence in the scale against him. The prestige of that triumph made him the foremost candidate for the Presidency, and he was universally looked upon as the successor to James Buchanan. But what of him now? Of the successful leader, eminent Senator, foremost Presidential candidate, there remains but a ruined politician, with only the prospect of being forced into retirement by his own State in the course of a few years. Whether he died of the Kansas-Nebraska bill, of anti-Lecomptonism, his Freeport speech or jealous politicians, does not matter—unless a mighty reaction should take place it is certain that there is no more hope for Stephen A. Douglas.

Several prominent politicians from this State have at various times tried a "change of locality" as a means of regaining their lost political eminence. Colonel Baker, the new Senator from Oregon, and General Shields[60] are the best known among these wanderers in search of office. Douglas will perhaps follow their example.

December 9, 1860

Springfield, 9 December 1860
[San Francisco *Bulletin*, 4 January 1861]

THE RECEPTION OF MR. BUCHANAN'S MESSAGE—
WHAT HIS SUCCESSOR THINKS OF IT

The conviction having settled upon Mr. Lincoln's mind that the burden of the present internal complications will devolve upon his Administration, an anxiety on his part to obtain material for an opinion as to the probable condition of the estate likely to be left to him, is natural. Inasmuch as the last Annual Message of his predecessor promised to furnish a way to that part of the future, it was not to be wondered that its appearance was awaited with considerable impatience.

Well, the parting effusion of the "Sage of Wheatland" [James Buchanan] was received in due time. A brief synopsis reached the President elect at a late hour on Tuesday evening [December 4]. The document *in extenso*, however, did not come to hand until Thursday morning [December 6], when the St. Louis paper brought it. Some people out here had the presumption to expect that Mr. Lincoln would be considered in Washington just as much entitled to an "advance" copy as the Governor of South Carolina.[61] But in this they proved themselves woefully mistaken. The "powers that be" had no courtesy to bestow upon those that "are to be," and hence Mr. Lincoln did not get the whole of the Message to read a minute earlier than other common folks.

The readers of the [San Francisco] *Bulletin*, who have doubtlessly digested and perhaps forgotten the Presidential peroration long before they will peruse these lines, could not well suppose from its tenor that it was apt to arouse an echo of approbation in the breast of Mr. Lincoln and his friends. Wishing to tell the truth, as to the impression it produced, I am obliged to state that the only agreeable sensation called forth by it originated in the knowledge that it was the last visitation of the kind its eminent author would be able to inflict. How could it be otherwise? It was nothing more nor less than a direct indictment of the party with which the President elect and his supporters sympathized. It was considered the vehicle of the deliberate charge, that upon its members the sole responsibility for the threatening dismemberment of the Union rested. It was judged to be unfair and factious, in all that portion which the alleged causes of the present disturbances are enumerated. Hence, it received no favor either at the hands of Mr. Lincoln or his intimate followers. The former was most decided in his condemnation of the accusatory tone of the Message towards the North. On Thursday morning [December 6], he refuted its allegations in reference to the Republican party most elaborately in the presence of a number of visitors. In his argument, he dwelt with particular emphasis upon the undisputable fact, that, while previous to the 6th of November his election was made the *conditio sine qua non* of the Union, at this moment that pretext is hardly any longer urged; but that, on the contrary, many of the leading fire-eaters now openly declare that his success is only the occasion and not the cause of their contemplated secession, and that, whether conservative or not in his Administration, they were determined to run the risk of disunion at all hazards.

His strictures were equally severe upon a certain phrase, in which, as he thought, Mr. Buchanan endeavored to make a personal fling at him, and to impress the public mind with the idea that there was actually something ultra to be feared from his (Lincoln's) administration. It was the passage referring to Mr. Lincoln's antecedents, as "being apt to produce some apprehensions," indeed, in the South. He pronounced the supposed insinuation unjustified, graceless, and uncharitable under the present circumstances.

He asserted, with a good deal of emphasis, that if Mr. Buchanan had at all entertained a desire to do him justice, and pacify the South, he would have done so without compromising himself, or simply citing his record. But to be wrothy is rather difficult with good natured "Old Abe," and hence he could not help interlarding his own remarks with a humorous one to the effect that "he would write Mr. Buchanan a letter, demanding an explanation."

As to the position Mr. Buchanan assumed towards the secession movements, Mr. Lincoln inclined to the opinion that having impliedly recognized a cause for it in the alleged aggressions of the North, it is somewhat inconsistent in his predecessor to attempt to frown it down; and that it is evident from the general spirit of the message, that as much countenance as possible will be given to the seditious plans of the Cotton States by a "masterly inactivity"—apparent assertions to the contrary notwithstanding.

LINCOLN, AND THE REPUBLICAN MEMBERS OF CONGRESS

It will perhaps be remembered that, in a former letter, I stated that a part of the programme agreed upon the other day, at Chicago, by Mr. Lincoln and the Republican leaders from the Northwestern States, for the guidance of Republican Congressmen, was the assumption of an entirely passive attitude. It was then, and is now believed, that by abstaining for the time being from all aggressive or offensive demonstrations, or measures, the cotton lords would be deprived of their most effective means of agitation, and in all likelihood be brought into a conflict with the conservative members from the border slave States, without involving the Republicans. The result, thus far, of this plan of operation has already proved its wisdom. The proceedings of yesterday and the day before shows that, instead of Southerners being arrayed against Northerners, the parliamentary arena was all but monopolized by Southern anti-secessionists, battling against secessionists.

Mr. Lincoln feels greatly gratified at this complexion of affairs, and expects the best results from a continuation of the part of "lookers on" in all controversies bearing upon the secession issue by his Congressional supporters. But he knows also that the ultraists among the latter are most restive under the restraint, and liable to burst out at any moment, consolidate the Southern ranks by radical onslaughts, and impart once more a sectional character to the strife.

The epistolary course between the President elect and Republican members of both branches of Congress, is most lively. Since the meetings of the Electoral Colleges in several States, they have deluged him with letters of congratulation and unsolicited advice. Those among them that can justly claim his confidence (Trumbull, Hamlin, Wade, Cameron, Corwin, Colfax,

[Isaac N.] Arnold,[62] and a few others) supply him faithfully, by mail and by telegraph, with all desirable information.

Mr. Lincoln is said to have received direct assurances within the last two days that Senator Seward does not approve the back downs of Thurlow Weed and Chevalier [James Watson] Webb, and will not embarrass his administration by undue forwardness in the *role* of a pacificator. From day to day, your correspondent's conviction grows stronger, indeed, that the compromises and concessions proposed by the above-mentioned journalistic worthies have no more effect upon the Presidential ear than "seed upon fallow ground," and that the New York *Tribune* has the most hearing.

THE CABINET

I am able to state, positively, that Mr. Lincoln has as yet made no proposition to any one in connection with seats in his Cabinet, but that such will be made within the next fortnight. Of the seven members, two will be taken from the Western States; one from Pennsylvania, one from New England, and three from the Southern States. Mark the prediction! The distribution is fixed, but the persons are not yet agreed upon.

THE REMOVAL TO WASHINGTON CITY—LINCOLN'S PROBABLE TIME OF DEPARTURE FROM SPRINGFIELD

Although the simplicity of the domestic life of the President elect will prevent the coming removal of himself and family to the Federal Capital from being a source of much tribulation, the female members of his household are nevertheless already busily engaged in preparing a proper "outfit" for the journey to the White House. His two boys are most impatient to see the grand sights of Washington City, having never been beyond the limits of this State. They think and talk of nothing else.

The time of departure is not yet definitely determined upon. It will probably take place on or about the 20th of February, as a visit [is contemplated] to some of the Atlantic cities, previous to the entrance into Washington.

VISITORS

There has been a great falling off in visitors during the last three days. Congress seems to absorb the attention of politicians so much as to let them forget, for the time being, even their claims and hopes for office. Ex Gov. Reeder is the only person of note arrived since my last. The rumors as to the object of his presence are very conflicting. The opinion preponderates, however, that it is a mere visit of congratulation. Mr. Lincoln at least would repel all other advances.

Col. Baker was expected to a strike a bee-line for this place on his arrival in New York. His failure to do so has created a considerable disappointment among the many old friends he has in this region.

December 10, 1860

Springfield, 10 December 1860

[New York *Herald*, 15 December 1860]

Since the adjournment of the Electoral College, rumors, speculations and theories as to the composition of Mr. Lincoln's cabinet have circulated more freely in and about the State House, and have assumed a more positive and reliable character. The President elect himself is even more reserved and cautious in his allusions to that delicate subject than before, which fact has been construed by some into evidence of his earnest occupation with the weighty matter in question. But his friends are now much more talkative and given to Cabinet making, as they no longer run the risk of compromising Mr. Lincoln by premature expression of their hopes, wishes and ideas with regard to the selection of his constitutional advisers previous to his actual election.

This morning a gentleman connected with the State government, and known to be in Mr. Lincoln's confidence, stated his views in reference to the complexion of the Cabinet, with a good deal of assurance, in one of the offices on the lower floor of the State House. He claimed that the seven members would be divided as follows among the several sections of the country: —The Northwest, two; Pennsylvania (as the banner State), one; New England, one; the South, three. It was hinted on the same occasion that although Mr. Lincoln had booked a number of gentlemen representing the above divisions of the country, he had as yet failed to determine definitely upon any one. Among the nominees from the Northwest and South the following names were alleged to be:—C[aleb] C. [B.] Smith, of Indiana; Tom Corwin or Tom Ewing, Sr., of Ohio; Edward Bates, of Missouri; C. M. Clay, of Kentucky; Robert E. Scott, of Virginia, and Mr. Etheridge, of Tennessee. On some of these names bets were offered by members of the same party.

I think one of your Washington correspondents reflected Mr. Lincoln's sentiments correctly when stating that he would not, in any emergency, endeavor to defeat the will of the people by offering office to members of Congress or state governments. He is said to have stated a few days ago, that he considered the position of a United States Senator more honorable and useful than any office within his gift.

There is a unanimous opinion and general acquiescence apparent among the politicians of this vicinity that Illinois will not be represented in the Cabinet.

The selection of a member from New England is expected to give the most trouble. Mr. Hamlin's judgment will probably decide the vexed question.

New York will be overlooked, inasmuch as Mr. Seward would be placed in an awkward position, if any other representative of the Empire State should be apparently preferred to him, who would be gladly appointed, were it not for the fear of throwing thereby a firebrand into the Southern states.

Congress is still all but monopolizing the attention of the President elect. His apprehensions of a split between the ultra and conservative republicans are said to have increased since the vote on the Boteler resolution.[63] I understand, however, that letters were received to-day from Senator Trumbull and other confidants representing the republican members to be a unit as to the attitude to be maintained toward the secession movement; that the Chicago programme of "masterly inactivity" will be strictly carried out by the members from the Middle and Western States, and that indiscretions are apprehended from a few explosive New Englanders only.

The [U.S. House of Representatives] Committee of Thirty-three is not looked upon very favorably in the State House. It is thought all together impossible that an understanding will be arrived at as to the proper remedy for the present condition of the country by so numerous and heterogeneous a body. The unacceptable ultimatum of the cotton States, it is believed, will be insisted upon, all possible conciliatory action of the committee to the contrary notwithstanding.

The Chicago *Daily Times* published a ridiculous *canard* on Saturday last about a secret visit of John Bell to Mr. Lincoln in the course of last week. The sensation story produced quite an outburst of laughter on being read in the President's room. The distinguished but unsuccessful rival has not and will not be seen in Springfield, as his chances for a seat in the Cabinet have grown beautifully less. His claims seem to be altogether overlooked of late.

During the last three days a truly extraordinary calmness has prevailed about the State House. With the exception of the gossiping conferences around the stoves in the first story, not the slightest symptom of the daily presence of the next President of the United States in the same building was noticeable. A Quaker meetinghouse can be no quieter than its halls since Saturday last.

Not even the ghost of a solitary place seeker haunted Mr. Lincoln to-day—a relief which is quite welcome to him.

It has now been raining, snowing, sleeting, blowing and freezing these eight days in this latitude. Springfield has got to be one grand mud hole, the daily navigation of which creates a good many melancholy feelings, from the President elect down to your humble correspondent.

December 11, 1860

Springfield, 11 December 1860

[New York *Herald*, 15 December 1860]

If the perception of similitudes and identities—the description of one thing by another—the power of illustration by comparison—be among the characteristics of true poetry, Mr. Lincoln may lay no mean claims to distinction as a minion of the Muses. A striking event, a happy thought, an opportune saying, never comes under his notice without eliciting an echo from among his own stores of observations and recollections.

Comparatively unruffled by any extraordinary fluctuations, as the current of his life has been up to the present year, the unusual clearness of his impressions and the tenacity of his memory enabled him, nevertheless, to gather an abundant crop of ideas and facts while pursuing the even grade of his way, and to use them as a standard wherewith to judge the present by the past.

With its aid he will render abstractions intelligible by pointing out their practical revelations in public and private life. He will facilitate the comprehension of complicated political situations by a reference to simple precedents. Nature and the material life of man are likewise often drawn upon by him for analogies and parallels. But his forte is the proper application he knows how to make of historical incidents, personal adventures, stories and anecdotes, in the course of conversations and set speeches. The rhetorical force of antithesis is unknowingly employed by him with happy frequency. The sublime and the humorous are nearly always coupled in his efforts. They uniformly contain a mixture of Attic salt [wit, humor] and logic, and hence are greatly relished. This is especially the case in his intercourse with the numerous callers that daily attend his receptions. Wit and simile then hold the balance to argument and narrative. He would consult his own interest, indeed, by checking his love of fun, as its constant manifestation always tempts visiters to protract their stay. It is true his drastic tales at times are rather crude, both as to form and substance. But they are regularly to the point, and hence never come short of effect.[64]

While the confusion, commotion and danger wax greater from day to day in the political arena, the President elect maintains his equanimity undisturbed. Quietly, fulfilling what he considers his present duties, he faces events with a philosophic calmness. Not that he does not feel intense anxiety as to what the future has in store for the people of this country; on the contrary, not a move on the public stage escapes his attention nor fails to be duly appreciated. But he evidently entertains the conviction that he can do nothing that is likely to stem the tide of the times. What is asked of him, in the way of public definitions of his policy, he would probably give, if he could persuade himself that it would do aught towards the adjustment of the present troubles. But he considers all such demonstrations futile, as the South, to use his own language, has "eyes but does not see, and ears but does not hear." As to the announcement of the composition of his Cabinet, it has been rendered impossible by the attitude of the South. How can he select three or whatever number of its members may be determined upon from that section, when the same men may be made foreigners by the progress of disunion even before the inauguration of his administration? How can he for this reason, on the other hand, choose but Northern men, without adding fuel to the secession flames?

Again, would it be becoming on his part to attempt to influence Congress by direct or indirect expressions of his desires as to its action in reference to the disunion movement, while such is yet Mr. Buchanan's privilege?

Many and absurd as the attempts have been to mis-impress the public as to the intentions and doings of the President elect, the following despatch sent over the country by the agent of the Associated Press, in Washington, yesterday, outshines them all:

"There is a rumor this evening that Jefferson Davis has received a despatch from Mr. Lincoln, the President elect, saying that he (Mr. Lincoln) was preparing a letter for publication defining his position on the questions now distracting the different sections of the country, which will, it is said, give entire satisfaction to the South."

Was a more stupid and transparent hoax ever perpetrated upon the newspaper reading public? I will not insult your readers by assuming that they gave credence to it even for a moment. Out here its effect was wonderful in a certain way. As soon as Mr. Lincoln had entered his room in the State House a crowd of friends made a rush at him with the morning papers containing the startling news. It being read to him, the Presidential sides shook forthwith with violent laughter, and it was a long time before the fit was over. The statement was considered so preposterous, that the insult its implied imputation of cowardice conveyed was altogether overlooked.

Judging from the drift of conversation in the State House, secession is now looked upon as a certainty. The President elect is prepared for the inevitable calamity, and his plans of action, it is said, are being adapted to it. A belief seems likewise to gain ground that the border slave States will be, *nolens volens* [i.e., willy-nilly], engulfed, and that the end will be a strict division of the country between the free labor and slave-holding interests.

The New York dailies that arrived here this morning brought copious extracts from English journals expatiating upon the result of the November election. The unanimous gratification therein expressed at the republican victory was received with a great deal of satisfaction in the State House. It was always claimed here that the hostile unanimity of European sentiment on the slavery question would do much towards impairing the prospects of a Southern confederacy, and that a collision between England and the cotton States was even more probable than a bloody conflict between the North and South.

The movements of place seekers appear to be controlled by the weather at present. While during the last eight or nine rainy days hardly any one was seen here, the clearing up in the course of yesterday afternoon brought a crowd here this morning.[65] They mostly hail from the northern part of this State.

E. Peck, Esq., the well known lawyer and republican leader, made his advent yesterday afternoon, and spent the entire evening with the President elect.

December 12, 1860

Springfield, 12 December 1860

[New York *Herald*, 17 December 1860]

For the sake of comment, I repeat the following paragraph, published at the head of the editorial columns of this morning's [*Illinois State*] *Journal* (Mr. Lincoln's recognized organ), and embodied in the special dispatch sent to the HERALD this afternoon. As stated in the despatch, "it is known to have emanated directly from the President elect,"[66] and hence deserves especial attention:

CABINET QUERIES

We see such frequent allusions to a supposed purpose on the part of Mr. Lincoln to call into his Cabinet two or three Southern gentlemen from the parties opposed to him politically that we are prompted to ask a few questions:

1. Is it known that any such gentleman of character would accept a place in the Cabinet?

2. If yes, on what terms does he surrender to Mr. Lincoln or Mr. Lincoln to him on the political differences between them? Or will they enter upon the administration in open opposition to each other?

These "Cabinet queries" appear to convey nothing more nor less than a decided hint to the effect, that—

1. The willingness of these "two or three Southern gentlemen" referred to accept seats in the Cabinet of the President elect is doubted.
2. It is feared that "any such gentleman of character" (mark the qualification) might take such an offer from a decided political opponent as an insult, it implying a supposition of their willingness to "modify principles for the sake of office."
3. That a mutual adaptation of principles is considered the condition *sine qua non* of administrative co-operation.
4. That Mr. Lincoln, at least, is indisposed to adapt his views to those of the members of his Cabinet.

Some of the readers will doubtlessly look upon this analysis as implying a broad and unmistakeable intimation that there is little probability of any representation of the Southern States in the Cabinet of the President elect, and that the meaning of the above semi-official interrogatories goes to confirm the Southern fears of aggressive intentions on his part. But it will be seen that only "two or three Southern gentlemen" are alluded to, while at least a dozen names from that section of the country have been connected with the Cabinet. My information warrants me, indeed, in stating that these queries are only intended as feelers, and should be simply looked upon as indicative of the delicacy felt by Mr. Lincoln at making propositions to open and ancient adversaries of the party that elected him.

John Bell's last letter did not improve his chances of being offered a seat, as its accusatory tone towards the North is not considered balanced by the subsequent anti-disunion sentiments.[67] He may be looked upon as fairly shelved.

To-day some of the oldest and most intimate friends of Mr. Lincoln gave it as their deliberate opinion in the course of a conversation during their usual rendezvous in one of the State offices, that peaceable secession was a matter of absolute impossibility. Their views were expressed in such a manner, as to convey the idea that they were the reflections of similar convictions in higher quarters. It was asserted that even though coercion were not employed by the federal government, a conflict would be made inevitable by the improbability of an agreement upon the terms of the separation between the two sections of the country. Secession and civil war were evidently thought contemporaneous contingencies by the parties in question. Reconciliation on the basis of Northern concessions was scouted with much vehemence; although aggression was deprecated, collision was confidently predicted.

During the last few days several outrages, perpetrated by Southern mobs upon quiet, conservative and inoffensive merchants of high standing in St. Louis and Chicago, who had attempted to give their personal attention to business matters in New Orleans and other points, were brought to the direct notice of the President elect. The grievances being substantiated by the most positive evidence, he took no pains to conceal his indignation at these arbitrary and altogether groundless persecutions, which reveals a despotism worse than ever practised in Russia, even in the palmiest days of Nicholas I.

Frank P. Blair, Jr., unexpectedly appeared here last evening on his way to Washington from St. Louis. He attended the private conferences held daily in Mr. Lincoln's room after candle light. This morning and afternoon he has likewise spent most of his time in the State House. He denounces all propositions to compromise, concede, backslide, &c., &c., with the utmost bitterness. He pronounces the idea of a peaceable secession preposterous. "The Northwestern States," he says, "cannot and will not allow the building up of a 'foreign Power' on each side of the main artery of their commerce—the 'Lower Mississippi'—nor submit to an interruption of the free navigation of that river."[68]

Frank has pluck evidently. He means what he says. He knows no dodging or blinking. But I doubt that his "eagerness for the fray" was properly responded to by the powers that are to be. His martial disposition might be taken as a qualification for the Secretaryship of the War Department. Stranger things have happened.

Springfield, 12 December 1860
[New York *Herald*, 17 December 1860]
The most noticeable fact that has occurred here in connection with the new regime, within the last few days, is the rapid succession of semi-official statements in reference to public matters, and even in the *Daily* [*Illinois State*] *Journal* of this place—the central organ of the republicans of this State, and now the recognized mouthpiece of the President elect. Present appearances warrant, indeed, the inference that it will be henceforth made the regular vehicle of the thoughts, wishes and plans of the "powers that are to be."

Yesterday I quoted and commented upon a paragraph from the organ in question bearing upon the drawbacks to the selection of representatives of the South for Mr. Lincoln's Cabinet. To-day I subjoin some no less significant strictures upon John Bell's last letter, also taken from this morning's *Journal.* They confirm all I said upon the same subject in my last:

MR. BELL'S UNION LETTER.

Hon. John Bell has written a long and able Union letter, and we trust that it may be instrumental in allaying the disunion fever. *We believe Mr. Bell to be a patriot. He loves his country, and will do what he can to preserve it from dismemberment. He gives Mr. Lincoln credit for sincerity; that he has not disguised, but expressed his real sentiments. But Mr. Bell is woefully in error in regard to the designs and feelings of the republican party. Mr. Bell should understand, and the whole South ought to know, that the republican party, the party which elevated Abraham Lincoln to the Presidency, is the only party in this nation undivided in its support of the Union.* Many who supported Mr. Bell are disunionists—a large number who supported Mr. Breckinridge, and not a few who supported Mr. Douglas, are now in the secession ranks. But of all the many thousands who supported Mr. Lincoln there is not known to be a single man in favor of disunion—not one. *We, the republican party, love the Union, and we will peril everything but honor to maintain it. We do not love slavery and we do love freedom; but we will protect the South in the enjoyment of every constitutional right. The republican party makes no war upon the South—cherishes no hatred of the South.*

Nearly a column of the same issue is devoted to the inflammatory effect upon the South of the radical abolitionism John Wentworth is known to affect for the purpose of embarrassing Mr. Lincoln's administration and breaking up the republican party. It seems that immediately after the result of the Presidential election had transpired, Long John [Wentworth] launched a furious diatribe against the South, of whose tenor the following quotations are fair specimens:

You have sworn that if we dared to elect such a man you would dissolve the Union. We have elected him, and now we want to try your little game of secession. Do it, if you dare! So long as you remain in the Union peaceably and decently you shall enjoy your constitutional rights. But every man of you who attempts to subvert this Union will be hung as high as Haman.

The chivalry will eat dirt. They will back out. They never had any spunk, anyhow. The best they could do was to bully, brag and bluster. John Brown and his fifteen men were enough to affright the whole mighty Commonwealth of Virginia out of its propriety, and to hold it as a conquered province until recaptured by the federal troops; and to this day his ghost is more terrible than an army with banners in the eyes of every Southern cavalier. Those knights of the sunny South are just such heroes as Sancho Panza was. They are wonderful hands at bragging and telling fantastical lies, but when it comes to action count them out.

This piece of John Brownism was by someone headed, "From the Chicago *Democrat*—Lincoln's home organ"—and reprinted in the form of a circular, of which thousands of copies were disseminated in several Southern States. Some of the circulars are said to have been sent to Mr. Lincoln from Georgia, and hence the *Journal's* demonstration. It denounces this disreputable attempt to feed the disunion flame in the most bitter terms, and after asseverating with much emphasis that the imputed feelings of taunt and defiance were foreign to Mr. Lincoln, says of him:

He stands firmly and immovably upon the platform of the republican party, and is a believer in the principles therein enunciated.... *We feel satisfied that he will do his duty fearlessly in any emergency that may arise; but he will do it with a constant* regard to all the rights guaranteed to the several States by the constitution.

The strangest part of the article is the passage by which a direct intimation is conveyed that J. A. McClernand,[69] the democratic member of Congress from this district, allowed his frank to be used for the distribution of the incendiary circulars in the South.

Your Washington correspondents had better keep an eye on the present movements of Senator Trumbull and N. B. Judd, the chairman of the Republican Central Committee of this State, who is at present sojourning in the federal capital. They are both known here to be engaged in "surveying planks for the Cabinet," and to be in daily correspondence on the subject with the President elect.

December 13, 1860

Springfield, 13 December 1860
[San Francisco *Bulletin*, 10 January 1861]

THE PRESIDENT ELECT ASKS SOME QUERIES
IN REFERENCE TO HIS CABINET

From the very hour of his election to the Presidency, Mr. Lincoln has been belabored with written and verbal entreaties, by so-called conservative members of his party, to select the representatives of the South in his Cabinet from among such men as John Bell, Robert E. Scott of Virginia, Emerson Etheridge of Tennessee,[70] John A. Gilmer of North Carolina,[71] James Guthrie of Kentucky,[72] Henry Winter Davis of Maryland, and several others. As the secession movement progressed their solicitations grew more urgent, and of late assumed so importun[at]e a character as to become a regular annoyance, rendering abatement in some manner highly desirable. With a view to this effect, the following significant editorial paragraph appeared in the *Daily [Illinois State] Journal* of this place—the central [Republican] organ of the Prairie State—of date 11th December:

CABINET QUERIES

We see such frequent allusions to a supposed purpose on the part of Mr. Lincoln to call into his Cabinet two or three Southern gentleman, from the parties opposed to him politically, that we are prompted to ask a few questions:

1st. Is it known that any such gentleman of *character* would accept a place in the Cabinet?

2d. If yes, on what terms? Does he surrender to Mr. Lincoln, or Mr. Lincoln to him, on the political differences between them? Or, will they enter upon the Administration in open opposition to each other?

What *is* the understanding on these questions?

Knowing most positively that the above queries originated with, and were published at the special request of the President elect, I beg to direct the particular attention of the readers of the *Bulletin* to their undisguised meaning, and the following comments, the material of which has come also from authoritative sources.

Although, as stated, there was a general cause for the above official exposition of the views of the President elect, on the subject of the representation of the South in his Cabinet, the special occasion was John Bell's last published letter on the present condition of political affairs. His (John Bell's) name having been urged upon Mr. Lincoln with particular persistency in connection with a place in the Cabinet, the appearance of this epistle (the full text of which will probably have reached you by Pony Express before you receive this) was thought an excellent opportunity to give the cabinet-making friends of the President elect to understand, that the proposed union of opposite political elements in the incoming Administration was looked upon as *unwise, discreditable, dangerous, and hence, altogether impossible.*

Mr. Lincoln is, indeed, fully aware that the *conditio sine qua non* of a successful Administration is the consonance of the convictions of all its members on all the vital questions of internal and external policy. He knows that the Chicago platform was the basis of his success; and hence, that the selection of such men for his Cabinet as have been and are now spitting upon it, would be a direct slap, not only in his own face, but in that of the party which elected him. He knows, that in view of the recent unmistakable declarations of vehement hostility towards the Republican party, by "two or three Southern gentlemen," they would not become his constitutional advisers without involving inconsistency, either on his or their part. He knows that the very offer of seats, to openly avowed adversaries, would imply his own humiliation, and, for all that he can judge by, be treated as an insult by those that were to receive them.

It should not be inferred, however, from the *Journal's* interrogatories, that Mr. Lincoln is actually animated by a sectional spirit, as alleged by his opponents, and does not desire to grant a voice to all the sections of the country in his ministerial council. Any such implication would do him gross injustice. He is, on the contrary, truly anxious to be counseled and assisted by Southern, as well as Northern men, in the discharge of his Executive duties. He only wishes the country to understand that most of the material thus far presented to him for selection, is of too heterogeneous a nature to answer his purpose, and that his unwillingness to make use of it arises not from sectional prejudices, but the fact of seeing his Administration wrecked at its very outset by the rock of dissension, on the most important issues it will have to meet.

LINCOLN ON BELL

That the chances of John Bell for a position in Mr. Lincoln's Cabinet are rather slim, will further appear from the subjoined direct strictures on his last epistolary performance. They will appear in tomorrow morning's *Journal*, (I copy them from a proof slip,) and are likewise inspired by the "highest authority." Says the *Illinois State Journal* of the 14th December:

HON. JOHN BELL'S UNION LETTER

The Hon. John Bell has written a long and able Union letter, and we trust that it may be instrumental in allaying the disunion fever. We believe Mr. Bell to be a patriot. He loves his country, and will do what he can to preserve it from dismemberment. He gives Mr. Lincoln credit for sincerity—that he is not disguised, but expresses his real sentiments. But Mr. Bell is wo[e]fully in error in regard to the designs and feelings of the Republican Party. . . . Mr. Bell should understand, and the whole South ought to know, that the Republican party—the party which elevated Mr. Lincoln to the Presidency—is the *only party in this nation undeviating in its support of the Union.* Many who supported Mr. Bell are Disunionists; a large number who supported Mr. Breckinridge, and not a few who supported Mr. Douglas, are now in the Secession ranks. But of all the many thousands who supported Mr. Lincoln, there is not known to be a single man in favor of disunion—not one. *We, the Republican party*, love the Union, and we will peril everything but honor to maintain it. We do not love slavery as we do love freedom; but we will protect the South in the enjoyment of every constitutional right. The Republican party makes no war on the South—cherishes no hatred of the South.

HOW THE DISUNION FLAME IS FED

For some weeks, Mr. Lincoln has from time to time received copies of a circular from divers Southern sources, containing a reprint of a rabid abolition leader, published immediately after the 6th November in the Chicago *Democrat*, John Wentworth's "own [organ]" in every respect. This notorious individual, it is perhaps known to your readers, has been affecting the most measureless abolitionism during the last four or five months, for the sole purpose of inflaming the Southern mind against Lincoln and estranging the conservatives from the Republican cause, and all that simply because the majority of the Republicans of this State prefer Trumbull to himself for re-election to the United States Senate.[73] Investigation being made by the friends of the President elect as to the source, from which the incendiary editorial referred to found its way into the Southern States, overwhelming evidence was obtained of the fact that hundreds of copies had been circulated in Georgia and North [and] South Carolina, *under the frank of J. A. McClernand, the Democratic member of Congress from this district.* This precious piece of partizan malice was openly denounced in to-day's [*Illinois State*] *Journal.* In speaking of the insincere ultra rant of the leader thus disseminated under Democratic auspices, it says:

Mr. Lincoln stands firmly and immovably upon the platform of the Republican party, and is a believer in the principles therein enunciated; but in the midst of the popular triumph which those principles have achieved, neither he nor the Republicans as a party assume to indulge in any such strain of offensive taunt and ridicule. We feel satisfied that he will do his duty fearlessly in any emergency that may arise; but he will do it with a constant regard to all the rights which are guaranteed to the several States by the Constitution.

CANARDS PLUCKED OF THEIR FEATHERS

Since the meeting of Congress, the Washington correspondents of the New-York press have let loose upon the public a number of outrageous *canards* in reference to Mr. Lincoln's position and intentions. As they will doubtlessly reach the Pacific in their flight, I have selected the most impudent for the sake of an authorized *pars-pro-toto* [a part taken for the whole] contradiction.

1. Says the Washington correspondent of the New York *Herald:*

There is a rumor this evening, that Jefferson Davis has received a despatch from Mr. Lincoln, the President elect, saying that he (Mr. Lincoln) was preparing a letter for publication, defining his position on the questions now distracting the different sections of the country, which will, it is said, give entire satisfaction to the South.

2. Says the Washington correspondent of the New York *Times:*

Private letters received from Mr. Lincoln by a special friend of his here, urge moderation and forbearance. *He desires everything done that is possible, without regarding his party at the North, to harmonize the sections. He speaks in high terms of the articles in the New York Times and the Albany Evening Journal.*

The first story is so absurd as to require in refutation only the simple statement that Mr. Lincoln contemplates a pilgrimage in sack-cloth and ashes to the realm of King Cotton, just as much as the imputed correspondence with Jefferson Davis.

As to the second, I can give your readers the most positive assurance that there is not an atom of truth in it. Mr. Lincoln has written no letters recommending any attitude or measure to the Republican members of Congress,[74] and he does not approve of the backsliding of the Albany *Evening Journal.* He desires reconciliation and pacification, but not at the cost of principle.

LOYALTY OF THE PACIFIC STATES—DISTINGUISHED VISITORS

Mr. Latham's[75] reluctant testimony to the loyalty of the Pacific States to the Union was not necessary to persuade Mr. Lincoln of that gratifying fact. He never doubted the sincere attachment of California to the Confederacy [i.e., the Union].

Frank P. Blair, Jr., was here on Tuesday and Wednesday last. He spent two entire evenings in private conference with the President elect. He asks nothing for himself, but will be largely consulted as to the distribution of the spoils west of the Mississippi. He is defiant and bellicose as to the secession movement. He says that the Northwest must not and will not consent to the establishment of a foreign power in the shape of a Southern Confederacy on both sides of the Lower Mississippi.

The Hon. Edward Bates arrived from St. Louis this evening. His visit is said to be "by invitation." More about him in my next.

[Another journalist described Lincoln's conversation with him and other visitors on December 13:

After nearly a week devoted to private business in this city, I yesterday visited Springfield and the President elect. At the State House, Lincoln was asked if he had any news from the South.

"No," he replied; "I have not yet read the dispatches in the morning papers. But, I think, from all I can learn, that things have reached their worst point in the South, and they are likely to mend in the future. If it be true, as reported, that the South Carolinians do not intend to resist the collection of the revenue, after they ordain secession, there need be no collision with the Federal Government. The Union may still be maintained. The greatest inconvenience will arise from the want of Federal courts, as with the present feeling, judges, marshals, and other officers, could not be obtained." On this point Mr. Lincoln spoke at some length, regretting its difficulty, but adding that his mind was made up as to how it should be overcome. His tone and language were moderate, good-humored and friendly towards the South.

He then went on to speak of the charges made by the South against the North, remarking that they were so indefinite that they could not be regarded as sound. If they were well defined they could be fairly and successfully met. But they are so vague that they cannot be long maintained by reasoning men even in the Southern States. Afterwards he spoke of the course pursued by certain Republican newspapers at the North, which I need not name, in replying to threats of secession from Southern States, by saying "Let them secede; we do not want them." This tone, he remarked, was having a bad effect in some of the border States, especially of Missouri, where there was danger that it might alienate some of the best friends of the cause, if it were persisted in. In Missouri and some other States, where Republicanism has just begun to grow, and where there is still a strong pro-slavery party to contend with, there can be no advantage in taunting and bantering the South. Leading Republicans from those States had urged him to use his influence with the journals referred to, and induce them to alter their present tone towards the South. He did not say he had promised to do this, and I only gathered from his manner and language that he would prefer to see the bantering tone abandoned.

There was no caution given in regard to keeping his remarks private, and as he knew my professional position, and yet gave no such caution, there can be no violation of confidence in publishing this very brief sketch of his remarks, omitting, of course, many things, but giving their general tone with fidelity. The only reservation he made was when he was expressing his views of affairs in the South. He said he had arrived at them after much study and thought; they were his views at the present time, but of course liable to be modified by his more mature judgment after further information and further study of the progress of events. Having thus discussed public affairs for some time, Mr. Lincoln then changed the conversation, making pleasant allusions to incidents of his recent visit to Chicago.][76]

December 14, 1860

Springfield, 14 December 1860
[New York *Herald*, 20 December 1860]

The leading topic in Presidential circles during the last twenty-four hours has been the Union demonstrations in New Jersey and in Philadelphia. The proceedings of the meeting in the last mentioned city especially attracted attention. Although it appears to be supposed that the leaders and members of the late [Constitutional] Union party were the prime movers and composed the bulk of the attendance on both occasions, and that comparatively few republicans participated, it is nevertheless evident that the tone of the speeches and resolutions then and there delivered produced an uncomfortable feeling. It is true the information received here from Washington and other sources warrants the belief that the republican ranks in both New Jersey and Pennsylvania are yet unshaken—panic and distress to the contrary notwithstanding. But, on the other hand, the moral effect of such peace offerings as the resolves of the Philadelphia meeting[77] upon the weak kneed members of the party in those two States is nevertheless feared. In the Quaker City particularly much quaking is expected among the sufferers from the commercial and industrial calamities entailed by the present crisis. But great reliance, however, is placed on the loyalty of the interior counties of the Keystone State, that rolled up such tremendous majorities for the republican candidates. The agricultural districts especially are believed to be unmoved, owing to their comparative natural independence.

Several intimate friends of Mr. Lincoln have taken no pains to conceal their disgust at the, as it seemed, authorized use of Gov. Curtin's name as an endorser of the Philadelphia platform.[78] Their hints at eating dirt, &c., &c., were very plain. They think it an altogether inexplicable shift from the Chicago to the Philadelphia platform.

All that I have seen and heard during the last six days goes to confirm the assertion made in a former letter, that owing to the uncertainty of the character of coming events, great hesitation is felt by the President elect to determine upon his constitutional advisers at the present moment, and that for the same reason a definite selection will be put off to the latest possible moment. The result of the secession conventions in the Southern States will be awaited, at all events. No difficulty will be experienced in choosing the representatives of the free States in the Cabinet. But I venture to say that with regard to those of the South, a good deal of perplexity is experienced. Advances from some of the Southern gentlemen, frequently mentioned in connection with positions, would probably prove very welcome. But they are not expected to be made by them, as none will be vouchsafed to them. A "coming together" seems a rather remote contingency.

I understand that the President elect has of late again been urged by many parties to come out with a letter defining his executive plans in reference to the slavery issue. But I do not think that he is at all disposed to change his resolution to remain silent until the time of his inauguration, and that principally in view of the growing frequency of the declarations of Southern politicians, to the effect that no assurance or concession could now induce the cotton States to forego their settled purpose to go out of the Union and attempt the construction of a Southern confederacy.

The appearance of Mr. Lincoln has somewhat changed to the worse within the last week. He does not complain of any direct ailment, but that he looks more pale and careworn than heretofore is evident to the daily observer. But whatever effect his new responsibilities may have had upon his body, the vigor of his mind and the steadiness of his humorous disposition are obviously unimpaired.

Quite a relaxation, no doubt, proved to Mr. Lincoln the jolly affair that he is said to have attended last night, on the occasion of the marriage of his friend and cordial supporter, Hon. O. M. Hatch, the Secretary of State, to Miss Enos, of this city.[79]

The [wood]cut on the first page of one of your illustrated contemporaries, claiming to represent the lady and the two sons of the President elect, is pronounced a wretched caricature by all that know Mr. Lincoln's interesting family.[80]

In my letter of the 5th inst., published in the HERALD of the 11th, while speaking of Hon. I. N. Morris, the democratic Congressman from this State, you made me say, "Mr. Morris was always looked upon by republicans as somewhat of a Douglasite on the slavery question." It should have read "somewhat ahead of Douglas on the slavery question."

Place seekers are once more "few and far between." No increased influx is looked for until the meeting of the State Legislature, in the course of next month, when "high tide is expected to set in."

December 15, 1860

Springfield, 15 December 1860
[New York *Herald*, 16 December 1860]
Edward Bates, of Missouri, arrived from St. Louis at a late hour last evening. He came by invitation of the President elect, with whom he spent most of his time to-day.

It is currently reported that the Secretaryship of the Interior was formally offered him.[81]

Mr. Bates takes very strong ground against secession, and says secession is treason and must be put down, and the authority of the government maintained at all hazards.[82]

Mr. Bates returned home this evening.

December 16, 1860

Springfield, 16 December 1860
[New York *Herald*, 20 December 1860]
If I were asked upon what element in the composition of the President elect I looked as the mostly likely source of apprehension, I would not mention in reply either his wrongly imputed hostility towards the South, nor the alleged aggressiveness of the party that elected him and expects faithfulness on his part to its tenets. Nay, odd as it may sound, I would name, on the contrary, a quality which is by common consent considered rather laudable than otherwise—viz: his good nature.

To receive everybody with uniform kindness—to indulge the general curiosity with untiring patience—to reply to all questions with unvarying readiness—to grant willing compliance to all requests—to heed endless suggestions—may be a very good and pleasing rule in private life. It is doubtlessly, likewise, an effective means of popularity in public spheres; but its general observation by so high-stationed a personage as the President of the United States, I venture to say, is fraught with many hazards, and that from the very abuse of those for whose benefit it is practised.

All that can claim the personal acquaintance of Mr. Lincoln will agree that he is the very embodiment of good temper and affability. They will all concede that he has a kind word, an encouraging smile, a humorous remark for nearly every one that seeks his presence, and that but few, if any, emerge from his reception room without being strongly and favorably impressed with his genial disposition. But, although his visiters may leave him all thus well pleased, is it not more than probable that the pleasure is only one-sided and unshared by him that produced it? It is true no man enjoys company more than Mr. Lincoln. It is true he loves argument, discussion, witty sayings, &c., &c., perhaps as much as any other mortal. But it may be, nevertheless, safely presumed that the sensations derived from his variegated intercourse are not all of an agreeable character, but that, on the contrary, they were largely intermingled with annoyance and perplexity.

Yet, notwithstanding the assertions of sensation writers—that never failing plague of political eminence in this country—the groveling tide waiters, fawners, sycophants and parasites combined in the genus "office seekers," have thus far affected him only in a slight degree. From present appearances, indeed, it may be inferred that it will not be visited upon him in all its virulence until after his advent in the White House. Delay and the unwelcome distance having sharpened their appetites, the place-wanting cormorants will then beset him in close file and with double fury. Reticence will then have to supersede, to some extent, unrestrained communicativeness. Reserve must take the place of indiscriminating affability. His ears and eyes must learn to be closed at certain times. His lips must be trained to less ready and unqualified responses. If not, the crowd will unbalance and overwhelm him.

The revelations of every hour since the publication of the significant paragraph in reference to the selection of representatives of the South for the Cabinet, in last Wednesday's [*Illinois State*] *Journal*, go to confirm my conviction that what was then said was unequivocally meant. The language publicly used by the friends of the President elect leaves no doubt as to his fixed intention not to offer any one a place among his constitutional admirers [advisors] that has lately placed himself on record against the party that elected him. The growing estrangement of the Southern States will rather strengthen than weaken this resolution. As the probability of secession gradually assumes the character of certainty, the conviction that all peace offerings will be scouted becomes correspondingly more settled. That a *porte feuille* [cabinet portfolio] will not be tendered to any citizen of any State that is likely to be carried off by the secession is certain, as it is not desired to run the risk of having a representative of a "foreign Power" in the proposed Cabinet.

The event of the day is the visit (by invitation) to the President elect of the Hon. Edward Bates, of Missouri. The venerable Judge arrived at a late hour on Friday evening. At an early hour on Saturday morning he repaired to Mr. Lincoln's room in the State House, and remained closeted with him until the public morning reception commenced. The interview was renewed at one P. M., and continued until three o'clock. The duties of his profession allowing but a short absence from St. Louis, the distinguished Missourian returned home on the evening train of the same day.

Mr. Bates' presence was solicited by the President elect: first, for an exchange of views on the present condition of public affairs; and, secondly, for making the formal offer of a seat in his Cabinet to the unsuccessful rival aspirant to the republican nomination. Frank P. Blair, Jr., had been deputed as mediator during his late stay between the two high contracting powers. Through him the invitation to repair to Springfield was extended to Mr. Bates.

As to Mr. Bates' views, I am able to state that they are most decided and uncompromising on the secession question. He proclaimed boldly that "secession is treason, and must be put down." He furthermore urged, with great energy, that the "majesty of the federal laws should be maintained at all hazards." It is said that he agreed with the President elect on all the leading points that became the subject of discussion.

It is universally asserted that the Secretaryship of the Interior was offered to Mr. Bates, and accepted by him. In some quarters his name was connected with the Attorney Generalship. The authentic information I possess warrants me, however, in contradicting the offer of the last mentioned office.[83]

In addition to Mr. Bates, several Eastern politicians of note have been invited hither. The invitations are reported to have been made through Senator Trumbull. The recipients are expected here in the course of the next fortnight.

John C. Fremont is strongly pressed for Secretary of War by Ohio influences.[84] The last pony express is also said to have brought several strong appeals in his favor from California.

December 17, 1860

Springfield, 17 December 1860

[New York *Herald*, 21 December 1860]

I mentioned in a former letter that among the most noteworthy phenomena in the political spheres of this latitude, at the present time, was the fact that the *Daily [Illinois State] Journal* of this city, the central organ of the republicans of Illinois, had of late been evidently made the authoritative vehicle of Mr. Lincoln's views on current events. Since the publication on Wednesday last of the paragraph bearing upon the proposed selection of representatives of the South of the John Bell school, hardly an issue appears without containing some editorial matter unmistakably stamped with a semi-official character. This morning's *Journal* again contains some very significant articles, the most interesting portions of which I embody in this letter. The vigorous exhortation following immediately after this will attract special attention. It confirms what I said in my last of the "growing mettle" in Presidential circles:

STAND FIRM—BE TRUE.

We feel indignant sometimes when we hear timid republicans counseling an abandonment, in part, of republican ground. We are asking for nothing that is not clearly right. We have done nothing wrong. We have nothing to apologize for, nothing to take back, as a party. We have fought a hard battle; we have come out of it victorious; and shall we now call back the routed, flying enemy, and basely surrender all that we have gained? Never. Let us stand firm as the eternal hills upon the republican platform, and "turn this government back into the channel in which the framers of the constitution originally placed it." Some there are who counsel Mr. Lincoln to take into his cabinet two or three gentlemen who do not agree with him politically. They do not know the man. On the 17th [16th] of June, 1858, in a speech delivered in this city, Mr. Lincoln said:

> Our cause, then, must be entrusted to, and conducted by, its own un-doubted friends—those whose hands are free, whose hearts are in the work—who do care for the result. Two years ago the republicans of the nation mustered over thirteen hundred thousand strong. We did this under the single impulse of resistance to a common danger, with every external circumstance against us. Of strange, discordant and even hostile elements, we gathered from the four winds, and formed and fought the battle through, under the constant hot fire of a disciplined, proud and pampered enemy. Did we brave all then to falter now?—now, when that enemy is wavering, dissevered and belligerent? The result is not doubtful. We shall not fail—if we stand firm, we shall not fail. Wise counsels may accelerate, or mistakes delay it, but, sooner or later, the victory is sure to come.

The victory has come—brilliant, glorious, overwhelming. Mr. Lincoln himself led the triumphant host. The people have entrusted their cause to him, knowing "his hands to be free," his "heart in the work," and "that he does care for the result." Will he entrust now, think you, to those who are not its own undoubted friends; will he call around him a hostile Cabinet, and reward with offices and honor the very men whom the people have repudiated? . . . Let there be no wavering, no faltering here—no treacherous counsel, no base surrender of principles. Let there be justice, moderation, prudence, but unflinching firmness.

Mr. Botts' Union letter was read with a good deal of satisfaction by the President elect.[85] Botts stock has since considerably risen among his friends, and the ever talking and ever writing Virginian's name is again prominently connected with a seat in the Cabinet. I doubt, however, that such a consideration will be made to answer this bid. The *Journal* prints the letter in full, with a strong complimentary notice. The organ this morning also had the following plain hint at the time when Mr. Lincoln will publicly define his views:

MR. LINCOLN WILL SPEAK.

We are often asked by strangers, "Why does not Mr. Lincoln speak? Will he say anything to allay the storm?" Yes, gentlemen, he will speak. He will define his position, and all the world will know his policy. He will speak in the city of Washington, on the 4th day of March, 1861, if he lives and should happen to feel like it.

The leading subject of conversation in hotel parlors yesterday continued to be the visit of Mr. Bates. There appeared to be a unanimity of approbation among republicans of the bold view he expressed in reference to the secession issue during his stay, and much gratification at the prospect of seeing him among the constitutional advisers of the President elect. That the Secretaryship of the Interior was formally tendered to the distinguished Missourian is disputed by no one. Mr. Lincoln is known to have been a strong admirer and personal acquaintance of Mr. Bates for many years, so that his selection was not a cause of surprise. It is said that he was [at] first decidedly disinclined to accept any appointment on account of the dependence of his large family on his professional labors, and that it was only upon the urgent entreaties of Frank P. Blair, Jr., that he consented to come up here and receive the offer at the hands of the President elect.

To-day the startling news of the resignation of General Cass,[86] contained in the morning dailies, set all the Presidential surroundings all agog. An intense excitement prevailed all the morning in the State House. The alleged cause of his retirement being a corroboration of the suspicion long entertained, that Mr. Buchanan was, in spite of the tenor of his last message, winking at the secession movement, Mr. Lincoln's predecessor was denounced in bitter terms. His obvious connivance, it was urged, afforded an excellent reason for his impeachment.[87]

December 18, 1860

Springfield, 18 December 1860
[New York *Herald*, 24 December 1860]
Disunion being looked upon in this portion of the globe as a certain future contingency, the question as to the attitude likely to be assumed by the Northwestern States in case that lamentable event should become a *fait*

accompli is freely discussed among the politicians that constantly congregate here from all parts of the free States west of the Alleghenies. Unrestrained as the exchange of views is, it is remarkable how little discrepancy is noticeable between the several conjectures, propositions and plans. The idea put forth by some Douglas democratic Congressmen, of an independent Northwestern confederacy, is pronounced preposterous with an emphatic unanimity. The coalescence and cohesiveness of the Northwestern and Atlantic States are believed to be so intimate and perfect by the ligaments of consanguinity, sympathy and material interest, that a disintegration and well being are thought to be no more of a simultaneous possibility than life in a human body cut in two. The Northwest, it is contended, will and must cling to the Northeastern States, if not from option, from necessity. The love of the Union is, indeed, nowhere stronger or purer than in the youthful and prosperous communities of States washed by the Ohio, Missouri and Upper Mississippi. Whatever Southern segregations may take place, they will adhere to the remnants of the beloved confederacy [i.e., Union] with all their characteristic vigor and ardor. Secession is a political heresy, whose professors will be found "few and far between" in the Northwest; and woe to the leaders that will attempt to persuade their followers into embracing that fallacious faith.

A noteworthy consonance of opinion in reference to the disunion issue is apparent in another respect. It is the universal conviction that the Northwest will never submit to the interruption of the free navigation of any of the Western rivers by a foreign Power that would arise in an independent Southern confederacy. Among the hundreds of intelligent and influential citizens of Illinois, Indiana, Ohio, Michigan, Wisconsin, Minnesota and Iowa—representatives of all parties—that I have met here during the last five weeks, I did not find a single disunionist, and they were not slow in asserting that the West would be first in drawing the sword in case of any attempt to blockade, by tariff or otherwise, the father of Western waters.

The [*Illinois State*] *Journal* of this morning contains the following official disclaimer, the substance of which I telegraphed you last night:

A FORGERY

The democratic papers are publishing a letter purporting to have been written to Hon. Thos. Ewing, of Ohio, by Mr. Lincoln. The letter pretends to indicate the line of policy that Mr. Lincoln intends to pursue. Mr. Lincoln is made to say that he will promptly and rigorously execute the Fugitive Slave law—that he will recommend the restoration of the Missouri Compromise line and its extension to the Pacific coast—that he will exert himself to secure a speedy repeal of Personal Liberty laws[88]—that the Territories shall be thrown open to slavery—that all agitation of the slavery question should be discountenanced—that he will earnestly urge ministers of the gospel to cease preaching upon the subject of slavery—that he is opposed to the celebration of the anniversary of the execution of John Brown—that he will appoint no John Brown sympathizer to office; and, finally, that he will recommend the Northern people to mind their own business. We have seen the letter in the [Cleveland] *Overland National Democrat*, and such is its import. It is hardly necessary, we presume, for us to say that the letter is a forgery. Mr. Lincoln has written no such letter to Mr. Ewing nor to any one else.

It is said that the attention of the President elect was directed to the fabrication that called forth this explicit disavowal by a prominent Ohio politician, who wrote about its injurious effect upon the republicans in the northern part of that State.

In support of what I stated in former letters as to the authoritativeness the editorials of the [*Illinois State*] *Journal* have lately assumed, I quote the subjoined paragraph from to-day's [*Illinois State*] *Register* (the central organ of the Douglas democracy of this State) in reference to the leader headed "Stand firm—Be true," as embodied in my communication of yesterday:

THE FIAT OF MR. LINCOLN

The *Illinois* [*State*] *Journal* yesterday, though disclaiming to "speak as one clothed with authority," has the article which we quote below. The *Journal*'s disclaimer is nothing. Its editor is Mr. Lincoln's kinsman; it is published under his eye, and it would be ridiculous to presume that its utterings in regard to matters of such moment, considering Mr. Lincoln's position, were not put forth under his direction, and with his sanction.

The *pronunciamento* Thurlow Weed concocted last night, in concert with Mr. Seward, and a synopsis of which was telegraphed all over the Union, was not, as the telegraphic despatches have led the people to infer, a reflection of Mr. Lincoln's views.[89] It should be understood in the East that Mr. Weed is not the spokesman of the President elect. It may have unknowingly foreshadowed Mr. Lincoln's ideas. But even on this point no certainty as yet exists, as the synopsis was a very unsatisfactory and unreliable means of comparison.

Messrs. D. D. Dana, of Boston,[90] and A. D. Vover, of New York city, called upon Mr. Lincoln to-day.

Quite a number of financiers are in town, for the purpose of depositing the additional securities required by the Auditor of [this] State from divers banks of issue to make up the deficiencies caused by the decline of State stock. Confidence in the soundness of the currency of this State is being gradually restored.

The weather is again unfavorable, and keeps place-seekers at a gratifying distance.

December 19, 1860

Springfield, 19 December 1860
[New York *Herald*, 24 December 1860]

Will there be any Southerners in Mr. Lincoln's Cabinet? A momentous question, to which, I presume, Mr. Lincoln himself could make no definite answer in view of the present juncture of public affairs. As to the border slave States, the offer of a seat to Mr. Bates secures a representation of at least one of them. But in regard to all others, the prospect seems to be rather dubious just now, and that not so much from any desire on the part of the President elect to exclude the representatives of any section of the country from among his constitutional advisers as from other causes. Mr. Lincoln is most certainly anxious to grant a full voice to the Southern as well as to the Eastern and Northwestern States in his ministerial council. But it appears that circumstances have already occurred, and are likely to occur, that will render it all but impossible for him to realize his wishes in this respect. How can he, indeed, surround himself, safely and consistently, with men whose political convictions on the leading question of the day are diametrically opposed to his own? Take all the Southern politicians of the late Union party that have been mentioned in connection with positions in his Cabinet—John Bell, Robert E. Scott, of Virginia; John A. Gilmer, of North Carolina; Judge Sharkey[91] and others; have they not all of late taken so hostile a stand towards the republican party that an agreement with Mr. Lincoln on matters of internal policy would be absolutely out of the question. John Bell put himself out of the ring by his last public letter. Robert E. Scott and John A. Gilmer have followed suit by effusions of similar tenor. At least the impression produced by them in the State House warrants such a belief. Other so called conservatives, that might have proved suitable, will probably be carried to a like distance before long by the secession movement. What, then, can Mr. Lincoln do? Either stultify, and paralyze himself by receiving dreaded political adversaries (whose willingness to serve is also questionable) into his Cabinet, or take up such men as John M. Botts, who would cause dissatisfaction both North and South, or draw his material only from the sympathizing elements of his own party. In the face of the fatality of Cabinet dissensions, demonstrated by the disruption of Mr. Buchanan's administration, he can hardly be presumed to be disposed to try the experiment of a "divided house."

Considerable sensation was produced to-day in the Capitol by the appearance of a live disunionist, wearing the emblem of secession. The gentleman, who called himself D. E. Ray, and claimed to be from Yazoo, Miss., stalked into Mr. Lincoln's reception room with a blue cockade displayed on his hat. He walked in with a sullen air, introduced himself, and plunged into a corner of a sofa, where he reposed for at least a quarter of an hour, without uttering a word, and with his eyes down, but all the while manipulating his tile [i.e., hat] so as to fasten the President's eye upon the cockade. Mr. Lincoln at first hardly noticed him; but one of the other visiters at last addressed some questions to the scowling Southron that induced him to open his lips. The conversation next turned to the secession issue. In its course the Mississippian remarked gruffly that they were not afraid down South of Mr. Lincoln himself, but of those who followed him. The President elect hereupon joined in the talk, and soon found occasion to remark "that the main differences between Northerners and Southerners were that the former held slavery to be wrong and opposed its further extension, while the latter thought it right and endeavored to spread it; that, although the republicans were anti-extensionists, they would not interfere with slavery where it existed, and that as to his own intentions, the slave States would find that their slave property would be as secure from encroachment as it had been under Mr. Buchanan." The Southron, having evidently softened down under the influence of these peaceful declarations, requested of Mr. Lincoln a copy of the debates with Senator Douglas, which was duly given him, with an inscription by the donor on the title page. Mr. Lincoln remarked, on handing the book to him, that he hoped its possession would not give him any trouble on his return to Mississippi. The recipient of the gift finally retired, apparently somewhat mollified by Mr. Lincoln's kind treatment.

I am told that the same cockade man had made himself rather conspicuous in the morning while disputing with a zealous republican at his hotel. The latter was induced by the remarks of the fire-eater to offer a bet that he (the Southron) did not hold, own, and never had owned, a single slave—which supposition was unwillingly acknowledged to be true. And yet the gentleman from Yazoo had been denouncing the "black republicans" most severely for attempting to "steal our niggers."[92]

Springfield, 19 December 1860
[San Francisco *Bulletin*, 14 January 1861]

VISIT OF EDWARD BATES TO MR. LINCOLN

It will perhaps be remembered by the readers of the *Bulletin*, that in my letter of the 8th [9th] instant I ventured to foreshadow an intention on the part of the President elect to take some decisive steps relative to the construction of his Cabinet in the course of the fortnight next succeeding the above date. An event that occurred within the last few days, and was briefly mentioned at the close of my last, verified the prediction. I refer to the visit of Edward Bates, of Missouri, to the President elect.

Mr. Bates came here at the express and urgent solicitation of Mr. Lincoln. The former's record as a rival aspirant to the Chicago nomination, indeed, would have rendered a visit altogether impossible under any other circumstances. Frank P. Blair, Jr., whose presence for several days in this place was also alluded to in a previous letter, had been deputed as the bearer of Mr. Lincoln's invitation to the distinguished Missourian. He is farther said to have been authorized to intimate, that an offer of a seat in the Cabinet was contemplated, and to ascertain Mr. Bates' views as to an acceptance. In consideration of the dependence of his family upon his professional labors, the recipient of the following proposition is reported to have felt disinclined at first to take a place among Mr. Lincoln's constitutional advisers. The entreaties of Mr. Blair and other friends, however, finally overcame his reluctance, and the trip to Springfield was accordingly undertaken.

Mr. Bates spent some six hours in private conference with the President elect, on Saturday [December 15]. A very full and free exchange of opinions on the present condition of political affairs and the composition of the Cabinet is said to have taken place. As to the latter part of their counseling, one fact has transpired with all but certainty, viz: that the Secretaryship of the Interior was formally tendered to Mr. Bates; and in reference to his views on the all-absorbing secession question, he expressed them so unhesitatingly and decisively, not only in the President's apartments, but in various places of general resort he frequented during his stay, that they were soon publicly known. He was bold and emphatic in his denunciation of all movements aiming at a dismemberment of the Union. With an energy, that made one forget the whiteness of his hair and flowing beard, he protested: "that secession is treason, and *must* be put down;" that "the majesty of the law *must* be maintained at all hazards," and that "peaceable secession is an impossibility." That he *meant* what he *said* was apparent.

The old Whig friends of Mr. Lincoln were not surprised at the selection of Mr. Bates for an important post in the Cabinet. Mr. Lincoln was known to them to have entertained for many years the highest regard for the public and private virtues of his unsuccessful rival for the Presidency, and that the question was not so much whether a seat would be offered as whether it would be accepted.

JOHN C. FREMONT PRESSED FOR THE CABINET

It will doubtlessly be gratifying to your readers to learn, that there is a strong probability of a tender of the Secretaryship of War to the Republican standard-bearer of 1856. Influences of a very potential character have lately been exercised here in his favor, voices from Ohio and New York, that are entitled to and have received an appreciative hearing, have pleaded his cause with an evident show of effect. It is, furthermore, asserted, that strong appeals in his favor were brought by the last Pony Express from your State, and made a deep impression on the appointing power. A leader on the same subject in the most influential paper west of the Alleghenies was read to the President elect by a prominent politician no more than three days ago, within your correspondent's own knowledge. Nor does it seem to me, from all I can hear and see, that there is any great disposition to deny the object of all these demonstrations. I am prepared to say, on the contrary, that in view of these fighting times, a military man of Col. Fremont's experience, pluck and renown is thought pre-eminently preferable to a civilian. I think, however, there is an apprehension of an unwillingness to serve. Were it removed, there would be little doubt as to the representation of the Golden State in the Cabinet by its most famous citizen.

TEMPER OF THE PRESIDENT ELECT ON THE DISUNION ISSUE

A month ago, there was a manifest disposition in Presidential circles, to treat the restive Cotton States with the indulgent forbearance usually employed with good effect in the treatment of irritated, fretting children. Their disunion spasms were ascribed to the flutters of excitement consequent to the humiliating and startling news of the election of a Republican President, and expected to be healed by the sobering influences of time alone, without necessitating the application of any more violent remedy. The President elect shared the belief with all his friends, that a short trial of the Republican Administration would satisfy the South of the groundlessness of their apprehensions, and induce her to some rash acts of lawlessness while laboring under the first impulses of disappointment, and defeat to the contrary notwithstanding, to return ultimately to her former loyalty. But the developments of the last four weeks have changed this disposition and belief altogether. The determined infatuation and stubborn deafness to all moderate counsel, with which the secession abyss is being approached, gradually produced less kind and conciliatory sentiments. The openly avowed purpose of Southern leaders to try their disunion experiment at all hazards, and the heedless indorsement of their seditious plans by the population of the Gulf States loosened sympathetic ties. The haughty, insulting tone with which impossible concessions were demanded, resulted in wounded pride and a spirit of hostility. The cruel proscriptions and persecutions of all Northern men, without regard to political convictions, throughout the Cotton and Southern States called forth feelings of deep indignation, and desires of retaliation. In fine, as the disunion movement grows in extent and violence, the firmness of the powers, that are to be, increases correspondingly. Those that imagine the President elect at all scared—indeed, will find themselves sadly disappointed after the 4th of March next. They will be more apt to find a roaring lion than an affrighted lamb in the White House. Its future occupant will show more pluck than they perhaps give him credit for. He is possessed of true Kentucky "grit," and will not fail to demonstrate it in a striking manner. Although ready and anxious to respect and protect the constitutional right of all sections of the country, he yet feels that he is in duty bound to uphold the Federal laws by all lawful means. Knowing himself to be right, consequences will have no terror for him, and he will strictly fulfill his constitutional obligations, and let the responsibility for whatever will arise from Southern resistance rest where the public sense of justice will place it.

The above may be deemed strong language, but your correspondent knows what he is writing; he fully understands the meaning of every word he uses. Being desirous of reflecting the views of the incoming Administration to the best of his opportunities for information, he would not employ other terms in the face of the overwhelming evidence daily appealing to his senses, in support of the fact that *concessions are scouted and that peaceable secession is looked upon as impossible in the State House.*

PRONUNCIAMENTO BY HIS ILLINOIS "ORGAN"

In proof of this assertion, an editorial from the *Daily [Illinois State] Journal,* of this place (the central organ of the Republicans of the Prairie State) is subjoined. It appeared yesterday and *is positively known to have been inspired by the President elect.* Says the *Journal:*

STAND FIRM—BE TRUE

[omitted—see above, entry for December 17, for the text of the *Journal* editorial]

EFFECT OF THE LETTER OF J. M. BOTTS, OF VIRGINIA

The last epistolary production of J. Minor Botts on the "State of the Union," is pronounced a very bold and patriotic document by the President elect. But J. M. B. writes too much and speaks still more. Were it not for this fact, his bid for a seat in the Cabinet might perhaps prove successful. As it is, Botts' stock is rising; but it is doubtful whether it will be bulled up to par by the few advocates of the loquacious Virginian's claims.

Yesterday Mr. Lincoln received from a prominent Ohio politician an extract from the *National Democrat*, a Breckinridge daily journal, published at Cleveland, containing what purported to be a "conservative" letter from the President elect to the Hon. Thomas Ewing, Jr. He read the forged message to a number of visitors, remarking—"So you see I have written a letter after all." In the evening, his private secretary telegraphed an official disavowal to the New York *Tribune.*

December 20, 1860

Springfield, 20 December 1860

[New York *Herald*, 21 December 1860]

The Springfield *Journal* of to-day has a startling leader on secession, which, from the peculiar relations of the paper to the President elect, has great significance.

It says that South Carolina cannot dissolve the Union by the simple passage of resolutions or other passive demonstrations. Her federal officers may resign, and she may close her courts and post offices, but she cannot get out of this Union until she conquers this government. While this government endures there can be no disunion.

If South Carolina does not obstruct the collection of the revenues at her ports, nor violate any other federal law, there will be no trouble, and she will not be out of the Union. If she violates the law then comes the tug of war.

The President of the United States, in such an emergency, has a plain duty to perform. *Mr. Buchanan may shirk it, or the emergency may not exist during his administration. If not then the Union will last through his term of office.*

If the overt act on the part of South Carolina takes place on or after the 1st [4th] of March, 1861, then the duty of executing the laws will devolve upon Mr. Lincoln.

The laws of the United States must be executed. The President has no discretionary power on the subject. His duty is emphatically pronounced in the constitution. *Mr. Lincoln will perform that duty.*

Disunion by armed force is treason, and treason must and will be put down at all hazards.

Springfield, 20 December 1860

[New York *Herald*, 25 December 1860]

The inhabitants of Springfield were to-day startled out of their habitual sedateness by two momentous events. In the morning the exciting news of the sudden advent of Thurlow Weed set them all agog, and in the afternoon the stirring report of the passage of the secession ordinance at Charleston ruffled their equanimity.[93]

The great republican chieftain, the liege lord of the Albany lobby [Weed], is come, and gone again. He flashed up like a meteor, moved some brief hours on this narrow stage, and was heard no more. There may be little "sound" or "fury" in these words, but they signify a good deal nevertheless. Vanished as the political halo that surrounded him in bygone times may have to a great extent, enough is left of his past prestige to make his pilgrimage hitherward an object of general interest. The republican Warwick[94] of New York may be straying, swerving, warping, but he is still a power in the land. The thousands of eyes that will steadily follow his wanderings; the thousands of lips that will anxiously inquire for the nature of his errand; the thousands of minds that are taxed to solve the mystery of his late recantations, prove him such. Will not every reader of the HERALD on opening to-morrow morning's issue wonder what Weed has been doing out here? Whether he came after the spoils, tried to make "Old Abe" embrace his new faith, met variance or coincidence of opinion? Most assuredly he will, and expect your correspondent to gratify his curiosity.

But to the particulars of the memorable visit.[95]

Weed arrived here from the East on the early morning train. He came by invitation, received upon a hint given to the President elect through Senator Trumbull of his desire to "compare notes." The spoils, it must be said to his credit, were not the only motive of his voyage hither. Not that he loved them any less, but that he has sense enough to see that other things must be attended to first before they can be quietly enjoyed.

Immediately after breakfast the distinguished visiter repaired to the private residence of the President elect who was prepared for his coming, and did not hold any levees during the day on his account. His reception was of the most cordial character. Two clever fellows, and why should they not treat each other cleverly?

The warlike champion of yore had come with an olive branch in his hand. He at once hauled his "compromise" out of his pocket and proceeded to business. It is said that each of its features was successively scanned by Mr. Lincoln with the utmost care, that they became the subject of a most earnest discussion, and that Weed soon found more points of divergence than agreement. It is stated that his idea of a stringent, but not odious, Fugitive Slave law was accepted; but that neither horn of the dilemma he proposed in reference to slavery in the Territories—viz: a sort of squatter sovereignty, or a geographical line of division—tempted the President elect. His opposition to these schemes—the acceptance of either [of which] would involve a flagrant inconsistency—is said to have been strenuous, and finally compelled Weed to consent to modifications in order to come to an understanding. The exact character of the substitute has not transpired; but it is asserted by good authority that Weed will proceed directly from here to Washington, and submit it to the approbation or rejection of the republican members of Congress, when its propositions will doubtless become generally known.[96]

Weed, with commendable propriety, made no allusion to the distribution of the fruits of victory until his opinion in regard to New York city and State appointments was solicited. He then recited the list of his friends he had been booking for his various positions during the last four or five weeks, accompanying it with a proper enumeration of their several qualifications and efforts in the cause. The talk of Mr. Lincoln's friends drifted in the course of the day towards Moses Grinnell as Secretary of the Treasury, Simeon Draper or General [James W.] Nye as Collector, and Chevalier [James Watson] Webb as Postmaster. It was reported that Weed made an authorized intimation during his visit of Mr. Seward's unwillingness to take a position in the Cabinet.

The air of the State House offices, hotel parlors and barrooms was pregnated all day with an infinity of rumors, conjectures and speculations. Their vagueness and contrariety induce me to pass them unnoticed.

Weed's interview with the President elect lasted from nine A.M. to three P.M., with a short intermission at noon. During the last two hours Judge Slosson[97] and J. H. Van Allen,[98] who had arrived from New York on the same train, were present. Cobb's last public letter[99] was the theme of elaborate comment in the afternoon. Mr. Lincoln's views are grossly distorted and misrepresented in that epistolary essay on the right and duty to secede. You may look for a semi-official refutation shortly after the return of the party to the East.

Weed will re-embark in an Eastern direction at half-past six o'clock this evening. I consign him to the tender mercies of your Washington correspondents.

The news of the passage of the secession ordinance, although expected with much certainty, made an immense sensation among all classes and political creeds. The "tug of war" is now supposed to be close at hand. The

President elect did not experience any extraordinary shock of nerves on hearing of the attempted legalization of open rebellion. It certainly did not make him any more willing to listen to compromises. Timidity is evidently no element of his moral composition.

Springfield, 20 December 1860

[New York *Herald*, New York *Tribune*, Boston

Daily Advertiser, 21 December 1860]

Thurlow Weed, Judge Slosson and J. H. Vanalin [Van Alen], of New York, arrived here from the East in the early morning train.

Weed was closeted with Lincoln from nine o'clock until three. He brought his compromise along, which was the subject of earnest discussion.

It is said that modifications were insisted on by the President elect relative to the recognition of the right of slavery in the Territories, and that the idea of a restoration of geographical lines of division was repudiated.

Weed returns East this evening. It is reported that he will take the modified programme to Washington, where it will be submitted to the republican members of Congress. He saw no one but Lincoln and a few of the latter's friends.

The New York city appointments were parceled out during Weed's interview with Lincoln.

Moses Grinnell is mentioned as Secretary of the Treasury, and Mr. [Simeon] Draper as Collector.

Seward's declination of a seat in the Cabinet is said to have been intimated.

The news from Charleston produced great sensation in political circles. Mr. Lincoln, however, received it calmly.

The President elect is grossly misrepresented in Cobb's last letter.

Springfield, 20 December 1860

[New York *Herald*, 24 December 1860]

Will the republican administration attempt to maintain the federal Union by force? Will secession be dealt with as treason? Will the federal army and navy be employed to protect the property of the United States and to secure the collection of revenues?

The answers to all these grave questions may be found in the subjoined startling leader of this morning's [*Illinois State*] *Journal*, the substance of which will be telegraphed to you to-day.[100] It is a "stunner." As to its authoritativeness, it will only be necessary to repeat that the *Journal* is edited by a nephew of the [wife of the] President elect, and published under his very eyes; facts which render it highly improbable that sentiments disapproved by Mr. Lincoln should be reflected by it:

THE UNION—IT MUST BE PRESERVED.

There are not a few who seem to think that the Union will be dissolved whenever the South Carolina secession Convention passes a resolution to that effect. The Union cannot be dissolved by the passage of resolutions. South Carolina may resolve that she is no longer a part of this Union. She may hold secession meetings, mount disunion cockades, plant palmetto trees, make palmetto flags, trample under foot the glorious flag of our country, and proclaim from the housetops her treason and her shame, but all this will not dissolve the Union. She may compel her citizens to resign official place held under the federal government, she may close her courts and post offices, and put her own people to a great deal of inconvenience and trouble, but she will still be in the Union, unmolested. She cannot get out of this Union until she conquers this government. The revenues must and will be collected at her ports, and any resistance on her part will lead to war. At the close of that war we can tell with certainty whether she is in or out of the Union. While this government endures there can be no disunion. If South Carolina does not obstruct the collection of the revenue at her ports, nor violate any other federal law, there will be no trouble, and she will not be out of the Union. If she violates the laws, then comes the tug of war. The President of the United States, in such an emergency, has a plain duty to perform; Buchanan may shirk it, or the emergency may not exist during his administration. If not, then the Union will last through his term of office. If the overt act on the part of South Carolina takes place on or after the 4th of March, 1861, then the duty of executing the laws will devolve upon Mr. Lincoln. The laws of the United States must be executed—the President has no discretionary power on the subject—his duty is emphatically pronounced in the constitution. Mr. Lincoln will perform that duty. Disunion, by armed force, is treason, and treason must and will be put down at all hazards. This Union is not, will not, and cannot be dissolved until this government is overthrown by the traitors who have raised the disunion flag. Can they overthrow it? We think not. "They may disturb its peace; they may interrupt the course of its prosperity; they may cloud its reputation for stability; but its tranquility will be restored, its prosperity will return, and the stain upon its national character will be transferred and remain an eternal blot on the memory of those who caused the disorder."[101] Let the secessionists understand it, let the press proclaim it, let it fly on the wings of the lightning, and fall like a thunderbolt among those now plotting treason in convention, that the republican party, that the great North, aided by hundreds of thousands of patriotic men in the slave States, have determined to preserve the Union—peaceably if they can, forcibly if they must.

December 21, 1860

Springfield, 21 December 1860

[New York *Herald*, 27 December 1860]

Contrary to general expectation, the great Albany lobbyist [Thurlow Weed] did not appear to have any anxiety to keep his visit to Mr. Lincoln a secret. He did not even attempt to preserve an incognito, and escape the attention of lynx-eyed correspondents, but defiantly inserted his name among the registered arrivals at the Chenery House, the favorite resort of visiting politicians. The supposition that he would endeavor to arrive and depart unnoticed was so universal that a colleague rushed frantically all over town in search of the very information he might have obtained by a mere glance at the register of his own stopping place. He had overheard a remark that Weed was on hand, and not believing for a moment that the distinguished stranger would put up at a public house, he exerted his legs and lungs for nearly an hour, early in the morning, trying to ascertain the name and residence of the resident friend of Mr. Lincoln, the guest of whom he supposed the object of his solicitation to be. In explanation of the freedom of Weed's movements, it is said that the fact of his arrival in Chicago having been noticed in an evening paper of that city precluded the practicability of secresy. But even if he had succeeded in reaching this place unobserved, he would have found concealment altogether impossible in view of the smallness of the town and the hundreds of eyes that are constantly on the lookout. Place seekers who contemplate visiting Springfield will do well, indeed, to abandon, like Weed, all idea of coming and going unrecognized, in order to save themselves a mortification at finding their names printed and their mission stated in the public prints.

There can be no doubt as to the correctness of the statement in my last that the President elect dissented most decidedly from the main points of Weed's compromise propositions. Since the latter's departure the friends of Mr. Lincoln talk more freely about the object and fruit of the conference, and all their remarks go to confirm what I said on the subject. Knowing—as I did—by the most direct means of information, the undisguised hostility of Mr. Lincoln to the re-establishment of any geographical divisions, and any farther territorial acquisitions by slavery, I could have well ventured an opinion as to the fate of Weed's programme at the hands of the President elect without waiting for the result of the former's personal plea in its behalf. Mr. Lincoln has been, and is now, a firm believer in the power of Congress to prohibit slavery in the Territories,—Mr. Weed's ingenious arguments to the contrary notwithstanding.

I have it from excellent authority, that, although Weed intimated Seward's intended disinclination of a seat in the Cabinet, he was nevertheless made the bearer of a letter from the President elect to the Senator from New York, offering him the Secretaryship of State. I doubt, however, the reliability of the statement.[102]

More credit deserves the report that Weed was merely asked to suggest names in connection with New York city and State appointments, and that he was unable to elicit any positive assurances. Senator Trumbull, who is known to have visited New York solely for the purpose of receiving and passing upon claims to office, has not yet reported, and hence nothing definite will be done at present.

I cannot resist the conviction that the passage of the secession ordinance by the South Carolina Convention has, instead of intimidating the President elect, only made him firmer and more decided in his views on the reckless and unjustifiable attempt to break up the Union. He will not swerve from the conscientious and rigorous fulfillment of what he considers his constitutional obligations, lest certain consequences might occur. He will not, like his predecessor, give way to unmanly terror and childish despair should events demand prompt and vigorous action. And that he will be called upon to strike, I believe, appears from hour to hour more certain to him.

There are many similarities and identities between the ideas embodied in Senator [Benjamin F.] Wade's last speech and those frequently expressed by Lincoln, that I am almost inclined to think that old Ben spoke by inspiration.[103]

I do not think the term "organ," in its usual interpretation, properly indicates the relations of the *Daily [Illinois] State Journal* of this place to the President elect. It should not be looked upon as a trumpet, by dint of which Mr. Lincoln daily proclaims all his ideas, opinions, plans, &c., &c., to the general public. Nor does he solicit or direct the editor to embody certain views in certain articles on certain occasions. But, on the other hand, it would be absurd to presume that a paper devoted for many years to the furtherance of his political fortunes, recognized as the central organ of the republican party of his own State, owned and edited by his kinsman,[104] with whom his intercourse is most constant and intimate, should say aught contrary to his sentiments.

The position of the New York *Tribune*, relative to the right to secede, does not find much favor with the republicans out here.[105] It is universally pronounced untenable. I am all but certain that Mr. Lincoln himself pronounces it dangerous and illogical.

It is stated that Mr. Lincoln is daily receiving large numbers of letters from prominent men of all the free States urging him to stand squarely and firmly on the Chicago platform, and not budge an inch.

Springfield, 21 December 1860
[San Francisco *Bulletin*, 16 January 1861]

VISIT OF THURLOW WEED TO THE PRESIDENT ELECT

At last the great Albany lobbyist is come! The Warwick of New York—the maker and destroyer of political fortunes—the prince of wire-pullers, has made his advent! Like hundreds of other hopeful pilgrims, he has turned his face towards the newly-risen political sun to bask for a brief time in its congenial light.

At an early hour yesterday morning, one might have seen numerous groups gathered in the State House, offices, hotel parlors and bar-rooms. The expression of their countenances showed that something startling had happened. Conjectures, surmises, speculations kept their tongues in steady motion. And what was the burden of their under-tone conversation and whispering? Weed—Weed alone, and nothing but Weed. Weed had arrived on the morning train from the East—had repaired immediately to the President's private dwelling and was closeted with him ever since. Was that not enough to set the many political quid-nuncs, permanently and temporarily sojourning in this place, nearly crazy?

But to the facts in reference to this memorable visit. Mr. Weed landed here at 5:30 A.M., in company with Judge Slosson and J. H. Van Allen of New York city. He had undertaken the journey upon a hint conveyed through Senator Trumbull, to the effect, that his visit to the President elect at the present time would not be undesirable. The hint was given out in response to an intimation of a desire on his part to interchange views on the threatening aspect of public affairs with Mr. Lincoln. Otherwise, his relations to Mr. Seward would have precluded a call of his own accord.

I believe I referred in my last to the fact, that the substance of an elaborate compromise leader in the Albany *Evening Journal* had been telegraphed all over the country on Saturday last [December 15], and that the agent of the Associated Press embodied the unfounded insinuation in his despatch, that the ideas set forth in the article in question reflected those of Mr. Lincoln.

The unexpected (not to the President elect and his friends, but to the public at large) appearance of Mr. Weed so shortly after the publication of his compromise propositions, was naturally connected with the alleged coincidence of his views with those of Mr. Lincoln, and a reputed intention to spread it in a more elaborate form with a sort of semi-official endorsement before the country. The main object of Mr. Weed's visit was, indeed, a conference with Mr. Lincoln as to the character of the remedies best to be applied in the present political crisis. But it originated more in Mr. Weed's anxiety to find a palliative for the troubles now distracting the country, than in any conviction on the part of the President elect of the necessity of further compromises. The result of the conference proves this most conclusively.

WHAT THE ALBANY SAGE PROPOSED— LINCOLN DIFFERS WITH HIM

It would, of course be tantamount to an attempt to impose upon your readers, should I claim that I am privy to all that passed between Mr. Weed and Mr. Lincoln. But my means of information are nevertheless such as to warrant me in submitting the following as a correct account, and I am confident that the sequence will bear me out in all I state.

The different elements composing Mr. Weed's panacea, were as follows:

1. That an *efficient, but not revolting* fugitive slave law should be passed, and that its passage should be followed by a repeal of Personal Liberty laws.
2. That when the Territories contain a population, which, under the census, entitles them to a representation in Congress, they may come into the Union with State Governments of their own fashioning—provided, of course, that they conform to the Constitution of the United States; or if this be inadmissible,
3. A renewal of the geographical division of the remaining Territory—as by virtue of the Missouri Compromise line.

All these propositions were the subject of earnest and protracted discussion between Mr. Weed and Mr. Lincoln. But all the requirements of the former would not induce the latter to give his assent to any but the first one. Mr. Lincoln, although strongly opposed to all further concessions by the free soil to the slaveholding interest, was disposed to take up with an amendment to the fugitive slave laws, in order to remove the pretext for a secession movement. But, on the other hand, *his faith in the right of Congress to legislate on the subject of slavery in the Territories, is unshaken, and he will never swallow the proposed Squatter Sovereignty or the restoration of geographical lines of division between free and slave labor.*

The interview of the Albany pacificator, by dint of back-downs and re-nunciations, and the unyielding exponent of unadulterated Republicanism, lasted from 9 A.M. until 3 P.M., with a short intermission at noon.

CABINET APPOINTMENTS—MORE OF WEED

I have it from good authority, that Mr. Weed was solicited to suggest names in connection with the New York City and State appointments; and that although his opinion as to the qualifications, devotion to the cause, etc., etc., was respectfully received, he did not succeed in eliciting any definite pledge or promise. Moses H. Grinnell is to-day mentioned by the friends of Mr. Lincoln as Secretary of the Treasury, Gen. Nye as Collector of the port of New York, Chevalier Webb as Postmaster, and Simeon Draper as Deputy-Treasurer.

Mr. Seward, it is stated, authorized Weed to express his determination, in case the subject should be broached, not to accept a seat in the Cabinet.

Mr. Weed returned East on yesterday's evening train. He carries a letter from Mr. Lincoln to Mr. Seward, the tenor of which has yet failed to tran-spire.

I have been assured this morning that Weed accepted certain modifi-cations of his programme as suggested by the President, and that he will proceed directly to Washington to lay it before the Republican members of Congress in its modified shape. The truth of this will, of course, be tested within the next few days.

I feel authorized to state that New York appointments will not be acted upon until Senator Trumbull, who is now on a sounding expedition in the Empire State, will be heard from.

POSITION OF THE PRESIDENT ELECT ON THE SECESSION ISSUE

It will be remembered that I directed the attention of the readers of the [San Francisco] *Bulletin* to certain authoritative statements in the *Daily [Illinois] State Journal* of this city. I enclose another leader from the same paper, headed the "Union Must be Preserved." (The substance of this article has already been published in the *Bulletin*.) It is a most significant article, for it advocates coercion, if need be, to preserve the Union, and distinctly states that Mr. Lincoln will use force against the Disunionists. Its source entitles it to the due consideration of the general public. It is true, the *Journal* is not Mr. Lincoln's "organ" in the usual interpretation of the term. The President elect does not write its leaders, nor give special instructions for certain strictures on certain occasions. But it would be preposterous to presume that a journal that is owned and edited by his [wife's] nephew, and published under his very eyes, that is the recognized central organ of the Republican Party of his own State, that has been devoted for years to the advancement of his political fortunes, should say aught contrary to his views. It should be borne in mind, however, that the article was written before the news of the passage of the secession ordinance by South Carolina was received.

WHAT HENRY CLAY SAID ON A SIMILAR ISSUE

Mr. Lincoln is known to be an old Henry Clay Whig. He calls the immortal Kentuckian his "beau ideal of a statesman." That his position in reference to the secession issue as indicated above is the identical one occupied by Mr. Clay in 1850, with regard to the then threatened nullification by South Carolina of the Compromise Measures of that year, will be seen by the following quotations from a letter and speech written and delivered by his prototype during the same period:

> But suppose we should be disappointed, and the standard should be raised of open resistance to the Union, the Constitution, and the laws, what is to be done? There can be but one possible answer: the powers, the authority and dignity of the Government ought to be maintained and resistance put down at every hazard. The moment a daring hand is raised to resist by force the execution of the laws, the duty of enforcing them arises, and if the conflict which may arise should lead to civil war, the resisting party, having begun it, will be responsible for all the consequences. . . .[106]
>
> I should deplore, as much as any man living or dead, that armies should be raised against the authority of the Union either by individuals or States. But, after all that has occurred, if any one State, or a portion of the people of any State, choose to place themselves in military array against the Government of the Union, I am for trying the strength of the Government. I am for ascertaining whether we have a Government or not—practical, efficient, capable of maintaining its authority and of upholding the power and interests which belong to a Government. Now, sir, am I to be alarmed or dissuaded from any such course by intimations of spilling of blood? If blood is to be spilled, by whose fault will it be? Upon this supposition, I maintain it will be the fault of those who raise the standard of disunion and endeavor to prostrate the Government. And, sir, when that is done, so long as it pleases God to give me a voice to express my sentiments, and an arm, weak and enfeebled as it may be by age, that voice and that arm

will be on the side of my country, for the support of the general authority for the maintenance of the powers of this Union.[107]

I have quoted these two passages, for the special reason that Mr. Lincoln has used them within my own hearing, in explanation of his position, to visitors.

THE PRESIDENT ELECT IS CALLED UPON BY A COCKADE-WEARING SECESSIONIST

A poltroon hailing from Yazoo, Miss., stalked into Mr. Lincoln's reception room on Wednesday afternoon last, decked with a blue cockade. He introduced himself as "Mr. D. E. Ray." He plunged into the corner of a sofa, and there sat, sullen and silent, for some twenty minutes. One of the other visitors at last addressed some questions to him, when he splurged out some disunion sentiments, which were promptly rebuked with a good deal of pungency by the questioner. The interchange of radical ideas waxing hot, Mr. Lincoln, who had previously taken no notice of the Southern churl, interfered to prevent serious consequences, and by letting off a timely joke or two, succeeded in doing so. Engaging in conversation with the Mississippian, he soon cooled him down to such a degree that the Southron begged him for a copy of his debates with Douglas, to take back to Yazoo. The book was procured, duly inscribed and handed to him by the President elect, who expressed the hope that its possession would not involve him in any trouble in Yazoo. The Southerner then retired, heartily ashamed of the insult he intended to inflict by the exhibition of his cockade upon him who treated him so kindly.

EFFECT OF THE NEWS OF THE PASSAGE OF THE SOUTH CAROLINA SECESSION ORDINANCE UPON MR. LINCOLN

The news of the resolution of the South Carolina Convention, to consider themselves out of the Union, was telegraphed to Mr. Lincoln from Washington on Thursday morning last [December 20]. He received it with the utmost calmness. Having expected this act of folly, rebellion and treason, it did not surprise him. He is evidently not afraid to look events in the face, like his pusillanimous predecessor. He deplores the event, but is prepared for its consequences.

THE NEW YORK *TRIBUNE* AND THE "RIGHT OF SECESSION"

The position assumed by the New York *Tribune*, recognizing the right to secede and recommending a passive "let them go," is pronounced untenable both by the President elect and his friends.

December 23, 1860

Springfield, 23 December 1860

[New York *Herald*, 27 December 1860]

Among the many prominent characteristics of the President elect, I think every impartial observer, of sufficient familiarity with the various elements of his moral temperament, will rank self-reliance, independence of thought and action, and straightforwardness of purpose. His whole career is a running illustration of the prominence of these traits. But, although unaccustomed to shape both resolution and execution according to the dictates of his own clear judgment—to measure and pass upon the merits of things with the aid of his own moral and intellectual standard—the efficacy of this guide, demonstrated by his success in life, never produced conceit enough to induce him to overlook altogether the ideas, motives, arguments, counsels and remedies of others. On the contrary, a coincidence of his own views with those of the master spirits of his and previous ages is always greeted by him with great satisfaction and consciousness of increased strength. No one can be more anxious to fortify his position by precedents. No one rejoices more in the knowledge of reflecting the sentiments of the statesmen and patriots that illuminate the pages of the history of his country.

It will be remembered that during the last ten days I have, at various times, sought to define the position of the President elect in reference to the secession issue. As one of the most unmistakeable indications of his temper on this subject, I quoted a leader from the *Daily [Illinois State] Journal*, of this city, headed "The Union must be preserved," and the substance of which was the bold declaration "that secession is treason, and must be put down at all hazards." In exemplification of what is said above, it may be well to state that a comparison of the manifesto in question with the anti-nullification letters and edicts of Gen. [Andrew] Jackson will reveal striking similarities and even identities. But the whig antecedents of Mr. Lincoln rendered it unlikely that he would content himself with supporting his position by democratic authorities. It is said, indeed, that the subjoined quotations from a speech and a letter of Henry Clay, delivered and written during and immediately after the agitation of the Compromise measures of 1850, have been frequently used of late by Mr. Lincoln in indirect explanation of his views of the disunion movement. They show conclusively that the position attributed to him by me is the identical one assumed by the immortal Kentuckian with regard to the threats of South Carolinian secession after the passage of the measures already referred to: [omitted—see above, entry for December 21, for the passages by Clay]

Such were the sentiments of the "gallant Harry of the West," and I venture to predict that he who looks upon him as his prototype will not fail to respond to them.

December 24, 1860

Springfield, 24 December 1860

[New York Herald, 31 December 1860]

About two weeks ago I took occasion to state in a letter to the HERALD that invitations had been sent out from here to divers political eminences to repair hither for the purpose of both counselling with the President elect on the present condition of public affairs and receiving offers of seats in the Cabinet. This announcement is now being rapidly verified. A week since Mr. Edward Bates made his appearance and was tendered the Secretaryship of the Interior. Last Thursday Thurlow Weed loomed up, to return with the authority to sound certain New York gentlemen as to their willingness to serve, and to-day David Wilmot, of Proviso renown,[108] made his advent, to become the recipient of the flattering offers of a place among Mr. Lincoln's constitutional advisers.

It is evident that in view of the location in Springfield of the fountain head of federal patronage, any political personage that undertakes the journey to this place renders himself liable to the imputation of tuft-hunting, and hence it may well be presumed that no gentleman of character and self respect is likely to come here unless invited to do so by the President elect. From this reason alone the just inference can be drawn that Mr. Wilmot came here at the special invitation of Mr. Lincoln.

But there is additional evidence of the correctness of this presumption. As soon as Mr. Lincoln had been apprised of Mr. Wilmot's arrival on the early morning train he repaired to the St. Nicholas Hotel, where the expected visiter had taken rooms, and welcomed the distinguished Pennsylvanian in the heartiest manner. The two at once retired to a private apartment, in which they remained until noon, when Mr. Lincoln returned to his residence for dinner. At two o'clock another conference commenced, and lasted until four, at which hour Mr. Lincoln reappeared in the public reception room at the State House.

That during the interview a proposition was made to Mr. Wilmot to accept a position in the Cabinet is looked upon as a *fait accompli* by all the friends of the President elect. It is likewise added by them that, as in the instance of Mr. Bates, no definite place was offered, but that the views of Mr. Wilmot as to what appeared most adapted to him were ascertained, with the mutual understanding of an ultimate agreement at a later date.

Rumor connects Mr. Wilmot both with the Secretaryship of State and that of the Navy. I would not be surprised if he should be found the holder of the most important *portefeuille* [portfolio] under the incoming administration.

The selection of Mr. Wilmot gives general satisfaction among the supporters of Mr. Lincoln in this latitude. It is looked upon as an earnest of the Territorial policy to be pursued by the republican regime. It is construed into an unmistakeable indication of the firm adherence of the republican President to the Chicago platform, and of his unshaken faith in the soundness of its most prominent plank, viz: the right of Congress to legislate prohibitorily on the subject of slavery in the Territories.

Mr. Wilmot, it will be remembered, was one of the most active supporters of Mr. Lincoln's claims to the republican nomination among the Pennsylvania delegation to the Chicago Convention.

He appears to be in excellent health, and well conditioned to bear the onerous duties of a Cabinet officer.

He will take the Chicago train at half-past six P.M., and return immediately to his home, in spite of the violent snow storm that has prevailed here for some days and rendered railroad travelling on the Western prairies a rather comfortless undertaking.

It is asserted, with some show of likelihood, that Mr. Wilmot was determined upon as the representative in the Cabinet of the republican banner State [Pennsylvania] because of his having been for some time off the political stage, and of his consequent relative independence from the numerous rival cliques and factions that are squabbling for the spoils under the guidance of ambitious leaders.

Simultaneously with Mr. Wilmot, Colonel E. D. Baker, the newly elected Senator from Oregon, arrived in this his old home, his first visit since his emigration to the Pacific coast, some ten years ago. "Ned," as he was familiarly called hereabouts in former days, was most cordially greeted by his old friend, the President elect, and a host of relatives and acquaintances. His visit is of a purely private character. He came to see a sister, married in this place, his mother and a brother, both of whom live a short distance from here [in Winchester]. His official duties not allowing any protracted absence from Washington, his relatives will all meet him here, where he will remain over the holidays. A public dinner in his honor has been spoken of to-day.

The holidays are close at hand, and we will, together with the inclemency of the weather, keep Springfield clear of office seekers during the remainder of the week.

Springfield, 24 December 1860
[New York *Herald*, 25 December 1860]

Senator Baker, of Oregon, and David Wilmot, of Pennsylvania, arrived here from the East this morning. Mr. Baker's visit is of a purely private character.

Mr. Wilmot came by invitation of the President elect, who called upon him at his hotel immediately after his arrival, and spent some five hours with him in the course of the day. It is certain that Mr. Wilmot will represent the republican banner State in the Cabinet, but no definite position is as yet assigned to him. He returns East this evening.

It is now understood that one after the other of the gentlemen selected for the Cabinet will be summoned hither.

December 25, 1860

Springfield, 25 December 1860
[New York *Herald*, 31 December 1860]

Your correspondent is no believer in things supernatural. He has no faith in goblins, ghosts, doubles and second sights, up to this time. But if Judge John Slosson really moved among the bulls and bears of Wall street on Thursday last, as per card in Saturday's *Tribune*, instead of hobnobbing at the Leroy House[109] in this city with Thurlow Weed, James H. Van Allen and the President elect, he confesses himself considerably confounded. He will to-morrow invest some of his spare cash in a copy of the "Footfalls on the boundaries of another world," [by Robert Dale Owen] to solve the mystery. But in the meantime he is ready to recant, as his knowledge of the travelling facilities from the capital of Illinois to the Empire City [New York] is sufficient to convince him that the intervening distance could not have been measured between Thursday afternoon and Friday morning. He is the more willing to make the *amende honorable* as a prospecting tour to Springfield is hardly apt, under the prevailing circumstances, to reflect credit upon political characters.

Mr. Wilmot having left, Senator Baker is the sole observed of all Springfield observers. He is certainly a remarkable man and has made a remarkable career. Of restless ambition, indomitable energy, true English perseverance, fine natural parts, great elegance and popular manners, he could not well fail to make his mark. Nor will he go anywhere without attracting general attention. Here he was at all times surrounded by people eager to be spoken to by him. But great as the desire apparently was to hear him talk, it is said he was rather reserved and cautious in all his public expressions of sentiments. He was urged to deliver a public speech—a request which he saw fit respectfully but firmly to decline. He evidently labored under the same restraining effect of the uncertain aspect of public affairs that signalizes the present course of most Congressional eminences. Some of Mr. Lincoln's friends are reported to be anxious to probe him as to his imputed popular sovereignty predilections—attempts which were, however, successfully dodged by him. In regard to the immediate prospect, he is said to have stated, as the prevailing opinion at Washington, that no peace offering whatever is likely to prevent the secession of the cotton States, and that before long the disunion question will be reduced with the North to the task of keeping the border slave States in the confederacy [i.e., Union].

The heavy snow fall during the last forty-eight hours in this latitude having rendered it impossible for Mr. Baker's mother to meet him here, he set out this morning for her place of residence, some seventy miles west of this. He expects to return on Friday and remain here over Sunday. A banquet in his honor will probably come off on Saturday.

Considerable relief is felt in republican circles by consequence of the appearance of Mr. Seward's disavowal of his alleged endorsement of Weed's compromise specifics. Although it went rather hard with some to believe in so flagrant an inconsistency on the part of the New York Senator, it was yet thought that stranger things might happen in these strange times, and hence the disappointment was most agreeable.

In this connection it may be well to mention that the cheap puff the great Albany lobbyist [Thurlow Weed] let off after his turn did not produce any sensible impression in the State House.[110]

For the last few days several prominent republican leaders of this State have been sojourning here. Their intercourse with the President is constant and intimate. It is said that the more important of the Illinois appointments have been allotted during their stay. Among them were Hon. Leonard Swett and Judge Davis, of Bloomington, and Senator Marshall, of Coles county.[111] Judge Davis was formerly a law partner of Mr. Lincoln and continues to be on the most intimate terms with him.[112] His opinion is said to be highly valued by the President elect. He is a man of great talents and solid acquirements, and I would not be surprised to see him fill one of the most influential positions under the republican administration.[113] He is certainly qualified to do credit to any office within the gift of his friend.

This being Christmas day, matters are rather quiet in and about the State House. A good many country people are in town, and but few find their way to Mr. Lincoln's reception room. This afternoon a party of St. Louis gentlemen all but monopolized the attention of the President elect.

Mr. James H. Van Allen has returned here, after an absence of several days.

Mr. Thomas W. Sweeney,[114] of Philadelphia, is also in town, and paid his respects to Mr. Lincoln.

Springfield, 25 December 1860

[San Francisco *Bulletin*, 21 January 1861]

PROVISO-WILMOT'S VISIT TO MR. LINCOLN—
WILL REPRESENT PENNSYLVANIA IN THE CABINET

Another distinguished arrival from the East in the course of yesterday morning demonstrated the correctness of my announcement some two weeks since, that invitations have been issued to a number of prominent Republican leaders to visit the President elect, for the purpose of both interchanging views and receiving offers of a seat in the Cabinet. David Wilmot, of Proviso renown, arrived here from his home in Pennsylvania by the early morning train, on a mission similar to that which brought Mr. Bates of Missouri hither last Saturday a week ago, viz: to be made the recipient of the flattering tender of a place among Mr. Lincoln's constitutional advisers.

So soon as the President elect had been apprised of the coming of his expected visitor, he repaired immediately to the St. Nicholas Hotel, where the distinguished Pennsylvanian had taken rooms. The two having exchanged salutations, they at once retired to a private apartment, where they remained engaged in earnest consultation until noon. The interview was resumed shortly after dinner, and continued until 3 o'clock, when Mr. Lincoln took his leave of Mr. Wilmot and proceeded to the State-house to open the public afternoon reception.

There is no more doubt as to the offer of a position in the Cabinet, on the part of Mr. Lincoln, and its acceptance by Mr. Wilmot, than there was in the instance of Mr. Bates, whose selection has since been officially announced. Mr. Lincoln's most intimate friends to-day, proclaim the fact openly, that Mr. Wilmot has been determined upon as the representative of the Republican Banner State [Pennsylvania] in the Republican administration. But although it is certain, beyond all gainsay, that he will be one of the members of the Cabinet, the exact position he will occupy has not been definitely agreed upon by the two high contracting powers. Both the Secretary of State and that of the Navy are claimed for Mr. Wilmot in Republican circles. I think the former is most likely to be assigned to him. It would be but natural, indeed, that the most prominent [position] should be given to the State that rolled up the largest majority for the Republican nominees.[115] Mr. Wilmot, it will be remembered, was one of the earliest and most zealous of advocates of the claims of Mr. Lincoln before the Chicago Convention. But this was not the only reason that impelled his choice. The principal one was his comparative retirement from the political arena during the last few years, and his independence from the many cliques and factions in which the Republicans of the Keystone State are arrayed around ambitious leaders. This selection, it was thought, would not excite any jealousy and dissatisfaction that any other man would inevitably produce. Mr. Wilmot gives great satisfaction to the Republicans of this region. He is taken as an earnest of the firm intention of the President elect to remain true to every article of the Republican faith laid down in the Chicago platform, and as an unmistakable indication of an intended adherence to the doctrine of the right of Congress to legislate prohibitor[il]y on the subject of slavery in the Territories.

Mr. Wilmot appeared to be in vigorous health, and well-condition[ed] to bear the onerous duties of a Cabinet officer on his shoulders. Having transacted the business that brought him here, he returned East on last evening's train, although a violent snow-storm, that augured anything but an agreeable trip, prevailed at the time of his departure.

ARRIVAL OF SENATOR BAKER

Simultaneously with Mr. Wilmot, the long-expected newly-elected Senator from Oregon landed in Springfield. The news of his arrival spread like wildfire among the politicians of this burg, and the parlor the St. Nicholas was soon filled with a crowd, eager to welcome "Ned" back to his old home. It is said that Mr. Baker was moved to tears when he found himself, after an interval of over ten years, once more surrounded by the intimate friends of earlier days. The first thing he did, after extricating himself from the friendly importunities of former acquaintances, was to call on his sister, who is married in this place. He remained at her residence the remainder of the morning, and at noon dined with a number of friends at his hotel. After dinner, he hunted up his old friend "Abe," who received him in the heartiest possible manner. What strange emotions these two men must have felt on meeting again, after so long a lapse of time, in view of the wonderful changes their political fortunes had experienced in the meantime! They had a long, cordial, private talk, and did not separate until after dark.

Col. Baker's visit is of a purely private character. He comes to greet his friends and relations, and that is all. His official duties precluding a protracted absence from Washington, his stay will be confined to a few days. Were it not for its shortness and desired privacy, a public demonstration in his honor would doubtlessly be got up. He starts to-day for Winchester, a small town some seventy miles west of this, where his aged mother resides. He is expected to return here on Friday, stay over Sunday, and re-embark for Washington on Monday next.

AUTHORIZED DEFINITION OF THE TERRITORIAL POLICY OF THE NEW ADMINISTRATION

On Saturday last the N.Y. *Tribune* was authorized from here by telegraph to contradict officially, the statement afloat in many eastern journals, that the President elect was, in view of the threatened severance of the Union, willing to abandon the Republican dogma in regard to slavery in the Territories. The same journal was also requested to intimate, that Mr. Lincoln would stand squarely on the Chicago platform, and not yield an inch either forward or backward. This accords precisely with what I remarked in my last letter on the result of Thurlow Weed's visit.

SENATOR SEWARD'S DISCLAIMER

W. H. Seward's emphatic disclaimer of his imputed indorsement of the compromise scheme of Thurlow Weed, has greatly relieved the friends of the Senator. Although they were hardly prepared for the implied flagrant inconsistency on the part of the radical propounder of the "irrepressible conflict" theory [i.e., Seward], the back-down was nevertheless regarded as among the possibilities in these times so fruitful with strange developments. The official disavowal, however, has restored their confidence in the firmness of his political convictions.

COL. FREMONT AND THE CABINET

From day to day, the opinion gains ground here that the Pathfinder [i.e., Frémont] will be found at the head of the War Department after the 4th of March next. The popular sentiment in his favor was very high throughout the West, and it is more than probable that Mr. Lincoln will defer to it. It is, however, unlikely that the journey he is at the present moment said to be making to New York has been induced by the offer of a seat in the Cabinet. Mr. Lincoln did not make any tenders previous to his *bona fide* indorsement by the electoral college. I would not be surprised if the Colonel should pay Springfield a visit shortly after his landing in New York.

CHRISTMAS IN SPRINGFIELD

A dreary, joyless Christmas we are having in Springfield. A furious snowstorm is blowing, and imparts a most melancholy and deserted aspect to the town. Mr. Lincoln is holding no levee to-day. He flatters himself that the inclemency of the weather and the holidays will give some days respite from the inroads of place-seekers.

December 26, 1861

Springfield, 26 December 1860
[New York *Herald*, 1 January 1861]

The developements of the last few days justify the belief that the work commenced in good earnest by the President elect immediately after the meeting of the electoral colleges, some three weeks since, is nearly completed. The long array of names, partly suggested by others and partly booked by himself, with a view to the construction of the Cabinet, has been carefully sifted. Information as to the antecedents and qualifications of the proposed members has been sought and obtained. The claims of the different States and sections have been duly weighed and a partial decision finally arrived at. I say "partial," because my information warrants the assertion that certain places in the Cabinet will be held in abeyance until events in the South will have reached a point of culmination, although the probability of a selection of members from the slaveholding States, in addition to Mr. Bates, evidently grows fainter, in view of the hostile attitude lately assumed by most political characters from that section mentioned in connection with the Cabinet. The possibility of a more favorable turn of affairs is not yet despaired of, and hence room is left for such as might, after all, be found acceptable.

As to the component parts of the fractional Cabinet already made up, the country has been apprised, first by the HERALD's Springfield correspondent [i.e., Villard], and subsequently, in an official manner, by the [St. Louis] *Missouri Democrat*, that the Hon. Edward Bates, of Missouri, has received the tender of and accepted a place among Mr. Lincoln's constitutional advisers. The post ostensibly assigned to him is claimed to be the Secretaryship of the Interior. But, although the signs confirmatory of that report were strong enough during and immediately after Mr. Bates' visit to induce my own belief in its truthfulness, I have yet of late received some unmistakeable hints to the effect that it was purposely given out to get certain parties on the wrong scent. I am really all but persuaded that your Washington correspondent stated the truth in the premises when asserting that "the Attorney Generalship was the *bona fide* position offered to and accepted by Mr. Bates."

The other memberships already positively disposed of are the Secretaryship of the Interior and that of the War Department. David Wilmot will hold the former, and John C. Fremont the latter. I am confident that the sequence will substantiate this statement.

John C. Fremont has not been heard in reply to the tender of what is but justly due him; but he is expected to manifest no resistance to the pleasure of the President elect, and the current of popular opinion, that, to all appearances, flows very strong in his favor throughout the free States. Thus we will have—

> Attorney General .... Edward Bates.
> Secretary of the Interior .... David Wilmot.
> Secretary of War .... John C. Fremont.

The head of the Treasury Department will doubtless be procured from among the financial republicans of your city. Either Moses H. Grinnell or Geo. Opdyke[116] will be the man.

New England will probably be represented by the Secretary of State, while the Postmaster General and Secretary of Navy will be taken from the South—provided, of course, that suitable material can be obtained from that quarter. If not, New England and the Northwest will each get an additional representative.

Although it is well known here that Mr. Lincoln had occupied himself thus far only with this composition of his ministerial council, gossipers have, nevertheless, been busy in distributing other appointments among prominent leaders of their party. The foreign missions have for some days furnished the staple of their conjectures. Disclaiming all authenticity, I yet subjoin a few of their "guesses," in order to show the drift of opinion hereabouts:

> Minister to London .... Wm. H. Seward.[117]
> Minister to the new kingdom of Italy.............. Wm. C. Bryant.[118]
> Minister to Berlin...G. Koerner, of Ill.[119]

Mr. Koerner[120] not being a politician of national reputation, the connection of his name with so high a station necessitates an explanation. He is German by birth; has resided in this State for over twenty years. Has held the offices of Supreme Judge and Lieutenant Governor, and is an intimate friend and ardent supporter of the President elect. He did yeoman's service for the cause during the last campaign, and hence may well expect a substantial reward at the hands of him to whose elevation to power he contributed so much. He is said to be a man of great natural parts and profound acquirements; an excellent linguist and a first class lawyer—qualifications which would certainly go a great way towards redeeming American diplomacy from the disgrace into which it has fallen in Europe; owing to the ignorance and boorishness of some of its present representatives.

Among the hotel arrivals of to-day are Chas. A. Morton and F. Hoyt, of New York city; F. Metcalf[121] and J. V. Fletcher,[122] of Boston; Abijah Fletcher,[123] from Westford, Massachusetts, and Jas. F. Sherron, from Philadelphia.[124]

December 27, 1860

Springfield, 27 December 1860

[New York *Herald*, 5 January 1861]

Senator Baker having returned from the visit to his mother at an early hour this morning, and announced his determination (in consequence, it is said, of a telegraphic recall from Washington) to re-embark for the East on the evening train, his friends, unwilling to see him depart without a formal manifestation of their regard and admiration, resolved to extemporize an ovation in the shape of a public reception. Accordingly, [hand]bills were hurried out requesting all the old acquaintances of the distinguished visiter to meet at two o'clock in the Court House. Pursuant to the call, a very large crowd assembled at the appointed hour, in spite of the shortness of the notice. Col. Baker having entered the hall surrounded by his most intimate friends, the meeting was called to order by Col. King.[125] Hon. James C. Conkling, a district elector, residing in this place, then welcomed Mr. Baker in a speech occupying about ten minutes. At its conclusion the latter took the stand amidst the most enthusiastic cheering and clapping of hands. He was expected to make a set speech, touching upon the present aspect of political matters. But I understand Mr. Lincoln intimated to him a desire to see politics avoided on the occasion, as probably all that Mr. Baker should say in reference to public questions would be construed into an expression of the sentiments of the President elect rather than his own. Hence the Colonel's effort dwelled mostly on "by-gone times," a recall of which, while among his former political associates and supporters, seemed eminently appropriate. But after all the current of thought carried him to political subjects at times. He spoke of his own fervid devotion to the Union. He pronounced the idea of an independent Pacific republic in case of Southern secession a calumniatory cheat and groundless presumption. He asserted most emphatically the loyalty of the people of the Pacific States. He said that now, when their dearest hope—the Pacific Railroad—was approaching realization, nothing was remoter than a severance of the ties that attached them to the Union, and that after the achievement of that grandest project of the century no power on earth would ever succeed in rending them asunder. He expressed, also, the belief that his old friend Lincoln would faithfully fulfill the high trust confided to him by the American people; that he would hold both the North and South to the discharge of their respective constitutional obligations; that he would see the federal laws maintained throughout the length and breadth of the land, and that no particular section or State need · have any fear of injustice or aggression on his part.

The speech lasted about an hour, and was frequently interrupted by hearty applause. It was evident that whenever the speaker made an allusion to politics he labored under a certain restraint, and was extremely cautious in the selection of his terms of expression. In the course of yesterday, however, he delivered a short address in the town of Winchester, the place of residence of his mother, in which his utterances were much more unreserved. He reflected the views of Mr. Lincoln in certain passages. He said:

> It requires neither concession nor submission by any part of our citizens to preserve the constitution. It only requires obedience to the laws; and that all men should be determined to render and secure. In spending a day at Springfield, I received impressions which fully satisfy me—indeed I know—that under Mr. Lincoln's administration the laws of the United States will be fairly and faithfully executed, North and South—that it will make no difference whether it be in Massachusetts or Georgia, Vermont or South Carolina. But while he will execute all the laws with promptness and fidelity, it will be done with that coolness and consideration which so eminently characterizes the President elect.

That popular mania—the collection of autographs of distinguished men— has proved of late a source of considerable annoyance to Mr. Lincoln also, and hardly a mail reaches here without bringing him numerous requests of specimens of his handwriting. Of course all of them wander unnoticed into his waste paper basket.

Within the last week a Boston genius sent him the most curious and at the same time uncomely present yet received by him. It is one of his speeches, transcribed in diminutive characters, so as to represent what is intended to be the outlines of the President elect. The penmanship is excellent, but the combination is such as to produce a frightful ensemble. The wretched caricature was encased in a costly frame. The perpetrator of the anomaly duly inscribed himself as an "artist."

To-day a considerable influx of strangers, among whom are many expectants, took place. Among the arrivals at the leading hotels are: Charles H. Noyes, New York[126]; Chauncey Bush, d[itt]o.[127]; Major Henshaw,[128] d[itt]o.; C. W. Kingsley, Boston[129]; R. F. Andrews, New York[130]; R. C. Parsons, Cleveland[131]; R. E. Coyle, Cincinnati; A. Grovenor, Wisconsin.

The ex-Rev. J. S. Kalloch, formerly of Boston notoriety, now of Leaven-worth City, is also in town, trying his best with the President elect.[132]

December 28, 1860

Springfield, 28 December 1860

[New York *Herald*, 3 January 1861]

Although your correspondent has no desire to claim any undue importance, he yet flatters himself that he has rendered, and is rendering, pre-eminent services to the President elect. The HERALD's faithful chronicles of whatever transpires in this region has saved many an hour of annoyance and perplexity to the "powers that are to be." It is solely owing, indeed, to the untiring vigilance with which he watches, and the regardless mercilessness with which he brings to publicity, the movements of place-seekers and tuft-hunters, that Abraham has not suffered any overwhelming attacks from the rapacious expectants among his supporters. No more efficient means of keeping the eager host at a safe distance could have been adopted than that which is now daily exercised to his benefit in the columns of the HERALD. The regular advertising of all political characters that venture hitherward in search of something in the way of Presidential favor is a most powerful scourge, that strikes terror to the hearts of all of them, and restrains them more than any apprehension of cold comforts at the hands of the Presidential elect. Several times your correspondent has already been besought with solicitations of mercy in the shape of silence as to the arrivals and manoeuvres in this locality of certain personages. But he is determined to do his duty without fear or favor, and protect "Old Abe" from the "black plague" of American politics.

In the wake of Thurlow Weed has followed the redoubtable ex-chief of the dark lanternites [i.e., nativists] of your State. Dan. Ullman is come.[133] It is stated that he is very anxious to hide his visit from the knowledge of his political confreres in New York. But in accordance with the above inflexible rule, his wishes could not be heeded. Ten minutes after his arrival last night his being here was known in the HERALD office.

The exact object of Dan.'s journey has not yet leaked out; but it may be naturally supposed that he did not come here merely to rest momentarily in Abraham's bosom. That he did not come by invitation I venture to say, and that the claims of himself and friends to a substantial recognition of their efforts during the Presidential campaign would not have suffered from not being urged until after the 4th of March is equally certain. I am, nevertheless, inclined to think that the American [i.e., Know Nothing] wing of the republican party in the Empire State will not be overlooked in the distribution of federal patronage, and doubtless even without the protest against its monopolization by the older republicans, that Ullman is to-day reported to have lodged in the State House.

Mr. Putnam,[134] the well known coadjutor of Ullman in the conversion of Americans [i.e., supporters of the American party, also called Know-Nothings] during the last summer, is expected to arrive here to-day, and assist the latter in laying the common wires in the Capitol. Will not Bobby Brooks[135] experience pangs of jealousy, and growl and show his teeth, on learning how hopefully his late political associates are licking their chops out here, and reflecting how easily he might have managed to share their coming juicy bones?

The wholesale robbery of the Indian Trust bonds did not excite as much amazement in Presidential circles as might have been expected under the circumstances.[136] The truth is that the republicans in this vicinity believe Mr. Buchanan's officials capable of almost everything in the way of malfeasance in office. They would not be surprised at seeing a general stampede with the public funds to the camp of the secessionists in South Carolina. No change to the better is expected previous to the inauguration of "Honest Old Abe."

The [Illinois State] Register of this morning contains a call by the Democratic State Central Committee for a convention of delegates from all the counties of the Prairie State, to be held in the second week of the coming month. It is said that the call was issued upon the suggestion of Senator Douglas, who desires to probe the sentiment of his followers in this State on the secession question before assuming a definite position in reference to the same issue.

Senator Baker, of Oregon, started for Washington this morning. During the last two days of his visit Hon. B. F. Harding,[137] the Speaker of the Oregon House of Representatives, was also here. He is mentioned in connection with the United States Marshalship of his State.

T. D. Jones,[138] the well known Cincinnati sculptor, has been in town for several days to prepare a bust of the President elect ordered by some citizens of Porkopolis [Cincinnati].

[Today Lincoln also met with Duff Green.][139]

December 29, 1860

Springfield, 29 December, 1860
[New York *Herald*, 3 January 1861]

The withdrawal of the Gulf States being now looked upon in the light of a certainty, rather than a mere probability, in Presidential spheres, the position of the border slave States in relation to the secession movement is watched with daily increasing interest. Missouri especially is regarded with peculiar anxiety, from her being our nearest slaveholding neighbor; for, although it is well known that her geographical situation renders the preservation of the Union the *conditio sine qua non* of the continuation of slavery within her limits, it is nevertheless evident, on the other hand, that there is a powerful and organized party of sympathizers with the Southern disunion flurry conspiring to draw her into the vortex of secession. There can be no doubt that the thirty thousand votes cast for [John C.] Breckinridge [in Missouri] on the 6th of November represent as many disunionists. It is furthermore certain that even a large number of the supporters of [John] Bell and [Edward] Everett are ready to countenance measures aiming at a severance of the ties connecting this State with the Union. Hence the developements likely to be made in reference to the disunion issue during the session of the Missouri Legislature that will convene on Monday next are awaited with the greatest concern by the friends of the Union, both in and without the State. That "secession" will be the all absorbing subject of the deliberations of that body is universally believed, and that deep apprehensions prevail as to this result is likewise true. This uneasiness is largely augmented by the impossibility to define with anything like accurateness the political complexion of the several members of the Legislature. To this fact the strange all but uninterrupted editorial silence the [St. Louis] *Missouri Republican* has cultivated since the outbreak of the secession fever in the South in regard to its probable bearings upon the State, the leading democratic paper of which it claims to be. Although individuals of large experience in politics and intimate acquaintance with men and matters within their own State are at its helm, they find themselves apparently puzzled whither to steer by a want of knowledge as to where the wind is likely to blow.

Alarmists seem to fear the enactment of special laws by the pro-slavery majority of the Legislature with a view to the arrogance [arrogation], if not oppression, of the strong free soil element in the city and county of St. Louis. Some talk of the impending legislative attempts to denounce and suppress the anti-slavery press of St. Louis as public nuisances, and to expel free soil leaders from the State. If any such measures should be entertained in the Legislature, lively times may be expected in St Louis. Such men as Frank P. Blair will be found tough customers to deal with. He and his thousands of backers will contest, if necessary, with swords and bullets, every inch of the ground they rightfully occupy.

Some days ago I took occasion to dwell upon the unanimity and determination of the anti-secession sentiment of the Northwest. Since then the voices in the public prints, and among the people of this section of the country, proclaiming utter hostility to the proposed dissolution of the Union, scorning the idea of peaceful secession, have become still more frequent. It is undeniable, indeed, that the sentiment of the overwhelming majority of both the republican and democratic masses of the Northwestern States runs in favor of maintaining the constitution and the laws throughout the country at all hazards. In evidence of this, it is but necessary to point to the fact that the propriety of an overhauling of the militia system of the several States by their respective Legislatures, about to meet, is advocated in Illinois, Indiana and other portions of the West, and that legislation in connection with this subject is all but certain in at least the two first mentioned States. The maxim of "in times of peace prepare for war" will doubtless be acted upon.

The republican newspapers and politicians of Indiana are already waxing clamorous over the distribution of the federal spoils—thereby living up to the hereditary and proverbial reputation of the Hoosiers for general want of knowledge as to what is proper. They should know that the President elect has, as yet, something more important to think of than subordinate appointments in their State, and stop their "nominations" and "recommendations" until after the 4th of March. Among the most noisy aspirants seems to be S. P. Oyler,[140] of Johnson county, who figured somewhat prominently in the Indiana delegation to Chicago, and is well known as an expert wirepuller. He has put himself up for United States Attorney. I hope "Old Abe" will give him the slip in consideration of his forwardness.

One Nat Usher[141] appears to be urged by a number of country editors, whose pulls are probably paid for at the rate of five dollars a piece, for the United States Marshalship. Such cheap endorsements won't effect much with Abraham.

Caleb B. Smith[142] is still thrust upon the President elect, in connection with a seat in the Cabinet, by Indiana influences. I should be woefully disappointed if he could be induced to select a man for so responsible a position whose only real qualification is a stentorian voice.

It is rumored that Hon. Edward Bates, of Missouri, is about repeating his visit to Mr. Lincoln for further consultation.

December 30, 1860

Springfield, 30 December 1860
[New York *Herald*, 7 January 1861]

As predicted in my last, a second visit of Hon. Edward Bates, of Missouri, to the President elect is now being paid. Mr. Bates arrived last evening, on [the] half-past nine o'clock train from St. Louis, for the purpose of spending the Sabbath with his Presidential friend. Last night and early this morning various rumors were in circulation as to the object of his repeated appearance. Some claimed to know that he came to make known the result of a fortnight's reflections as to the position he was to select in the Cabinet—the choice between the Secretaryship of the Interior and that of State being left to him. Others asserted, with the best show of probability, that he had an appointment, made during his first visit, to meet certain Eastern politicians. And so it turned out. The noon train from the East landed among us no less a personage than the greatest of Pennsylvania wirepullers—the renowned Gen. Simon Cameron, accompanied by Mr. Sanderson, of Harrisburg, one of his most faithful henchmen.

The unexpected arrival of the General was somewhat of a stunner, not only to your correspondent, but to the majority of the political schemers and intriguants of Springfield. "Proviso Dave" [Wilmot] had been here but a few days ago. He was supposed—nay, seriously believed on the very best authority—to have been offered a place among Mr. Lincoln's constitutional advisers. The universal impression was that he had promptly and gladly accepted the flattering tender. What, then, did Cameron's sudden apparition mean? Was the Keystone State to be rewarded for the republican laurels it had won so gloriously by a double representation in the Cabinet? An altogether improbable inference. Had Wilmot, after all, been only summoned hither for consultation? A hardly more tenable supposition. Had he declined the propositions of the President elect and recommended the appointment of the Pennsylvania Senator in his stead? A possible, but not very probable contingency. There was, indeed, a puzzle that bid fair to allow of a solution with the aid of future events only. An apparent bit of diplomacy of which unsophisticated "Old Abe" was not thought capable. A seeming antagonism of facts difficult to explain.

Mr. Cameron having been in town only a few hours at the time of this writing, your correspondent does not feel warranted to state anything beyond the palpable facts connected with his visit and the multifarious conjectures indulged in by gossipers as to the import of his advent in this latitude. He is, however, confident that he will be able to furnish "full and reliable particulars" in his next.

Shortly after the General's arrival he repaired to the private dwelling of the President elect, in company with Mr. Bates, who had evidently looked for him all morning. Mr. Lincoln, who was kept duly apprised of the progress of his Eastern visiter's journey by telegraph, and immediately notified of his presence in town, was awaiting their call, and received them with his customary artless Western heartiness. The trio forthwith entered a retired apartment, where they are said to be still engaged in close consultation at the present moment.

In reference to the subject of their deliberations, surmise, of course, is all that has as yet transpired. It is stated, on the one hand, that Cameron came to reiterate in person his reasons for declining to serve in the Cabinet, to a place in which he is believed to have been invited more by mere courtesy and formality than otherwise, and with a full knowledge of his unwillingness to fill it. *Per contra*, it is claimed that Wilmot actually backed out to make room for Cameron, and that the authorized disclaimers, heretofore periodically disseminated through the agency of the latter in regard to imputed aspirations to a *portefeuille*, were mere shams, put forth while secretly intriguing to get rivals out of the way, and intended to impress the powers that are to be more strongly in his favor, though on his assumed disinterestedness and reticence. Again, it is asserted that his object is to learn the views of the President elect as to the propriety of getting Pennsylvania ready for the now seemingly inevitable bloody conflict between Northern maintenance and Southern defiance through special enactments during the coming session of the State Legislature.

These rumors are all given for what they may be considered worth. But although your correspondent is as yet without positive information on the subject, he ventures to express the unshaken conviction that Mr. Cameron will not occupy a seat in the Cabinet. He may be mistaken in this. But if so, the error will be excusable, as it is based on the well known rigid adherence to honesty of both purpose and means of the President elect, and the presumption that he, as a well informed politician, cannot be ignorant of the character of the agents employed by Cameron in promoting his political fortunes.

The developements of the next twenty-four hours will doubtless dispel the fog now surrounding the premises.

It is reported that both Mr. Cameron and Mr. Bates will return to their respective homes in the course of to-morrow.

Springfield, 30 December 1860
[New York *Herald*, 7 January 1861]

As predicted in my last, a second visit of Hon. Edward Bates of Missouri has now been paid. Mr. Bates arrived last evening from St. Louis for the purpose of spending the Sabbath with his presidential friend. Last night and this morning various rumors were in circulation as to the object of his repeated appearance. Some claim to know that he came to make known the result of a fortnight's reflections as to the position he was to occupy in the cabinet—the choice between the secretaryship of the Interior and that of State being left to him. Others asserted with the best show of probability that he had an appointment made during his first visit to meet certain Eastern politicians. And so it turned out.

December 31, 1860

Springfield, 31 December 1860

[Cincinnati *Commercial*, 1 January 1861]

Senator Cameron and Mr. Sanderson,[143] of Pennsylvania, arrived here on Sunday, on a visit to Mr. Lincoln.

The President elect has abandoned his public reception room at the State House, and receives few friends at his own house.[144]

Hon. Edward Bates has been here all day.

Senator Cameron left at noon.

Springfield, 31 December 1860

[New York *Herald*, 1 January 1861]

Simon Cameron, of Pennsylvania, arrived here yesterday, and J. P. Sanderson with him. Mr. Lincoln's headquarters have been changed. There are to be no more receptions.

CHAPTER THREE

JANUARY 1861

January 1, 1861

Springfield, 1 January 1861

[New York *Herald*, 7 January 1861]

The fog in which the object of Senator Cameron's visit was wrapped has cleared away to a certain extent since my last. It is now certain that his journey hither was prompted by the consideration of his claims to a position in the Cabinet. But although it is positively known that he came here for the purpose of settling his account with the President elect, the precise manner in which this was done has not yet transpired. Mr. Lincoln's friends themselves do not seem to agree as to the result of the negotiations between the distinguished Pennsylvanian and the dispensing powers. Quite a number cling to the opinion that a tender of a seat was made to Cameron as a matter of mere formality, a non-acceptance having been intimated in advance, and that the trip out here was undertaken by him with a view to a personal explanation of the reasons of his declination, and to present the claims of his followers. They also express the belief that Mr. Wilmot's acceptance of a place in the Cabinet was conditioned on the previous refusal of Cameron to serve, and that this being now officially announced, the former's appointment was the more certain. A majority of those that move about the State House is, however, evidently impressed with the idea, on the other hand, that Mr. Cameron did not come here to decline, but to accept, and that his selection for the Secretaryship of the Treasury may be considered a foregone conclusion. They assert that Wilmot had waived an appointment in favor of Cameron; that the rather positive declarations heretofore made as to the latter's unwillingness to figure in the Cabinet were unauthorized, and that he was not only willing but anxious to be elevated to a like position. They further appear to think that the knowledge of this desire, and its all but unanimous endorsement by the republican leaders of the Keystone State [Pennsylvania], made its fulfillment all but imperative on the part of the President elect, in view of the decisive influence of the supporters of Cameron, exercised in the Chicago Convention.

Now it may be that the key to Uncle Sam's empty cash box has been actually offered to Mr. Cameron. It may be that the loud and violent opposition made to his appointment has been quieted down by the promise to some leading rival of the United States Senatorship to be vacated by him. But your correspondent, although appearances are now against him, still adheres to the belief embodied in yesterday's letter. He still remains persuaded that Cameron's visit was made for the purpose of consultation on the condition of the country, and securing the share of the federal spoils demanded by his friends, and not of receiving the offer or accepting the post at the head of the Treasury Department; and this not from a presumption of an infallibility of opinion, but from a firm conviction that Mr. Lincoln is determined to construct a pre-eminently pure Cabinet—to select his constitutional advisers from among public men free from all taint of corruption, and to scorn the thought of surrounding himself with characters whose political success has been achieved, not by uncommon talents, comprehensive acquirements and unswerving honesty of purpose and means, but mainly by the prestige and judicious use of wealth.

Again, the writer is inclined to think that the antecedents of Mr. Lincoln furnish little ground for the supposition, that in the choosing of the material for the more important offices within his gift, he will act in strict conformity with those party rules and usages according to which services to the cause, and not capacity, constitute the principal qualifications for office. Nor does the plea of peculiar obligations on the part of the President elect to Mr. Cameron appear to be tenable; for it is well known that shortly after the adjournment of the Chicago Convention Mr. Cameron made a speech in Harrisburg, in which he openly avowed that Mr. Seward had been his first choice for the republican nomination.

Whatever the truth in the premises may be, it is certain beyond all gainsay that Mr. Cameron's selection would produce some "tall" growling among Western republicans. Already now I can hear some undertone grumbling and strong hints at expectations of something better, called forth by the credence placed by many in the report of this definite assignment of a place in the Cabinet to the Pennsylvania Senator. He is obviously looked upon in no better light than Thurlow Weed, and there can be no doubt that Wilmot would have given the best satisfaction.

The story telegraphed from Harrisburg to the press, and announcing an impending awful catastrophe between Senator Cameron and some other Pennsylvania politicians, excited a good deal of merriment out here. The imputation of Mr. Lincoln's telegraphing for Mr. McClure,[1] announced as "bitterly opposed to Cameron's appointment," to explain the visit of the latter, is especially refreshing.[2] The reliability of the information conveyed in the despatch may be inferred from the fact that Mr. Cameron had re-embarked for the East long before the hoax was sent out from Harrisburg.

Mr. Bates returned to St. Louis on last evening's train. All day yesterday his name was generally connected with the Secretaryship of State, to which position he is said to have been transferred, in consideration of the increasing intricacy of public affairs.

Springfield, 1 January 1861
[Cincinnati *Commercial*, 3 January 1861]

Is not Abraham of late keeping rather bad company? Thurlow Weed has hardly shaken the Springfield mud off his boots, when up looms his Pennsylvania counterpart—the more notorious than noteworthy Gen. Simon Cameron. What does it mean, this rushing from the Albany Scylla into the Harrisburg Charybdis? Have the two all-powerful political managers caught unsophisticated "Old Abe" in their wires? Have they succeeded in getting him under their thumbs, and squeezing appointments out of him at their will? Surely not, unless your correspondent be altogether mistaken in his appreciation of the character of the President elect. Yet he must confess that things out here have assumed a rather puzzling shape. Although Sphynx-like mysteriousness and diplomatic reticence and tortuousness are elements foreign to Abraham's intellectual composition, it is yet obvious that certain cabalistic complications are now exercising the Presidential circles.

The cause of their tribulations seems to be the selection of the representative of the Republican Banner State [Pennsylvania] in the Cabinet. Wilmot appears to be the first choice of the President elect and his more intimate friends. That his recent visit was made in compliance with a special invitation by the former, and for the purpose of receiving a formal tender of a position of the Cabinet, is also certain. But it is now stated, on good authority, that he (Wilmot) conditioned his acceptance on the refusal of Cameron to serve, and gave the disinterested advice of first probing his imputed disposition to decline to the very bottom, before determining upon some one else. This advice was doubtlessly based on some reliable private information as to Cameron's real desires, and the knowledge of his vindictiveness in case of disappointment. At all events, it is certain that immediately after the departure of Mr. Wilmot, an invitation to visit Springfield at the earliest possible moment, was despatched to Mr. Cameron, agreeably to which he made his advent on Sunday evening last.

That he spent most of the time, during which he remained here, (from the evening before last until yesterday noon,) in company with the President elect, is, of course, but natural. That their interviews were protracted and devoted exclusively to the earnest discussion of public matters is likewise known. But as to the results of their deliberations nothing positive has yet transpired. Mr. Lincoln's friends, however, show little reserve in their expressions of opinion on the subject. Some contend that Cameron, from the very beginning, intimated his unwillingness to exchange his Senatorial *toga* with a portfolio and occupied himself principally with the advocacy of the substantial recognition of the services to the cause of his most faithful friends, the discussion of current events, the suggested propriety of providing by special enactment of the Pennsylvania Legislature for the emergency of an enforcement of the federal laws in the South *vi et armis*.[3] Others—and, it must be acknowledged, they seem to be in the majority—assert with a good deal of assurance, that Mr. Cameron came here expressly and solely for the purpose of receiving the tender of and accepting the Secretaryship of the Treasury, and that he and no one else will echo the voice of Pennsylvania in Mr. Lincoln's ministerial council.

Now, your correspondent does not presume to deny flatly and absolutely the possibility of Mr. Cameron's appointment to the post referred to. He has not authoritative information to the contrary. But he will, nevertheless, record his firm conviction that the Pennsylvania Senator will not figure in the Cabinet, and that Wilmot will after all be the man. This assertion may be found rather bold, in view of the confessed lack of positive knowledge on the subject. Yet it is founded on his well-known honesty of both purpose and means, abhorrence of political trickery, and detestation of the employment of corrupting influences for the promotion of personal ends; and hence, not quite so illogical as it may first appear. Mr. Lincoln is anxious to combine [nothing] but *pure* elements into his Cabinet. He knows, on the other hand, the character of the levers used by Cameron to lift himself into political prominence. Why, then, should the writer's conclusions prove fallacious?

Whatever may be the ultimate solution of the question as to whether Mr. Wilmot or Mr. Cameron will represent Pennsylvania in the Cabinet, it is true beyond all contradiction, that *the former would be much preferred to the latter by Western Republicans, and that the appointment of Proviso Dave [Wilmot] would be hailed with delight while that of the wealthy political parvenu [Cameron], that has been in the habit of buying Conventions and Legislatures, would be considered a rather bad omen as to the success of the Republican Administration.*

The ridiculous *canard* started from Harrisburg in a dispatch to the Associated Press, published in this morning's papers[4] and [several illegible words][5] other Pennsylvania politicians opposed to his appointment to the Cabinet, may be pronounced exploded, in view of the fact that the former had started upon his return trip East before the telegraphic yarn reached this point.

The idea of an array of hostile elements about the President elect by his citation [invitation], is highly creditable to the ingenuity of the perpetrator of the hoax.

Those that place credence in Cameron's appointment, derive a very plausible argument from the fact that Mr. Bates met Mr. Cameron here according to a previous arrangement. The distinguished Missourian attended all the interviews between the latter and the President elect. He returned to St. Louis yesterday morning.

January 4, 1861

Springfield, 4 January 1861
[New York *Herald*, 5 January 1861]

The fog which has shrouded the movements of the President elect, in connection with the Cabinet, for the last few days, is now clearing away, and matters are becoming more distinctly understood. Modifications were necessitated by Southern events, and the case now stands as follows:

Alexander K. McClure, of Harrisburg came here greatly excited to protest against Cameron's appointment. His wounds were plastered over with promises, and he returned home apparently satisfied.

Cameron's appointment to the Secretaryship of the Treasury is now a fixed fact. He was urged by nearly all the republican leaders of his State, who desire to step into his shoes in the Senate. Wilmot waived his claims in his favor, and will be supported by his friends for the Senate. Bates will be Attorney General, as previously announced. Mr. Lincoln announced this himself.

Caleb B. Smith, of Indiana, is strongly urged for Secretary of the Interior by Pennsylvania and Indiana influences, and will doubtless be appointed.

Amos Tuck, of New Hampshire, is here.[6] Either he or Mr. [Nathaniel P.] Banks[7] will be Secretary of the Navy.

Governor Chase, of Ohio, arrived here to-night. He comes by invitation of the President and will probably be tendered the Secretaryship of State.

Mr[s]. Lincoln will go to New York next week to make purchases for the White House. Lincoln will start for Washington about the middle of February, and will probably go by way of Pittsburgh and Harrisburg.

Springfield, 4 January 1861
[Cincinnati *Commercial*, 5 January 1861]

Cameron's appointment as Secretary of the Treasury is certain. It was solicited by nearly all the leading Republicans of Pennsylvania, Wilmot included. The latter declared in his favor, and will take his place in the Senate.

Alexander K. McClure, of Harrisburg, came here in great excitement, to protest against Cameron's appointment. His feelings were soothed by assurances of the President elect, and he returned home apparently satisfied.

During Bates' last visit he determined on accepting the Attorney-General-ship. He stated this himself in public. Caleb B. Smith, of Ind., will certainly be Secretary of the Interior. Amos Tuck, of New Hampshire, is here to-day. Either he or N. P. Banks will be Secretary of the Navy. Should [John C.] Fremont be found willing to serve, he will be Secretary of War.

Mrs. Lincoln will go to New York next week, to buy outfit[s] for [the] White House.[8]

Mr. Lincoln is expected to start for Washington about the middle of February. The route is yet unfixed. The Pittsburgh, Ft. Wayne and Chicago Road have tendered a special train.

The news of an impending attack on Fort Sumter produced great excitement.

Mr. Lincoln keeps himself very retired now.

Ex-Gov. Chase, of Ohio, arrived here to-night, by invitation of the President elect.

January 6, 1861

Springfield, 6 January 1861

[New York *Herald*, 10 January 1861]

The object of Gov. Chase's visit is no longer a mystery. I have it from the most direct and reliable source, that he was summoned hither by the President elect for the mere purpose of consultation on national politics, and the policy to be recommended to the North Western States, as represented by the republican majorities in their several Legislatures. It is true the Governor's relations to Mr. Lincoln have been of the most intimate character during his present stay in Springfield. The attention[s] shown to him by the President elect were of the most marked character. But a tender of a seat in the Cabinet was, nevertheless, not included in the kind things extended to him. As to the result of his deliberations with the President elect it is stated that *it was agreed to urge upon the legislative bodies of Ohio, Indiana, Illinois, Michigan, Wisconsin, Minnesota and Iowa, to take common ground in the shape of the passage of strong and explicit Union resolutions; and, should the course of events in the South require it, prepare for the necessity of maintaining the republican administration and the federal laws vi et armis, by getting their militia system into working order.* As to national politics, a perfect coincidence of opinion was arrived at. Compromise propositions are looked upon unfavorably, not from any feelings of hostility towards the South, but from the conviction that the cotton States are determined to go out of the Union, no matter what peace offerings in the form of Northern concessions may be offered to them.

The certainty that Ohio was not to be represented in the Cabinet, in the person of Mr. Chase, as Secretary of State, has again placed Seward at the head of the names connected with that position by the friends of Mr. Lincoln. A number of these have insisted, from the very beginning of speculations as to the composition of the Cabinet, that he was to be the man. Chase's sudden arrival shook their confidence a little, but at this moment it is not only fully restored, but imparted to many others that heretofore doubted the probability of his appointment to the position in question, in view of the threatening attitude of the Southern States. I feel warranted, indeed, in stating most positively, on the same unquestionable authority that disclosed the import of Governor Chase's visit, that influential post under the federal administration has been actually tendered to him. But nothing definite has as yet transpired as to his own predilections in the premises. It is only known here that a final reply to the flattering proposition of the President elect has not been made by him up to this time. The general impression appears to be that his acceptance will be made to depend on the developement of the secession movement. It is believed that in case the cotton States should all follow in the wake of South Carolina in the course of the next four weeks, so as to preclude the possibility of an amicable adjustment, he will yield to the solicitations of his friends and accept the offered *porte feuille* [portfolio]; but that, on the other hand, the manifestation of a more conciliatory disposition on the part of the restive States will induce him to decline, in order not to obstruct the attempts at pacification likely to be made by the incoming administration.

It is now evident that the Greeley faction is altogether off the track here. Thurlow Weed seems to have played his game so well during his late visit to Springfield, that he managed to produce impressions unfavorable to the claims of his antagonists within the ranks of his own party. It seems that little was really wanted to recall the Douglas preferences of the *Tribune* in 1858 to the memory of the President elect. That *faux pas* has not been and never will be forgotten. Open hostility, as in the instance of Seward's supporters in the Chicago Convention, appears to be overlooked, while the desertion of supposed friends in the very hour of need is still vividly remembered.

The President elect does not approve of the advocacy, by certain republican Congressmen, of the scheme of admitting New Mexico as a State, with its territorial slave code unimpaired.[9] His faith in the Chicago dogma of the right of Congressional prohibition of slavery in the Territories is as firm as ever.

Any amount of button holing and wire pulling is now going on in the hotel parlors and State House offices, among the members of the Legislature and a countless swarm of lobbyists. The hard times have brought here an immense number of aspirants to the few offices within the gift of the Legislature. The scramble is, of course, confined to the republican majority. The democrats are said to be brewing filibusterism, to prevent any legislation likely to injure the prospect of recovering their lost political fortunes in this State.

Among the recent hotel arrivals are:

G[eorge] A. Dunlap, J. D. Moxley, B. C. Webster,[10] Charles H. Weller, E. V. McMaken, J. Henry Bulger, all of New York city; L. W. Sharpe, of Philadelphia, and Benjamin Ward Dix, of Boston.[11]

[This day Lincoln met with Gustav Koerner and Norman B. Judd to discuss cabinet matters.][12]

Springfield, 6 January 1861

[New York *Herald*, 8 January 1861]

I am able to state on the most direct authority that Governor Salmon P. Chase has not been tendered a seat in Mr. Lincoln's Cabinet, and that Mr. Seward will certainly be Secretary of State, should he desire the position. The Greeley faction is evidently off the track.

Mr. Lincoln disapproves of the proposition to admit New Mexico with her Territorial slave code unchanged.

Springfield, 6 January 1861

[Cincinnati *Commercial*, 10 January 1861]

The ingenuity of our political newsmongers was fearfully taxed during the last six days. Their inquisitiveness and gar[r]ulity fairly ran riot. The visits of Senator Cameron, Ex-Governor Chase and Amos Tuck, of New Hampshire, in the short space of one week, were almost too much for them. It was wonderful to behold the range of their Baconian inductions, the caustic plausibility of their reasoning—the Machievel[l]ian logic of their conclusions. Their brains were racked night and day; their tongues moved with restless glibness. The atmosphere of hotel parlors and bar rooms was pregnant with rumors, conjectures, inferences, probabilities and possibilities, and all felt obviously relieved when the last of the distinguished trio had taken his departure.

But great as the commotion and confusion has been all week owing to the nebulousness of the doings in "high quarters," light gradually superceded the fog and the import of the journey hither of the three political eminences became well understood. The object of the visit of Senator Cameron and Amos Tuck I have already pretty fully indicated in my last. As to that of Mr. Chase, I am able to speak with still more positiveness. That his name was connected by gossipers with the Secretaryship of State, was but natural. But although I should feel truly gratified to record his selection for the position in question, as a well authenticated fact—a feeling which is doubtless shared by the bulk of Western Republicans—as a faithful chronicler I am yet compelled to state that my information to the contrary is unequivocal and authoritative. The Ex-Governor did not come here to receive a tender of a seat in Mr. Lincoln's Cabinet. He was invited hither for the sole purpose of consultation as to the attitude best assumed by the Republican party and the incoming Administration in reference to the impending disrupture of the Union. The conviction appears to be settled in Presidential spheres, that the question is now no longer how "to forestall attempts at," but "how to meet the accomplished fact of disunion?" The days of concessions and compromises are believed to be passed, and those of action to come, and hence, a desire is felt to counsel with the foremost of sympathizing minds as to the most efficient mode of confronting the issue of aggression, treason and rebellion. The question of recommending to the several Legislatures of the Northwestern States now assembled, the propriety of re-organizing the militia systems so as to be prepared for any emergency, was discussed. I learn, however, that less warlike demonstrations, namely, the passage of a uniform set of strong anti-disunion resolutions, were thought more advisable for the present.

Some of Gov. Chase's expectant friends probably suppose that during his stay he took occasion to bring their claims before the President elect. But, judging from the manifest disinclination of the latter to listen to any propositions in relation to inferior appointments previous to the 4th of March, it is hardly possible that their wishes have been realized.

Mr. Chase was the object of marked attention on the part of Mr. Lincoln. The latter spent most of his time in company with his visitor and improved every opportunity to manifest the high regard he entertained for, and the implicit confidence he placed in, the counsels of the distinguished Ohio Statesman.

I feel authorized to state, that it now lies altogether with Mr. Seward whether he is to occupy a place in Mr. Lincoln's cabinet or not. There can be no doubt that he can have the Secretaryship of State if he wants it.

Appearances now indicate the out-generaling of [Horace] Greeley, [David Dudley] Field[13] & Co., by the [Thurlow] Weed faction, in this latitude. It is understood that there is considerable dissatisfaction felt in the camp of the former, at the apparent composition of the Cabinet. But Douglas seems to be the hostile phantom that prevents any close approach of the "Tribune people" to the "powers that are to be." Greeley has many and bitter enemies among the immediate surroundings of the President elect, that think the time has come for repaying him for his anti-Lincolnism in '58.[14]

The log-rolling and wire-pulling, usually preceding the meetings of legislative bodies in this country, is now going on in our hotels. The number of lobbyists is legion. The session, which is to commence at 12 M., to-morrow, will be a very interesting one. There is a rumor to-day that the Democratic minority propose to make a bolt, whenever political legislation will be attempted by the Republican majority.

January 7, 1861

Springfield, 7 January 1861
[Cincinnati *Commercial*, 9 January 1861]

I am able to say to-night, on positive authority, that Mr. Cameron has not been tendered the appointment to the Secretaryship of the Treasury. He came here on his own invitation, not at Mr. Lincoln's suggestion, and went away disappointed. The report of his appointment was the result of intimations dropped by him here and elsewhere, and for a while was generally believed even here, and by Mr. Lincoln's friends. No small indignation is felt in certain quarters that he has permitted the reports to go uncontradicted . . . and the letters which came here from Washington describing his self-satisfaction when congratulated on his elevation . . . do not allay the irritation.

This is the exact truth in the matter, and may be implicitly replied on by your readers. Most emphatic protests against Cameron's appointment have been received here from prominent Republican Congressmen, which show that the matter is altogether misunderstood.

Leading republicans from all parts of the State are putting influences to work to secure Mr. Chase's acceptance of the place which Cameron did not get. They are writing and telegraphing all over the Union to-night. They say that he is the man to stop the leaks and introduce economy into the Government, and that they must have him.

[Freeport attorney John Anderson Clark (1814–81) and Charles Henry Ray of the Chicago *Tribune* called this day on Lincoln. On July 26, 1861, Clark was appointed surveyor general of the New Mexico territory.]

Springfield, 7 January 1861
[New York *Herald*, 12 January 1861]

Let Thurlow Weed look to his laurels. He has found his equal, if not superior. A cabal just disclosed, in reference to the reported appointment of Senator Cameron to a place in Mr. Lincoln's Cabinet, shows the great Pennsylvania politician to excel no less in political cunning than the great Albany lobbyist. A bolder scheme was never conceived nor more adroitly executed. Its history should find a conspicuous place in the political records of the country. It furnishes a counterpart to the best strokes of diplomacy of a Talleyrand, and its ultimate explosion is a matter of wonder rather than of natural consequence.

Will it be believed, after being fed for days, nay, weeks, with rumors, reports, and even apparently positive announcements, all bearing upon the alleged tender of the Secretaryship of the Treasury to General Cameron, the public will now be asked to rid itself of its already settled conviction as to the certainty of that appointment? And yet the developements of this day render it absolutely certain that *there was not the least foundation to the thousand and one stories afloat during the last fortnight in relation to the same subject; that a direct offer was not made nor thought of at any time by the President elect; that he did not even extend an invitation to come here to Cameron, but that he came on his own motion, and that, although Mr. Lincoln was ever inclined to take the propriety of his appointment into consideration, owing to the circumstances hereafter related, he has now definitely and permanently dismissed all propositions to that effect.*

As this is the substance and result of this grand office hunting conspiracy, the subjoined details of it, learned by me from the very highest sources, are of a strikingly interesting and instructive character. They prove at once the utter recklessness of the Cameron faction, and the certainty that their *regime* will have to go unrecognized under the incoming administration. They will doubtless startle the Pennsylvanians out of their habitual sedateness—open their eyes as to the plot that has been brewing undiscovered in their midst—and they may thank the Lord that the danger of a monopoly of the federal spoils by the followers of Cameron's political fortunes is removed.

It appears that Cameron's first move in pursuit of his Cabinet aspirations was to strew sand in the eyes of the republican public by causing an authorized declaration to be made some five weeks since, through the Washington correspondence of the New York *Tribune.* Having thus surrounded himself with the halo of disinterestedness, he set his friends to work secretly circulating petitions for and recommendations of his appointment. Dozens of them arrived here daily for a long while, during the last month. His antagonists being thrown off their guard by his intimated and apparent intentions to decline, did not suspect his propaganda, and hence took no measures to counteract its effect. The seeming unanimity of the republican sentiment of Pennsylvania, as reflected in the numerous written appeals in favor of his appointment, first produced an impression on the President elect, and he was inclined, as already stated, to take its propriety into consideration. But in the meantime Cameron grew impatient. He expected an immediate response to the pleas of his friends, in the shape of an invitation to repair hither. This not being forthcoming as early as he wished it, he waxed apprehensive of a discovery of his machinations by his opponents, and hence came out here uninvited to look in person after the interests of himself and friends. He probably supposed that his personal appearance would exact a tender of what he was after. But in this he was disappointed. As soon as his journey became known to his republican adversaries they fairly overwhelmed the President elect with despatches protesting against his appointment. Although the violence of their protests did not impress the latter favorably, common prudence induced him to delay any definite action in the premises, and hence Cameron had to return without the desired commission in his pocket. He was kindly received and treated with the utmost respect throughout his visit. But that was all.

How well Cameron played his game may be judged from the fact that even Mr. Lincoln's friends in this place, with very few exceptions, all believed in his rumored assignment to be the Secretary of the Treasury, and for the last six days it was generally looked upon as an accomplished fact, and those who discredited it were charged with allowing their feelings of disapprobation to prevail over their judgment. As to myself, it will be remembered that I insisted on the falsity of reported appointment until the "signs of the times" appeared to demonstrate it so plainly as to render further denial facti[ti]ous. Yet, although I reluctantly acknowledged what had seemingly become an undeniable fact, I yet could never shake off all doubts in regard to it, and that simply because of my previously acquired knowledge as to an intense detestation on the part of Mr. Lincoln of the school of politicians whose maxim is that the "end justifies the means," and whose prototypes are Weed and Cameron. The sequence has now shown that my original impressions were correct.

It will perhaps be asked what evidence I have to offer of the correctness of this last version of the Cameron affair. To satisfy the doubting in this respect, I will state that, although Mr. Lincoln did not first deny the reported elevation of the Pennsylvania Senator to a place among his constitutional advisers, in order not to increase the smarting of his already wounded feelings, the profound dissatisfaction this alleged selection caused among his best friends did not remain concealed to him, and finally elicited a semi-official disavowal during the last twenty-four hours. I state this positively and authoritatively, and the readers of the Herald may place implicit reliance in it.

Just after the contradictory hint was given out, emphatic protests arrived from Washington. They emanated from republican Congressmen, and were couched in the strongest possible terms, and directed to persons who would not fail to make the contents known in the proper quarter. These demonstrations, and the all but universal feeling of relief manifested by the numerous prominent Illinois politicians now in town, must convince the President elect that Cameron is an impossibility, and hence the old fox may be considered caught in his own traps, and fairly disposed of.

The greatest indignation is now felt here at the unaccountable neglect of Senator Cameron to put a stop to the unrestrained use by his friends of his own name and that of the President elect in connection with this matter. The wholesale deception he thus indirectly tolerated is not likely to redound to his credit.

Springfield, 7 January 1861
[Cincinnati *Commercial*, 9 January 1861]
It is to-day stated on good authority that Gov. Chase intimated a preference for retention of a seat in the Senate in response to an inquiring hint at a possible offer of a seat in the Cabinet. W. B. Ogden, receiver, and D[aniel] W. Boss, general agent of the Pittsburgh, Ft. Wayne and Chicago Railroad, are now here, presumptively in connection with the tender of a special train to the President elect. Pennsylvania influences are at work to induce his passage through that State. Apprehensions of Southern attempts to prevent Lincoln's inauguration by force are now felt. They are based on letters received here from responsible parties in Virginia, revealing plots to that effect. Organization of the Legislature was prevented to-day by intentional absentation of Democratic members—I presume they will come in to-morrow.

January 8, 1861

Springfield, 8 January 1861—1 A.M.
[New York *Herald*, 8 January 1861]
The general impression here now is, that the South will be represented in the Cabinet by two members at least, including Mr. Bates.

It is understood that Governor Chase intimated a preference for the retention of a seat in the Senate, in response to a hint at a probable offer of a place in the Cabinet.

The tender of a special train over the Pittsburg[h], Fort Wayne and Chicago Railroad has not been formally made. D. W. Boss, the general agent of the road, and W. B. Ogden, receiver, are now here, presumptively in connection with the matter. Pennsylvania influences are at work to induce Mr. Lincoln's passage through that State.

Apprehensions of attempts to prevent Mr. Lincoln's inauguration by force are felt. It is said that letters have been received here from responsible parties in Virginia revealing plots to that effect.

The organization of the Legislature was prevented to-day by the intentional absentation of the democratic members. The Governor will recommend the reorganization of militia in his message.

Springfield, 8 January 1861
[Cincinnati *Commercial*, 10 January 1861]

Among the most successful political cheats practiced upon the newspaper reading public of this country, will be hereafter cited the great Cameron Cabinet bubble of last week, pricked last night by my special dispatches to the [Cincinnati] "Commercial," and more elaborately so in the following. A more deliberate wholesale imposition was never attempted. With an absolute nothing as a basis, a fabric of seeming facts was reared by dint of deceptive ingenuity, regardless effrontery, presumed credulity, that kept the public for a whole week not only in a state of suspense, but persuaded [by] far the largest portion of it to look upon an utterly imaginary matter in the light of a reality and accomplished fact. How many of your readers, indeed, were inclined two days ago to question the appointment of Senator Cameron to the Secretaryship of the Treasury? Why, even here in close proximity to the fountain head of intelligence as to the composition of the Cabinet, it was considered a foregone conclusion on the part of the President elect, and openly proclaimed as such by parties whose relations to him were of an intimate character. But all this only goes to show that the deception at the bottom of this grand sell was a masterpiece of political cabal. *For I can now state positively and authoritatively, that Mr. Cameron has never received the tender of Secretaryship of the Treasury, nor of any other position in Mr. Lincoln's Cabinet; that his visit to Springfield was undertaken on his own initiative, and not that of the President elect; and that, although his appointment was once favorably thought of by the latter, in view of recent developments there is now no longer the slightest probability of his being found among Mr. Lincoln's constitutional advisers after the fourth of March next.*

Some of your readers will doubtless be slow to place credence in the above explicit statement owing to the all but equal positiveness with which previous assertions to the contrary were made. But they should remember that your correspondent's knowledge of Mr. Lincoln's proper appreciation of Cameron's political character, induced him from the very start to question the possibility of his appointment, and that even at the time of its reluctant acknowledgment, as an apparent fact, he did not altogether yield his doubts on the subject, and as to the foundation of the above contradiction, it will perhaps suffice to say that the supposed election of Mr. Cameron called forth disapprobationary feelings and demonstrations of so decisive a character, not only here but throughout the west, in Pennsylvania and Washington that a semi-official disavowal was almost necessitated. In the course of the last three days, the symptoms of dissatisfaction became so strong among the many western politicians now congregated here, and epistolary protests from Washington so frequent, that a certain uneasiness commenced being felt in "high quarters," in consequence of which a contradictory hint was given out. The immediate relief manifested by all those that wish the incoming Administration well, on learning its meaning, furnished a decisive evidence of Cameron's unpopularity and impracticability. The somewhat shaken confidence in the judiciousness of the President elect has been fully restored hereabouts by the denial, and a similar effect will probably be produced in your latitude.

Now, as to the history of this Cabinet swindle. According to well informed parties, it was prepared as follows: Five weeks ago, Cameron had the apparently authoritative report put in circulation, that he was unwilling to accept a seat in the Cabinet. After thus blinding those that knew not his insatiable ambition, his friends were required, in order to give him the appearance of a reluctant object of solicitation, to circulate numerous petitions and recommendations, urging the propriety of his nomination upon the President elect. They were passed around so slily that his antagonists remained ignorant of their existence. Being duly spread before Mr. Lincoln, their number and unanimity naturally produced a belief that the wily demagogue actually was the choice of the Keystone State for the Cabinet. But fortunately, the habitual prudence of the President elect, prevented him from acting immediately upon the matter. Cameron, having quietly waited several weeks for an invitation to come to Springfield, at last grew impatient, and undertook the journey of his own accord. At the same time he had rumors started that he went by request and to receive the offer of a place in the Cabinet, so as to prevent counteraction. But his opponents knew their man. As soon as it had leaked out that he was *en route* for this point, telegraphic remonstrances— brief, but pointed—were showered upon the President elect, so that Cameron found him, on his arrival, so far influenced as to render his journey fruitless.

Great indignation is felt here and known to be shared in Washington, at the reckless and compromising use Gen. Cameron allowed his friends to make of the President elect, in connection with his office-hunting conspiracy. The universal opinion is that the man has fully lived up to his reputation, and that the desperate card he undertook to play has shelved him forever.

The feeling here in favor of Mr. Chase's appointment to the position Mr. Cameron unsuccessfully aspired to, is very general and enthusiastic. His friends in Ohio and Washington have been written to from here, to persuade him into acceptance. But, although I believe that the Governor can have the post in question if he desires it, I think on the other hand he will adhere to his resolution to retain his seat in the Senate.

Springfield, 8 January 1861
[Cincinnati *Commercial*, 9 January 1861]

The exposition of the Cameron cabal, showing the false pretences of that gentleman, produces feelings of evident relief among many Western Republican leaders now assembled here.

An Iowa delegation is in town to-day, pressing Fitz Henry Warren for Postmaster General.

Both Houses of the Legislature perfected their organization to-day.

A committee of Chicago merchants is here to urge a change of the banking laws of this State. There will doubtless be some legislation on the subject.

January 9, 1861

Springfield, 9 January 1861
[Cincinnati *Commercial*, 10 January 1861]

Protests against Cameron's appointment continue to arrive from all parts of the country. Their emphatic language show[s] that it is looked upon as discrediting the incoming Administration in the eyes of the Republicans.

Caleb B. Smith's appointment is likewise received with evident disfavor.

The President elect, who has been lately greatly pestered by applicants for local offices, has given out that he will pay no attention to petitions and recommendations for subordinate offices until after his inauguration.

Senator Trumbull's re-election to-day, did not occasion any special demonstration. To-night the different Republican coteries have their several private sprees. Lincoln was present during the voting. S. S. Marshall was voted for by the Democrats.[15]

January 10, 1861

Springfield, 10 January 1861

[New York *Herald*, 15 January 1861]

I notice in the telegraphic despatches from Washington, as well as in the letters and correspondence from this place, that a great deal is being said about the selection of Mr. Cameron, of Pennsylvania, for the important office of Secretary of the Treasury in the Cabinet of Mr. Lincoln. There have been so many reports published and put into circulation, and so many contradictory statements made, that it has occurred to me that the truth would not be out of place; and as I think I am a little posted in the matter I will give you the facts.

Some time ago the Hon. David Wilmot, of Pennsylvania, came on a visit to Springfield on the invitation of the President elect, who desired to consult with him on the affairs of the nation in general, and on the prospects of the incoming administration in particular. In the course of that conversation Mr. Lincoln offered to Judge Wilmot a position in his Cabinet, either as Secretary of the Treasury or of the War Department, as he might choose. Judge Wilmot's reply was that he preferred going into the Senate rather than the Cabinet, as, in his opinion, he was better adapted to the former position than to the duties of a more administrative office. After some further conversation on this point, he suggested to Mr. Lincoln that Mr. Cameron was the fittest man to be selected from Pennsylvania for a seat in the Cabinet, both from his intrinsic ability and from the fact that he had contributed more efficient service than any other man in that State towards Mr. Lincoln's election. He also dwelt on the sagacity and intelligence of Mr. Cameron as qualities fitting him for such a position. Soon after Mr. Wilmot's return home, Mr. [Leonard] Swett, who appears to be the travelling confidential agent of Mr. Lincoln in the Cabinet business, arrived in Washington with an invitation to Mr. Cameron to visit Springfield. On being thus invited, Mr. Cameron immediately started for this Mecca of the republican party, and had a long, full and interesting conversation with the President elect, on which occasion Mr. Lincoln told as many as a dozen capital stories and cracked an infinity of first rate jokes, winding up with the same offer which he had previously made to Judge Wilmot. He also said to Mr. Cameron, "Don't leave to-day. Stay here over to-night and you will see Judge Bates, whom I expect by the next arrival from St. Louis, and as he is also to go into the Cabinet it would be as well for you to see each other." Mr. Cameron consented to stay, but at the same time suggested to Mr. Lincoln the propriety of giving him a formal invitation in writing to the seat in the Cabinet which he had verbally proposed. Mr. Lincoln said he would do so, and accordingly wrote an invitation to Mr. Cameron and handed it to that gentleman, who put it in his pocket, and I suppose it is there to the present moment, as I do not think that he is in the habit of losing important papers by hanging up his overcoat in too public a place. The interview with Judge Bates took place, according to appointment, after which Mr. Cameron went back to Washington.

In the course of time—a very short time, for the telegraph hurries up everything now-a-days—it came out that he had been offered a seat in the Cabinet, and not long after there was a terrible hullabaloo among all the politicians, great and small, and mostly of the latter class, in consequence of this appointment, because it had effectually spiked the guns of some, as Major Anderson did at Fort Moultrie,[16] and because it compelled others to make new deals for the federal spoils. The result was that all sorts of protests and letters were sent to Mr. Lincoln, emanating from one or two sources, whose business and prospects had thus been completely frustrated. Among those who felt most aggrieved by this selection were Governor Curtin, the new chief magistrate of Pennsylvania,[17] and Alex. McClure, of Philadelphia [Chambersburg], both old line whigs, and therefore opposed to Messrs. Cameron and Wilmot, who are old line democrats; for it may not be known to the public at large that, in addition to the "irrepressible conflict" between the North and the South, there is also an "impending crisis" in regard to the spoils, between the old line whigs and the old line democrats who help to make up the republican party.

So, in the course of a train or two after the return of Mr. Cameron to Washington, Alexander McClure turned up one fine morning at Springfield, but not till after the letters, and petitions, and protests against Cameron began to pour in. Then there was a long talk with the President elect, and then the whole matter was reconsidered. What Mr. Lincoln had said and done was turned over in his mind several times; and I understand from the best authority, such as has never yet deceived me, that he wrote to Mr. Cameron stating that he had found it necessary to reconsider his offer, and make out a new slate, and that he would like him to give up the appointment he had promised him. Out of this grew all the rumors and reports and noise that have crept into the columns of the immortal Herald, as well as into the mortal journals of Pennsylvania and elsewhere, and which have created such a hubbub among the spoils and place hunters of this present unhappy country. I am led to believe from the Post Office waybills that up to the moment I write these lines to you Mr. Cameron has made no reply. It is understood that he is a very cautious, discreet and careful man, and is probably turning the whole affair over in his mind. There is no doubt but that he reads the original letter of Mr. Lincoln daily after his morning devotions, and before he goes to the Senate chamber, because that letter and the Bible are the two great authorities which he consults, and to which, of all places, he looks for truth.

So much for the great hullabaloo about the incoming Cabinet, the Hon. Simon Cameron, Senator from Pennsylvania, and the President elect.

Springfield, 10 January 1861

[Cincinnati *Commercial*, 14 January 1861]

Yesterday afternoon the prize, that next to the electoral vote of the State, was the object of the greatest concern to Illinois Republicans during the late canvass, was finally carried off. Senator Trumbull was duly re-elected for the term of six years from March next, by the Republican majority in the Legislature. The vote of the first session stood 54 to 46, the Democrats bestowing the empty honor of their votes upon S. S. Marshall, the well known Congressman from this State, although the fruit of the strenuous political labors of many months was gathered on the occasion, no particular exultation was indulged in. An outburst of applause upon the announcement of the result of the voting by the Speaker of the House was all that occurred. Mr. Trumbull had wisely chosen to remain in Washington. Otherwise his legislative friends would have taken good care to run up a respectable wine and whisky bill for his special benefit. As it was those of their number that are in the habit of demonstrating joyous emotions by free indulgence in things spirituous, severally got elated in their own way, subject to the relative plethora of their respective purses.

The President elect witnessed the triumph of his former rival. He first came up into the gallery; wedged himself into the rather mixed crowd therein assembled, and entertained the by-standers with his usual humor. Some members discovered him, however, from below and brought him to the floor, where he was presented with a seat among the State officers.[18]

Just two years ago, your correspondent watched from the identical position he occupied yesterday afternoon, the proceedings resulting in the return of Stephen A. Douglas to the United States Senate. Little did he then dream of the wonderful changes, the political fortunes of the main actors in the election drama of that day, would undergo in the short period intervening between then and now. If any one would have ventured at that time the prediction that the gallant, but vanquished opponent of the "Little Giant" would rise to the highest place in the land, in spite of his then discomfiture, he would have been pronounced afflicted with a sickly exuberance of imagination. Even his most faithful friends looked upon his defeat as a fatal blow to his political aspirations. Yet—his past loss proved the means of his present gain. For who will question, that if he had then supplanted Douglas in the United States Senate, his name would never have appeared before the Chicago Convention?

The official announcement of Mr. Seward's acceptance of the Secretary-ship of State, sent a thrill of delight through the hearts of all that wish the incoming Administration well. We can see nothing but glad faces this morning among our Republicans. These glad tidings will call forth an echo of gratification not only throughout the free States, but all over Europe, where Mr. Seward's statesmanship has as many admirers as in his own country. This glorious piece of news coupled with the certainty of the utter failure of Cameron's intrigues has wonderfully increased "Old Abe's" popularity hereabouts. He is being fairly overwhelmed with the heartiest congratulations. Would that Governor Chase's friends, like those of the New York Senator, prevailed over him to forego his preferences for his present position [in the U.S. Senate], and join Mr. Seward in the Cabinet. With Seward, Chase and [Nathaniel P.] Banks among Mr. Lincoln's immediate advisers, those that elected him could safely trust in the pre-eminent success of his administration.

It is understood here that Mr. Seward was at first very firm in his determination not to accept the tendered post at the head of the foreign department, and that Weed, as stated by me at the time, intimated as much during his visit to the President elect, but that the latter appeared so solicitous about securing the counsels of his unsuccessful rival as to induce the former, together with other friends, to renew their efforts urging an acceptance until they at last prevailed.

Present appearances warrant the statement that the rumored appointment of Caleb B. Smith meets no more favor among most of Mr. Lincoln's friends in this region than that of Gen. Cameron. It is fervently hoped that the sensible portion of the Indiana Republicans will, before it is too late, counteract the attempts of the noisy clique that has been straining every nerve for weeks in the undertaking to saddle the aforesaid incompetency upon the Republican Administration. Smith and Seward are as far apart as night and day and the light of the latter should not be diminished by the former's obscurity. Your [i.e., the Cincinnati *Commercial*'s] frank leaders on the subject are an example that should be promptly imitated by those that do not desire to see worse than mediocrity fill the most responsible offices in the country.

It is now evident that the politicians of Pennsylvania and Indiana think their claims to office paramount to those of any other State. Their placeseeking pretensions evince a manifest anxiety to be looked upon as regular warwicks— President makers, to whose influence and support the powers that are to be, owe their existence. I trust that their vaulting ambition will not overleap the President elect.

It is a source of merriment out here, that the New York "Tribune" has also, of late, betaken itself to Cabinet-making. It is generally believed, that its apparently authoritative dicta are sent forth to cover up its actual destitution of knowledge on the subject, arising from the prevalence of Seward influences in this quarter.

Springfield, 10 January 1861
[Cincinnati Commercial, 11 January 1861]

To-morrow morning's [*Illinois State*] Journal will contain an authorized announcement of Mr. Seward's acceptance of the Secretaryship of State. Lincoln was apprised of it by this morning's mail. The tender was made through Weed. Republicans consider it glorious news. I reiterate my previous statement that Cameron received no appointment. The disclosure of his intrigues has rendered him an impossibility. Intelligence is received here that Chase withdraws his declination of the Secretaryship of the Treasury, and will make his ultimate decision known after consultation with his friends. The desire to see him in the Cabinet is daily growing stronger here. Mr. Julian, of Indiana, is here to urge Smith's claims.[19] A strong opposition is now at work to secure his substitution by N. B. Judd, of this State.

The news of the firing into the Star of the West,[20] threw the Legislature and citizens into feverish excitement. Lincoln is greatly exercised about it.

VILLARD.

Springfield, 10 January 1861
[New York Herald, 11 January 1861]

The [*Illinois State*] *Journal* of to-morrow will contain an authorized announcement of Mr. Seward's acceptance of the Secretaryship of State. Mr. Lincoln received it by this morning's mail. The offer was made through Mr. Weed. The republicans are in ecstacies.

My statement that Mr. Cameron received no appointment is correct to the letter.

Advices have reached here that Mr. Chase withdraws his definite declination of the Secretaryship of the Treasury, and that he will make his ultimate decision known after consultation with his friends.

Geo. W. Julian, of Indiana, is here to urge the claims of C. B. Smith. There is now a strong counter pressure for N. B. Judd.

Mr. Lincoln takes the news from Charleston very gravely. It is thought that the Rubicon is now crossed.

January 11, 1861

Springfield, 11 January 1861
[New York *Herald*, 17 January 1861]
The *Daily Illinois State Journal* of this morning contains the following official announcement of Mr. Seward's acceptance of the Secretaryship of State:

MR. LINCOLN'S CABINET.

The Albany *Evening Journal* having announced that Mr. Seward has accepted the position of Secretary of State under the President elect, it may not be out of place to state that official advices to that effect have been received by Mr. Lincoln. The portfolio of the State Department was tendered to Mr. Seward several weeks ago, and the selection cannot fail to receive a cordial response from all who love and are determined to stand by the Union. Mr. Seward's wisdom as a statesman of ability, as a diplomatist, will directly tend to strengthen confidence in the incoming administration at home and abroad. The *Journal* properly remarks, "that on no former occasion has a President offered, or a Secretary accepted, that department in a manner more delicate and respectful to each, or more independent and honorable to both," and it puts on record the prediction "that President and Premier will so discharge their duties amid all the difficulties that surround them as to preserve the blessings of Union, and to deserve and receive the homage of their countrymen." We have confidence that the sequel will verify the prophecy.

It is known that Mr. Lincoln received Mr. Seward's formal acceptance only by this morning's mail, and that the paragraph in Thurlow Weed's paper was inserted simultaneously with the mailing of the letter. Mr. Lincoln immediately acknowledged its receipt by special telegraphic despatch to Washington.

Candor compels me to state that the construction put upon Mr. Seward's appointment in a late editorial of the Herald is not endorsed by the friends of the President elect. They look upon it as an earnest of the firm adherence of the new *regime* to the dogmas of their party, as laid down in the Chicago platform, rather than as a symptom of readiness to compromise and renounce. The radical republicans of this section, at all events, augur from Mr. Seward's premiership the strict fidelity of the incoming administration to the principles to the triumph of which it owes its existence. It may be safely presumed, nevertheless, that Mr. Seward's profound statesmanship and catholicity of views will enable him to understand the exigencies of the times, and prevent any clashing act of the administration of which he will, doubtlessly, be the most prominent and influential member.

The last twenty-four hours have developed the probability that Mr. Chase may, after all, not accept the Treasury Department, offered to him by the President elect during his recent stay in this city. The ex-Governor himself would greatly prefer the Senatorial toga to a ministerial portfolio. But it seems that an acceptance is urged upon him by many of his most intimate and faithful friends, and that he is not unlikely to yield to their counsel. Advices to that effect reached here last night.

The partisans of N. B. Judd, of this State, who are now assembled around their leader at this point, are working with might and main to secure the place informally tendered to Caleb B. Smith, of Indiana, for him. The jealousy of rival republican chieftains from this State paralizes, however, their efforts to some extent. But it is very possible that their representations will prevail in the end.

Mr. Judd is an old and tried friend of the President elect, and Mr. Lincoln's personal preferences will not conflict with the wishes of the advocates of the former's cause. Nor is the country likely to suffer by the substitution of the shallow-brained Hoosier [Caleb B. Smith] for so able a man as Mr. Judd.

The news of the firing upon the Star of the West threw both Legislature and citizens generally into intense excitement. The tug of war is believed to be come—the Rubicon crossed—civil war inevitable. Legislative business was all but suspended. The "overt act of treason and rebellion" occupied the minds and mouths of all.

The President elect looks very gravely. He says little in reference to the startling events in South Carolina, but it is obvious that he is nevertheless most deeply concerned and exercised about their probable consequences.

The Legislature has thus far confined itself to the formation of committees and introduction of petitions and bills.

Springfield, 11 January 1861

[Cincinnati *Commercial*, 15 January 1861]

I have glad tidings for your readers. There is now a strong probability that Mr. Chase will be, after all, one of Mr. Lincoln's Constitutional advisers. Information reached here by the last eastern mail, that many of his Ohio friends recommend an acceptance of the portfolio tendered to him, in view of the desirability and necessity of surrounding the first Republican President with the strongest possible Cabinet, and that the ex-Governor shows a disposition to yield to their urgent solicitations. Should the telegraph substantiate this welcome news, all doubts as to the success of the Republican Administration will be at once removed. A structure supported by such pillars as Seward and Chase, cannot come short of commanding firmness. The Ohio statesman will certainly acquire a strong title to the lasting gratitude of the Republican party by sacrificing his personal preferences for the sake of the common weal.

Cameron's machinations still occupy the minds and mouths of our politicians. Racy developments are still being made in reference to his attempt to foist himself upon Mr. Lincoln as Secretary of the Treasury. It appears that, as stated in a former letter to the [Cincinnati] *Commercial*, Mr. Wilmot was the original choice of the President elect, as the representative of the Republican [Banner] State in the Cabinet; and that upon an indication of his hopes and wishes for the United States Senatorship, Mr. Cameron was mentioned as a possible substitute, and at once heartily endorsed by "Proviso Dave," who supposed himself pretty sure of success in case the places of both Bigler[21] and Cameron should have to be filled.—Upon his advice mainly, a letter, couched in very general terms, and making no definite promises or pledges, but merely holding out a vague prospect of a possible tender of a seat, was despatched to Cameron by Mr. Lincoln. This is the letter that is now known to have been extensively "shown around" by the discreet General, and that induced him to come here, although it did not contain an invitation to do so, upon which all his more or less positive hints and assertions were based.

The advices, that will have reached you by this time from Washington, have doubtlessly convinced your readers, that my denial of his ever having been definitely offered either the Secretaryship of the Treasury, or any other position, was well founded; although his personal appearance in Springfield made the omission of a tender during his stay, exceedingly embarrassing. Mr. Lincoln was all but forced to refrain from it by the energetic telegraphic remonstrances, that reached him from Pennsylvania, even before Cameron's arrival.

The report of the offer and acceptance of the Secretaryship of the Treasury, so busily and widely circulated by Cameron himself, and all his friends, was not contradicted by Mr. Lincoln, simply because he was unwilling to hurt the feelings of the Pennsylvania Senator, and furthermore, because he well knew that the impression it was likely to produce, would enable him to judge correctly of the estimate placed upon Cameron by the people of his own and other States. By this, Abraham caught the foxy Simon in his own trap, for, instead of general rejoicing, universal indignation reached his ears, and made it incumbent to banish all ideas of making him one of his ministers.

It cannot be concealed that the President [elect] finds it very difficult to find sound Southern timber for his Cabinet. While in the North the abundance of names pressed upon him is a source of perplexity, just the reverse troubles him in the South. A number of individuals, it is true, have been suggested to him. But those among them whose capacity and worthiness would make their selection desirable, are not only supposed to be unwilling to serve, but also known to have assumed, of late, a position of so decided hostility towards the party that elevated Mr. Lincoln to power, as to be rendered utterly impossible. Material of inferior quality could doubtless be obtained with ease. But such is considered worse than nothing, and hence does not diminish the embarrassment. I feel warranted in asserting that even at this moment this delicate question is no nearer a solution than six weeks ago, and that all the prominent statesmen that were summoned hither in the course of the last four weeks, were freely and anxiously consulted on the subject, but were unable to afford the relief sought for. As the case now stands I think it more than likely that no further Southern appointment will be made until after the arrival of the President-elect in Washington.

The selection of the route to be followed hence to the federal capital, will be definitely made within the next two weeks. Mr. W. B. Ogden, the well known Chicago financier and receiver of the Pittsburgh, Fort Wayne & Chicago Railroad, who is here in the capacity of a State Senator, is said to be very solicitous to see Mr. Lincoln pass over the road he represents. All the Pennsylvania politicians that have visited the President elect since his election, also urged his passage through their State. Per contra, many of his friends here desire him to take a more southerly route, namely, via St. Louis, Cincinnati, and over the Ohio & Baltimore Railroad, and that because of the threats of armed prevention that have lately been made.

The present session of our Legislature promises to be a working one. The members have commenced in good earnest, and do not appear to be afflicted with the usual anxiety of newly-fledged legislators for notoriety by dint of oratorical buncombe. They meet three times a day and work away with a will. The most important measures introduced up to this time are, a bill amending the banking laws and [one] providing for the re-organization of the militia of this State. A preliminary discussion has taken place, that revealed a disposition to act upon both subjects. The bills in question are now in the hands of committees, but will be reported back at an early date.

January 12, 1861

Springfield, 12 January 1861
[New York *Herald*, 17 January 1861]

Frequent allusions have been made by me in preceding letters to the position occupied by the President elect in reference to the various modes and means, proposed by patriots in Congress and elsewhere, for the pacification of the country. I took occasion to state at different times that he had distinctly and emphatically expressed his firm adhesion to the Chicago platform in general, and the republican doctrine of the Congressional right to legislate prohibitively on the subject of slavery in the Territories; that he was decidedly opposed to the Crittenden resolutions,[22] and equally so to the scheme of admitting New Mexico as a State with its Territorial slave code unchanged—in fine, that he was as resolute and outspoken an anti-slavery extensionist as ever. That such are really his views no one that has ever enjoyed the privilege of his frank, unreserved conversation on public matters will deny; but I have reason to think—in fact, I know—that should he be called upon, after assuming his place at the helm of the ship of State, to subordinate, for the sake of the harmony and peace of the country, his private opinions to public measures, he will not fail to make a patriotic response. I believe, to illustrate the meaning of this assertion, that although entirely loath to see slavery spread over another inch of ground, he would yet affix his signature to a Congressional enactment embodying the propositions of Mr. Robinson,[23] or even the restoration and extension to the Pacific coast of the Missouri compromise line, provided he could be satisfied that it was demanded by the bulk of the nation, and the only means of saving the Union.[24] On the other hand, it will be but simple justice to state that neither he nor his friends have any longer faith in the availability of any of the suggested compromise measures. They appear to incline to the conviction that not only all the cotton States will follow in the wake of South Carolina; that no peace offering of any description will ever induce them to retrace their steps, and that the question with the republican administration will not be, how to forestall secession, but how to deal with it as an accomplished, stubborn, irrevocable fact.

It is now considered certain in Presidential circles that at least one, and perhaps two places, will be left open in the Cabinet with a view to the representation of the South, and that they will not be filled until after the arrival of the President in the federal capital. The statement of the New York *Tribune* that Robert E. Scott, of Virginia, and William A. Graham[25] would be taken from the slaveholding States, is totally unfounded. No such selections have been made; nor is it at all likely that Mr. Scott will be one of Mr. Lincoln's ministers. His last epistolary effort, in which he placed himself determinedly and bitterly on record against the party that elevated Mr. Lincoln to power, has rendered him altogether impossible.[26]

It would be vain to conceal the fact that the most intricate and delicate question to be solved by Mr. Lincoln previous to his inauguration is now this very representation of the Southern section of the country in his ministerial council. There is evidently an absolute want of Southern planks likely to fit into the already constructed portion of the Cabinet. That this difficulty has already proved very vexatious to Mr. Lincoln is certain, and that he will put off his ultimate decision in the premises until a point of culmination will be further approached, either one way or the other, is more than probable.

Judging from present appearances, the session of the Legislature of this State will be a pre-eminently working one. The legitimate business for which it has been convened will be first disposed of; politics will only be dabbled in in case the legislation proper shall not absorb the forty days within which the session is wisely confined by the constitution. The most important measures thus far introduced are bills for the amendment of the banking laws and the reorganization of the militia of this state.

Charles Botier, the well known financier of your city [New York], was here during yesterday.

Springfield, 12 January 1861
[New York *Herald*, 18 January 1861]

In a preceding letter allusion has already been made to the probability that the South would be at best represented by only two members, including Mr. Bates, in Mr. Lincoln's Cabinet. That its restriction to that number now appears to be all but certain may well be stated. This contingency would doubtless fill the minds of many with grave apprehensions. But the cool observer of the course of Southern events will be apt to acknowledge that, unless a great reaction takes place within the next four weeks, they will render such a complexion of the Cabinet inevitable. The present condition of Mr. Buchanan's ministerial council foreshadows this. When he—the democratic President—the yielding friend of the South—finds himself unable to retain more than the stated number in his Cabinet, how can it be expected that his republican successor will be able to secure the services of more representatives from the section of the country now arrayed in hostility against the federal government? The truth of the matter is, that as the disunion fever spreads, the possibility of finding suitable material is growing less, and that, in the face of Mr. Buchanan's experience, the danger of dissonances in his Cabinet is more dreaded by Mr. Lincoln than the risk of being unjustly charged with sectional preferences.

Although the President has been enjoying much more rest and peace since the abandonment of his daily levees than while they were in full blast, his appearance plainly indicates that an *otium cum dignitate* [leisure with dignity] is not exactly the thing he is now enjoying. The concerned expression of his pallid features tells a meaningful tale. I understand that petitions and recommendations for office come upon him in daily increasing showers as the time of his inauguration approaches. The politicians of the Keystone State [Pennsylvania] are said to be particularly impatient to secure their share of the spoils. They seem to claim the sole merit of nominating and electing the republican President.

The rebellious movements in the South naturally give the President elect the most concern. Not that he feels in any way responsible for them. But the prevailing uncertainty as to the final issue of the Southern crisis greatly embarrasses him in the first and most consequential of his duties, viz: the construction of his Cabinet and the preparation of his inaugural.

Considerable pipelaying and logrolling are now doing, both in legislative and Presidential spheres, by State politicians. The division of the federal patronage will doubtless be made previous to the departure of the President elect for Washington.

The only business thus far transacted by the Legislature has been the passage of a bill making certain appropriations for expenses incurred during the last session, and the re-election in the course of this afternoon of Lyman Trumbull to the United States Senate for another term of six years, commencing on the 1st [4th] of March next. The affair came off unaccompanied by any extra demonstrations, with the exception of an outburst of enthusiastic applause when his election was formally proclaimed by the Speaker. No speeches were made on the occasion. Mr. Lincoln was present while the vote was being taken. He first went up into the gallery and stood among the general crowd. On being noticed, however, by some members on the floor, he was taken down and furnished with a seat. Just two years ago an act was consummated in the same hall that was then looked upon by him as the greatest political disaster of his life. And yet that very misfortune made him what he is now. For had he then succeeded in supplanting Douglas in the United States Senate he would never have attained to the highest station in the land.

The official announcement of Mr. Seward's acceptance of the Secretaryship of State was made here simultaneously with the appearance of the paragraph in the Albany *Evening Journal* telegraphed to the press last evening. The feeling of satisfaction it produced among our republicans was intense. It dispelled at once all doubts and apprehensions as to the character of the Cabinet. It was received as an earnest that capacity and honesty really formed the standard of the President elect in selecting its component elements, and raised the latter immensely in the eyes of his supporters. The lips of all overflowed with his praise. The members of the Legislature, above all, appeared to be delighted with the encouraging intelligence. They all think that, with Mr. Seward at the head of the Department of State, Mr. Lincoln's administration will at once command general respect and confidence both at home and abroad.

It is understood here that Mr. Seward's inclination ran in the direction of a foreign mission, and that his reluctance to serve at home was indicated, as stated by me at the time, during Thurlow Weed's visit. But the President elect did not abandon the hope of securing his administrative co-operation upon this intimation, but gave him ample time to reconsider, during which the Senator's friends wrought the change of resolution just made known. The result would doubtless have been different did not the Southern imbroglio render a conflict all but inevitable. The management of our foreign relations is likely to require just as much statesmanship, in case a general secession of the slaveholding States should take place, as that of our internal affairs.

A hue and cry, almost as great as that levelled at Cameron, is now being brought to bear upon the President elect in connection with his alleged intention to invite Caleb B. Smith, of Indiana, to a place in his Cabinet. The mental calibre of that choice of the Hoosier politicians seems to be thought altogether inadequate to a creditable fulfillment of the duties of Secretary of the Interior; but the pressure in his favor is headed by Henry S. Lane and other Indiana matadors, who claim more than ordinary significance for themselves, and more than ordinary prominence for their claims, and hence the result of the agitation, *pro* and *con*, is doubtful.

The office seeking representatives of Indiana and Pennsylvania, the two States that pretend to have done more towards nominating and electing Mr. Lincoln than any others, have already caused trouble enough to the President elect by their impudent forwardness and dictatorial presumptions to square any claims for extra allowances they may possibly have. Their wrangles for place are disgusting to behold. It is obvious that they only want an intellectual nullity in their representation in the Cabinet, in order to be least interfered with in the appropriation and distribution of the subordinate spoils.

It has been rumored about town for some days that the President elect is making the first draft of his Inaugural Address. This report is, however, without any foundation in fact. The change the posture of public affairs is now daily undergoing renders it necessary for him to put off the discharge of this important task to the latest possible moment.

The few visiters he now receives seek him at his private dwelling. To his correspondence he attends, however, with his secretary, in an office rented by him a few days ago [in Johnson's Building] in the business part of the city.

The *elite* of the political world of this State are now here. Among the more prominent characters are Judge Davis, W. B. Ogden, N. B. Judd, Governors Moore[27] and Yates, G. Koerner, Judge Catron, J. M. Palmer, Dr. [Charles Henry] Ray, of the Chicago *Tribune*[28]; E. [Charles L.] Wilson, of the Chicago *Journal*,[29] Young Scammon and others.[30]

The Eastern arrivals at the leading hotels are: Charles G. Wilson, G. W. Jenks, of New York city; R. D. Allen, of Boston; W. D. Bunting,[31] of Cleveland, and G. Bigler, of Lebanon county, Pennsylvania.

Springfield, 12 January 1861
[Cincinnati *Commercial*, 14 January 1861]
(The following despatch from our Springfield correspondent, has been lingering by the way, but is still news matter.)

Gov. Yates was inaugurated this afternoon. His message is the most decided anti-slavery, anti-compromise and anti-secession document sent to any Northern Legislature since the beginning of the crisis. Although delivered under the very eyes of Mr. Lincoln, its tone is so radical as to make it hard to believe that it has his sanction. Cameron matters are still in *status quo*. Judd is still energetically pressed for the place in the Cabinet assigned by rumor to Smith of Indiana, but I think Mr. Lincoln will be the only member from Illinois. Mr. Jones, the sculptor of your city [Cincinnati], has been professionally engaged with Mr. Lincoln for some days.

Springfield, 12 January 1861
[New York *Herald*, 14 January 1861]
Ja[me]s Appleton, Jr., of Boston, and Edgar Cowan,[32] and J. P. Sanderson, of Pennsylvania, arrived at a late hour this evening. The visit of the last mentioned two [men] is in reference to the Cameron imbroglio. Sanderson, who was here with Cameron ten days ago, is direct from Washington. Some racy developements will doubtlessly be made to-morrow.

The report that Henry Winter Davis was to be in Lincoln's Cabinet was authoritatively denied here to-day. It is understood that no Southern appointments will be determined upon until after Lincoln's arrival in Washington.

The conviction prevails now in Presidential circles that the day of compromise is passed, and that nothing but force will bring the rebellious States back into the Union.

Mr. Lincoln was presented this forenoon with a gold-headed rosewood cane valued at two hundred and fifty dollars, by Messrs. Ja[me]s Churchman[33] and Samuel Gamage[34] of San Francisco, in the name of C. M. Young, of Nevada city [California].[35]

W. Jones, an Indiana farmer for whom Mr. Lincoln split rails thirty years ago, is here on a visit to his former hired hand.[36]

January 13, 1861

Springfield, 13 January 1861
[New York *Herald*, 17 January 1861]

There is another excited flutter among our political *quid nuncs.* All the pangs of curiosity—all the uncertainties of rumors, conjectures, implications and deductions, that deprived them of their peace of mind and rest of body only a fortnight ago, are being renewed. The Cameron cabal is revived. The more feared than fearful Pennsylvania chieftain has once more entered the lists in the person of his most devoted henchman—J. P. Sanderson. That faithful squire, who had followed his liege lord hither but a few days ago, landed a second time in this republican Mecca at a late hour last evening. The news of the bombardment of Charleston would have produced no more amazement than that of his sudden apparition. In a mere whiff it had penetrated the remotest biding place of politicians. "What does it mean?" escaped the lips of all. "Is he come as a harbinger of peace or war?" "Has the vehement opposition to his master's appointment stirred up his mettle and excited his ire, or induced him to forego his Cabinet aspirations?" These were the questions—more easily asked than answered.

Not a little was added to the irritation by the fact that Edgar Cowan, the newly elected United States Senator of Pennsylvania, had not only arrived on the same train, but also engaged apartments in common with Sanderson. There was another puzzle. It had been universally believed that Cowan's triumph was tantamount to a defeat of Cameron, as Wilmot had received the support of the Cameron men in consideration of services rendered during his late visit to this place, and hence the apparent harmony and co-operation of supposedly hostile elements proved a profound mystery and no mean source of disconcert and confusion.

Thus it was not to be wondered at that this holy Sabbath was desecrated by general and persistent attempts to solve this seemingly inexplicable enigma. So many experienced noses being on the scent, it could not be a matter of surprise that, ere the distinguished visiters had dwelled twenty-four hours in our midst, the mist of discordant circumstances that first shrouded their intents and purposes has cleared away and the case all but fully understood.

It appears that Mr. Sanderson came here in a direct rush from Washington City, as the envoy plenipotentiary of the great Pennsylvania cabalist. Frightened, beyond all doubt, by the intensely hostile demonstrations that have been brought to bear upon the President elect during the last ten days, the latter instructed his *fidus Achates* to undertake the journey to Springfield once more, and bring matters to a head either one way or the other. And thus the confidential messenger hied hither, and giving himself hardly time for a hasty lavation and repast, sought the Presidential presence at the earliest possible moment. He found Mr. Lincoln at his private residence, and was closeted with him from eight to eleven o'clock P.M. The interview was renewed this forenoon, and likewise lasted several hours.

As to the tenor of the alternative presented by the deputy, it was framed with Mr. Cameron's habitual prudence and cunning. It neither asserted nor demanded anything in offensive or imperious terms. It was couched, on the contrary, in the most respectful and conciliatory language. It left everything to the pleasure of the party to whom it was addressed, and expressed a willingness to abide by his ultimate decision. While a readiness to serve was intimated, no anxiety for office was manifested. In fine, the document was so held as to enable the author to come well out of the affair, no matter what its upshot would be.

The President [elect] received Mr. Cameron's representative with his usual kindness, and listened to all he had to say with attention and respect. But it is well understood that he failed to respond directly or definitely, but expressed his intention to take the matter under further advisement.

It is not improbable that the question whether or not Mr. Cameron will occupy a seat in Mr. Lincoln's Cabinet will be ultimately decided before Mr. Sanderson re-embarks for the East. In the meantime the President elect finds himself in a disagreeable predicament. On the one hand, the disregard of the numerous emphatic remonstrances against the appointment of the Senator from Pennsylvania threatens to become a means of serious offence to their prominent and influential originators; while, on the other, the knowledge of Cameron's secret desires and easily wounded pride and great power opens the unpleasant prospect of equally grave consequences in case of his disappointment. Nevertheless, I venture to say that—Mr. Sanderson's visit to the contrary notwithstanding—the failure of the Cabinet aspirations of his principal is greatest [i.e., most likely], and that a plaster in the shape of a first class foreign mission will be offered.

As to the import of Mr. Cowan's visit, it is known that he met Mr. Sanderson by accident at Pittsburg[h], while on his way here, and being an intimate acquaintance, came on with him; but, although the main object of his trip is to become personally acquainted with the President elect, that he intended, with a generosity truly creditable to the victor, to urge Cameron's claims in order to secure for his defeated rival [David Wilmot] a place at his side in the United States Senate.

Mr. Cowan did not attend last night's interview between the President and Mr. Sanderson, but was formally introduced to the former in the course of the morning.

Springfield, 13 January 1861
[Cincinnati *Commercial*, 14 January 1861]

Gossip has been busy all day with the visit of Senator Cowan and J. P. Sanderson to the President elect, as they represent antagonistic factions. It was first supposed that they came here to renew the struggle over Cameron's appointment. But it is now known that the former's object is merely to make the acquaintance of the President elect. The latter brought Cameron's ultimatum. It is reported that he expresses himself willing to withdraw from the field. Mr. Lincoln holds the matter under advisement.

January 14, 1861

Springfield, 14 January 1861
[New York *Herald*, 15 January 1861]

The all absorbing subject of speculation is the visit of Senator Cowan and J. P. Sanderson to the President elect. As they are known to represent antagonistic factions, it was first supposed that they came here to renew the struggle over Cameron's appointment; but it is now known that they accidentally met while on the way hither.

Mr. Cowan's object is merely to make the acquaintance of Mr. Lincoln.

Mr. Sanderson brought Mr. Cameron's ultimatum, in which a readiness to withdraw from the field is said to be expressed. Mr. Lincoln is holding the matter under advisement.

Mr. Judd is still energetically pressed for the place assigned by rumor to Mr. Smith, of Indiana; but I think Mr. Lincoln will be the only member of the Cabinet from Illinois.

Governor Yates was inaugurated this afternoon. His message is the most decided anti-slavery, anti-compromise and anti-secession document sent to any Northern Legislature since the beginning of the crisis. Although delivered under the very eyes of the President elect, its tone is so radical as to make it altogether improbable that it has his sanction.

Springfield, 14 January 1861
[Cincinnati *Commercial*, 18 January 1861]

Another excitement is raging among our politicians. Cameron is again in the field. More cabalistic than a Chinese Mandarin, and nothing daunted by his ill success ten days ago, he has once more commenced his Cabinet intrigues. Having changed his plan of operations, he did not undertake to relay his wires about the President in person, but intrusted one of the most devoted of his followers (the faithful J. P. Sanderson) with the job. At a late hour on Saturday evening he (Sanderson) most unexpectedly emerged from an Eastern train. Having been here but a few days since in company with his lord and master, he was at once recognized, and the news of his arrival spread with wonderful rapidity. Crowds of newsmongers forthwith flooded in the Chenery House to persuade themselves of the reality of his advent by a personal inspection of the hotel register, and ascertain, if possible, the meaning of his second visit. But eager as their curiosity was, they had to be satisfied for that evening at least with the fact that immediately after his arrival he repaired to the private residence of the President elect, and did not leave him until after eleven o'clock.

Here was a mystery that promised to tax their powers of inference and deduction to the utmost. Nor was its solution rendered any more easy by the still more puzzling fact, that Edgar Cowan, the newly elected State [U.S.] Senator from Pennsylvania, had not only arrived simultaneously with Sanderson, but also taken apartments in common with him. Politics, it is true, are known to make strange bed fellows. But it looked altogether unprecedented, that the representatives of two rival factions yet hot with the fierceness of an antagonistic strife just ended, should have made peace and come out here to further common objects. Their coming and rooming together was certainly good evidence of such being the case. And yet it soon became known on the other hand, that Mr. Cowan did not accompany Mr. Sanderson to the house of the President elect on the evening of their arrival. What, then, in view of these confounding circumstances was the real import of their visit?

All day yesterday, and all this forenoon, the efforts of those that take an interest in what is going on in Presidential circles, to ferret out the matter, were unrelenting, and at the moment of this writing the respective intentions of the two distinguished visitors are pretty well understood. Sanderson is known to have come here direct from Washington City at the behest of Cameron, to bring matters between the President elect and the Pennsylvania

Senator to a conclusion. He was the bearer of a letter in the latter's hand-writing touching upon the aspiration to a seat in the Cabinet.—Without reference to or excuse of the unwarrantable freedom, with which his friends undertook to claim his appointment by Mr. Lincoln to the Secretaryship of the Treasury, he simply assents in it, in terms most humble, to forego all claims to a seat and leave this ultimate selection of a member from his State altogether with the pleasure of the President elect.

Now this is in exact keeping with the foxy ways of old Simon. He could not well insist on his claims, in the fear of the vigorous protests against his appointment that have been fairly showered upon Mr. Lincoln during the last fortnight. A withdrawal was the only thing he could do, with credit to himself and benefit to his cause. For, his apparently disinterested declina-tion could not fail to refute, to some extent, the charge of office-hunting, so successfully brought against him by his opponents, while at the same time the pleas and representations to the contrary, of him who presented his mission, would counteract any disposition on the part of the President-elect to accept his voluntary retirement from the field of competition.

How little is meant by the proposed withdrawal, is fully illustrated by the developments made in the course of yesterday, in regard to the portent of Mr. Cowan's visit. It was first supposed that he and Sanderson had met by sheer accident, and that he (Cowan) made the journey merely for the purpose of making the personal acquaintance of the President elect. But it is now known that, although they did not start together, they met by appointment in Pittsburg[h], and that Cowan came here to redeem a pledge given to the few Cameron men whose support, first promised to Wilmot, was afterwards transferred to him, and secured his election, to the effect that he would use the influence of himself and his friends to secure the appointment of Cameron to a place in the Cabinet.

Thus the case now stands according to the very best authorities. Lin-coln is thereby placed in a sort of quadrangular dilemma. On one side this unfortunate, indefinite epistolary hint at the possibility of an appointment to Cameron, proves a source of embarrassment. From another, emphatic remonstrances stare at him. On a third he is met by Cameron's letter offer-ing to waive all claims—a seeming generosity that is more exacting of an appointment than the former direct demand of it—while on a fourth Sand-erson's and Cowan's exertions perplex him. I venture to say that Abraham is most heartily tired of this Cameron cabal and anxious to shake it off at the earliest possible moment. But, as it is, he finds himself in a quandary, from which it is difficult to escape. His ultimate decision in the premises will doubtless be made before long.

Mr. Cowan was formally introduced to Mr. Lincoln on yesterday morning. Both he and Sanderson since spent most of their time with him. They are still here, but expected to leave this evening.

Springfield, 14 January 1861
[Cincinnati *Commercial*, 21 January 1861]

According to constitutional provision, the Republican State officers elected last November, were duly installed into their respective offices in the course of this afternoon. Some of the citizen-soldiery had unfortunately conceived the idea of a military pageantry [pageant] on the occasion, in consequence of which part of the inauguration ceremonies partook more of the ludicrous than the solemn. The retiring officers were induced to allow themselves to be escorted in carriages to the Gubernatorial mansion, where they called for their successors, and brought them to the State House.—All this had been well enough, had not the dilapidated carriages in which they rode, and the wretched appearance of the three companies of infantry and artillery— numbering together about sixty men, all told—imparted to the performance the character of a masquerade. As it was, the spectacle inside the State House was far more attractive and impressive than the outside fizzle. At least two thousand people, embracing, to use a common-place expression, the "intelligence, wisdom, wealth and beauty" of the State, crowded every nook and corner of the Hall of the House of Representatives, in which the formal installation took place. After entering and reaching their seats on the dais around the Speaker's desk, the oath of office was successively administered by Chief Justice Caton to Richard Yates, the Governor elect; Francis A. Hoffmann, the Lieutenant Governor[37]; O[zias] M[ather] Hatch, the Secretary of State[38]; J[esse] K. Dubois, Auditor[39]; M. [William] Butler, Treasurer,[40] and N[ewton] Bateman, Superintendent of Public Instruction.[41]

This being over, Gov. Yates proceeded to deliver his inaugural address. Although the novelty and solemnity of his situation evidently affected and embarrassed him so much as to render his delivery the worst possible,[42] the character of the production was yet such as to rivet the attention of the audience. As you will doubtlessly extract the leading passages of that portion that treats of national politics, for the benefit of your readers, I will confine myself to a few comments. It cannot be denied, that the tone of some sentences and even whole paragraphs was unexpectedly radical. The ideas therein reflected were more boldly conceived and more emphatically and unsparingly expressed, than in any other contemporaneous Northern State paper. Outspokenness, although in reality a virtue, sometimes becomes a fault in public life, and such seems to be the case with the message of Gov. Yates. Not that it contained a solitary fallacy—nay, only the truth strongly and bitterly told, so that it cannot but jar upon the ears of those for whose special benefit it is intended. There was no diplomatic evasion or circumscription about the document. It conveyed exactly what the author meant. It reminded one frequently by its impassioned fever of the vigorous philippics of [Henry Ward] Beecher, [Wendell] Phillips, [Charles] Sumner and other anti-slavery champions par excellence. Its effect upon the audience proved conclusively that it was looked upon as no ordinary composition. The Republican element was [at] first surprised at its unlooked for rigor of thought and expression; but the subsequent applause, with which its most salient points were greeted, plainly demonstrated that they coincided with their own sentiments. The Democratic listeners seemed [at] first amazed, and then gratified with the warmth and decisiveness with which firm adherence to Republican doctrines was proclaimed; compromise and secession denounced. They all appeared to be struck with the idea of being furnished with a most formidable means of continuing their malicious, but cherished labors in fastening the abolition odium upon their hated opponents.

I have no doubt, indeed, that Gov. Yates' message will be extensively used for disunion propaganda. The fact of its having originated with a prominent and intimate friend of the President elect, will most certainly be used for the imputation, that it embodies his sentiments. The *Enquirer*, of your city [Cincinnati], which, like the *Gazette*, found itself obliged to follow in the wake of the *Commercial*, and provide "Springfield correspondence," will surely attempt it. To forestall its and other misrepresentations, I will say, *that I am able to state authoritatively that neither Mr. Lincoln nor any other political friend of Gov. Yates* saw or heard anything of his message before its delivery. The Governor, for reasons best known to himself, saw fit to assume the entire responsibility of it.

The President elect has just been presented with a rosewood cane, headed with a most beautiful specimen of polished gold-bearing quartz weighing over half a pound, and valued at over two hundred dollars. The presentation was made by Judge Churchman, of Nevada City, and Mr. Samuel Gamage, of San Francisco, Cal., who came here from the East for the purpose, in the name of and for C. W. Young, an enthusiastic Republican jeweller of the former place. The cane bears the inscription:

To ABRAHAM LINCOLN,
First Republican President of the United States.
FROM C. W. YOUNG, Nevada City, Cal.

Abraham was so embarrassed on receiving the rich gift, that he could hardly express his obligations.

An unsophisticated Hoosier farmer [William Jones] arrived here on Saturday last from the [southwest Indiana] "pocket,"[43] on a visit to the President elect. He was the object of special attention on the part of the latter, inasmuch as it was the identical party for whom, over thirty years ago, Lincoln mauled rails for 37½ cents per day and board.

January 16, 1861

Springfield, 16 January 1861

[Cincinnati *Commercial*, 17 January 1861]

Senator Cowan and J. P. Sanderson left yesterday morning, after laying close siege to Mr. Lincoln for nearly three days. The universal opinion here is that their mission was not successful, and that Mr. Lincoln thought best not to decide the question of Cameron's appointment definitely during their stay. The pressure exercised by them now being removed, there is no longer any probability of an ultimate decision in Cameron's favor, as strong counter efforts are daily made. Cameron's offer to withdraw was evidently only made, not meant. Both Cowan and Sanderson worked at any rate like beavers for him. The former's support was extended in return of obligations to Cameron for members of the Pennsylvania Legislature. The anti-Cameron men, received as powerful reinforcement in the persons of George Opdyke, Hiram Barney,[44] and Judge Hogeboom,[45] of New York City; they are all decidedly opposed to Cameron's appointment and did not hesitate to make their opinion known to the President elect. The same parties express themselves very strongly against compromise propositions. They came here on a friendly visit to Mr. Lincoln with no special intentions. The pressure for [Norman B.] Judd is growing tremendous. If the Hoosiers want to save [Caleb B.] Smith they had better hurry out here.

Springfield, 16 January 1861

[New York *Herald*, 21 January 1861]

If it be true that mirthfulness is a sign of good health, the most gratifying conclusions as to the bodily *status* of the President elect may be drawn from the effect the racy leader in last Saturday's HERALD, on Cameron's discomfiture,[46] is said to have had upon the President elect. I am informed that he laughed over it until tears coursed down his cheeks. Bothered and perplexed as he is, the frequent application of such healthy medicine cannot but prove a relief and relaxation to him.

There was a rumor afloat to-day that Governor Chase's declination of a place in the Cabinet was received in last night's mail by Mr. Lincoln. If this be so, it will only go to show that the Governor's ambition has got the better of his patriotism. The President elect, and the whole country, would be gratified to see the Ohio statesman in the Cabinet; and that as much reputation can be made in these revolutionary times out of the Secretary-ship of the Treasury as that of State, is obvious. Why, then, not accept the guardianship of Uncle Sam's cash box?

Judd stock has greatly improved within the last two days. I would not be surprised, indeed, to see his appointment to the Interior Department officially announced within the next twenty-four hours. The plea of the Indiana and Pennsylvania place seekers, that they nominated and elected Lincoln, does not certainly hold good with regard to Illinois; for his nomination by the delegation of this State in the Chicago Convention was the initiatory step on which his final success was conditioned. Judd's claims to the Cabinet are, therefore, entitled to as much consideration as those of Smith and Cameron, and even more, as he was principally instrumental in bringing forward Lincoln in his own State.

Among the late arrivals are T. B. Thoe, Toledo; P. W. Abbott, Boston; H. D. Colby, Rochester, N.Y.; Wm. H. Blood, New York city; W. Mattoon, Springfield, Mass.; W. H. Johnson, Utica, N.Y.; J. J. Broom and L. A. Busich, of New York city.

Senator Cowan and J. P. Sanderson, Esq., have left for home, the latter shaking off the mud of Springfield as he entered the cars with an air which plainly said, "Once, twice, but never again." How could he feel otherwise? Will the result be a faction fight between the Pennsylvania republicans?

Springfield, 16 January 1861
[New York *Herald*, 22 January 1861]

In glancing over the list of arrivals at our principal hotel this morning, my attention was arrested by a somewhat dubious and unusual entry. There stood, "Mr. Barney and two friends, of New York." What did it mean? Was this a careless, accidental generalization, or an intentional, premeditated mystification? Evidently the latter. To be sure, there are many Barneys, and many may be the friends of each; but was it probable that a "Mr. Barney and two friends" would come all the way from New York to Springfield, and, without due cause, let neither the hotel keeper nor anybody else know who they were? There was at least ground for suspicion; familiarity with the wiles of politicians excited mine, at any rate. The mystery had to be solved. Beckoning the clerk, I pointed to the strange registration. He did not speak, but there was a sly wink in his right eye that sufficed to me. It told me plainly that there was something up, and that was all I wanted. I quietly turned around to survey the loungers in the portico, and glancing leisurely about—lo! there sat the solution of the registry enigma in the persons of George Opdyke, Hiram Barney and Judge Hogeboom. There they were, placidly smoking their segars and engaged in an undertone conversation, little suspecting, evidently, that the eye of the HERALD's correspondent was upon them, that their attempted incognito had failed, and that in less than twenty-four hours not only the fact of their presence in Springfield, but the object of their mission, would be known throughout the Empire City [New York]. How could they expect, indeed, to escape discovery? Did I not tell them through the HERALD, many weeks ago, that any attempt to come to Springfield and dance attendance upon the President elect was preposterous and should not be made? Had they heeded my disinterested counsel the mortification of being laughed at by their friends in New York for being thus exposed would have been saved to them. The enormous mustache which forms the distinctive and unmistakeable characteristic of one of them should have been done away with, at all events, if concealment was desired.

The distinguished trio were presented to Mr. Lincoln shortly after nine o'clock this morning, by a prominent politician of this State, and remained closeted with him until noon. The interview was renewed after dinner, and continued until nearly dark.

As to the object of their mission, the "damned New York free traders," to use the graphic language of an indignant Pennsylvanian, came here in the first place to protest against the appointment of Senator Cameron to the Secretaryship of the Treasury. Being men of wealth and standing in the commercial and financial world, their representations doubtless had the desired effect.

As representatives of the genuine radical democracy of New York, the delegation furthermore took occasion to express the decided hostility of themselves and followers to any compromise propositions that involved a renunciation of the republican creed, as laid down in the Chicago platform. Herein they found an exact coincidence of their own views with those of Mr. Lincoln.

Would I be believed if I asserted that the three abstained altogether from touching upon the "spoils?" Probably not. Nor is it at all likely that Mr. Lincoln should not have improved the opportunity of sounding their wishes and expectations as to distributing the federal patronage in New York. But I do not think that definite promises and pledges were either asked or given.

The Democratic State Convention, that met in the House of Representatives at ten o'clock A.M., and had three sessions in the course of the day, was remarkable not so much for the number as for the mental calibre of those that attended it. Hardly half of the counties were actually represented. It was, indeed, more a gathering of politicians than representatives of the people. But among the attendance were the most respectable and eminent members of the Douglas democracy of this State. The occasion was evidently looked upon as a most momentous one. Even the Judges of the Supreme Court, including Chief Justice Caton,[47] who had not participated in any political demonstration in the last twenty years, were present and took active part in the proceedings.

A strong Union sentiment—much stronger than might be inferred from the resolutions adopted—pervaded the Convention. There were, it is true, a number of sympathizers with the secession movement in the South, but they were in a wo[e]ful minority, and were prevented from evaporating [espousing] their disunion sentiments in speeches.

As to the resolutions, the principal [ones] of which will be telegraphed to you this evening, they were gotten up in the time-honored fashion by a committee, the members of which had been agreed upon in advance and understood each other. I do not deem them very creditable. They lament evils, but propose no available remedies. They were obviously inspired by Douglas and Pugh,[48] and reflect the sentiments of those ex-popular sovereigns rather than those of the democratic masses of this State.

The principal actors in this democratic drama were Wm. H. [A.] Richardson,[49] Judges Caton and [Samuel] Treat,[50] Ex-Governors Casey[51] and Moore, Don Morrison,[52] O. B. Ficklin,[53] A. Shaw,[54] S. Breese[55] and Wm. French.[56]

Isaac N. Morris is said to have telegraphed here that the assembled democracy must endorse Major [Robert] Anderson or go to the devil. It seems that they preferred the latter.

Henry Fitch, Jr. made the most decided Union speech on the occasion. He is the son of Senator Fitch.[57]

Springfield, 16 January 1861

[Cincinnati *Commercial*, 17 January 1861]

The Democratic Convention was numerously attended, although several counties were not represented. The flower of the Douglas Democracy was in attendance. Considerable dignity was added to the proceedings by [the] participation of Chief Justice [John Dean] Caton, his two associates and the United States District Judge. Some members from the extreme South of the State evinced strong sympathies with the South, but were prevented from embodying them in the resolutions by the Union majority. The speeches all had a strong Union flavor. The resolutions show that the Democracy of

Illinois follows wherever Douglas goes. The following are the most important of the resolutions adopted in full.

3d. That we deny the Constitutional right of any State or any portion of the people thereof, to secede from the Union and that we are equally opposed to nullification at the North and secession at the South as violative of the Constitution of the United States.

4th. Resolved that is the opinion of this Convention that the employment of military force by the Federal Government to coerce submission of the seceding States, will inevitably plunge the country in civil war, and entirely extinguish all hope of a settlement of the fearful issues now pending before the country. We therefore earnestly entreat as well the Federal Government as the seceding States to withhold and stay the arm of military power, and on no pretext whatever to bring on the nation the horrors of civil war until the people themselves can take such action as our troubles demand.

That we recognize the power and duty of the Federal Government to protect the property of the United States, and we recognize and declare the duty and power of the Federal Government through the civil authorities within the jurisdiction of the States, to enforce all laws passed in pursuance of the Constitution, but we distinctly deny that the Federal Government has any constitutional power to call out the military to execute these laws, within the limits and jurisdiction of any State, except in aid of the civil authorities.

Springfield, 16 January 1861

[New York *Herald*, 17 January 1861]

Senator Cowan and Mr. Sanderson left this morning disappointed, after laying close siege to Mr. Lincoln for three days. It is now understood that Mr. Cameron's offer to withdraw was not absolute. He merely expressed his willingness to forego his claims should they prove a source of embarrassment to the President elect. Both Cowan and Sanderson worked like beavers in Cameron's interest, but Mr. Lincoln thought best not to commit himself definitely while they were here. The pressure exerted by them now being removed, there is no great probability of an ultimate decision in Cameron's favor, as strong counter efforts are constantly being made.

It is believed here that Cowan's support of Cameron's claims was exerted in return of obligations to Cameron members by the Pennsylvania Legislature.

The probability of Mr. Judd's appointment is increasing.

A test vote was taken in the Legislature this morning on Mr. Crittenden's compromise proposition. The republican majority voted down resolutions embodying them.

The Democratic Convention to-morrow will be very largely attended. There is a prospect of a hard struggle as to which of the compromise measures now before Congress should be endorsed.

Three mysterious gentlemen arrived early this morning, and registered themselves at the St. Nicholas Hotel, as Mr. Barney and friends. They were apparently very anxious to preserve an incognito, but were soon recognized as Messrs. George Opdyke, Hiram Barney, and Judge Hogeboom, of New York city. The distinguished trio had a protracted interview with the President elect both this morning and afternoon. The object of their mission is to protest against Cameron's appointment, and express the decided opposition of the republican masses of the Empire State to any compromise involving an abandonment of the Chicago Platform. That the distribution of federal patronage in New York city also received their attention may be well supposed.

Mr. Edwards's speech is an exact reflection of Mr. Lincoln's views.

January 17, 1861

Springfield, 17 January 1861
[San Francisco *Bulletin*, 12 February 1861]

MR. LINCOLN'S CABINET

Since my last [December 25], considerable progress has been made by the President elect in the discharge of his first and most important duty—the formation of his Cabinet. That a good deal of difficulty and perplexity would attend the fulfillment of this delicate task, not only from the present intricacy of Southern affairs, but also from the spirit of rivalry and jealousy likely to be engendered within the ranks of the party that elevated him to the Presidency, could be well predicted. Nor have the developments of the last two weeks failed to substantiate this view of the case.

THE GREAT CAMERON COMMOTION

About a fortnight ago, a despatch was sent to the Associated Press from Harrisburg, Pa., conveying the intelligence, in rather positive terms, that Senator Cameron had been offered and accepted the Secretaryship of the Treasury. A day or two after the announcement, another despatch emanated from the same locality, casting a doubt upon the correctness of the first one, and stating that there was a violent opposition among many Republican leaders to Cameron's appointment, and that Judge Alexander K. McClure, and other anti-Cameronites, were about embarking for this place to enter their personal protest against his preferment. These despatches had hardly been digested here, when our political quidnuncs were thrown into a feverish excitement, by the unexpected arrival of Cameron and his *fidus Achates*, John P. Sanderson. His appearance in this latitude could be construed only into a confirmation of his reported election for a place in the Cabinet. The obvious cordiality with which he was received by, and the constant and intimate relations he had with, Mr. Lincoln during his stay of two days, could likewise but strengthen the belief in his appointment. Nor was the non-committal, but nevertheless significant smile with which he received inquiries addressed to him by anxious politicians on the subject apt to weaken it. Unwelcome as the fact of his appointment was to many, they yet did not allow their prejudices to prevail over their judgment in the face of all these corroborative circumstances, but made up their minds to see Cameron in charge of Uncle Sam's cash-box after the 4th of March next. This conviction was disseminated both by mail and telegraph, and thereby impressed upon the public at large.

Cameron had hardly started upon his return trip, amidst the congratulations of the numerous tuft-hunters now sojourning in this town, when up loomed the aforementioned Judge McClure. He arrived evidently much exercised and indignant at the seeming triumph of his hated antagonist. He asserted with more emphasis than discretion in the parlor of his hotel previous to calling upon Mr. Lincoln that "Cameron should not and would not be appointed"—"it was an absolute impossibility"—that "his appointment would result in a permanent disintegration of the Republican party of his State"—and sought the Presidential presence with defiance in his eyes and determination on his lips. Everybody expected to hear of a rumpus as the result of the interview from the supposed definiteness of Cameron's appointment. But contrary to general belief, the excited protestant issued from Mr. Lincoln's room and returned home a quieted and apparently satisfied man. There was a puzzle, admitting of but two solutions: his irritation had either been soothed with assurances and promises of liberal remembrances in the distribution of Federal patronage, or Cameron's appointment was, after all, no certainty, but merely a possibility.

McClure had hardly shaken the Springfield mud off his boots, when a crowd of Western politicians, attracted by the meeting of the Legislature, made their advent and took up the cudgels in opposition to Cameron. Many of them holding very intimate relations to the President elect, they remonstrated against his appointment both with frankness and persistency. They boldly claimed that it was decidedly unpopular throughout the West. It would greatly diminish, they said, the confidence of the bulk of the Republicans of the Northwest in the incoming Administration, and hence they demanded a recall of the portfolio supposed to have been tendered and accepted. Their efforts were strongly seconded by epistolary protests that commenced pouring in upon the President elect from Washington City and New York, New England, Pennsylvania, and most of the Northwestern States. Those from the Federal capital especially, were distinguished for vigor and unreservedness of expression. Many of them originated with prominent Republican Congressmen, who seemed to look upon the appointment in the extravagant light of a fatal stain upon the character of the new *regime*, and who wrote accordingly. As time passed on, these verbal and written demonstrations of hostility only grew greater in number and stronger in tone. At first, little attention was paid to them by Mr. Lincoln; but they crowded upon him at last so thick and fast, that he could not help taking notice of them.

What was the surprise of those who had made the alleged preference of Cameron a cause of indirect reprehension, when a hint was given out by him to the effect that there was no occasion for complaint and protest; that, although an intimation of the probability of an appointment had been conveyed to Cameron, nothing definite had been determined; that the matter was still under advisement, and would not be ultimately decided without fully hearing both those who desired and those who opposed his selection for the Cabinet. Here was another puzzle! There were the friends of Cameron, who had for nearly three weeks loudly and positively proclaimed their chieftain as the future custodian of the Federal Treasury. There was Cameron himself, who, although never directly affirming the correctness of the report, had never denied it, but had chosen to preserve a meaningful silence. There was *per contra* the above authoritative disclaimer of any binding promises in the premises. How was this discrepancy to be explained?

For several days the matter remained in a fog; but towards the close of last week the true merits of the case became known through the agency of some politicians of this State, who are among the oldest and most esteemed friends of Mr. Lincoln. It appears that, some three weeks since, Mr. Lincoln wrote a letter to the Pennsylvania Senator, embodying a desire for a consultation on the condition of public affairs, and a hint of an intention to select him as a representative of the Republican banner State [Pennsylvania] in the Cabinet. This letter was seen by a number of Cameron's friends, and although it did not convey a formal tender of any particular position, the despatches above alluded to were sent over the country on the strength of it, in order to stifle possible opposition by representing the appointment as a fixed Cabinet. But Cameron's adversaries were not to be silenced in that way. So soon as the despatches in question were published, they also put the telegraph in requisition and transmitted a "brief, but pointed" protest to Springfield. It reached Mr. Lincoln before Cameron arrived here, and although it did not induce him to make an immediate change of his programme in regard to his visitor, his habitual prudence caused him to abstain from carrying out his original intention of making a formal offer during the latter's sojourn, and leave the matter an open question until the "other side" was heard.

Thus Cameron had to return without a commission in his pocket, but still with a good prospect of getting it in due course of time. Being preceded by the report of a formal arrangement of the terms with the President elect, upon which he was to occupy a seat among his constitutional advisers, he was overwhelmed with congratulations in Pittsburg[h], Harrisburg and Washington, which, not being declined by him, made his reputed appointment appear in a still more positive light. He had, however, hardly reached Washington when a storm that had gathered in the meantime in Springfield broke loose over his head. His opponents in this region, waxing indignant at his failure to contradict the report of his unconditional appointment as Secretary of the Treasury, and learning the true state of affairs, through the above-mentioned semi-official declaration, commenced opening their batteries upon them. Denunciatory leaders, letters and telegrams were hurled at him with relentless vigor, and with so much effect, that his organs in Pennsylvania began to mistake significant allusions to injured feelings, profound indignation, probability of a declination, etc. The Washington correspondence of the Eastern press, which was theretofore fraught with daily assurances of the positiveness of his appointment, also changed its tone on the subject. From day to day the possibility of the General's retirement was represented as growing greater, and now there seems to be a general understanding that he has eventually withdrawn from the field.

HOW THE PENNSYLVANIA SENATORIAL ELECTION COMPLICATED MATTERS

Not a little was added to the complication of the case, by the unforeseen result of the struggle for the United States Senatorship in the Pennsylvania Legislature. David Wilmot was supposed to be sure of the succession to Bigler, in view of the support of his claims by the Cameron faction. He had been invited, it will be remembered, to Springfield, about a month since, to receive the offer of a *portefeuille* [portfolio], and it was generally believed that he had accepted it. But it leaked out afterwards that he waived his claims in favor of Cameron, whose cause he embraced, in order to secure the countenance of the almighty Simon in the pursuit of his Senatorial aspirations. Thus, it was the universal impression that, in return for services rendered here, he would be unanimously voted for by the Cameron members of the Legislature. But this proved a mistake. Enough of them went over to the opposition to elect Edgar Cowan. The cause of this unexpected turn of fortune was immediately understood here, when the fact of the sudden advent on Monday evening last, of Mr. Cowan and the same J. P. Sanderson that had accompanied Cameron himself, and the nature of their mission, became known. They both came here to jeopardize the impression produced upon Mr. Lincoln, by the violent opposition to Cameron's appointment. Mr. Cowan worked with a zeal for his reputed adversary that proved the making up of former differences, and the late formation of an alliance in accordance with the terms of which Wilmot was dropped, and Cowan elected upon the promise of the co-operation of himself and friends in pressing Cameron for the Cabinet. But although both he (Cowan) and Sanderson laid close siege to the President elect for nearly three days, they did not succeed in exacting a surrender—that is, procure the desired commission for the Cabinet. They had to return with the simple assurance that Lincoln had the matter under advisement.

Thus the great Cameron imbroglio—with which the newspapers have been occupied here nearly three weeks, so accounts have doubtlessly reached you likewise ere this—stands at this moment. The counter pressure having again full play since the departure of Sanderson and Cowan, there is now no great probability of an ultimate decision in Cameron's favor. Your correspondent could never persuade himself of its certainty, and that because of his personal knowledge of the detestation in which Mr. Lincoln holds the politicians that owe their success to the practical application of the axiom that "the end justifies the means." Mr. Lincoln was induced to make advances towards Cameron by the representations of certain parties, who made him appear as the unanimous choice of Pennsylvania for the Cabinet. But since the strong opposition to him became manifest to him, he would be glad to see the informal tender, that caused all this commotion unmade. That this matter has greatly bothered him, all his friends acknowledge.

There can be no doubt as to the unpopularity of Cameron's rumored appointment in the Northwest. A marked feeling of relief was evinced, indeed, throughout Ohio, Michigan, Wisconsin, Illinois and Iowa, when the disclaimer was given out. That there will be deep and loud disaffection in these States should he, after all, manage to get into the Cabinet is certain. It is, however, also probable on the other hand, that the overlooking of his claims will provoke a rumpus between the incoming Administration, himself and his friends.

EX-GOV. CHASE TENDERED A SEAT IN LINCOLN'S CABINET

How unfounded the original report of Cameron's appointment to the Treasury had been, was shown by the visit, in the course of last week, of Ex-Gov. Chase of Ohio, for the purpose of receiving the tender of that identical Department. That this has actually been, has since been publicly admitted by the recipient. But although the Governor felt highly flattered at this mark of distinction, he had no hesitation to say to Mr. Lincoln, that his preference was for service in the Senate, to which he had been but recently elected. Since his return home, however, he has been prevailed upon to withdraw his absolute declination, and request Mr. Lincoln to hold the matter in abeyance until he could have fully consulted with his friends on the subject. The Governor's appointment would be immensely popular throughout the West and East, and it is hoped that he will eventually accept.

PRESENTATION BY A CALIFORNIA DELEGATION

Messrs. James Churchman of Nevada, and Samuel Gamage of San Francisco, came here on Saturday last [January 12] to pay their respects to the President elect. During their stay they presented him with a splendid gold-headed, rosewood cane, valued at $250, in the name of C. W. Young of Nevada [City, California]. The gift was received with much gratification. Both Mr. Gamage and Mr. Churchman asserted emphatically that they were not after office—a fact which, as redounding to their credit, I will state.

BACKWARDNESS OF NEEDY CALIFORNIANS

Although a number of expectants from the Golden State are known to be in Washington, they seem to be afraid of coming out here. The frequently expressed determination of the President elect not to consider any applications for subordinate offices until after the 4th of March, probably has something to do with this backwardness

ABUNDANCE OF WESTERN POLITICIANS

Since the meeting of the Legislature on the 9th inst., the influx of Western office-seekers has been tremendous. The details of their operations in my next.

Springfield, 17 January 1861
[Cincinnati *Commercial*, 22 January 1861]

It has been supposed here for a long while that in the face of the decided displeasure of the President-elect at the impatience, obtrusiveness—nay, outright impudence of certain applicants for subordinate offices, no politician of character, possessed of any respect for himself would venture to Springfield, unless especially invited by Mr. Lincoln. Some official hints have, indeed, been given out from time to time, duly recorded for the benefit of all concerned, in the [Cincinnati] "Commercial," that the President-elect would not pay the slightest attention to any petitions, recommendations or applications not bearing upon the composition of the Cabinet, and that all visitors having the furtherance of personal interests in view, and not belonging to the list of those booked for the Cabinet, would be unwelcome and run the risk of receiving the cold shoulder.

Mr. Ben Eggleston[58] (not knowing whether the Col. or Hon. is most appropriate in his instance, I simply use the Mr.,) being a reader of the *Commercial*, it may be well inferred, that he was aware of the danger in which he placed his reputation and prospects by a pilgrimage to Springfield *without* "special invitation." Hence, it may be logically concluded from the fact of his journeying hither, unprovided with a Presidential citation [invitation], that his self-imposed mission was in reference to the only subject now occupying Mr. Lincoln's mind, viz: the Cabinet.

So it was—at least apparently. Having been safely discharged by last night's train from Chicago, and stored his bodily self under the hospitable roof of one of our hotels, he quietly commenced looking and feeling about to ascertain the run of popular opinion on the Chase question in this latitude. He soon found that the Republicans out here are all but universally sound on it. Being among the wolves, it was, of course, but wise to howl with them, and hence it was not to be wondered that Ben was looked upon and pointed out as a strong Chase man.

But the sequel, as detailed to me by—to use the expression so familiar to a Springfield correspondent—good authority, went to show that he was viewed in the wrong light. Will you believe it? He has been denounced to me as a secret emissary in the interest of no smaller bird than D. K. Cartter.[59] I was [at] first loath to credit this awful charge, but the evidence offered in support of it was so strong as to make it imperative on your correspondent to reiterate it. He left Ohio with a petition for or recommendation of the appointment of the abovesaid mediocrity in his pocket. The signatures of a number of Republican politicians are said to be attached to it. He was enjoined to present it only in case he found the declination of Ex-Gov. Chase to be definite, and keep altogether quiet about it if the question of the former's appointment to the Treasury Department was still open.

The latter being the case, my informant contends the document never saw the daylight during Ben's stay in Springfield, and will be carried back to Cincinnati in the envelope in which it was originally enclosed, and under the address of the President elect.[60]

Serious as the above exposition of Ben's double-dealing may appear, I have still worse things to tell of him. A malicious fellow who pretends to have known him for many years, has whispered into my ear, that he never had any idea of presenting the written request to take care of Cartter, and that the principal object of his visit to the President elect was to make an argument *ad hominem* in favor of his own fitness for [a] place in the Cabinet.[61]

If this be so, Ben might have saved all the trouble and expense of coming to Springfield, had he remembered what I stated weeks ago in the "Commercial," that Mr. Chase and Mr. Chase alone could represent Ohio in the Cabinet.

Being deeply impressed with the virtues and capacities of Mr. Eggleston, that qualify him pre-eminently for any office within the gift of Mr. Lincoln, I was not a little surprised at the rumor which has just reached me, that ambition had got so much the better of Ben's judgment as to induce him to make a significant—but, alas! unheeded allusion to the Postoffice in your city during his last interview with the President elect. Can it be possible?

Whatever the upshot of Mr. Eggleston's several private chats with the President in the course of to-day may have been, his hasty departure to-night, together with the cloud of disappointment, that had settled on his countenance, indicated that it was not of a very satisfactory character. I venture to say, indeed, that Ben goes back to Porkopolis [Cincinnati], not as Minister, and still less as Postmaster, and that he will have reason to curse his suicidal folly of coming out here, after the 4th of March, for that he has been booked by Abraham under the head of "bores," is certain.

The least that is said about the Democratic State Convention that met here on yesterday, and the pith of whose proceedings were telegraphed to you, the better. It was an altogether discreditable affair. The craven, malignant spirit that pervaded the resolutions, proved that the Douglas Democratic politicians of this State are as full of meanness, inconsistency and party bitterness as their leaders. The assemblage consisted altogether of politicians. Fossils that had rested quietly in obscurity and oblivion for twenty odd years had been dug up and made to attend, to impart a sort of dignity to the body. But they only succeeded in giving it a cadaverous aspect.

January 18, 1861

Springfield, 18 January 1861
[New York *Herald*, 19 January 1861]

George Opdyke, Judge Hogeboom and Hiram Barney left last night for Columbus, Ohio, to urge Gov. Chase to accept the Treasury Department.

Ben. Eggleston, of Cincinnati, has been here to offer his services in case of Chase's declination. He is ready to compromise for the Cincinnati Post Office.

A prominent member of the Ohio Republican Central Committee is here working against Chase.

A strong California delegation, headed by D. Crittenden, of San Francisco, is laying close siege to the President elect.

There is a big scramble among Illinois politicians for the Chicago Post office. George W. Gage, of the Tremont House,[62] seems to have the inside track.

There is a prospect of serious trouble in the Legislature. Senator [Austin] Brooks[63] resigned to-day, and it is rumored that his democratic colleagues will do likewise, to prevent the passage of a bill to reorganise the militia by the republican majority.

The New York resolutions were introduced to-day and referred to a committee after an exciting debate.[64]

Springfield, 18 January 1861
[New York *Herald*, 23 January 1861]

The distinguished trio from the Empire City—George Opdyke, Judge Hogeboom and Hiram Barney—whose arrival and movements I recorded in my last, returned home on last night's train. That their expectations of the President elect had been realized could be easily divined from the joyful expression of their countenances. Cameron they found still suspended half way between the Cabinet and the cold of disappointment, with a fair prospect of a speedy consignment to the latter. The assurances they received of the President elect satisfied them that there was no imminent danger of a renunciation of the republican creed by the incoming administration; and, as to their share of the "fat of the land," I venture to say that they had nothing to complain of. It is true George did not button his coat over a commission for either the Postmaster or Collectorship. But it may be nevertheless regarded certain that he will have one of these two positions, and that his two companions have likewise good reason to rest easy until the day of the distribution of the New York city spoils will have arrived.

During their stay the three visiters were the objects of special attention on the part of the numerous Illinois politicians of prominence now sojourning here. All the limited resources Springfield could afford were lavished upon them. But although much sought after, they kept [to] their rooms as much as possible—doubtless from their foolish notion of being able to preserve an incognito. Yesterday's HERALD will probably convince them of the utter failure of their attempts in this respect.

Seward's speech has been assiduously and elaborately discussed during the last forty-eight hours in our political circles.[65] While it is generally known that the President elect approves of its every sentence, it is yet thought that he (Lincoln) would have made a much less general and more positive and decided effort had he been in Seward's place. As to republican opinion outside of Presidential spheres, I must say that the comments of the *Tribune* are endorsed by many. Greater firmness was expected, and hence partial disappointment is frequently met with.

Ben Eggleston, a well known Cincinnati politician, has been here for the last twenty-four hours. He came here with a petition, signed by many influential republicans of Southern Ohio, including four or five electors, recommending the appointment of David K. Cart[t]er to a seat in the Cabinet. The petition was to be offered by him only after ascertaining definitely whether or not ex-Governor Chase had declined to serve. Some who knew Ben of yore appear to believe that the petition would have quietly remained in his pocket had he at all found an opening for another representative of Ohio; but he soon discovered that Chase, and Chase alone, could represent Ohio, and hence had no further hesitation to present the document referred to. It is believed that he did not allow the opportunity to pass without throwing out some significant hints as to the federal offices in his native city. Had he received any encouragement at all he would surely have given the President elect to understand that he would have no conscientious scruples whatever to serve as Postmaster of Porkopolis [Cincinnati] for four years after the 4th of March next. As it was, Benjamin found that there was nothing to be done at present with "Old Abe," who is still absorbed in the construction of his Cabinet, and hence returned home disappointed.

A strong California delegation is now here, headed by D. Crittenden, of San Francisco, and Judge Churchman, of Nevada City. They all assert most vehemently that they did not come here in quest of office; but, although these assertions of disinterestedness may be made in good faith, I regret to say that they seem to be received with "many grains of allowance." They seem to be very anxious for the arrival of Col. Fremont in New York—probably to secure the proper endorsement of their claims. They evidently entertain strong hopes that either he or Mr. Sullivan[66] will represent California in the Cabinet.

A great scramble is still going on among local politicians as to their several portions of the federal spoils. The Chicago Post Office is a particular bone of contention. George W. Gage, the well known host of the Tremont House, is here after it. But I am sorry to say that the prize is hotly contested by about twenty-five competitors.

A greenish fellow arrived here day before yesterday from North Carolina, and sought and found accommodations for himself and wife at one of our hotels. Entering himself and companion on the register, he astonished the clerk by adding the word "abolitionist" to his name. Being pumped, he confessed that he supposed "they were all abolitionists where Lincoln lived, ready to lynch any Southerner," and hence thought best, while being among the wolves, to assume the airs of one.

Springfield, 18 January 1861
[Cincinnati *Commercial*, 22 January 1861]

If it be true that evil-doers seek darkness, it was but just to infer that the intentions of three travelers that arrived here on yesterday morning's train from the East, were of a sinister character. Their movements were decidedly suspicious. On reaching one of our hotels, they firmly declined entering their names on the register, but straightway demanded rooms, and retired to them in a manner that plainly indicated their anxiety to shun observation. These facts being duly communicated to your correspondent, he was at once satisfied that there was something in the wind, and forthwith went to work ferreting out the matter.

It did not take me long to ascertain that my suspicions were well founded, and that the three mysterious gentlemen had come here on a mission to the President elect. Their desire to preserve a strict incognito was obviously great, but ere they had sought the Presidential presence, they were known to us as George Opdyke, Hiram Barney and Judge Hogeboom, of New York city. Let their example be a warning to those of your readers that contemplate a visit to Springfield. Let them imitate Ben Eggleston, who boldly and fearlessly spread his name in large characters. It is neither sensible nor practicable to come to Springfield unobserved. The town is too small and the reporters too vigilant.

As to the object of the visit of the trio from New York, it turned out to be of such a nature, as to make it hard to understand, why they desired to keep their coming and going secret. It is true, being advertised in the public prints is not very agreeable, especially as the inferences drawn from the journeys of politicians in this direction are not always creditable. Yet, as their consciences were clear, that is, as they did not come after office, but merely to give the President elect the benefit of their counsel, it is difficult to see why they did not wish the world to know that they had been to see "Old Abe."

Their business with the President elect was to enter their gentle protest, as free traders, against the appointment of such an embodiment of [the] protective tariff humbug as Cameron. They furthermore took occasion to assure Mr. Lincoln that no matter what compromise-schemes were concocted in Albany and the Federal Capitol, the Republican masses of the Empire State were true to the Republican faith, pure and undefiled, and ready to rise in arms in support of the incoming Administration. No allusion whatever was made by them to the subject in which they were supposed to be most interested, viz: the distribution of the federal patronage in New York city. But I understand that, what they did not endeavor to exact, was voluntarily given. I dare say, indeed, that George Opdyke will be the successor of Schell[67] in the Custom House.

Ben. Eggleston had hardly accomplished a disgusted exit, when up turned Mr. Baber[68]—well known, I presume, in a negative way, to most of your Ohio readers. Mr. Baber, like Ben, came here on his own intimation [invitation]. Mr. Baber, like Ben, carried something in his pocket. Mr. Baber, like Ben, was charged with the delivery of a petition in reference to the representation of Ohio in the Cabinet. Mr. Baber, like Ben, thought Mr. Chase might do better service in the Senate; but unlike Ben, felt sure that [Robert C.] Schenck and not Cartter should be substituted. Mr. Baber, like Ben, was subcharged with patriotism, and ready to serve his country in any capacity, from the United States Senatorship down to a mail agency.

Nor was this all. Mr. Baber carried something besides that petition for Schenck's appointment. He had his other pocket full of clippings of the [Cincinnati] *Commercial*. Some of them bore upon the refusal of its publishers to insert in their columns a certain correspondence in reference to Lincoln's debates. Others were intended to fix the awful crime of past Douglasism upon them. He desired to read these extracts to the President elect. He thought they would convince him that the *Commercial* had been and still was his bitter foe. Again he taxed his powers of persuasion to demonstrate that the very men that now urged Chase, had opposed his (Lincoln's) nomination from the very start, and that the true and original Lincoln men did not desire the ex-Governor's appointment to the Cabinet.

And what was the upshot of all this bother, you will ask? Simply, that Mr. Baber produced a vivid impression in certain circles, as to what impudence and stupidity combined could do, and imparted a thorough idea of his boring capacity, which, to use the pointed illustration of a prominent Illinois politician, are "equal to those of a hundred and fifty gimlets."

Springfield, 18 January 1861
[Cincinnati *Commercial*, 19 January 1861]

Owing to derangement of the wires, I was unable to inform your readers of the operations of Mr. Eggleston at this point. He arrived here from Chicago night before last, and after besieging Mr. Lincoln all day, on Thursday re-embarked on the evening train. It is understood that he called here on his own invitation, ostensibly to press D. K. Cartter's appointment in case of Mr. Chase's declination, as the representative of Ohio in the Cabinet, but really to show his own fitness, if not for the Cabinet, at least for the Cincinnati Post-Office. Be it said that he goes home, without either portfolio or commission.

Geo. Opdyke, Judge Hogeboom and Hiram Barney, of New York, left last night for Columbus to urge Chase to accept the Treasury Department.

A California delegation of place seekers is here headed by D. Crittenden, of San Francisco.

There is a big scramble for the Chicago post office; some 20 competitors are in the field. Trouble is brewing in the Legislature. Austin Brooks, editor of the Quincy *Herald*, resigned to-day, and it is rumored that his Democratic colleagues will follow suit to prevent the passage of a bill to re-organize the militia.

Mr. Baber, of the Ohio State Central Committee, is here to undermine Chase.

January 19, 1861

Springfield, 19 January 1861
[New York *Herald*, 25 January 1861]

Few mortal beings ever carried a heavier load than that already resting, and likely to rest hereafter, upon the shoulders of Abraham Lincoln. Nor can it be concealed that, although he stands up manfully under its weight, the burden is taxing at times his patience and power of endurance to the utmost. It is evident that he is not yet fully accustomed to the idea of being placed at the head of a nation of thirty millions of people in less than sixty days, and that the grandeur of the mission he will be called upon to fulfill is at present more a source of anxiety and embarrassment than of hopeful and exalting emotions to him. He feels, in a measure, like one who, after groping in comparative dark[ness], suddenly emerges upon scenes of intense brightness, and finds himself at first less at home amidst light than dimness, but gradually loses his bewilderment and realizes his position and surroundings.

As during the last four weeks, the occupations of the President elect consist now principally in receiving visiters, conducting negotiations for the completion of his Cabinet and attending to his correspondence. As to visiters, those that come here on his special invitation are called upon by him at their respective hotels, while those that come of their own accord are either received at his private dwelling or in his down-town office— according to their several political stations and the object of their calls. The general crowd of place-seekers has to content itself with one hour each day, during which alone the Presidential ear is open to their selfish, annoying whisperings. The fact that they are hardly ever granted a separate and private hearing, but admitted into his office in a bulk, usually prevents them from making their desires and expectations known.

As to his correspondence, it has increased so wonderfully during the last fortnight that he finds it utterly impossible to read, not to speak of answering it all. I met his servant only last evening in the vestibule of the Post Office carrying a good sized market basket full of letters. His private secretary opens them, and from the signatures determines their relative importance. Those emanating from obscure sources are invariably consigned to the stove without the least mercy. Petitions for office especially share this fate.

Since the departure of his spouse for the East [on January 10], the President elect has been keeping house alone. Whatever his other qualifications may be, it is well known that in the management of the kitchen and other domestic concerns he is sadly destitute of both talent and experience. Hence it is more than probable that, upon the return of the master spirit of his home, whose functions he so imperfectly exercises, anything but praise will be bestowed upon him for the result of his administration during her absence.

It was but yesterday that I had occasion to converse with Mr. Lincoln on the subject of his impending trip to Washington city. He stated that he had as yet neither fixed the day of his departure nor selected the route, but that the former would probably take place on or about the 15th proximo. As to the latter, I think Mr. Lincoln's preferences are for a southerly route, via Cincinnati, Wheeling and Baltimore, doubtless to demonstrate how little fear he entertains for his personal safety. But there is a great pressure brought to bear on him in favor of a more northerly one, via Pittsburg[h] and Harrisburg, and it is most likely that this will be ultimately determined upon. Stoppages will be made by him at all the principal points. He knows that those who elected him are anxious to see how he looks, and hence is willing to gratify this, their excusable curiosity.

A number of the lady friends of Mrs. Lincoln have, with characteristic feminine solicitude, taken up the newspaper rumors of intended attacks upon the President elect while on his way to the federal capital, and used them as arguments to induce her to delay her removal to Washington until her husband was safely installed in the White House. But the plucky wife of the President met all these well meant propositions with scorn, and made the spirited declaration before she started upon her Eastern trip that she would see Mr. Lincoln on to Washington, danger or no danger.

There is a prospect of the breaking up of the Legislature in a grand row. The democratic members, like the Southern disunionists, are restive under the rule of the majority, and are said to contemplate revolution to prevent its legislative exercise. Some of their leaders avowedly sympathize with the secession movement, and express their determination to forestall hostile republican action in reference to it at all hazards. The prospective passage of a bill for a reorganization of the militia seems to be especially obnoxious to them. To-day Austin Brooks, a member of the Senate and the well known editor of the Quincy *Herald*, resigned. His resignation was accompanied by a speech, in which he frankly acknowledged that he retired because he could not endure to witness the enactment of "black republican" laws. It is rumored that all his colleagues, both in the upper and lower house, will follow his example in the course of the next week, so as to leave the Legislature without a quorum.

Springfield, 19 January 1861

[Cincinnati *Commercial*, 21 January 1861]

R. P. L. Baber, of your Ohio State Central Committee, is exhausting his wits in attempts to create an impression, in Presidential circles, against Salmon P. Chase, and for Robert Schenck, of Ohio. He is trying to convince Mr. Lincoln that the very advocates of Chase's appointment, were bitterly opposed to his (Lincoln's) nomination, and that Ohio should be represented in the Cabinet by a more conservative man than Chase.

He brought a pocket full of extracts from the [Cincinnati] *Commercial* along, to prove that it does not favor Mr. Lincoln's Administration, and that hence its advocacy of Chase's claims should not be heeded. His efforts had no better effect than to persuade everybody he came in contact with that his boring capacities, to use the language of a prominent Illinois politician, are equal to one hundred and fifty gimlets.

A. H. Conner, Wm. T. Otto and R. H. [William G.] Coffin, of Indiana,[69] came here in hot haste, this morning, to look after Smith's chances, evidently in response to the warning lately given in the *Commercial*.

John C. Fremont is expected here in the course of the next fortnight, to receive the tender of the War Department. It is not believed that he will accept.

A large meeting of Illinois bankers was held here yesterday, at which resolutions were passed recommending an amendment of the Banking laws, by which a central point of redemption and a restriction of securities to stocks of the United States and Illinois.

Springfield, 19 January 1861
[New York *Herald*, 20 January 1861]

A. H. Conner, Wm. T. Otto[70] and R. K. [William G.] Coffin, of Indiana, came here this morning to counteract the pressure of Illinois politicians to supplant Smith by Judd. Efforts to undermine Chase and substitute Robert D. [C] Schenck or D. H. [K.] Car[t]ter, are still being made; but Mr. Chase, or no one else will represent Ohio in the Cabinet.

Hon. Lawrence Weldon[71] will be United States District Attorney for the Southern District of Illinois. S. A. Hurlbert[72] and Col. Collamer are prominent applicants for the same position in the Northern district. J. Russell Jones, of Galena,[73] and Dr. Back, of Aurora, are in for the Marshalship.

Horace Greeley is expected here next week.

Springfield, 19 January 1861
[New York *Herald*, 21 January 1861]

Judge Kellogg, member of Congress from this State,[74] and one of the Committee of Thirty-three, arrived from Washington this morning, and immediately sought an interview with the President elect, which was continued throughout the day. He comes here to obtain a definite and authoritative announcement of Mr. Lincoln's views in reference to the compromise propositions.

The result of this visit will determine the ultimate action of the Republican members upon them.

Mr. Kellogg is opposed to Judd's appointment. The leaders of the anti-Judd forces are all here, and co-operate with the Indiana delegation in favor of Smith.

January 20, 1861

Springfield, 20 January 1861
[New York *Herald*, 25 January 1861]

How many ambitious souls do not at this moment look upon Abraham Lincoln with the eyes of envy? How many aspiring minds are not disposed to chide fate for placing, with comparatively little effort on his part,[75] that dearest boon, immortality, within his reach, for which they vainly yearned and struggled for a lifetime? True, a striking partiality has been shown to him by the power that shapes the destinies of man. The gates of fame are thrown open to him at its bidding. With a single step he is transferred from the narrow, obscure sphere of a provincial politician to the proudest position any mortal being can occupy. But there are no roses without thorns. The very lustre that suddenly surrounds him may dazzle and lead him, instead of to success and glory, to failure and degradation. The very tide of fortune that carried him so unexpectedly to the highest place in public life may sink the inexpert steersman. Shoals and rocks without number are ahead of him, and the chances for utter wreck are equal to those for safe landing. Instead of saving the Union, he may but be called upon to bury it. Time, indeed, alone will decide whether the bestowal of the highest political prize within the gift of the people is justly a source of envy.

It is evident that, in the opinion of the President elect and his immediate advisers in this locality, the issues to be dealt with under the republican administration are now narrowed down to the question whether the federal laws should be enforced, and the outrages already perpetrated upon them by the rebellious States repelled and punished, or the right of secession individually acknowledged, and the formation of an independent confederacy within the limits of the Union tolerated by assuming and preserving a merely defensive attitude. *They believe that all past party divisions will be altogether lost sight of, that "Union" and "disunion" alone will be made the rallying cries of two great parties, and that present appearances render the ultimate decision of the supremacy of either by the sword more probable than by the ballot.* That the President elect will be found ready after the 4th of March next to exhaust all means at his command to uphold the majesty of the law and the authority of the federal government is certain. But that *his efforts in this direction will have to be seconded, not only by Congress, but by the masses of the North, in order to prove successful, is equally so. The possibility of being crippled by a desire of a majority of the North to preserve peace, even at the expense of disunion, is dreaded, indeed, as likely to involve a paralysis and serious failure of the incoming administration.*

Early this morning A. H. Connor, the Chairman of the Republican State Central Committee of Indiana, arrived here, accompanied by Wm. T. Otto, one of the electors, and A. K. [William G.] Coffin, a prominent politician from the same State. They came in a great hurry, in evident excitement at the prospect of a substitution of Caleb B. Smith by N. B. Judd in the Interior Department. They all but monopolized the Presidential ears to-day, and express themselves in public, without much reserve, that Indiana will and must have Smith. But the Judd faction is strong and wide awake and will hotly contest the prize.

The slicing off of the federal spoils in this State has already divided the republicans into a number of factions, the leaders of which are now congregated here trying to undermine each other. The principal bone of contention is now the appointment of Judd to a seat in the Cabinet; and the result of the wrangle for and against will determine which of the coteries is to control the remainder of the patronage likely to be awarded to Illinois. The Judd men are led by Judd himself and Dr. [Charles Henry] Ray, of the Chicago *Tribune.* The anties by Judge Davis, L. Swett and Chas. Wilson, of the Chicago *Evening Journal.*

I have just learned that about two weeks ago a scandalous painting on canvas was received by Mrs. Lincoln per express from South Carolina. It represented Mr. Lincoln with a rope around his neck, his feet chained and his body adorned with tar and feathers. Comment is unnecessary.

Among the latest Eastern arrivals are W. S. Wood, of your city[76]; W. W. Stephenson, of Pittsburg[h], Pa., and L[eander] Holmes,[77] of Oregon.

Springfield, 20 January 1861
[Cincinnati *Commercial*, 24 January 1861]

On Monday last [January 16] I despatched to the *Commercial* the following item:

"The pressure for Judd is growing tremendous. If the Hoosiers want to save Smith let them hurry out here."

It was, obviously, upon this warning that Messrs. A. H. Conner, Chairman of the Republican State Central Committee, Wm. T. Otto, and R. R. Coppin [William G. Coffin], put a change of linen in their carpet-bags, one day last week, and started. They arrived early yesterday morning. Mr. Conner, having been here once before, some six weeks ago, was evidently anxious to hide his second visit from your correspondent, who had advertised him and his doings pretty liberally in the columns of the *Commercial.* He did not exactly try the non-registering dodge, but entered his name in an altogether illegible manner. The characteristics of the outward man being, however, known to every body, was also of very little practical benefit. For not only the fact of the presence of himself and companions, but also the object of their joint mission, leaked out in the course of the very morning of their arrival.

It appeared that they actually came out here in view of the unfavorable turn Smith's prospects had taken within the last fortnight. Being determined that Caleb B. should represent Hoosierdom in the Cabinet, the "Commercial" and that "vile conspiracy" to the contrary, notwithstanding, they resolved to push matters with Abraham to a head. Nor did they find that their visit was any too early. They soon ascertained that their favorite was all but unhorsed by the zealous, wide-awake partisans of Judd, and that the chances of the latter were at least equal, if not better than those of the former. To their credit be it said, that they lost no time whatever, but rolled up their sleeves and went to work with a will. Nearly all day yesterday they plied the President elect with both verbal and written arguments bearing upon the propriety of a tender of a *porte feuille* [portfolio] to the aforesaid "pure patriot and distinguished statesman." Nor was this all. They soon found sympathizers in the shape of prominent politicians from this State, who were here to counteract the efforts of Judd's friends, and a mutual adaptation of plans and junction of forces was readily accomplished. The result of these joint operations I am unable to indicate at the time of this writing. Mr. Lincoln holds the matter under advisement. I venture to say, however, that persistency and exaction is not likely to succeed with him, and that to those who ask most he will grant least.

The anti Judd element of this State is now concentrated here in unusually strong numbers. It is headed by Judge Davis, of Bloomington; L. Swett, one of the electors at large, and Charles Colsen [Wilson], of the Chicago *Evening Journal*, Gov. Yates, and others. But every inch of ground is most vigorously contested by Judd's adherents led by such expert tacticians as Ebenezer Peck and Dr. [Charles Henry] Ray, of the Chicago *Tribune*.

Judge Kellogg, the well known Congressman from this State, was landed here by this morning's Eastern train. The Judge is a relentless anti-compromise member of the Committee of Thirty-Three, and it is understood that he comes out here to ascertain definitely and positively the views of the President elect upon the different remedies prescribed by the Thirty-Three. Mr. Kellogg is said to be strongly opposed to Judd's appointment, and likely to remonstrate against it during his present stay.

I just learned of an incident of Mr. Chase's visit, that although not [the] latest news, is still worth relating. The Ex-Governor attended, it will be remembered, divine service in company with the President elect. During the prayer preceding the sermon, the pastor invoked the blessings of Heaven upon the "President elect and his Constitutional advisers." The last expression had hardly escaped his lips when the whole congregation turned and fixed their eyes upon Governor Chase, of whose presence they were aware.

A striking illustration of the brutality that distinguishes the conduct of Southerners towards Northerners has just come to my knowledge. A box shipped from Charleston, S. C., and directed to Mrs. Lincoln, was received here a few days ago. On being opened it was found to contain a picture representing Mr. Lincoln with a rope around his neck, his feet manacled, and his back adorned with a coat of tar and feathers. I am informed, but find it hard to believe, that the shippers were ladies.

Mr. Baber has returned to his customary haunts in Columbus. Messrs. J. W. Donohue, of your city,[78] and P. Mitchell, of Dayton, are here.

January 21, 1861

Springfield, 21 January 1861

[New York *Herald*, 26 January 1861]

Never since the 6th of November has there been so much commotion among our politicians as within the last twenty-four hours. Such a buzzing, buttonholing, running to and fro was never before heard of. So many rumors, reports, conjectures and presumptions were never before afloat. It was a real harvest day for gossipers. At all points, groups of eager talkers and listeners could be seen. Every nook and corner of the hotels were occupied by individuals with grave and excited countenances, and busy, restless tongues. At the Chenery [House], especially, strange scenes were enacted in the course of the afternoon. At about three o'clock there might have been seen the President elect standing in one corner with General [James K.] Morehead [Moorhead], of Pennsylvania, M. C.[79] In another, sat portly Judge [David] Davis, with A. H. Connor, of Indiana. In a third, Alexander Cummings, editor of the New York *World*, was observed in a conversation with W[illiam] T. Bascom, Chairman of the Ohio Republican State Central Committee.[80] In a fourth, Wm. Kellogg, member of Congress from this State, was holding forth to a circle of legislators—in short, there was evidence all around of an unusually numerous influx of prominent men from abroad and extraordinary excitement among the politicians at home.

And what was the upshot of all this evident flutter and agitation? There was, in the first place, the visit of Judge Kellogg, the Illinois member of the Committee of Thirty-three. It had become known that he came here to obtain the endorsement of the President elect of some one of the compromise propositions now before Congress. It having always been supposed that Mr. Kellogg had been one of the most immovable of the republican members of the House, and hence the announcement of his faltering produced no little amazement. It was further known that he had been almost constantly with Mr. Lincoln since his arrival on yesterday morning, and that the Congressional recommendations for settling the present difficulties were the main subject of their consultations. The radical republicans were indignant at the supposed sudden weak-backness of Kellogg and his seeming attempts to exact the consent of the President elect to compromise and concession. A number of members of the Legislature from the northern part of the State forthwith sent a telegraphic inquiry to Mr. Farnsworth,[81] at Washington, to ascertain whether the [members of the] Congressional delegation from this State were really ready to yield. The negative reply at once propped up their hopes, and they at once went to work to counteract the effect of Kellogg's counsels.

They soon found, however, that their apprehensions had been groundless. They learned that, although Mr. Kellogg suggested the propriety of taking up with the border States' propositions,[82] after slight modifications, he merely intended the suggestion as a feeler, and that he was far from pressing Mr. Lincoln to accede to anything inconsistent with the spirit of the republican faith as reflected in the Chicago platform. Mr. Kellogg himself pronounced, indeed, all reports to the contrary "unmitigated lies," during the afternoon, which emphatic declaration set him all right again with his republican friends.

Another cause of to-day's excitement was the advent early this morning of Gen. J. K. Moorhead, M. C. from the Allegheny district, Pa., accompanied by "Mother [William J.] Robinson," a well known political character of the Keystone State,[83] and Alexander Cummings, editor of the New York *World*. That the former's visit was in relation to the Cameron incident leaked out without delay. The appearance of a third delegation representing his claims to a seat in the Cabinet, in the wake of Senator Cowan and J. P. Sanderson, was not construed, however, into a very auspicious symptom as to the probability of his ultimate appointment. It is looked upon as warranting the presumption that constant appliances are necessary to prevent the triumph of the opposition.

Mr. Moorhead sought and obtained separate interviews, extending over several hours, both in the forenoon and afternoon.[84] His return East on the evening train proved that the object of his journey—viz., to ascertain something definite in reference to Cameron matters, and the views of the President elect on the remedies best applied in the present crisis—was speedily accomplished.

As to Mr. Cummings, of the *World*, he was introduced to Mr. Lincoln in the morning and called upon by him at his hotel in the afternoon. Mr. Cummings is said to have come here as the representative of commercial conservatism, intermixed with party, to respectfully submit to the President the views and wishes in regard to the secession question of the class of which the *World* is presumed to be the mouthpiece. It is also stated that

Mr. Cummings, true to his Pennsylvania interests, took occasion to urge Mr. Cameron's cause. He re-embarked for the East in company with General Moorehead [Moorhead].

The Indiana agitators for Smith are still here. They have formed a sort of offensive and defensive alliance with the anti-Judd men from this State, now concentrated here in full force under the leadership of Judge Davis, Kellogg, Swett, Governor Yates and others. Judd himself is here, and leads his partisans in person. The strife for supremacy is fierce, and a source of great tribulation to the President elect. A decisive battle is expected to be fought within the next forty-eight hours.

A rather unexpected visitor to Mr. Lincoln arrived here to-day, in the person of Senor M. Romero,[85] the Mexican Minister at Washington. The object of his journey is to make himself familiar, in an unofficial way, with the policy of the incoming administration in reference to his own country, and exchange views as to the probable effect of the formation of an independent Southern confederacy upon Mexican affairs. He was received with great courtesy, not only by the President elect, but by all the State officers, who vied with each other in extending the hospitalities of Springfield. He will proceed hence to St. Louis.

Martin H. Cassell[86] has been appointed one of the Canal Commissioners of this State, in place of Dr. [Charles Henry] Ray, of the Chicago *Tribune*, whose term of office expired the other day.

Mr. [William T.] Bascom's visit is believed to be bearing upon the question of Mr. Chase's appointment to the Cabinet. It is claimed by well informed parties that he brought the ex-Governor's final declination to Mr. Lincoln.

Springfield, 21 January 1861
[Cincinnati *Commercial*, 25 January 1861]

No better evidence in support of the fact, reiterated in several of my preceding letters, that the appointment of Senator Cameron to the Cabinet was, at best, but a remotely possible contingency, could be furnished than the rapid succession of delegations representing his interest to the President elect. Senator Cowan and J. P. Sanderson have hardly left, and yet already this morning an additional set of propagandists for the great Pennsylvania cabalist made their advent. It consists of Gen. J. K. [Moorehead], M. C. from Allegheny District, "mother" [William J.] Robinson, another political celebrity from the Keystone State, and Alexander Cummings, who, although he may be considered a *de facto* New Yorker from being one of the Editors of the *Daily World*, is still, at heart, a Pennsylvanian, and devotedly attached to the political fortunes of Cameron. Mr. Moorehead sought and obtained an interview with Mr. Lincoln immediately after his arrival. Mr. Cummings was introduced in the course of the forenoon, and called upon by Mr. Lincoln at his hotel in the afternoon.

As to the special object of their mission, it is understood that they come here armed with formidable documents in the shape of petitions, signed by two-thirds of the Pennsylvania delegation to Chicago and a majority of the Republican members of the Legislature, and recommending Cameron for the Treasury Department. Mr. Cummings, it is said, also took occasion to express the sentiments of the religious conservatives his paper claims to represent in reference to the secession question.[87]

The visitors were received and treated with great civility by Mr. Lincoln. But, like Cowan and Sanderson, they failed to secure his positive committal on the Cameron question. They returned East on the evening train.

The most interesting movement on the political chess board in this vicinity at the present moment, is the struggle between the Judd and Smith factions. The quantity of buzzing, whispering, button-holeing, and boreing done by their respective partisans, is wonderful.—But secret machinations of every description and without number are employed to achieve success. The anti-Judd leaders of this State are now all here and operate with a good deal of skill and vigor. Judge Davis, Gov. Yates, L. Swett, Judge Kellogg, M. C., especially distinguish themselves among them. They seem to co-operate with the Smith delegation from Indiana, who are evidently determined not to leave Springfield until their object is fully accomplished. The united forces appear to be too strong for the Juddites to cope with, although their chieftain has placed himself in person at the head of his followers. To-day at least the indications are that their defeat is a rather probable emergency.

A good many rumors have been afloat yesterday and to-day in regard to the purport of the unexpected visit of Judge Kellogg from Washington to the President elect. It was asserted by usually well informed parties that he had come here to persuade Mr. Lincoln into a sort of semi-official endorsement of the Border State propositions. I am, however, to-day enabled to state, by authority, that *he has not and will not approach Mr. Lincoln with any such intentions.* I feel safe, indeed, in claiming to know that his main object is to thwart Judd's aspirations to the Cabinet.

One of the most prominent Republican politicians of this State addressed a direct inquiry to the President elect within the last forty-eight hours as to his views on the Border State propositions. His frank reply was *that they would only be worth noticing in case a proposition for a Constitutional amendment, requiring the consent of two-thirds of all the States to any additional acquisition of territory, should be incorporated.* This is authentic.

I learn from a direct source, that on yesterday Mr. Lincoln, in his vexation at the relentless obtrusions of both the Judd and Smith factions, told his persecutors, with more emphasis than his usual good nature, that *"no further Cabinet appointments would be definitely* agreed upon until after his arrival at Washington City."

This morning's Daily [Illinois] State Journal contains an elaborate leader, which I know to have been inspired by the "highest authority." It treats of the "right of coercion and making war on a State." It is rather foggy, but evidently means to convey the following propositions:

1. The right to secede does not exist.

2. Its assertion by State Legislatures and Conventions is of no consequence, as all enactments to that effect are null and void.

3. The President of the United States is bound to enforce the Federal laws with all the means at his command.

4. The incoming President will discharge this duty. He will not send a Federal army to invade any State for the purpose of exacting the repeal of unconstitutional enactments, *vi et armis*, but simply see that due respect is rendered to the revenue and other Federal laws.

M. Romero, the Mexican Minister at Washington, is here. He brought a letter of congratulation from President [Benito] Juarez to Mr. Lincoln.[88] The letter is couched in respectful, but rather pompous terms. The Mexican Senor has been the object of general courtesy and attention, both of the President elect and the many prominent political characters now sojourning here.[89]

Springfield, 21 January 1861
[New York *Herald*, 22 January 1861]

Another delegation, representing the Cameron interest, and consisting of General J. K. [Moorhead], M. C., and Alex Cummings, of the N.Y. *World*, arrived here this morning. They had a protracted private interview with the President elect this afternoon. Their exertions in behalf of Cameron are seconded by the anti-Judd faction of the State, headed by Judge Kellogg, M. C., Judge Davis, and Governor Yates.

One of the of republican members of the Legislature from the four republican Congressional districts of this State telegraphed to Mr. Farnsworth, M. C., to ascertain the feeling at Washington as to the compromise propositions, and his reply was, "No concessions."

The Indiana delegation are still here and untiring in their pressure for Smith.

The excitement produced by the presence of the many distinguished pipe-layers from abroad, and the strife between the several factions, is intense.

Blanton Duncan, the Chairman of the Bell Everett State Committee of Kentucky,[90] has written a letter to the Chairman of the Democratic Central Committee of this State, in which he says that no compromise likely to be offered by the North will arrest the secession movement, and that Kentucky will be out of the Union in less than three months.

James W. Sheahan,[91] the right bower of Senator Douglas, and formerly editor of the Chicago *Times*, is here, expressing strong Union sentiments.

Mr. Powers [Romero], the Mexican Minister at Washington, is paying a visit to Mr. Lincoln. He was the recipient of marked courtesy, although his visit has not a political bearing.

W[illiam] T. Bascom, the Chairman of the Ohio State Central Committee, is in town.

January 22, 1861

Springfield, 22 January 1861

[Cincinnati *Commercial*, 23 January 1861]

The President elect said, within the last 48 hours, to a prominent politician of this State, that the Border States proposition would be worth considering only in case a provision could be incorporated prohibiting the acquisition of any more territory without the consent of two-thirds of the States. Mr. Kellogg, M. C., authorizes a contradiction of the report that he came here to urge Mr. Lincoln's endorsement of any of the compromise measures now before Congress. Mr. Lincoln threw out a strong hint yesterday, in repelling the impertinent advances of certain politicians who are pressing Cabinet appointments. He said that Bates and Seward were the only members directly agreed upon, and that none others would be until after he arrived in Washington.

R. A. Cameron,[92] D. C. Branham,[93] and W. March,[94] a special committee of the Indiana Legislature, arrived here this morning, to extend an invitation to Mr. Lincoln to pass through Indianapolis on his way to Washington. He received them very courteously, and expressed himself willing to comply with their request. A definite answer will be given in the course of the next fortnight. The Committee of Invitation are strongly opposed to Smith, and would like to see him supplanted by Colfax. The Illinois Republican delegation to Congress, telegraphed again to-day, to make no concessions, and pass no resolutions. The Republican and Democratic members of the

Legislature, to-day, made a compromise, and passed bills calling a Constitutional Convention, and re-districting the State. W. T. Bascom is understood to be operating for Schenck.

Springfield, 22 January 1861

[New York *Herald*, 28 January 1861]

The *Daily State Journal* of this morning contains a lengthy leader under the heading "The Right of Coercion and Making War on a State," which not only bears external evidence of being carefully prepared under the eyes of the President elect, but is so universally received by republican politicians as an authoritative exposition of Mr. Lincoln's views, that I feel fully justified in subjoining its substance:—

The article begins with a refutation of some of the points made in President Buchanan's last annual message and Attorney General Black's judicial opinion on the right to secede. The following propositions are then made:

1. No State has the right to secede.
2. It is the duty of the President of the United States to enforce the laws thereof.
3. The first republican President will discharge that duty fearlessly and faithfully.
4. In its discharge he will confine himself to enforcing the laws in which the country at large is interested, viz: the collection of the revenue and the protection of the federal property. He will not invade a State to secure the repeal of unconstitutional enactments by its Legislature, but merely resist aggressive encroachments upon the federal authority.

The article is not very luminous. The *animus*, however, is clear. It breathes the determination of the incoming administration to do its duty, and oppose the resumption by the Southern States of the sovereign powers delegated to the federal government at all hazards, and assert its authority with all means at its command.

Several significant declarations have been made by the President elect within the last forty-eight hours. A prominent republican took occasion to allude in his presence to the many rumors afloat as to his readiness to endorse the border States' propositions. His remarks elicited a vigorous reassertion of the strict adherence of the President elect to the Chicago platform; that the policy of the republican administration would be conducted on that basis, and that the border States' propositions should be entertained by republicans both in and out of Congress only in case a constitutional prohibition of the acquisition of any more territory without the consent of two-thirds of the States could be simultaneously secured.

The importunities of the different cliques now engaged here in pushing the claims of divers aspirants to Cabinet appointments drew out another noteworthy dictum from Mr. Lincoln, who seems to be growing justly impatient with the solicitousness of certain parties. He stated in as many words that in the selection of his constitutional advisers he had to consult the feelings and wishes, not of a few friends, but of the people at large; that Messrs. Bates and Seward were the only members of the Cabinet definitely determined upon, and that it was highly probable that no other names would be officially announced until after his arrival in the federal capital.

Judge Kellogg is greatly mortified at the character of the reports circulated and credited so generally during the last three days as to the object of his visit to Springfield. He has to-day authorized a flat and unequivocal contradiction of the rumor that he came out here to urge upon Mr. Lincoln the propriety of committing himself on some of the compromise propositions, in order to secure their endorsement by the republican members of Congress. He also denies the truthfulness of the statement that he came here to counteract the efforts of the friends of N. B. Judd in connection with the Cabinet. He says that his back is as sound as ever, and seems to deem attempts on the part of any person to influence the action of the President elect upon the Cabinet question no less than impertinent intermeddling.

Before this contradiction was given out a number of republican leaders had again telegraphed to Messrs. Farnsworth, Washburn[e][95] and Lovejoy, at Washington, to sound their feelings on the compromise issue. They replied laconically, but unmistakeably: "Make no compromises—pass no resolutions." This telegraphic exhortation will doubtless put a stop, for the present, to the contemplated legislative action on the subject of disunion.

Another Indiana delegation made their appearance this morning, consisting of a legislative committee, appointed under a joint resolution, to invite Mr. Lincoln to pass through the capital of the Hoosier State while on his way to Washington. They were received by the President elect in the course of the forenoon. In reply to their invitation, he stated that circumstances had as yet prevented him from definitely selecting any particular route; that he had seriously thought of going via Indianapolis, and would let them know his final decision in the course of the next fortnight.

A rich revelation has been made in regard to the committee in question. It seems that the Speaker of the lower house of the Indiana Legislature

[Cyrus M. Allen] had flattered himself at one time with an idea of going into the Cabinet, and that it was only with a view to obtain a general legislative endorsement that he accepted his present position. After being elected, however, he found that the friends of Smith had voted for him merely to get him out of their way in Springfield. Knowing that Conner and others were out here, belaboring the President elect in favor of Smith, he appointed, out of revenge, none but strong anti-Smith men on the Committee of Invitation, in order to paralyze the exertions of the former. It is stated, indeed, that the members improved their opportunity, and entered an emphatic protest against Smith's appointment during their stay, and that apparently with good effect. One of them, at least, asserted most strenuously that Caleb would never enjoy the honors and emoluments of the Secretaryship of the Interior.

W. T. Bascom, Chairman of the Ohio State Central Committee, is here operating for Schen[c]k.

Dr. W. W. Gitt, a Virginia delegate to the Chicago Convention, is here to demonstrate his own fitness for office under the cover of advocating the claims of Montgomery Blair to the Cabinet.

Frank P. Blair, Jr., has just arrived from St. Louis.

Springfield, 22 January 1861
[New York *Herald*, 23 January 1861]

A committee of Indiana legislators are here to invite Mr. Lincoln to pass through Indianapolis on his way to Washington. He promised a definite answer within the next fortnight. The committee are all strong anti-Smith men.

The Illinois delegation to Congress again telegraphed to-day to republican members of the Legislature to make no concession and pass no resolutions.

The President elect said, within the last forty-eight hours, to a prominent politician of this State, that the border States proposition would be worth considering only in case a provision could be incorporated prohibiting the acquisition of any more territory without the consent of two thirds of the States.

Mr. Kellogg authorizes a contradiction of the report that he came here to urge Mr. Lincoln's endorsement of any of the compromise measures now before Congress, and to oppose Judd.

Mr. Lincoln threw out a strong hint yesterday, in replying to the impertinent advances of certain parties pressing Cabinet appointments, that Bates and Seward were the only members definitely agreed upon, and that none others would be until after his arrival in Washington.

Springfield, 22 January 1861
[San Francisco *Bulletin*, 14 February 1861]

LINCOLN'S PREMIER, SEWARD

The news of the formal acceptance by Senator Seward of the Secretaryship of State, tendered to him by the President elect some time in December, has doubtless reached you ere this will come to hand. Although the fact of the tender had been known to the more intimate friends of Mr. Lincoln for many weeks, but few of them believed that Mr. Seward would be found willing to serve in the capacity in question. It is now known here, indeed, that the New York Senator's predilections ran in a different direction, and that he was made to yield only by the most urgent and persistent appeals of his oldest and most confidential advisers.

The official announcement of this acceptance in the Albany *Evening Journal* was telegraphed hither nearly two days in advance of the mail carrying Mr. Seward's formal advice to Mr. Lincoln. The exultation produced among the many Republican politicians from all parts of the Northwest, sojourning here in attendance on the Legislature and the President elect, was wonderful. They congratulated each other as heartily as though the Presidential battle had been won over again. It added immensely to the popularity of Mr. Lincoln. For nearly three days his private office was all but constantly filled with prominent characters, expressing their gratification at the auspicious intelligence. They all appeared to think that, with the support of such a main pillar as Seward, the success of the incoming Administration is certain.

GOVERNOR CHASE AND THE CABINET

The question whether or not Mr. Chase will consent to exercise the functions of Secretary of the Treasury, after the 4th of March, is still unsettled. His friends, upon whose counsels his ultimate decision will depend, seem to be very much divided on the subject. Some contend that the United States Senate offers a much larger and more gratifying field for the application of Mr. Chase's eminent abilities, while others claim that all these considerations should be forgotten in view of the imperiled condition of the Federal Government and the country at large. The matter is most likely to be definitely settled in the course of the present week.

In the face of the authoritative announcement of the informal offer of the Treasury Department to Mr. Chase, it must certainly appear strange that parties should come here from Ohio to urge the appointment of other representatives of that State to the Cabinet before his definite declination has been made known. Such has nevertheless been the case. Ben Eggleston, the well-known Cincinnati politician, came here last Friday [January 18] with a petition signed by several Electors, and recommending D. K. Cart[t]er of Cleveland, and on Saturday R. L. Baber of Columbus, a member of the Republican State Central Committee, arrived with a similar document endorsed by a number of Ohio Legislators, in favor of R. D. [C.] Schen[c]k, in his pocket. Both these gentlemen soon found out that Chase and no one else will represent the Buckeye State in the Cabinet, and hence, did not make a very protracted stay.

THE CAMERON IMBROGLIO AGAIN

That the probability of the selection of Senator Cameron as one of Mr. Lincoln's Ministers is by no means great, is fully shown by the advent this morning of another Pennsylvania delegation in the wake of Senator Cowan and J. P. Sanderson, and likewise in the Cameron interest. It consists of General J. R. [K.] [Moorhead], Pittsburg[h], Pa., and Alexander Cummings, formerly one of the proprietors of the Philadelphia *Evening Bulletin*, and now of the New York *World*. This visit proves conclusively that constant appliances are thought necessary to secure the final recognition of his (Cameron's) claims. Yet, this continued pressure in his favor to the contrary notwithstanding, I think that he will be substituted in the end by a man that will give more general satisfaction.

A REPUBLICAN WRANGLE

A bitter strife for the mastery has been raging for some time in this Republican Mecca between two factions, battling for the success of the Cabinet aspirations of their respective leaders—Norman B. Judd, of this State, and Caleb B. Smith, of Indiana. Early in December a Hoosier delegation, headed by A. H. Connor, Chairman of the Republican State Central Committee, came here, and with more energy than modesty demanded the award of a place in the Cabinet to the aforesaid Smith. They received no definite promises, but warm assurances that their wishes would be duly considered and probably fulfilled. They returned quite elated, and spread the news all over their State, so that Smith's appointment was universally looked upon as a certain though future contingency.

But in the meantime the friends of Judd, a prominent Chicago lawyer— Chairman of the State Central Committee—and an old and warm personal friend and supporter of the President elect, were not idle. They quietly matured their plans to unhorse Smith and put their own champion in his place, and upon the meeting of the Legislature commenced executing them. For the last fortnight they have been busy like beavers, and made such advances under the supreme command of Judd himself, who has been here all that time ostensibly engaged in the Supreme Court, as to create a general conviction, even in well-informed circles, that their efforts would be crowned with success. On Saturday last, it was even asserted that, the formal offer of the Secretaryship of the Interior had been made, notwithstanding the remonstrances of Judge Davis, Gov. Yates, Leonard Swett, and other anti-Judd leaders of this State. But all this was unexpectedly changed within the last forty-eight hours. Another Indiana delegation, again headed by Mr. Connor and other prominent Hoosiers, who had been informed of the maneuvers of the Judd [supporters], and taking a sudden alarm, rushed over here in hot haste to thwart the consummation of the Smith cabal. The Judd men having strongly sympathized with the anti-Cameron movement, the Pennsylvania delegation they found here at once concluded an offensive and defensive alliance with them. The anti-Juddites also joined issue with them, and the united forces, led on by master tacticians, have made a succession of vigorous onslaughts upon their antagonists with visible success, and at the moment of this writing the result of the squabble is very doubtful. An intense excitement exists, both among the participants in and the lookers-on this interesting struggle. The President elect being thereby placed between two fires, finds his position rather uncomfortable. I dare say that he is heartily tired of the annoyance to which the cross-firing of the contending factions exposes him.

THE SOUTHERN MEMBERS OF LINCOLN'S CABINET

It will be seen from the above that Mr. Lincoln is far from resting on a bed of roses, free from thorns, at the present time. But, although his Northern supporters have proved somewhat troublesome in the construction of the Cabinet, a greater source of perplexity is yet the selection of its Southern members. It cannot be concealed, indeed, that he finds sound southern timber exceedingly scarce. While he can complain in the North of an oppressive abundance of names, just the reverse prevails in the South. A number of individuals, it is true, have been suggested to him from that section of the country; but those among them whose capacity and worthiness would make their selection desirable, are not only supposed to be unwilling to serve, but shown to have lately assumed a position of such decided hostility towards the party that elevated Mr. Lincoln to power, as to become utterly impossible. Material of inferior quality could probably be obtained; but such is considered worse than nothing, as the case now stands. I think it more likely that no further Southern appointments, in addition to that of Mr. Bates, will be made until after the arrival of the President elect in Washington, and due consultation with the Republican leaders therein assembled.

COMPLETION OF THE CABINET

I am able to state most positively that Messrs. Seward and Bates are the only members of the Cabinet that have been definitely determined upon and assigned positions. Within the next ten days, however, two additions are expected to be made. Their character will depend altogether on the upshot of the Chase question and the Judd and Smith complication.

A CALIFORNIA DELEGATION

D. Crittenden of your city arrived here on Saturday, accompanied by James Churchmen and Sam Gamage, who had been sojourning in St. Louis since their first visit to the President elect. The trio had several interviews with the latter, and went away apparently satisfied. They did their best towards the representation of California in the Cabinet by Mr. [Eugene L.] Sullivan, but I know without the desired effect. Col. Fremont alone has a chance in that respect.

Mr. Gamage had a native Californian in the shape of a son some five years old with him. The youngster was duly introduced to the President elect, whom he coolly informed that he had been a "Bell-Everett man."

On informing Mr. Gamage that I had acquainted your readers with the earnest declaration that himself and companions had made, to the effect that they had come without any desire for or expectation of office, he replied: "They won[']t believe a word of it in San Francisco."

DEPARTURE OF THE PRESIDENT ELECT FOR WASHINGTON

Mr. Lincoln will start for Washington on or about the 13th of February. His route is not yet selected. A number of railroad companies have tendered special trains. He will probably travel by way of Pittsburg[h] and Harrisburg.

Mrs. Lincoln is now in New York making purchases for the White House. She will return in the course of a week, and accompany her spouse to the Federal Capital.

January 23, 1861

Springfield, 23 January 1861
[New York *Herald*, 24 January 1861]

Strong remonstrances against Chase's appointment have been received by the President elect from Pennsylvania and Maryland. The Pennsylvanians say they carried their State on the protective tariff question, and hence do not want an avowed free trader in the Cabinet.

Frank P. Blair arrived to-day. He says the day of compromise is gone, and the day of fighting come. He has no apprehension of the secession of Missouri.

W. W. Gitt, a Virginia delegate to the Chicago Convention,[96] is here to urge Montgomery Blair for the Cabinet, and secure something for himself.

Springfield, 23 January 1861

[New York *Herald*, 28 January 1861]

It is now nearly a month since the opening act of the Cameron melodrama was performed by the old stager himself in this village. The newspaper reading public having been treated diurnally from that [time] up to the present date with accounts of the progress of the tragic-comical play, a surfeit may be well presumed. It is true a constant shifting of scenes and change of actors relieved the monotony of the performance to some extent. But in these piping times the appetite of the public for novel excitements is so keen that such protracted ringing the changes on a single individual and a single subject cannot but produce a sort of intellectual nausea. It has been your correspondent's devout prayer, indeed, for many a day already, that the curtain be dropped in this all but farcical piece of political chicanery. Yet it seems that there is to be no end of it. Instead of a denouement, a great entanglement is *in prospectu.* The number of performers is to be increased, and the cabalistic knots double tied. Seward and Weed are now to be dragged upon the stage; at least, I learn to-day from a direct source that the Premier [Seward] has been solicited by the President elect to communicate his views as to the propriety of Cameron's appointment, and that his reply, strongly endorsing the Pennsylvania aspirant, has been received within the last forty-eight hours. I am further informed that this favorable certificate of character is but a portion of a programme agreed upon in Washington among Cameron's whippers-in to secure an ultimate recognition of his claims. Sufficient time will be allowed for its operation upon the Presidential mind, after the lapse of which a grand and last assault is to be made by the master tactician of the [Albany] *Evening Journal* [Weed] in case "Old Abe" should still be restive. A second visit of Thurlow Weed is, indeed, expected to take place toward the latter part of this week (the Washington correspondents are all mistaken as to the time of his intended arrival), when it is hoped the man that made Mr. Lincoln's Premier will find a place for the disconsolate Simon.

I trust that the great Albany lobbyist will settle this vexation in one way or another. There are many individuals to be found about here that think it might have been done much sooner, with credit to both Mr. Lincoln and Mr. Cameron, and that the variety of reports and rumors circulated these four weeks as to the nature of their relations did not by any means raise either in the opinion of the nation.

The Chase question is almost as badly mixed up as the Cameron complication. Every day brings a new version of what occurred between the ex-Governor and the President elect during the former's visit. To-day an otherwise well informed politician of this State told me an entirely new one, insisting, of course, that it alone was entitled to credit. According to it, Mr. Chase availed himself of a standing invitation and came out here to remonstrate against the alleged fishing of Cameron for the object. The President elect, who is, and has always been, a warm admirer of the Ohio statesman, listened respectfully to the arguments of the free trader against the protectionist, but in his frank, blunt manner asked him the rather embarrassing question, "How he himself would like to accept a seat in the Cabinet?" The circumstances of the occasion rendered, of course, a declination of the proposition imperative. This, it is said, was the very thing Abraham—whom this adroit movement stamps an intuitive diplomatist—was driving at.

However this may be, it is certain that Chase's reported appointment is calling forth as many protesting demonstrations as that of Cameron. For the last week politicians from the southern part of Ohio have been besieging the President elect with petitions against Chase and for some more conservative man. The Pennsylvanians that visited Springfield also showed a great anxiety to pay him back for his opposition to Cameron by making vigorous remonstrances. They urged that the Presidential battle had been fought and won on the protective tariff issue, and that it would at once discredit the incoming administration in the eyes of the protectionists of their State. That Seward is also averse to the colleagueship of Chase is well established by the fact that the representatives of the New York radicals—George Opdyke, Judge Hogeboom and Hiram Barney—visited Gov. Chase both before and after coming out here, and pressed his cause with manifest enthusiasm.

Frank P. Blair is now paying a second visit to Mr. Lincoln. Frank is down on all proposed concessions and compromises. He says they cannot possibly stay the tide of secession, but only weaken and demoralize the North. He evidently thinks "Fight we must, and fight we shall," and is ready to buckle on his armor and draw his sword. On the other hand, he does not seem to apprehend the engulfing of his own State in the vortex of disunion. He believes the Union sentiment strong enough to frown down all attempts at such by demagogues and traitors like Green,[97] Polk,[98] Gov. Jackson[99] and others.

To-morrow both houses of the Legislature will make an excursion to the neighboring city of Bloomington, for the purpose of attending the opening of the State Normal School. A grand spree may be expected, as the city authorities will foot the bills.

Springfield, 23 January 1861[100]

[Cincinnati *Commercial*, 26 January 1861]

Mr. [A. H.] Conner and his two squires had hardly retired from the field of their labors in behalf of Smith, in the course of night before last, when another trio of Indiana politicians loomed up in the persons of Messrs. Branham, March and Cameron, constituting a special committee, appointed under a joint resolution of the Indiana Legislature to invite the President elect to visit the Capital of their State, on his journey to Washington. They delivered their errand during yesterday morning. The President elect was, of course, glad to see them, and receive the courteous and flattering invitation of which they were the bearers. They did not, however, succeed in obtaining its unconditional acceptance. They were frankly told by Mr. Lincoln, that he had as yet determined upon no particular route, but had, nevertheless, already thought of going via Indianapolis, and would probably conclude to do so. A definite answer at an early date was promised.

The members of the Committee expressed themselves delighted with the manner of their reception by the President elect, and pronounced him a "perfect brick." They all three protested most emphatically, that the tender of the hospitalities of the body they represent, was the only business attended to by them during their stay. It is, however, rumored that they improved their opportunity to convey to the right quarter their notions as to the fitness of the Hon. Caleb B. Smith, for a seat in the Cabinet,—which, I dare say, is viewed by them in the exact light, the [Cincinnati] "Commercial" has been throwing upon the subject during the last three weeks. Whether this report is true or not, yet it is certain, that they were selected with an eye to the efforts Conner & Co. were known to be making out here for the great railroad manager [Smith]. The Speaker of the [Indiana] House of Representatives [Cyrus M. Allen], it is said, was himself an aspirant to Cabinet honors and profits, and was only elected to his present position owing to the desire of Smith members of the Legislature, to get him out of the way of their favorite. He found out the true motive of his elevation to the Chair too late to get the start of Smith, and hence, appointed unrelenting Anti-Smith men on the Committee. An unfavorable influence as to Smith's prospects might well be drawn from the fact, that one of the Committee stated with a good deal of vigor after the interview with Mr. Lincoln *that Caleb B. would never go into the Cabinet.*

Some of the Cameron partizans in this latitude have apparently derived great comfort from and felt in fine spirits ever since the official announcement of Senator Seward's appointment to the Secretaryship of State. They argue that Seward's well known intimacy with Cameron renders the latter's triumph in the protracted wrangle about his claims to the Cabinet certain, as the Premier's advice would be solicited and acted upon with reference to its further composition. They even say that Gen. Morehead [Moorhead] came here with Seward's indorsement of Cameron's aspirations, and that Mr. Lincoln is now so closely cornered, that even should he feel indisposed to gratify the wishes of the former's friends, an escape is no longer possible. Whatever foundation there may be to this assertion, your correspondent is free to confess that he is heartily tired of this Cameron cabal, and that it would do no harm to either the President elect or Cameron to put a stop to all the contradictory reports as to their mutual relations by permitting an authoritative exposition of the merits of the case.

Your St. Louis and Chicago exchanges doubtlessly furnished you sufficient evidence of the general credit the report received that Judge Kellogg had repaired hither from Washington to ascertain the views of the President elect upon the different compromise propositions now before Congress, and that the result of his mission would determine the action of the Republican members in the premises. The story was so universally told and believed that Mr. Kellogg was fairly overwhelmed with remonstrances against his supposed attempt to commit Mr. Lincoln, by Republican members of the Legislature, during yesterday. In response to them, he authorized a flat and full denial of both imputations, the benefit of which is herewith cheerfully granted.

Representatives Washburn[e], Lovejoy and Farnsworth again telegraphed on yesterday to the Republican majority of the Legislature "not to make any concessions nor pass any resolutions." Trumbull is also reported to have despatched to the same effect. These exhortations will probably preclude legislation on federal subjects for the present.

Frank P. Blair is here on a second visit to the President elect. He has no faith whatever in the practicability and desirability of compromises, and takes no pains to conceal his conviction that the present difficulties will have to be settled with the sword.

Dr. W. W. Gitt, one of the Virginia delegates to the Chicago Convention, is trying to convince Mr. Lincoln of the propriety of a proper reward of past services.

W. M. Edwards, Esq., of Terre Haute, Ind., arrived here yesterday morning.

January 24, 1861

Springfield, 24 January 1861
[New York Herald, 25 January 1861]

There is a strong rumor that Seward's endorsement of Cameron's claims has been received by the President elect. Weed is expected here every hour to bring the Cameron business to a head.

George G. Fogg, of New Hampshire, is paying a second visit to the President elect. He monopolized Mr. Lincoln's time throughout the day. His visit relates to the selection of the New England member of the Cabinet, and the action of the republican Congressmen upon the compromise propositions.

A Philadelphia delegation, consisting of [Dr.] H. G[ale] Smith, O. N. P. Parker,[101] P[eter] Ford and C[harles] Adams, arrived this morning to present the resolutions of a republican meeting, and a strong recommendation of Cameron for the Cabinet.

Mr. Lincoln talks of spending a few days in the country previous to his departure for Washington.

Mrs. Lincoln and son are expected home to-night.

January 25, 1861

Springfield, 25 January 1861
[New York Herald, 31 January 1861]

The political town talk is now turning about the efforts certain parties are making to entangle Mr. Lincoln in the controversy likely to distract Congress during the remainder of the session, upon the various compromise propositions now awaiting action in both houses. It is known that Mr. Lincoln has been plied for several days most vigorously, not only with written representations from prominent Eastern republicans of conservative predilections, but also with the verbal appeals of many of the distinguished visiters that lately made their appearance in this latitude. But as yet no signs of wavering or irresolution have become manifest. He evidently holds his ground as firmly at the present moment as he did ten weeks ago. Now as then, he gives it to be understood that he was elected on the anti-slavery extension issue; that he will profess and practise the faith whose followers elevated him to the Presidency, until he becomes convinced of its fallacy, not by threats, treason and rebellion, but his own sense of justice, and that he will hold himself altogether aloof from attempts to intermeddle with the strife of Congressional factions and the troubles of the present administration, until he shall have eventually assumed the reins of government.

It is true he takes no pains to conceal his views on the compromise prescriptions, compounded by the Congressional doctors at Washington. Any caller, seeking him under the aegis of a proper introduction, can elicit them by a few pertinent questions. But Mr. Lincoln will always tell the questioner that he expresses, on such occasions, the opinion of a private individual, and not that of the President of the United States. The strictures embodied in his replies upon the justness and practicability of the said suggestions as to the best mode of settling the present political difficulties will at once convince that as yet nothing has been brought forward that coincides with his hopes and wishes, and that he is not disposed, in the face of Southern lawlessness, to relish anything smacking of renunciation and humiliation.

The commander-in-chief of the cohorts of Pennsylvania office seekers has sent another storming party into the trenches that have been opened under his guidance around the President elect within the last four weeks. The assault is made this time by [Dr.] H. G[ale] Smith, O. H. P. Parker, P[eter] Ford and Charles Adams, all of the City of Brotherly Love and corrupt politicians. They came armed with unanimous resolutions of certain republican associations of Philadelphia, recommending Cameron for the Cabinet. The fact that this endorsement might have been sent under the auspices of Uncle Sam just as expeditiously and much more cheaply than carried by themselves warrants that the resolutions were merely the pretext, and the Philadelphia federal offices [were] the true objects, of their journey. But whatever the real motives of their pilgrimage may have been, it is certain that Abraham Lincoln did not give them any encouragement to realize any place hunting intentions, but contented himself with granting a short interview, in the presence of others, for the delivery of the resolutions only.[102]

The anti-Cameron feeling hereabouts has been greatly strengthened by his late somewhat mystical acceptance of the compromise ideas of his democratic colleague [Pennsylvania senator William Bigler].[103] That his Cabinet prospects are not improved by this unexpected exhibition of backsliding, and that the President elect most decidedly disapproves of Bigler's plan, are absolutely certain. What, then, did Cameron mean by placing himself in antagonism to the administration of which he desires to become a member, by the advocacy of a policy that will never be adopted by it? Many construe this strange movement on his part into a demonstration of the spitefulness he already expresses in consequence of the tardiness of the President elect in issuing his commission to the Cabinet.

It may now be considered definitely settled that Mr. Chase will not go into the Cabinet, and that hence the Buckeye State will remain unrepresented among Mr. Lincoln's constitutional advisers.

Colfax's friends have been making strong efforts in his behalf during the last week, by dint of Congressional, electoral and legislative certificates of character and fitness. But it is altogether improbable that he will secure the prize for which he is contending. The recollection of his Douglasism in '58, and Batesism previous to the Chicago Convention, is still rankling in certain minds, and likely to prevail over all other considerations.

[Gideon] Welles, of Connecticut, the aspirant to the same place on which Colfax has his eyes, has been most frequently mentioned by the public prints, and yet I know that he has never been earnestly thought of in connection with the Postmaster Generalship, or any other position in the Cabinet.

George G. Fogg, the well known New Hampshire politician, and Secretary of the National Republican Committee, has paid a second visit to the President elect in the course of to-day. He came to inform Mr. Lincoln of the true feeling prevailing among the republicans of New England and New York, and to impart any amount of backbone needed. Mr. Fogg is decidedly opposed to compromises and concessions, and thinks that all peace offerings will be spurned by the rebellious States. Some say that he improved his opportunity, and slipped a number of recommendations for office into Abraham's pocket. But I am inclined to doubt this. George G. knows better.

Mr. Jas. O. Putnam, the well known republican leader of your State [New York], has been here during the last twenty-four hours. The only thing that has thus far transpired in reference to the object of his mission is that he brought a whole satchel full of letters along—the reading of which to the President elect occupied some three hours this morning. They are supposed to contain partly the opinions of eminent Eastern men on the causes and remedies of the national crisis, and suggestions as to Cabinet and other appointments.

Mr. Oscanyan, the popular lecturer,[104] visited Springfield in the course of the present week. He called upon Mr. Lincoln, and was received with marked courtesy. He emphatically disclaims all aspirations to office.

Other hotel arrivals are: H. Hinkson, New York; H. S. Hubbell, Buffalo; F. S. Massey, Watertown, N.Y.; J. M. Anderson, H. Wallette and C. B. Robbins, of St. Louis; J. H. Terrill, Kentucky, and Col. W. Jameson, O. P. Gilham, R. A. Herr and R. L. Cobbs, of Ohio.

Springfield, 25 January 1861
[New York *Herald*, 26 January 1861]

It is evident that influences are now at work here to commit Mr. Lincoln on the border State propositions; but he as yet manifests no signs of yielding. He thinks it beyond his province to influence the action of Congress at the present time.

The clamor against Mr. Cameron has been strongly revived since his endorsement of Bigler's compromise scheme, but Mr. Lincoln has just declared to a Pennsylvanian that the principal opposition to his appointment came from New York, Ohio and Illinois, while in his own State [of Pennsylvania] it was comparatively trifling.

A prominent republican of this State expressed himself, after an interview with Mr. Lincoln, that Cameron was evidently a man that could be killed three times and yet would always come up anon.

Jas. O. Putnam, of New York, arrived here last night. He read an immense amount of letters to Mr. Lincoln this morning.

A member of the New York Legislature came here day before yesterday, and was closeted with Mr. Lincoln for several hours and returned East immediately after. He succeeded in maintaining a strict incognito.

It is not true that Mr. Romero brought a letter of congratulation from President [Benito] Juarez to Mr. Lincoln.

Mr. Colfax may not go into the Cabinet. His former Douglasism is too well remembered.

Mr. Lincoln will not go to Washington under a military escort, if his own desires be consulted.

Col. W. Jameson, of Ohio, is here.

Mr. Judd has returned to Chicago. He thinks he has a sure thing of the Secretaryship of the Interior.

January 26, 1861

Springfield, 26 January 1861

[New York *Herald*, 1 February 1861]

In my intercourse during the last few days with a crowd of Western politicians that are now all but constantly hovering about Springfield, I could not help being impressed with the fact that a reaction has taken place in regard to the sentiments many of them entertained towards Senator Seward. But a fortnight ago they all overflowed with measureless praise upon the announcement of his acceptance of the Secretaryship of State; but since the delivery of his last speech in the Senate a perceptible change has taken place in the tone of their views.[105] They do not express any direct disapprobation, nor indulge in open denunciation of his present course; but it is nevertheless evident that they do not exactly like it. The second sober perusal of his effort appears to impress them with the idea that he might have done better; that a little more firmness and decision would have entailed no harm; that a strong rebuke of the rampant treason practised by Southern Senators and politicians generally would have been in place; that its mean nothingness in the face of the momentous events in the South would tend to demoralize the republican party. Nor is the tenor of the speech in question the only cause of their fault-finding now manifested towards the New York Senator. His seeming gradual identification with Thurlow Weed's efforts in hatching out his compromise eggs is looked upon with apprehension and even disgust. Many already express their open regret at the impending fall of the great republican star, and seem to be prepared to find him before long at the extreme end of the right, instead of the left wing of his party, after the 4th of March.

N. B. Judd returned to Chicago on last night's train. Although retiring from the field of aspiration to the Cabinet, his air at the time of his departure was that of a victorious rather than a vanquished competitor. His friends claim, indeed, with the utmost assurance, that he is fully and irrevocably booked for the Secretaryship of the Interior. But, although my own personal observation has convinced me of the consummate tact and skill with which he laid and pulled the wires during the last three weeks, and of the untiring devotion and exertion of his many supporters, I must yet say that I cannot share their confidence. I still adhere to my original conviction, that Mr. Lincoln will be the only member of the Cabinet from Illinois, and shall continue to do so until an official announcement to the contrary will be made.

A good deal of newspaper talk has lately been made in reference to the alleged military escort under which Mr. Lincoln is reported to intend to go to Washington. A company of so-called Zouaves, lately formed in this place, is mentioned in connection with this supposed martial cortege. Now, I wish to state, for the benefit of all concerned, that this whole story, out of which so many rude and unjustifiable attacks upon Mr. Lincoln have grown, has no other foundation in fact than the conjectures, hopes and wishes of the youthful members of the said company. The matter may have been talked over in their drill room, and crept into a local paper in the shape of a rumor. But Mr. Lincoln has too much common sense to entertain so ridiculous a scheme for a moment. He utterly dislikes ostentatious display and empty pageantry, and the military association referred to will never be seen in the federal capital, if their visit is made to depend on the pleasure of Mr. Lincoln and the advice of all sensible friends. The raw disciples of Mars that constitute it would certainly afford but little real protection if such should be wanted.

The President elect was delighted last evening by the arrival on the Eastern train of Mrs. Lincoln and his oldest son [Robert], the Harvard student. He had been awaiting their return for the last three days. Dutiful husband and father that he is, he had proceeded to the railroad depot for three successive nights in his anxiety to receive them, and that in spite of snow and cold.

Mrs. Lincoln returned in good health and excellent spirits; whether she got a good scolding from Abraham for unexpectedly prolonging her absence I am unable to say; but I know that she found it rather difficult to part with the winter gayeties of New York city.

"Bob," the heir apparent to the President elect, has been observed of all the observing Springfield girls to-day. He walked the streets this morning, bringing up the rear of the "old man." The effect of a residence within the improving influences of genteel, well dressed and well behaved Boston is plainly noticeable in his outward appearance, the comparative elegance of which certainly presents a striking contrast to the loose, careless, awkward rigging of his Presidential father.

Among the latest arrivals are J. P. Bliss, Boston; S. S. Saunders, of Michigan; Charles W. Pratt, St. Louis; Benjamin Ward Dix, of Boston; E. Young and H. D. Sharpe, New York; George H. [W.] Haz[z]ard,[106] E. Locke and D. Root, Indiana; H. Z. Street, Ohio, and J. S. Copes, New Orleans.

Springfield, 26 January 1861
[Cincinnati *Commercial*, 29 January 1861]

Since the compromise movement in Congress has been brought to a head by the reports of the committees, the evident anxiety of many Republican members to steer in exact congruity with the course of the future helmsman of the ship of State, has again called forth various efforts to ascertain the views of the President elect, in reference to the propositions now awaiting final action. During the last three days, indeed, both written and verbal appliances have been brought to bear upon the object of this solicitude, to induce his committal on some of the measures contemplated in connection with the adjustment of the present internal difficulties. But, although this is done by influential parties, I am free to say, that Mr. Lincoln very properly and determinedly refuses to add the momentum of his opinion, officially expressed, to the Congressional machine. He thinks it both his duty and his privilege to abstain from any interposition in the deliberations of the National Council, until he shall be duly installed in the White House. Yet, this disinclination to speak as the President of the United States in the premises to the contrary notwithstanding, he does not hesitate to express his opinions on the subject in question *privately*, whenever called upon to do so in a proper manner. Hence, without pretending to speak by special authority, I can yet state positively, that he is utterly opposed to Crittenden's resolutions; that Bigler's scheme finds no more favor with him; that Senator Douglas's last remedy is not relished by him[107]; that he has many objections to Tom Corwin's report,[108] and that the Border State propositions alone would receive his countenance, provided a constitutional amendment could be secured conditioning the farther acquisition of territory by the Federal Government on the consent of two-thirds of the States. But I believe that he would even affix his signature to a Congressional enactment, coming up to these requirements, only in case he should conceive his approbation to be the *conditio sine qua non* of the peace, harmony and unity of the country. It may be, that a measure conceding more to the South would receive his sanction, for the same reason. But in that emergency he would certainly subordinate his individual preferences and sympathies to a sense of supposed duty. For the present, however, no signs of any such disposition are manifest. He firmly holds, that the question whether the right of secession exists, and whether the Federal laws are to be maintained, should be brought to a practical test, before the justness, necessity and practicability of concessions and compromises is definitely determined upon. In the face of the impatience and rashness of the leaders of the Cotton-secession, he thinks that both honor and wisdom require it of the North not to come down in the dust only to be ignominiously and spurningly kicked.

The everlasting Cameron embroglio was again brought up in the course of yesterday, by the arrival of another batch of emissaries in the service of the irrepressible Simon. A delegation from the City of Brotherly Love, made their appearance in the capacity of bearers of a set of Cameron resolutions, adopted by some Republican Club. That not much importance was attached to their mission, was proved by the fact, that they had to wait an entire day, before the President elect received the momentous documents in their charge. As to the effect of their resolving propaganda, I would say, that the time of their advent, so shortly after Cameron's inexplicable endorsement of Bigler's compromise plan, was anything but auspicious. For the outcry against that flagrant piece of back-sliding, among the Republicans of this vicinity, is extremely loud and vehement, and has already reached and influenced Mr. Lincoln. The Anti-Cameron men now openly and emphatically declare, that in view of that direct denunciation of the Republican faith, Cameron could and should not become a member of Mr. Lincoln's Administration. On the other hand, I have it from the best authority, that Mr. Lincoln expressed himself, within the last three days, to the effect that the opposition to Cameron principally came from parties outside of Pennsylvania, and that —— him, was relatively trifling.

The report that Thurlow Weed is coming out here to take up Cameron's case, is unfounded.

George G. Fogg, the Secretary of the Republican National Committee, spent [the] day before yesterday in close intercourse with Mr. Lincoln. George asserted most energetically that he had nothing to claim for himself, and that his visit only bore upon the condition of public affairs. I feel warranted to say that he came here to give Lincoln an inside view of matters at Washington, and make some suggestions in regard to the New England member of the Cabinet. He is a decided anti-compromise politician of the Hale school,[109] and is obviously held in high estimation by Mr. Lincoln.

James O. Putnam, one of the New York Electors, has also been in attendance on the President elect since yesterday morning. He had a good many letters to read to him; of what import has not yet transpired.

The members of the Legislature, together with all the State officers, have been indulging in a three-days' spree at Bloomington and Joliet.

January 27, 1861

Springfield, 27 January 1861

[New York *Herald*, 1 February 1861]

In view of the close approach of the inauguration of the incoming administration, the attitude it is likely to assume in reference to the overt acts of rebellion of the seceding States in seizing upon and preparing to seize by force of arms the federal property within their respective limits becomes a question of paramount interest.

Will the republican President use the army and navy of the United States for the protection and recovery of the forts, navy yards, arsenals, custom houses and post offices located within the States that will have renounced their allegiance to the federal government after his installation? Will he attempt to enforce the revenue laws? Will he allow the seditious members of the confederacy the further enjoyment of the benefits of the federal mail system? That the peace of the country depends on his treatment of these issues is obvious, and hence the general anxiety of the public to learn his intentions in the premises.

The most distinctive element of Mr. Lincoln's moral composition is his keen sense and comprehensive conscientiousness of duty. Upon taking his oath of office he will not be guided so much by his party predilections as by the federal constitution and laws. But these clearly and unavoidably define his line of action. They require him to secure obedience to their injunctions with all the means provided by them. That he will endeavor to fulfil[l] the obligations thus imposed upon him faithfully and fearlessly may be expected with the utmost certainty. Hence I venture to say that one of the first acts of his administration will be to renew the attempt to reinforce Fort Sumter, should Major Anderson and his gallant band be found still holding out; to demand the restoration of the federal property of the rebellious sovereignties; to collect an imposing naval force to blockade the Southern ports and collect the revenues in case of a refusal; to thoroughly sift the army and navy of officers sympathizing with the secession movement, and to put a stop to postal operations in all the States that refuse to recognize the authority of the general government. He does not propose to wage a war of aggression and subjugation. He will invade no State to bring about the overthrow of unconstitutional laws and authorities. He will observe a strict defensive, but nevertheless repel and defeat resistance to the execution of the above measures with all the power at his command.

Such, at least, is the import of all his late declarations on the subject. Influences may possibly be brought to bear upon him after his advent in the federal city that will effect a change of programme. But his present determination is certainly to test the strength of the federal government in the indicated manner. As the refractory States are not likely to comply with his excessive demands, civil war may be considered imminent.

I am able to announce authoritatively the programme of the journey of the President elect to Washington. Some modifications may be made previous to the day of departure, and perhaps on the way. For the present the plan is as follows:—

Mr. Lincoln will leave on the 11th proximo—a fortnight hence. He will go over the Great Western and Wabash Valley Railroad to Lafayette, and thence to Indianapolis. In the Hoosier capital he will stay one day, and be made the recipient of the hospitalities of the State authorities. From Indianapolis he will proceed to Columbus via Dayton, and perhaps via Cincinnati. At Columbus he will make a stay of only a few hours, and thence go to Cleveland and Buffalo. At Buffalo he will take the New York Central Railroad for Albany, where he intends to spend another day. From the capital of New York he proposes to make a direct strike for Harrisburg. But his friends in New York and Philadelphia are not likely to submit to such a slight. Washington will be made via Baltimore.

The agents of the several roads over which Mr. Lincoln will pass have been here and ascertained his wishes. Special trains will be provided all the way through, and the fewest possible changes made. The entire trip is expected to be completed inside of ten days. As previously stated, military escorts are not desired and will not be accepted.

Mrs. Lincoln and her three sons will embark a few days after the departure of the head of the family, and proceed directly to Washington by the shortest possible route, under the protection of a number of friends. The pressure upon Mr. Lincoln on his trip is expected to be so great as to render a joint journey undesirable.

A perfect lull has prevailed here during the last forty-eight hours. The Legislature has adjourned for a few days to indulge in a spree to Bloomington and Joliet, in this State, and but few obscure political characters from abroad are in town.

Written applications for office are now flooded upon the President elect with unusual vigor and frequency. Fifty are received per day on an average. Mr. Lincoln turns them all over to the tender mercies of his private secretary, who remorselessly consigns nine out of every ten to the stove.

Being anxious to prevent a waste of labor by your expectant readers, I herewith give them due warning that no notice whatever will hereafter be taken by the President elect of any epistolary supplication for subordinate appointments likely to reach him previous to his departure for Washington city.

Springfield, 27 January 1861
[Cincinnati *Commercial*, 1 February 1861]

From the subjoined programme of the journey of the President elect to the Federal Capital, the details of which have been officially given out within the last twenty-four hours, it will be seen that Mr. Lincoln has, with his usual kindness, consulted the pleasure and curiosity of his friends, rather than his own convenience, in determining upon the time and mode of going. The innumerable invitations, that have been poured upon him from all parts of the East, during the last four weeks, demonstrated to him in a most unmistakeable manner, the desire of his political supporters to see and render him what they consider due honor, previous to his assuming the Chief Magistracy of the country, and being unwilling to withhold what seems to be so universally and urgently demanded, he has consented to visit the different localities when invitations have reached him—not out of any craving for public orations, but a self-sacrificing disposition to gratify the wishes of his Republican friends. But laudable as the motive is, I am afraid that Abraham will have reason to regret his resolution ere he arrives at the end of his travels. He may fall a victim—not to the dagger of Brutus Pryor,[110] and other sanguinary patriots, but the irrepressible enthusiasm and obtrusiveness of a curious populace. Let, therefore, the crowds that are eager to swoop upon him be entreated in advance to show mercifulness to kindhearted "Old Abe."

The President elect will leave Springfield on the morning of the 11th prox. He will be accompanied by Col. Sumner of the First Cavalry,[111] and Major Hunter,[112] (both belonging to the Western Division U.S. Army) who have been detailed as aid-de-camps by special order of the War Department; a number of old political adherents, and last, not least, by a reportorial staff, representatives of New York, Boston, Philadelphia, Cincinnati, St. Louis and Chicago papers, inclusive of the correspondent of the [Cincinnati] *Commercial.* The President and his cortege will embark on a special train, to be provided by the Great Western and Wabash Valley Railroad, under the supervision of F[rancis W.] Bowen, Esq., the superintendent of the former road. No change of cars, and no protracted stoppages will be made between this point and Lafayette, and it is now probable that the same train will take the party on to Indianapolis.

At Indianapolis, Mr. Lincoln will give himself up for twenty-four hours to the tender mercies of the executive and legislative authorities of the "Hoosier State." The particulars of his entertainment by them, however, has not yet transpired.

From Indianapolis the journey is intended to be continued to Columbus via Richmond and Dayton. Should the people of your city show any solicitude to welcome Mr. Lincoln in their midst, a detour will doubtlessly be made to Porkopolis [Cincinnati]. At Columbus a public reception by the State Government will probably take place and the public at large be given an opportunity for a few hours to squeeze the Presidential fingers. From Columbus a Northern train will be taken for Cleveland, where another stoppage of a few hours will be made. From Cleveland another run will be made to Buffalo, where a public reception will again be held. From the city of the Lakes a special train of the New York Central Railroad [will] take the party to Albany, where Weed will take his friend Abraham into his keeping and present him to the legislative wisdom of the Empire State. Two days will probably be devoted to a consultation with the chieftains that will be gathered and the king of the Albany lobby. From Albany the present intentions are to strike a bee line for Harrisburg in order to avoid the overwhelming pressure likely to be experienced in New York and Philadelphia. But it is all but certain, that the New York Wide Awakes will not be put off in any such manner, but carry off the great rail splitter down the Hudson to the Empire City. Should such be the case, at least two days will be spent in the latter. If New York receives a visit, the city of Brotherly Love will not be overlooked, but only a day is likely to be granted to the Philadelphians for a sight at the future occupant of the White House. The next stopping place to be made from Philadelphia is Harrisburg, where legislative amenities will again be endured for twenty-four hours. From the capital of Pennsylvania a train is expected to be run through to Washington with but a few minutes stoppage at Baltimore.

It is not definitely settled, as asserted by some parties, that Mrs. Lincoln and her three sons will accompany the head of the family on his circuitous tour to Washington. The numerous *suite* of, and the public homage to the latter, would render the trip anything but agreeable to them. They will probably leave here on the 16th prox., and travel so as to meet Mr. Lincoln at Harrisburg, when the journey will be jointly pursued.

Various military companies, both here and abroad, have offered to do escort duty. But, as martial display would tend to add to the irritation of the public mind, none of the offers have been accepted. Arrangements for special trains have only been perfected from here to Indianapolis. The agents of the other roads, over which the President elect intends to travel, are, however, expected to appear at this place in the course of the present week, and tender the courtesies of their respective companies.

Springfield, 27 January 1861
[New York *Herald*, 28 January 1861]

It is now positively settled that Mr. Lincoln will depart for Washington on the 11th of February. He will go hence via Lafayette to Indianapolis, where he will receive the hospitalities of the Indiana Legislature, thence he will proceed, probably, by way of Cincinnati to Columbus, Cleveland, Buffalo and Albany. From Albany he intends to make for Harrisburg direct, thence to Baltimore and the federal capital, but a [de]tour to New York and Philadelphia is not impossible.

Arrangements for special trains all the way through are [in the] making. No military escort will be accepted. The entire journey is expected to be made inside of ten days. The Presidential family will start a few days after Mr. Lincoln's departure, under the protection of some friends, so as to reach Washington simultaneously with him.

Place seekers will consult their own interests by abstaining henceforth from both personal and epistolary applications for offices. The President-elect desires the utmost privacy during the remainder of his stay.

Springfield, 27 January 1861
[New York Herald, 28 January 1861]

Telegraphic advices have been received by Governor Yates, from the Governors of New York, Pennsylvania and other Northern States, suggesting the propriety of joining in a Convention, to be held at Washington in February, to devise proper remedies for the adjustment of the present difficulties.[113] The appointment of five Commissioners from each State is recommended. Governor Yates has finally decided to join in the movement. In this it is supposed he has acted upon the advice of Mr. Lincoln.

January 28, 1861

Springfield, 28 January 1861
[New York *Herald*, 29 January 1861]
The first draft of the Inaugural Message is now being made by the President elect. The Chicago platform will be the basis of its reflections and recommendations in reference to the internal affairs of the nation. It will not be finished until after consultation with the republican leaders in Washington.

Colonel Sumner, of the First Cavalry, and Major Hunter have been detailed by the War Department to accompany the President elect to Washington. The length of Mr. Lincoln's stoppage on the way to Washington will depend on the demonstrations likely to be made in his honor in different localities. His friends here look for tenders of the hospitalities of the Ohio, New York and Pennsylvania Legislatures. No further invitations will be issued to prominent politicians to visit the President elect, and none are desired here. The Cabinet will be completed in Washington.

Springfield, 28 January 1861
[New York *Herald*, 29 January 1861]
Telegraphic advices have been received by Governor Yates from the Governors of New York, Pennsylvania and other Northern States, suggesting the propriety of joining in a Convention, to be held at Washington in February, to devise proper remedies for the adjustment of the present difficulties. The appointment of five Commissioners from each State is recommended. Governor Yates has finally decided to join in the movement. In this it is supposed he has acted upon the advice of Mr. Lincoln.

January 29, 1861

Springfield, 29 January 1861
[New York *Herald*, 4 February 1861]
The President elect has entered upon the discharge of a duty next in importance to the construction of his Cabinet, viz: the preparation of his inaugural address. Already last week two or three days were devoted to this delicate and

difficult task, and it is understood that during the remainder of Mr. Lincoln's stay in this place his time will be principally absorbed in it. The material for this portentous undertaking was being assiduously collected ever since the beginning of the present month. Historical and other researches were made with great diligence, and a basis being thereby gained, the erection of the argumentative structure can now be completed in a comparatively short period. The ground from which the issues of the day will be viewed is already marked off. Abstract rights are ready to be asserted and wrongs to be pointed out; but the remedies to be recommended have not been determined upon, in view of the rapidity of events and the consequent dangers in the aspect of public affairs.

As to the party merit of the inaugural address, I venture to predict that the straight out republicans will have to find but little fault with it. There can be no doubt that, unless the present opinions of the President elect undergo a radical transmutation within the next four weeks, its tenor will be in strict conformity to the doctrines of the Chicago platform.

Only a first draft of the message will be made here. Suggestions of modifications are expected to be received on the journey to and in Washington, and the finishing touch will probably not be applied until a very few days before the inauguration.

Cabinet negotiations have been altogether suspended for the time being, owing to the commencement of the message. It is evidently the intention of the President elect to postpone the completion of the Cabinet until after his advent in the federal capital. A semi-official hint to this effect, indeed, has been given out. In pursuance of it, the hostilities between the partisans of the different aspirants have been interrupted. The Judd and anti-Judd men have both lowered their arms and lean on their shields, quietly waiting for an opportunity of making another assault previous to the 11th proximo. The retainers of Smith have altogether retired from the field, but a few faint efforts are still making by the backers of Colfax. Even Cameron seems to be willing to wait the final decision of his claims to the Cabinet with folded arms. Altogether, the newspaper reading public may confidently expect a total subsidence for the next fortnight of the countless rumors bearing upon the Cabinet making of the great railsplitter.

For this welcome relief the President elect is certainly indebted to a great extent to the disinterested vigor with which the HERALD's correspondent has labored during the last few days towards the dispersion of the hungry, howling crowd of solicitors for themselves and friends, that have plagued Abraham so remorselessly these many weeks. It is true Abraham's gain will prove his own loss, the impudence of place seekers having furnished almost exclusively his stock in trade since the holidays. But our humane instincts of the pitiful sight of Abraham's sufferings did not allow us to act otherwise.

Although the number of distinguished bores from abroad has been for some days growing refreshingly less, the influx of written supplications for executive favors is still as voluminous as ever. Baskets full of petitions and recommendations continue to arrive with every mail, much to the chagrin of Mr. Lincoln's private Secretary, upon whose shoulders the main burden of this overwhelming Presidential correspondence rests. Nor is the number of the applications their worst feature—their size is nearly always equally objectionable. Documents covering from twenty to thirty and more pages, setting forth the claims and merits of the several expectants, are frequently received. Some fools even went so far as to enclose essays on the duty and destiny of the republican party and the republican administration. To all such indiscreet individuals I wish to say again that neither Mr. Nicolay nor Mr. Lincoln are equal to the task of opening, reading and answering a hundred or so letters every day, and that hence their epistles run the ignominious risk of being transferred to the paper basket unnoticed. If they are determined on being heard, let them get their papers ready and station themselves at some convenient point along the route selected by Mr. Lincoln for his journey to Washington. A box for the reception of their applications will doubtless be attached to the Presidential train. But by all means let them abstain from addressing anything to Mr. Lincoln previous to his embarkation for the East. It will do no good, and may do a good deal of harm.

Mr. Lincoln intends to start to-morrow morning upon a two days' excursion to Charleston, the county seat of Coles county, in the southern part of this State. He proposes to pay a short visit to his aged stepmother [Sarah Bush Johnston Lincoln], who resides at the point mentioned, and expressed a strong wish to see him before he left Springfield for Washington. The strictest privacy being desired by Mr. Lincoln, no reportorial shadows will follow him.

Among the latest hotel arrivals are A. L. Mansom, David Bards, W. W. Cowes, all of Cincinnati; D. V. Bennett and W. L. Patton, New York, and Geo. C. Carbleman and I. N. Mardsham, of Kentucky.

Springfield, 29 January 1861
[New York *Herald*, 4 February 1861]

This morning's [*Illinois State*] *Journal* has the following leaded notice at the head of its first column:

MR. LINCOLN ON COMPROMISES.

At a late hour last night we received the following telegraphic item [from the Associated Press]:

> It is now certain that private letters have been received from Mr. Lincoln urging his friends to conciliation and compromise, and it is stated that he indicates the border States resolutions as a reasonable basis of adjustment. Assurances are given that this information is reliable. As soon after the electoral vote shall be counted in the presence of Congress, on the second Wednesday in February, he will acquaint the public with his views on the pending crisis. He heretofore has not felt it proper, in advance of official information of the declaration of his election, for him to take a prominent part in the direction of political affairs.
>
> We, of course, have had no opportunity to converse with Mr. Lincoln, but such is our knowledge of his views and feelings that we have no hesitation in declaring that Mr. Lincoln has committed himself to no compromise whatever, and that the whole thing is a canard of the first water. He has steadily refused to accede to the demand of those who insisted upon his giving his inaugural in advance.
>
> The country may rest assured that in Abraham Lincoln they have a republican President, one who will give them a republican administration. Mr. Lincoln is not committed to the border States compromise nor to any other. He stands immovably on the Chicago platform, and he will neither acquiesce in nor counsel his friends to acquiesce in any compromise that surrenders one iota of it.

The above is so decidedly and forcibly to the point that it will probably set at rest, until the delivery of Mr. Lincoln's inaugural address, all the idle and totally unfounded gossip that has been floating through both the East and West in connection with a supposed willingness of the President elect to renounce part of the principles, the prevalence of which secured his election to the chief magistracy of this country. He stands now where he stood on the day of his election. He has neither advanced nor retreated a solitary inch, and the public mind might as well be made to realize this incontrovertible fact by those who claim to influence it.

The pressure of place seekers from both at home and abroad continues unabated, although the President elect is not much less disposed to allow the absorption of his now so valuable time by their selfish, provoking importunities. But neither his coolness nor his anger, nor the various devices he has resorted to within the last fortnight to keep the expectants at a safe distance, have altogether relieved him from this worst of Presidential tribulations. The common herd of solicitants of second class post offices, consulships, clerk-ships, &c., &c., is got rid of easily enough. But a certain class of visiters to the President elect have been coming here for the last two months that are not to be baffled in this attempt to encroach upon Mr. Lincoln's time and good will. They are the "distinguished men" that make their advent in Springfield for the ostensible purpose of giving their disinterested but unsolicited advice in regard to appointments to the Cabinet and other leading positions and the policy of the incoming administration. These volunteer counsellors appear to think that their patriotic motives give them a perfect title to the attention of Mr. Lincoln during their respective stays in Springfield. They will first en-deavor to hunt him up and besiege him in his downtown office. If unsuccessful there, they will call at his private residence, and if admission to the Presidential presence be denied to them upon the first application they never fail to make a second, third, &c., &c., one, until their wishes are, *nolens volens*, gratified by the object of their obtrusiveness. Nor are they hardly ever satisfied with the privilege of one interview. They either exact an invitation to call again by conversational tactics or persuade Mr. Lincoln to return their call at their hotels, where, once got hold of, he is seldom able to cut himself loose with-out the loss of several hours' time. It is true Mr. Lincoln's inexhaustible good naturedness is mostly at fault in this. But then common decency should teach the visiting bores of distinction not to improve this excusable shortcoming.

Abraham knows that there is no safety for him from this infliction, either in his office or his house, and hence he has been looking out for other places of retreat, to which the irrepressible impudence of distinguished strangers would not follow him. Knowing his present anxiety for privacy I would cer-tainly not reveal them, but that the prelude of the Presidential drama, that is, his sojourn in Springfield, is so near its end. One of his secret haunts is the studio of Mr. T. D. Jones, the Cincinnati sculptor, whither he repairs now almost every morning, not for sittings, but to open and read his morning mail. The other is the sanctum of the [*Illinois State*] *Journal* office, where he also spends many a quiet hour.

J. T. [L.] Williams, of Fort Wayne, Indiana, whose principal stock in trade seems to consist in the fact that he sent the first telegraphic despatch an-nouncing the triumph of the republican State and electoral ticket in Indiana to Mr. Lincoln,[114] and Mr. [William] Mitchell, member of Congress elect,[115] are here urging Colfax's claims. Could any advice reach them, I would tell them to pack up their traps and go home. They can do no good, but a good deal of harm, to the cause they represent at this stage of affairs.

Messrs. John T. Dowling and M. M. Truman, of your city, arrived last night.

Springfield, 29 January 1861

[Cincinnati *Commercial*, 1 February 1861]

At the head of the editorial columns of this morning's "Daily [*Illinois State*] Journal" appears a significant and evidently authoritative explanation in reference to the position of the President-elect on the Compromise positions, the substance of which I shall telegraph you this evening. The occasion of it is a dispatch to the Associated Press from Washington City, published this morning, and representing it as a fact that Mr. Lincoln has written to his Congressional friends, recommending a conciliatory disposition toward the South and expressing a readiness to acquiesce in an adjustment of the present difficulties on the basis of the Border State propositions. The "Journal" pronounces the dispatch a canard of the first water, and declares with much terseness and emphasis, that Mr. Lincoln is not and will not be prepared to acquiesce in the Border State or any Compromise propositions, and is decidedly opposed to their indorsement by Congress.

It is to be hoped that this unmistakable declaration will extinguish the many idle stories sent out both from here and Washington in connection with the same subject. It confirms all I have heretofore stated as to the views of Mr. Lincoln on the question of exacted compromise and concession. He *may* possibly give his sanction to a new compact between the South and North, involving a partial renunciation of the doctrines of the party that elected him, provided a majority of the nation should assent to it. But he will certainly not do it in the face of the attempts of the refractory States to dictate terms by open treason and rebellion.

Mr. Lincoln has thought best to suspend temporarily the cause of so many weeks botheration—the construction of the Cabinet—and turn his attention to his next important duty, the preparation of the first draft of his inaugural address. I understand that already this week, two days have been devoted to this matter, and that within the next fortnight, that is, previous to his departure for Washington City, the message will be as far completed as the rapid progress of events will permit.

In view of his present occupation, Mr. Lincoln is doubtlessly inclined to dispense with the services of the distinguished political artizans that have been volunteering their assistance in Cabinet-making, during the last two months. It is to be devoutly wished, indeed, that your correspondent shall be no more obliged to hold up the patriotic motives and actions of eminent visitors to the President elect, to the admiration of the readers of the [Cincinnati] *Commercial*.

In consequence of the broad hint conveyed in my yesterday's dispatches to the effect that "place seekers will consult their own interest by abstaining hereafter both from written and verbal applications for office," and that "the President elect desires the strictest privacy during the remainder of his stay in Springfield," the tide of expectants has already dwindled down to a comparative ebb. The dread of a fatal registry in Old Abe's "black book" has most likely produced this greater backwardness as to personal inflictions upon the dispenser of all good things in the shape of federal offices. But epistolary supplications continue to arrive with alarming frequency. Baskets full of them—in the literal sense of the term—are daily transferred from the postoffice to Mr. Lincoln's room, and Mr. Nicolay, his private Secretary, has almost given way under the task of daily opening, reading, filing and answering this superabundance of correspondence.

What a record of human indiscretion, folly, selfishness, cupidity and stupidity does not this mass of missives contain. Just think of men expatiating upon their private virtues and public services for the special benefit of the President elect, covering from two to twenty-six pages of foolscap. It is almost impossible to believe that any human being could be so destitute of common sense as to be guilty of perpetrating the like mentioned enormity. Yet instances of a like kind have not by any means been rare occurrences. But a few days since a package was received from a letter writing monster in California containing a petition for place, filling twenty-three quarto pages, and in addition, a written copy of a campaign speech the shipper had delivered in some mining district during the Presidential campaign. The contents of the package will doubtless form a part of the collection of political curiosities the President elect will take on to the White House.

Although your correspondent does not greatly sympathize with the pains of place-hunters, he nevertheless feels humane enough to state for their guidance, that all written applications for subordinate office will be mercilessly consigned to the stove, until after the arrival of Mr. Lincoln in Washington.

Mr. Lincoln intends to start to-morrow morning for Charleston, the county seat of Coles county, in this State, for the purpose of visiting his old step-mother, who expressed a strong desire to see her Abraham before he enters on his four-years' absence in Washington. He will be absent only two days. I hope that the Indiana politicians will not be tempted by the short distance of Charleston from the State line, to invade him during his short stay.

The source of the Springfield correspondence of the [Cincinnati] *Enquirer*, in which Mr. Potter[116] is put up for the Post Office of your city, may be inferred from the fact that its representative out here accompanied the Legislature on their spree to Bloomington, and has been laid up there ever since Wednesday last—in consequence of what, your readers will readily suppose.

[This morning, according to the Chicago *Tribune*, Lincoln was supposed to meet with General John B. Rodgers of Tennessee.][117]

Among the late arrivals are, J. P. Bliss and B. J. Ward, of Boston; Z. Street, Salem, O; Geo. H. [W.] Haz[z]ard, E. Locke, and D. Root, Ind.; F. Young and H. D. Sharpe, of New York; J. S. Copes, of New Orleans, S. S. Saunders, Michigan; Geo. C. Castleman and J. N. Marksham, Ky.

Springfield, 29 January 1861
[New York *Herald*, 30 January 1861]

This morning's [*Illinois State*] *Journal* contains an authoritative contradiction of a Washington despatch to the press, stating that Mr. Lincoln had written to his Congressional friends recommending conciliatory measures. It says the country may rest assured that in Abraham Lincoln they have a republican President—one who will give them a republican administration. Mr. Lincoln is not committed to the border State compromise, nor to any other. He stands immovably on the Chicago platform, and he will neither acquiesce, nor counsel his friends to acquiesce in, any compromise that surrenders one iota of it.

Mr. Lincoln will leave to-morrow morning on a two days' visit to his step-mother, living near Charleston in this State.

J. T. Williams and W. Mitchell, M. C. of Indiana, are here, pressing Colfax for the Cabinet.

The tender of the services of Col. Sumner and Major Hunter upon the journey to Washington, was made by General Scott.

A proposition to accompany Mr. Lincoln to Indianapolis is now being discussed by the members of the Legislature.

There is a perfect inundation of Chicago politicians. Deacon Bross, of the Tribune,[118] figures conspicuously among them.

[A. L. Manson, David Burd, and W. W. Cones of New York were also reported to be in Springfield.]

January 30, 1861

Springfield, 30 January 1861
[New York *Herald*, 31 January 1861]

Judge Pettit, of Kansas, arrived last night.[119] He is on his way to Washington to look after his chances for the new Judgeship, created by the Kansas bill. He had a long interview with Mr. Lincoln, whose indorsement he is anxious to obtain, with a view to his confirmation by the Senate. He started east this morning in the train which Mr. Lincoln took for his two days' visit to his step-mother.

Quite a number of place seekers are again in town, sorely chagrined at the departure of the President. Among them are Mark W. Delahay of Kansas,[120] General Larimer, of Denver City[121] and J. P. Usher, of Indiana,[122] who is after a Marshalship. Judge [Edward] Bates is here on professional business.

Springfield, 30 January 1861
[New York *Herald*, 7 February 1861]

Considerable agitation has been produced in legislative circles during the last forty-eight hours in consequence of the introduction on yesterday morning of a joint resolution, by a prominent democratic member of the Senate, calling for the appointment of five Commissioners to the Convention to meet at Washington next week for the purpose of devising some means of adjusting the present difficulties. It was offered in response to the refusal of Governor Yates to recommend similar action. After considerable debate in the course of yesterday, the resolution was referred to a committee, by whom it was returned this morning to be tabled by the republican majority. While the subject was debated in the Senate yesterday forenoon, the President elect most unexpectedly appeared on the floor. His call is attributed to a desire to see the proposition defeated. The final refusal of his supporters to accept it is ascribed to his influence.

That the "powers that are to be" are opposed to the meeting of the Commissioners is furthermore demonstrated by a strong leader on the subject in this morning's *Daily [Illinois] State Journal*, in which the ground is taken that the appointment of Commissioners by the republican majority would be an indirect acknowledgment of the justness of Southern demands upon the North, and hence humiliate and demoralize the supporters of the incoming administration, that stands pledged to the Chicago platform. The article winds up: "We say to Virginia, and to all other States that are asking us to compromise and concede something, that we are not aware of having done any wrong to their people. That we propose to do no wrong either to her or them, or to any of the States of the South. That being our position, we do not propose to make either concession or compromise, for in doing so we are required to yield up every essential part of republican faith."

Considerable commotion was created this morning by the revelation of the fact that John Pettit, Chief Justice of the United States Court of Kansas, was here for a few hours last night on a secret visit to the President elect. If it be true that evil doers seek darkness, the Judge's conscience cannot be very clear. He landed here at six P.M., and left before daylight. Most of the evening he spent in private consultation with Mr. Lincoln. He is on his way to Washington, where he proposes looking after his nomination for the judgeship created by the amendment to the Kansas bill. It is reported that he came to see his friend Lincoln, to whom he had been so remarkably courteous as to excite general comment, during his stumping tour in Kansas in the fall of 1859, to secure the endorsement of the new administration of his aspirations to the sinecure created with a special view to his own wants. But it is rather difficult to see how the Judge will manage to curry and win favor with both the incoming and outgoing regime. Maybe his call on Lincoln is intended not to be known to his friend Buchanan. If so, I should feel sorry for foiling the Judge's schemes by thus giving publicity to it. It is true, at all events, that some of his enemies have been long asserting his inclination to go over to the republican ranks.

Almost simultaneously with the rotund Chief Justice of Kansas, Mr. Bates, of Missouri, made his third appearance here. His visit was, of course, connected with that of Pettit. But the departure of Mr. Lincoln for Charleston on this morning's Eastern train, the presence of Mr. Bates to the contrary notwithstanding, proved conclusively that the distinguished Missourian's visit was not of an official character.

Quite a number of expectants got here this morning, and were sorely chagrined to find the Presidential bird flown. Among them were Mark W. Delahay, a professional wirepuller, and original Lincoln man, from Kansas, where he hopes to be elected to the United States Senate, on the strength of his supposed ability to furnish a commission to every member of the Legislature that will vote for him and Gen. Wm. Larimer, Jr., formerly a prominent citizen of Pittsburg[h], Pa., but now of Denver City, who came all the way from Pike's Peak to make his wants known to the President elect. They and several others, nothing daunted by their disappointment, forthwith concluded not to be dodged by Abraham, and await his return from "Egypt."

Mr. T. D. Jones, the well known Cincinnati sculptor, who has been here these last six weeks, has nearly completed the modelling of the bust of Mr. Lincoln, which, for genial conception, vigor of handling, pose, fidelity to the original and elevated expression, far surpasses all his previous works. The bust is commissioned by an association of gentlemen called the republican citizens of Kentucky, Ohio and Indiana, and when finished will be cut into marble. It will greatly add to the artistic lustre of its author, already distinguished for many noble successes in sculpture portraiture. It will be exhibited in due season in your city.

G. F. Wright, the well known "Governor painter," has also been professionally engaged here for some time.[123] He is commissioned to execute the portraits of the ex-Governors of this State, and is now rapidly completing a most creditable gallery of "half lengths" paintings in oil.

January 31, 1861

Springfield, 31 January 1861
[New York *Herald*, 7 February 1861]

Truth can never be too readily told. Why then the studied attempts of certain parties in Washington to impress the public with the idea that the President elect is not only anxious for, but also actively engaged in, promoting a settlement of the present misunderstandings between the two sections of the country, by making epistolary appeals to his Congressional friends to accept the border States propositions as a basis for such? Why insist on a misrepresentation of Mr. Lincoln's views in the face of authoritative disavowals of the imputed motives and actions? For the sake of removing a false impression that seems to prevail to a great extent in the political circles of the East, I will say again that the President elect is firmly, squarely and immovably set against any compromise proposition that will involve a sacrifice of republican principles, and that even the proposed Convention of Commissioners, upon the suggestion of the Virginia Legislature, previous to his inauguration, is looked upon unfavorably by him. He desires to see the somewhat uncertain disposition of the border slave States to yield the rights of the majority and obedience to the federal constitution and laws thoroughly tested by his inauguration, before his friends shall make any move for a reconciliation upon the basis of Congressional enactments or constitutional amendments.

The question of the appointment of Commissioners promises to become a seed of discord in the republican party in the Legislature of this State, as in that of Ohio, New York and Pennsylvania. The northern members are most vehemently opposed to any action in the premises. Those from the central and more southerly counties, however, are inclined to respond to the call. Caucuses have been held every night for the last four days, and hardly anything else is at present talked of in the legislative halls and lobbies.

The conservatives prevailed on Judge Bates, whose presence on professional business I mentioned in my last, to address the caucus held last evening. But the Judge disappointed their expectations. He made an altogether non-committal speech. He spoke of the value of the Union to both sections of the country, of his own attachment to it, and of the duty of all patriotic men to unite in efforts for its preservation. He denounced the secession movement with great decision and vigor, and advocated the enforcement of the federal laws as the first and main duty of the republican President. But he saw best not to commit himself on any of the compromise propositions, and requested his hearers to hold him alone responsible for what he said, and not to look upon his remarks as an authoritative expression of the views of the President elect.

A prominent Kansas politician, now in this place, stated openly in the course of yesterday, in a place of public resort, that he had written a letter to Senator Trumbull urging the support of Judge Pettit's aspirations to the Judgeship created by the Kansas bill. This confirms what I stated yesterday, in reference to the Judge's readiness for conversion to the faith of the party about obtaining [to obtain] possession of the federal spoils. But I venture to say that, this epistolary endorsement to the contrary notwithstanding, he will not be touched by the republican Senators. As to the interference of the President elect in his behalf, that is beyond all plausibility. He (Mr. Lincoln) knows that the majority of Kansas republicans detest John Pettit, and will not stultify themselves by buying with place one of their most relentless and uncompromising foes.

There was a great flutter in political circles to-day in consequence of an apparently well authenticated report from Washington that Mr. Lincoln had written a letter to Schuyler Colfax, to be used by him in urging the adoption of the border State propositions upon the republican members. By those who know the deep grudge the President elect entertained against Colfax ever since the latter's advocacy of Douglas' claims to a re-election in 1858, the statement was at once pronounced improbable and absurd. Yet it obtained considerable credence until its public and emphatic contradiction this afternoon by one of Mr. Lincoln's most confidential friends, who thought it incumbent to disclaim the authorship for the President elect, as the story promised to affect the action of the republican legislators upon the border State propositions.

Applicants for subordinate offices are still arriving, in [a] vain quest of the dispensing power. The pangs of disappointment must be great, judging from the loud swearing of a number of them. A horde of the expectants are especially chagrined at the untimely absentation of the President elect. The inadequacy of their "cash on hand" to the unexpected prolongation of their hotel bills, is doubtless the main cause of their disquietude.

Joseph A. Nunes, a well known San Francisco, California politician,[124] has just arrived from the East. He also remains on the lookout for the Presidential traveller.

Springfield, 31 January 1861

[New York Herald, 1 February 1861]

A report from Washington, that Mr. Lincoln has written to Schuyler Colfax, and other republican Congressmen, urging the passage of compromise measures, is authoritatively contradicted.

Judge Bates made a speech before a republican caucus. He expressed himself strongly against secession, but did not commit himself on any of the compromise propositions, and disclaimed to speak for Mr. Lincoln.

Gov. Yates is not absolutely opposed to the appointment of Commissioners in response to the Virginia invitation, but objects to their meeting before Lincoln's inauguration. This is known to be the view of the President elect. There is a good deal of agitation on the subject in the Legislature, and Commissioners may yet be appointed.

Joseph A. Nunes, of San Francisco, was here to-day to see the President [elect].

The following despatch shows Mr. Lincoln's movements:

Charleston, 31 January 1860—1 P.M.
The President elect arrived last night and left early this morning for the residence of his step-mother.

Springfield, 31 January 1861
[Cincinnati *Commercial*, 4 February 1861]
Every Eastern newspaper that has reached me within the last two days, is replete with rumors and reports bearing upon the alleged interference of Mr. Lincoln, by dint of letters to Republican Congressmen, in behalf of "concession and compromise;" and hence I feel it incumbent on me, although I have already made several allusions to the same subject in previous letters, to state that all these stories are without the slightest foundation in fact. I am at a loss to understand how such canards as the subjoined item from your telegraphic Washington correspondence, can get abroad, in the face of the direct and unmistakeable official disavowals given out from here, during the last week. I quote the following passage, for the sake of *pars pro toto* [a part taken for the whole] illustration and refutation.

"Reliable advices were received from Mr. Lincoln this morning, by some leading Republicans. He advises his friends to compromise at once upon a basis satisfactory to the border States, and which will be perpetual."

Mr. Lincoln has not written a solitary line to any Republican Congressman conveying such instructions. On the contrary, he is firmly and decidedly opposed to granting anything, until the South abandons its rampant treason and rebellion, no longer makes insolent threatenings and impossible demands, and manifests a disposition to counsel coolly, temperately and forbearingly with the North. He is anxious, above all, to see the readiness of the slave-holding communities to yield the rights of that majority, and obedience to the Constitution and Federal laws, practically tested by his inauguration, before his friends shall make any move for the adjustment of the present difficulties called forth, as they are, by the sole agency of the Southern members of the confederacy.

An intense flurry was experienced last night, by our politicians, in consequence of the announcement that the notorious John Pettit, D. D., and United States District Judge of Kansas, had been paying a secret visit to Mr. Lincoln. The story sounded strange, and yet it turned out to be true. The above minister of Justice had actually landed late in the evening, hurried to and rested in Abraham's bosom for a few hours, and left again before day-break.

Being anxious to shun observation, the Judge put up at an obscure hotel. His plans were well laid withal; but the bird was too fat not to be smoked out by your vigilant correspondent. Be it known then to all concerned, that John Pettit, late a pillar of the Breckinridge party and still in enjoyment of the executive favors of Mr. Buchanan, came here for the purpose of sounding the Republican President as to his aspirations to the Judgeship created by the Kansas Bill. Unsophisticated people may be at a loss to see how the Judge is going to straddle both the Buchanan and Lincoln nags. But it is, nevertheless true, that he came here with the indorsement of certain Kansas Republicans, and that he would like to have his old friend Abraham, with whom he played many a social game of billiards in Kansas last fall a year ago, say a good word in favor of his confirmation to Trumbull, Seward *et al.* I dare say, however, that Abraham did not quite take the Judge's hint, and that he (Pettit) continued his journey to Washington with hopes rather subdued than otherwise.

Mr. Bates, upon invitation, addressed a caucus of Republican members of the Legislature last night. He took strong anti-secession ground, but did not commit himself upon any of the compromise propositions and disclaimed to speak for Mr. Lincoln.

The President embarked to-day at 10 A.M. for Charleston in the Southern part of this State. He was accompanied to the depot by Mr. Bates. He will return on Friday evening.

His departure was known to very few persons only and caused great dismay to a number of place-seekers, who arrived in the course of the morning. Among those that are now impatiently awaiting his return are Mark W. Delahay, of Kansas; J. P. Usher, of Indiana; and Gen. Larimer, formerly a well known Pittsburgh banker, and now of Denver City. Delahay would like to have his claims to the United States Senatorship of Kansas indorsed by Mr. Lincoln; Usher wants a United States Marshalship, and Larimer desires a commission as Governor of the prospective Territory of Idaho, (Pike's Peak) Territory.[125]

Springfield, 31 January 1861

[San Francisco *Bulletin*, 19 February 1861]

[The microfilmed version of the San Francisco *Bulletin* containing this dispatch is defective. A fold in the newspaper hides many words, whose omission is indicated in this transcription thus: [something]. Conjectures about the missing words are also enclosed within square brackets.]

LINCOLN ON THE COMPROMISE P[LA]NS

The observer of the doings in Pres[idential cir]cles during the last week could not help be[ing impre]ssed with the fact that influences of no [something w]eight, were brought to bear upon the Pr[esident ele]ct to exact an official endorsement o[f something] compromise propositions embodied in t[something]nt reports of the Committee of Thirty-[three] now awaiting final action in the House. [Written] and verbal appeals were made with s[something]y and constancy, by parties of high po[sition something], that there was good reason to beli[eve their] efforts would be crowned with success. [At the] hour of this writing it is, nevertheless, [something] little impression has been produced up[on the m]ind of Mr. Lincoln. The amount of back[bone with] which he is happily endowed is so great, t[hat] the extraordinary appliances that have be[en made to] operate upon him did not succeed in [something hi]m. I am enabled, indeed, to state by direc[t authorit]y that the Republican President [elect] is as y[et unprepar]ed to yield one inch of the position which [he has oc]cupied since the day of his election. His [something th]e justness of the principles, the preva[iling of] which caused his elevation to the highest o[ffice in th]e land, is still unshaken. The inconsidera[tene]ss, and rebellious defiance, and unreasona[ble deman]ds of the Cotton and Sugar States, hav[e con]vinced him that compromise was not only [impossi]ble, but would evidently come utterly shor[t of the] desired effect, and only humiliate and demo[ralize the] North. Hence, he has taken no pains t[o something tho]se who lately solicited an expression of [opinio]n on this subject from him, that of all the [something s]chemes now under Congressional consid[eration] the so-called Border State propositions al[something]yed notice, and they only, after the inc[lusion] of an amendment prohibiting the acquis[ition of a]ny more territory without the consent of [two third]s of the States.

This is authentic, and can be re[lied upon im]plicitly by your readers. I have though[t it nece]ssary to allude again to this matter, alrea[dy something]ed upon in my last, as the Eastern press ha[s something]led for the last few days with unwarrante[d something]ents to the contrary. Mr. Lincoln, I [something] will not, under any circumstances, go furth[er than] indicated in the above.

ON THE DISUNION ISSUE

I have the most positive evid[ence tha]t, in the opinion of the President elect, the [something] be dealt with under the Republican admin[istration some-thing] are now narrowed down to the question w[hether t]he Federal laws should be maintained [against e]ncroachments upon them, already per-petr[ated by t]he seditious States, repelled and punish[ed something] right of Secession indirectly acknowledge [something th]e formation of an inde-pendent confed[eration wit]hin the limits of the Union tolerated by [some-thing] and preserving a merely defensive attitude [something] understood to believe that all past par[ties something] will be altogether lost sight of, and t[hat "Uni]on" and "Disunion" alone will be made [rally]ing cries of two great parties, and that pre[something]arances render the ultimate decision of [the legiti]macy of one of the two by the sword mo[re proba]ble than by the ballot. That the Presid[ent elect] will be found ready after the 4th of Marc[h to] exhaust all means at his command to uph[old the] majesty of the Constitution, and the laws an[d the aut]thority of the Federal Government is a [something] certain. The most distinctive element of [his] composition is a keen and comprehensi[ve sense] of duty; and, in accordance with its impul[se he wi]ll fulfill his constitutional obligations fir[mly and] fearlessly, and, knowing himself to be right [something l]et consequence take care of themselv[es. Th]ough not especially commissioned by the [President] elect to define his position, in regard to th[e secessi]on issue, for the benefit of people of the P[acific coa]st, I yet feel convinced from all I saw an[d heard] of late in stating that:

1. He will immediately after [his acce]ssion to power make a most thor-ough sift[ing of] Federal officers, both civil and military; [and sym]pathizers with and abettors of the Secession [will be f]orthwith set adrift.

2. He will demand the restora[tion of] Federal property unlawfully seized upon [something] by the authorities of the seceded States.

3. He will collect a sufficiently [strong na]val force to secure the enforce-ment of reven[ue laws].

4. He will reinforce Major [Anderson] at all hazards in case he should be still [in po]ssession of Fort Sumter after the 4th of March.

5. He will not invade any State [with a] Federal army, to force the repeal of unc[onstitution]al laws and the overthrow of authorities [something] federal functions; but protect, and if n[ecessary] recover, the forts, arsenals, navy yards, m[ints], postoffices and customhouses within the [seceded] Southern State[s].

If this were [to cause a] civil war, then your [readers] may remain satisfied that the tug of wa[r something ca]me after the installation of the Republican [something ad]ministration.

CAMERON'S PRESENT POSITION [SOMETHING] CABINET

The recent endorsement of Bigl[er's pro]positions by Senator Cameron has taken ev[erybo]dy by surprise in this latitude. The clamo[r against] him is once more heard with increased str[ength]. Many of Mr. Lincoln's friends think, with [the Ne]w York *Tribune*, that this inexplicable ste[p of] the Senator from Pennsylvania has entirely sep[arated h]im from the Republican party. That the [Preside]nt elect does not share his views in the pre[mises is] certain, and that his gyrations will not imp[rove his] chances of going into the Cabinet is equally [certain.]

DISTINGUISHED VISITORS

During the last week Mr. Lincol[n has] suffered extensively from the importunities [of] anxious and illustrious political characters [who] besieged him in large numbers for the purpo[se of re]warding their respective interests. Among [the latt]er were George G. Fogg, of New Hampshi[re a leadi]ng anti-compromiser, who called here to g[ive] Lincoln an inside view of things and matter[s in Was]hington, and James O. Putnam, the well know[n Ne]w York politician, who bored Abraham for [almost a]n entire day with a satchel full of recom[mendati]ons for office, and epistolary expressions o[f the vie]ws of a number of Eastern politicians [on the] present crisis. The rumor of Thurlow Weed [being] here a second time is unfounded.

A special committee of the Ind[iana leg]islature was here to tender the hospitalities [of the] Hoosier State to the President elect, du[ring his] passage through it on his way to Washingt[on. The] invitation was accepted, as detailed farth[er something].

A Philadelphia delegation, cons[isting of Dr.] H. G[ale] Smith, O. P. Parker, P[eter] Ford, an[d Charles Ad]ams, arrived on Thursday last [January 24], with a [set of re]solutions passed by some Republican Associa[tion of] the city of Brotherly Love, and recomm[endations of] Cameron for the Cabinet.

JOURNEY OF THE PRESIDENT ELECT [TO THE] FEDERAL CAPITAL

For the last eight days Mr. Linc[oln has] been engaged in arranging his plans for [the] pending transportation of himself and fami[ly from] his small frame cottage to the White Hous[e and] yesterday the programme of the journ[ey was] officially announced. From the subjoined [something it] will be perceived that Mr. Lincoln has, [with h]is usual kindness, consulted the pleasure [and cur]iosity of his friends, rather than his own co[nvenienc]e, in determining upon the time and mode [something]. The innumerable invitations that have [been] pressed upon him from all parts of the East [during] the last month, demonstrated to him, in [an unmista]kable manner, the desire of his political S[something]'s to see and render him what they consider [something]or, previous to his assuming the chief M[agistr]y of the country, and being unwilling to d[ecline] what seems to be so universally and urgen[tly de]manded, he has consented to visit the di[fferent lo]calities whence invitations have reached h[im, no]t out of any longing for public ovations, [but a se]lf-sacrificing disposition to gratify the wi[shes of] others. But laudable as the motive is, I d[something]d that Abraham will have reason to regret [his re]solution ere he will get through with his [something]. I trust that he may not fall a victim—not t[o Roger] Pryor, and other sanguinary patriots—but t[he irrcp]ressible enthusiasm and obtrusiveness of a co[something po]pulace.

Mr. Lincoln will leave Springfield [something] morning of the 11th of February. He [will be] accompanied by Colonel Sumner and Major [Hunter] of the United States army, who have been [detaile]d to accompany him as a sort of aides-de-[camp by] special order of the War Department; a n[umber o]f more intimate friends; and, last but not le[ast, a] reportorial staff, consisting of represen[tatives] of New York, Boston, Philadelphia, Cincinn[ati, St.] Louis and Chicago papers, and the corres[pondent] of the San Francisco *Bulletin.*

The President [elect] and his cortege wil[l embar]k on a special train over the Great Western [and] Wabash Valley Railroad. No change of ca[something]tio protracted stoppages will be made betw[een thi]s point and Lafayette, and it is probable that [something]ty will go on the same train as far as Ind[ianapol]is. At Indianapolis Mr. Lincoln will give [himself] up for twenty-four hours to the tender m[ercies] of the Executive and Legislative author[ities] of the Hoosier State. From Indianapol[is the] journey will be continued to Columb[us, Ohi]o, via Richmond and Dayton. At Colum[bus a] public reception by the State and city a[uthoriti]es will probably take place, and the publi[c at la]rge be given an opportunity for a few hou[rs to s]queeze the Presidential fingers. From Col[umbus a run to] Cleveland will next be made. From Cleve[land a]nother run will be taken to Buffalo, where a reception will again be held for a few hou[rs. Fr]om the city of the Lakes, a special train of t[he New] York Central Railroad will take the par[ty to A]lbany, where Weed will take his friend [Lincol]n into his keeping. Two days will probab[ly] be devoted to a consultation with the Republic[an chie]ftains that will be gathered around the [leader] of the Albany lobby. From Albany, the pre[sent i]ntention is to strike across to Harrisburg. Bu[t it is] all but certain that the New York Wide-A[wakes] will not be put off in any such manner, but [something]off the great Railsplitter down the Hudson t[o the Em]pire City. Should such be the case, at l[east tw]o days will be spent in the latter. If New [York] receives a visit, Philadelphia will not be over[looked]. The next stopping place to be made from [Philad]elphia is Harrisburg, where legislative co[something] will again be rendered for a day. From [Harris]burg a train is expected to run through to [Washi]ngton, with but a few minutes' stoppage at B[altimor]e.

Mrs. Lincoln and her three sons wil[l accom]pany the head of the family. Mrs. Lincoln [and B]ob, her eldest son, arrived from the East but [a few] days ago—the former from a purchasing [trip to] New York, the latter from Harvard Univer[sity].

Special trains will be used all the [way thr]ough. Various military companies, both here [and a]broad, have offered to do escort duty; but [since a m]artial display would tend to add to the irrit[ation] of the public mind, the offers have not been a[ccepte]d.

CHAPTER FOUR

FEBRUARY 1861

February 1, 1861

Springfield, 1 February 1861—11 P.M.
[New York *Herald*, 7 February 1861]

The visit of the President elect to the haunts of his youth, in the vicinity of Charleston, in the southern part of this State, terminated, as foreseen, without any incidents of great interest. After spending the night at the residence of his old and intimate friend, Senator [Thomas A.] Marshall, he set out in a carriage on Thursday morning [January 31] for the residence of his aged stepmother, who received her dutiful son with the utmost joy and gratification. Several hours were devoted by the affectionate two to the contemplation of the cherished past and the portentous future. The President elect then visited the grave of his father, situated a short distance from the old homestead, and spent some time in prayer. At three o'clock in the afternoon he returned to Charleston, accompanied by his mother. In the evening a public reception was held by him in the court room, upon the request of his republican friends. A large assemblage, consisting of several hundred ladies and gentlemen, congregated to exchange greetings with him. Being called upon for a speech, he stated in response that the time for a public definition of his views was not yet come, and hence he would content himself on the present occasion with an expression of his gratification at the manifestation of the kindness and sympathy of his friends. He then shook hands with all present, and retired amidst the hearty cheers of the gentlemen and the waving of handkerchiefs by the ladies.

Having embarked early in the morning, he reached this place at eleven A.M., in company with Senator Marshall. At Decatur, some forty miles east of this, he met a committee of Cincinnatians, composed of Messrs. Benjamin Eggleston, Charles S. Moore and A. McAlpin,[1] who were on their way to Springfield, for the purpose of tendering him the hospitalities of their city while on his way to Washington. He immediately accepted the invitation, and after arriving here wrote a letter to that effect, with which the committee started upon their return trip this evening. The visit will take place on the 13th inst. A special train will carry the President [elect] and his cortege from Indianapolis to the Queen City of the West [Cincinnati].

The all absorbing question of legislative discussion within the last twenty-four hours continued to be the proposition to appoint Commissioners to the

Washington Convention. The President [elect] being known to be adverse to the appointment of such, both the Governor and the State officers, and a majority of the republican members of both houses, were at first disinclined to take action in the premises. The example of New York, Pennsylvania, Ohio and other Northern States, and the urgent counsels of a number of conservative republican leaders, however, brought about a different view of the case on the part of Mr. Lincoln, as well as the Governor and the Legislature, and hence the series of joint resolutions was agreed upon in a republican caucus last night, and of the passage of which you will be advised by telegraph.

Mr. Lincoln not being in town, they were not introduced, as the majority report of a joint special committee, until after he had returned and expressed his approbation. Upon the report being made in the afternoon, a most lively discussion sprang up in the Senate, in consequence of the presentation of a minority report, in which the appointment of two democrats and three republicans was recommended. Senator Marshall made a vigorous speech, which derived peculiar significance from the fact that he had been in close intercourse with Mr. Lincoln during the preceding two days. In its leading passages he said:

> If this Union is to be held together, it is not by being ready to take up with any proposition that may be made, and to yield to any terms that may be demanded. By so doing you will never be done yielding, and you will never preserve the Union. I love the Union as dearly as any man, but there is something dearer even than Union—dearer than peace. It is manhood—it is principle. I believe that the preservation of this government depends upon our exhibiting firmness in this crisis; not stubbornness; not entire absence of conciliatory feelings; not stolidity, but firmness tempered with conciliation. No man, no country, ever gained anything by exhibiting a truckling weakness. * * * *
>
> I confess that I have but little hope of any good from this Conference of Commissioners. I fear it will amount to nothing, because the Southern Commissioners, as far as I know, will demand terms that cannot be conceded.

The minority report was tabled by a strict party vote, and that of the majority adopted, only one democrat—Senator Underwood[2]—voting for it.

In the House the resolutions did not come up until late in the evening. Long and telling speeches were made by both democrats and republicans, and the discussion did not terminate until eleven P.M., when the republican majority carried their passage.

Springfield, February 1, 1861
[New York *Herald*, 4 February 1861]

Mr. Lincoln returned home this morning after visiting his step-mother, and the grave of his father at Charleston.

He held a public reception in the town hall at Charleston, attended by hundreds of people. Being called upon to make a speech, he stated that the time for a public definition of the policy of his administration had not yet come; and that he could but express his gratification at seeing so many of his friends, and give them a hearty greeting. Most of those in attendance then shook hands with him and dispersed, amid enthusiastic cheering.

On his way here he met a deputation from Cincinnati on their way to Springfield to tender him the hospitalities of the city. The invitation was accepted, and the time of the visit fixed for the 13th inst.

A bronze medal, with the head of Henry Clay, has been sent by Daniel Ulmann to Mr. Lincoln, with a letter stating the gift was intended for the first President that represented the views of the great whig leader.

Mr. Lincoln expressed himself to a visiter yesterday, that if Pennsylvania be represented in the Cabinet it will be by Cameron and no one else.

J. A. Nunes, of San Francisco, had a protracted private interview with Mr. Lincoln to-day. He is anxious to see California represented in the Cabinet. The appointment of a member from the Pacific coast is looked upon here as very probable. No communication has passed between Mr. Lincoln and Colonel Fremont since the latter's arrival in the East.

The report that General Scott has detailed Colonel Sumner and Major Hunter to accompany Mr. Lincoln to Washington is based upon a misapprehension, only a few personal friends will compose his *cortege.*

Springfield, 1 February 1861
[Cincinnati *Commercial*, 2 February 1861]

The discussion of the proposition to send Commissioners to the Washington Convention was brought to a head to-day, in the Legislature, by the passage of the following resolutions: *They are understood to be prepared under Mr. Lincoln's supervision:*

Whereas: Resolutions of the State of Virginia have been communicated to the General Assembly of this State, proposing the appointment of Commissioners, by the several States, to meet in Convention, on the 4th day of February, A.D., 1861, at Washington.

Resolved, By the Senate, the House of Representatives concurring herein, that with an earnest desire for the return of harmony and kind relations among our States and out of respect to the Commonwealth of Virginia, the Governor of this State be requested to appoint five Commissioners on the part of the State of Illinois, to confer and consult with the Commissioners of other States, who shall meet at Washington, provided that said Commissioners shall at all times be subject to the control of the General Assembly of the State of Illinois.

Resolved, That the appointment of Commissioners by the State of Illinois, in response to the invitation of the State of Virginia, is not an expression of opinion on the part of this State that any amendment of the Federal Constitution is requisite to secure to the people of the slaveholding States adequate guarantees for the security of their rights, nor an approval of the basis of settlement of our difficulties proposed by the State of Virginia, but it is an expression of our willingness to unite with the State of Virginia in an earnest effort to adjust the present unhappy controversies in the spirit in which the Constitution was originally formed, and consistently with its principles.

Resolved, That while we are willing to appoint Commissioners to meet in convention with those of other States, for consultation upon matters which at present distract our harmony as a nation, we also insist that the appropriate and constitutional method of considering and acting upon the grievances complained of by our sister States, would be by the call of a convention for the amendment of the Constitution in the manner contemplated by the 5th Article of that instrument; and if the States deeming themselves aggrieved shall request Congress to call such convention, the Legislature of Illinois will and does concur in such call.

Messrs. Eggleston, Moore, and McAlpin—the Committee of Invitation from your city—met Mr. Lincoln on the way here.

The invitation was at once accepted, and a letter to that effect prepared by Mr. Lincoln on his arrival here, and handed to the Committee.

They left for home this evening.

The visit will take place on the 13th.

I am informed that Eggleston told Mr. Lincoln, that the leader in the Commercial on the 31st, was written by Mr. Chase. The article has created a great sensation here.

February 2, 1861

Springfield, 2 February 1861
[Cincinnati Commercial, 4 February 1861]

Mr. Lincoln expressed himself to a visitor [William Larimer] yesterday, that if Pennsylvania be represented in the Cabinet, it will be by Simon Cameron and no one else.

J. A. Nunes of San Francisco had a protracted private interview with Mr. Lincoln to-day. He is anxious to see California represented in the Cabinet. The appointment of a member from the Pacific coast, is looked upon here as very probable. No communication has passed between Mr. Lincoln and Col. Fremont, since the latter's arrival in the east.

A report that Gen. Scott had detailed Col. Sumner[3] and Major Hunter to accompany Mr. Lincoln to Washington is based upon a misapprehension. Only a few personal friends will compose his cortege. Governor Yates appointed to-day Ex. Governor [John] Wood, Judge [Stephen T.] Logan, B. C. Cook,[4] John M. Palmer, and Thos. J. Turner,[5] all decided anti-compromise Republicans, commissioners to the Washington Convention.

Springfield, 2 February 1861
[Cincinnati Commercial, 5 February 1861]

The President-elect returned from his excursion to Charleston at 11 A.M. yesterday. The two days' exemption from the cares and perplexities of his office, and especially from the importunities of place seekers, proved quite a relief to him. He comes back very much improved in appearance by the refreshing prairie air, ready to resume his labors with renewed vigor. The particulars of his adventures in Egypt [i.e., southern Illinois] having been telegraphed to you, an account is not deemed necessary in this connection.

On the way to this place Mr. Lincoln came up with Messrs. Eggleston, Moore and McAlpin, the Committee of invitation from your city, who were on their way hither for the purpose of inviting him to deviate from his designated route, and make a detour from Indianapolis to Columbus via. Cincinnati. The bearers of the flattering tender of hospitalities of your people were received with great kindness and courtesy, and an acceptance at once vouchsafed. The Committee accompanied Mr. Lincoln to this point and received shortly after arrival, a letter from him formally accepting the invitation, with which they started upon their return trip at 6 o'clock.

I was informed yesterday afternoon that the visit was to take place on the 13th inst., and telegraphed you to that effect. I learned, however, this morning, from Mr. Lincoln himself, that the day had not been definitely determined upon; but would be made known within the next few days.

A party, traveling on the same train with the President elect and the Cincinnati Committee, informed me, that shortly after the company had taken seats in the cars, Ben Eggleston pulled a copy of the *Commercial* of the 31st out of his pocket, and read the leading editorial of that issue to the President elect. I also learn from the same source that he apprised Mr. Lincoln of the real or fancied existing belief in Cincinnati, that the article in question was the product of Ex-Governor Chase's pen. Although yourself as well as your patrons would, doubtlessly, be glad to number the distinguished statesman among your contributors, I have yet felt no hesitation to declare to those that interrogated me during the day, that I thought Benjamin had made a grievous, although well-meant mistake. But, whoever the author of the remarkable leader may be, it is a fact that it created a good deal of sensation in the State House. It was read aloud twice by prominent politicians to a circle of attentive hearers, and wherever your correspondent went in the evening, he had to hear allusions to it. As to the opinions expressed in regard to the views conveyed in it, I must say, that the novelty of some of them on the one hand, and the boldness of phraseology on the other, elicited more of wonder than approbation. A proper digestion of its meaning will probably result in a better appreciation.

The agitation in the Legislature upon the proposition to send Commissioners to Washington, was brought to a close in the course of yesterday afternoon by the passage of the resolutions telegraphed in full. There was at first a strong disinclination, both on the part of the Governor and the General Assembly, not to join in the movement, and that simply because of the conviction, that the Convention should not be held previous to the inauguration of the Republican Administration, and that it had been fixed at so early a date, in order to present an ultimatum in the shape of impossible concessions, the refusal of which would be seized upon to rush the border slave States out of the union before the 4th of March. This opinion was also shared by Mr. Lincoln. But it seems that the example of the Republican Governors and Legislatures of New York, Pennsylvania, and your own State [Ohio], and the urgent counsel of conservative home politicians, brought about a change after a few days of fermentation, in consequence of which the Republican caucus of the night before last agreed to force the passage of resolutions alluded to. They were submitted to Mr. Lincoln after his return, and having his approbation, were pressed in the Senate during the afternoon, and in the House late in the evening. A very excited discussion arose in both Houses, owing to the persistent attempts of the Democratic minority to amend them, by requiring the Governor to take two of the five Commissioners from the Democratic ranks. The proposed amendments were voted down and the resolutions as agreed upon by the Republican caucus, passed by a strict party vote; only one Democratic member of the Senate voting for them.

Senator [Thomas A.] Marshall made a very forcible speech on the occasion, which derived considerable interest from the fact, that he is one of the oldest and most confidential friends of Mr. Lincoln, and had just been in two days close intercourse with him upon the excursion to Charleston. The leading passages of his effort were thus: [omitted because it is quoted in a previous dispatch]

February 3, 1861

Springfield, 3 February 1861
[New York *Herald*, 8 February 1861]

Of all human vocations newspaper writing is doubtless the most thankless. While in every other intellectual pursuit the capable worker not only enjoys the fruits of his labors, but also receives due credit for them, the journalist runs his professional career without the all powerful stimulus of an individual recognition or appreciation of his efforts in disseminating intelligence and culture. Having become fully reconciled and accustomed by many years' service in the reportorial traces to this relative obscurity, your correspondent never dreamt of possessing any great significance until he learned, a day or so ago, that, unknown to himself, he has acted a prominent, and, it seems to be supposed, consequential part in the grandest office hunting play, performed during his stay in Springfield, viz: The Cameron melodrama. Will you believe it?—your most humble representative has been denounced to the President elect as one of the main instruments of a hideous conspiracy concocted to run Cameron off the track to the Cabinet; one of a "vile band of corruptionists"—to quote the expressive language of one of your Washington correspondents—combined for the purpose of defaming and defeating the illustrious political *impressario* of Pennsylvania. The announcement may sound strange, but it is nevertheless based on facts. During the last fortnight several bills of indictment have been received by Mr. Lincoln, consisting of copious clippings from the HERALD and lengthy revelations as to the alleged anti-Cameron plot. One of the main counts is the charge that the HERALD's correspondent was fed by Alexander R. [K.] McClure, of Harrisburg, during his (McClure's) visit to this point, to make onslaughts upon the Senator from

Pennsylvania. This and other accusations of minor import are unworthy of any extended refutation. Suffice it to say that the partisans of Mr. Cameron have convicted themselves by their obsequious information of the very malfeasance they attempted to fix upon your correspondent, viz: wholesale mendacity and slander, and that they have written themselves down, in the eyes of the very parties they sought to impress, as both fools and knaves.

Your correspondent will not allow this matter to rest here. Having fortunately got possession of names, he will fully expose the operations of these wheedling libelers as soon as he shall have heard from certain parties in Pennsylvania.

The President elect has announced his intention not to do anything further towards the completion of his Cabinet until after his arrival in Washington so frequently and openly within the last week that it is really to be wondered how visiters can continue to interrogate him as to his purposes in the premises. Yet a number of such have succeeded in exacting reiterations of them since his return from Charleston. His replies show that his mind is unchanged on this subject.

I do not think that the New York *Tribune* had "positive information from Springfield by which it could feel authorized to" contradict the rumor that "Mr. Cameron has been or is to be reinvited to a seat in Mr. Lincoln's Cabinet." For I am able to announce with equal if not more positiveness that the President elect informed Gen. Wm. Larimer, Jr., late a prominent citizen of Pittsburg[h], Pa., and now of Denver City, only the day before yesterday, that if Pennsylvania was to be at all represented in the Cabinet, it would be by Mr. Cameron, and no one else.

I deem it highly probable that the Pacific States will have a representative among Mr. Lincoln's constitutional advisers. It is certain, at all events, that the demands of that section of the country are still held under advisement. As to Col. Fremont's prospect, it is now understood here that he is disinclined to serve in the Cabinet, and will be more likely to accept a foreign mission. If Mr. Lincoln should conclude to gratify the wishes of California and Oregon, Mr. [Eugene] Sullivan will doubtless be the man.

Mr. Joseph A. Nunes, of San Francisco, had a protracted private interview with Mr. Lincoln in the course of yesterday in reference to the appointment of a California member. He is highly gratified with the result of his visit, and rather confident that success will crown his efforts. Mr. Nunes made hosts of friends among our politicians during his short stay. He addressed a large audience in the Hall of Representatives last evening on the questions of the day, and his speech was pronounced by all present the best oratorical effort made here in many days.

The Governor appointed to-day Judge Logan, John M. Palmer, Hon. Thos. J. Turner, ex-Governor Wood and B. C. Cook Commissioners to Washington. They are all prominent politicians, and rather radical in their republican professions. They go with no hope of a successful mission.

Mrs. Lincoln has been presented with a splendidly ornamented sewing machine.

Major W. Harrow[6] and J. G. Bowman,[7] of Indiana, and Colonel W. Jameson, of Ohio, are in town. The former two are after local appointments in the Southern part of this State.

Springfield, 3 February 1861
[New York *Herald*, 16 February 1861]

How are the mighty fallen! Just three months ago the great republican party, after a most desperate and protracted struggle, routed the disjointed ranks of the divided democracy, and secured the dearly coveted prize of the succession to the federal administration. The conquerors then stood in deep and solid columns—flushed with victory—shouting with triumph—exulting at the prospect of the spoils, and deriding their vanquished opponents. How different is the present aspect of the victorious host. Noisy exultation has died away. Assurance has given room to doubts and apprehensions. Loud defiance has resigned its place to gentle sounds of conciliation. Unconditional surrender of the federal power is no longer insisted on. Unwavering firmness can no more be boasted of. Discouragement and defection are visible in every direction—in short, the nearer the fruits of victory are approached, the smaller the chances of their undisturbed enjoyment seem to grow.

It is not only in Congress that dissonances are audible in the republican ranks in reference to the compromise question. It is not only in their party organs that flagrant discrepancies of opinion are becoming manifest—nay, in almost every State that rolled up a majority for Lincoln and Hamlin, a division of the party in power into pro and anti-compromisers, or conservatives and radicals, appears to be imminent. New England seems to hold out best. But the Northwest—the firm, faithful Northwest, to which the leaders of the party pointed with so much pride and confidence upon the inauguration of the secession movement—bids fair to come altogether short of expectation. In Ohio the agitation of the proposition to send Commissioners to the Washington Convention in the Legislature resulted in a virtual split of the republican majority. Even here—under the very eyes of the President elect and the stiffening influences of his display of a most respectable amount of backbone—discord, arising from the same sources, threatened at one time to drive the conservative republicans into affiliation with the democratic members, in order to secure the appointment of Commissioners, and although harmony has been restored, it is more than likely that dissensions will break out with greater violence as soon as the question, whether to compromise or not, will be brought to an actual head by the necessity of a decision either one way or the other.

That profound apprehensions of a wreck of the republican party against the compromise rock prevail in Presidential circles is certain. The President elect, indeed, cannot help being impressed with the existence of dangerous variations of opinion as to the character of the remedies best applied in the present crisis, by the flagrant incongruities in the counsels daily offered to him by both the rank and file of his supporters in this region. He must be aware that anything but a unanimity animates those that endeavor to point out a line of policy to him, and it may be well presumed that the prospect of a fatal rupture in the very element that was expected to support and strengthen his administration is not apt to lessen the already existing perplexities of his position.

The *Tribune* philosopher [Horace Greeley] arrived at last, at an early hour this morning. His advent in the capacity of a lecturer having been previously announced, the event did not produce the flutter among politicians it would have caused had he arisen in another *deus ex machina.* Having an engagement at Jacksonville for this evening, his stay in Springfield was confined to a few hours. He had just time to hobble up to the State House, shake hands with a few members of the Legislature, learn the news of his defeat at Albany,[8] and make an appointment with the President elect for a long interview in the course of to-morrow, and catch the Western train. A detailed account of his operations after his return to-morrow morning may be confidently looked for by the readers of the HERALD in my next letter.

Mr. Lincoln received an invitation from the authorities of the Empire State and the citizens of Albany to visit the capital of New York, while on his way to Washington, on yesterday morning. It was at once accepted. The day of his visit, however, is not yet fixed.

It may now be considered certain that the Presidential party will stop two or three days in your city [New York]. I learn that orders have already been sent to engage apartments at the Metropolitan Hotel.

February 4, 1861

Springfield, 4 February 1861
[New York *Herald*, 5 February 1861]
Grave apprehensions prevail in Presidential circles of fatal dissensions in the republican party on the compromise question, and consequent embarrassment

of the incoming Administration. The Chicago *Tribune* reads Mr. Kellogg, of Illinois, out of the party on account of his compromise propositions. Much feeling is manifested here among the radical republicans in view of the apparent discrepancy between his declarations during his late visit to this place and the position now occupied by him.

Mr. Washburn, of Maine,[9] telegraphed to Gov. Yates urging him not to appoint Commissioners to Washington, as the appointment would demoralize the republican party. This and other appeals of the same nature prevented the departure of the Commissioners until this evening.

Horace Greeley arrived here this morning, and went west after a few hours' stay, without seeing Mr. Lincoln. He is expected back to-morrow morning, when he will make his wishes known to the President elect. He is very severe on Mr. Cameron and Mr. Kellogg. A positive declaration, in reference to the compromise movement, will doubtlessly, be elicited by him. Mr. Lincoln received the news of Greeley's defeat at Albany with his usual complacency.

A Pennsylvania delegation is here[10] to urge Gov. Reeder in case of Cameron's withdrawal.

Mr. Lincoln has received and accepted an invitation from the State authorities and citizens of Albany to visit that city. The trip to New York from Albany is now definitely determined upon. The Presidential party will stop at the Metropolitan Hotel while in New York city.

Springfield, 4 February 1861
[New York *Herald*, 16 February 1861]

There has been no more noted character in Springfield, next to Mr. Lincoln himself, than Colonel E. E. Ellsworth, commander of the celebrated corps of the United States Zouave Cadets, of Chicago.[11] He is now studying law with the law partner of Mr. Lincoln [William Herndon]. I recently called upon him at his office, and found him engaged in replying to the numerous letters which had accumulated during the last few weeks in which he has been engaged in stumping Illinois for the republican cause. I found the Colonel to be very thoroughly posted on military matters, and, in my opinion, his love for the military will override his intentions to become a lawyer. Finding his opinion on military matters eagerly sought by the leading military men of the country, I obtained from him a statement, which in substance is as follows:

We have in this country an institution which is referred to occasionally in Fourth of July orations, as the "bulwark of our country's liberties," &c., which all unite in pronouncing indispensable. While they believe a certain degree of fitness, education and practice necessary to the success of men in any other pursuit or profession, they persist in maintaining that our militia, with no means, comparatively, of educating themselves to their duties, and laboring under the weight of an organization defective in principle and detail, are "well enough," and it only requires the emergency to call into play this immense power which our people believe exists somewhere, to give life to a force of two million defenders of our government armed, disciplined, equipped and serviceable. This does very well to talk, looks very pretty on paper, and conveys a pleasant sense of security; but the facts tell a very different tale. Some one turns to the register, and triumphantly tells you to look there, and sure, enough, it foots up an aggregate of almost three million of men; but you ask your triumphant friend, "Is that correct?" "Certainly," he replies. "How large a force has Illinois, for instance?" you ask further. "Why, sir," he responds, "Illinois has 257,000 men, an army of itself." "When was that report made?" "In 1855." Pursuing this subject, you inquire still further, "Of what do you understand that force to be composed?" "Why, sir, of uniformed men, armed, drilled, and disciplined, and ready to respond to their country's call." Assuming that, with the exception of a few States, this is a fair example, let us look at the facts. That report embraces the number of men in the State in 1855 capable of bearing arms, and, instead of 257,000, we have not one thousand uniformed and equipped men in the State, and they, having no incentive to exertion, pay but little attention to military matters; and the whole system has fallen into disuse and decay. This is not an isolated instance by any means. "Well," says our friend, "admitting that to be the fact, we all know that we have the most military spirit of any people on the globe, and if we are assailed the whole nation would fly to arms. Look at the Revolution; look at Mexico." "Well," we ask, "what do you prove?" "Why, that if a people of between three and four millions can successfully combat with Great Britain, one of the strongest nations on the earth, or march through an enemy's country with a small army, fighting against the odds our men encountered in Mexico, that now, when we have thirty millions of people, we are equal to any emergency."

Very true, but does it not also prove that, had the men of the Revolution, added to the advantage of fighting on their own ground, and with the motives which sustained them, enjoyed at the onset the advantages of thorough organization and discipline, the war of seven years might have been brought to a termination in half that time? Or does it disprove the fact that our army in Mexico was indebted for its efficiency to the labor of educated and competent officers, without whose services the volunteers would have been but little better than an armed mob, and their valor, great as it was, would not have enabled them to combat successfully against even the partially disciplined troops of Mexico? "Oh, but stop," says our friend again, "you will admit that the men, by the aid of educated officers, were made good soldiers in the field?" "Certainly." "Well, then, haven't we the same abundance of officers now?" "Undoubtedly, and if men were again required for a foray of the same nature—requiring comparatively a small number of men—we should not realize the incomplete nature of our militia system more than we do at present; but wars with Mexico, with Kansas and with Utah, don't constitute the full measure of our liabilities. Why do we appropriate immense sums to fortify our coasts, and for the manufacture of arms and munitions of war? Is it not proof that the policy of our government, while decidedly opposed to standing armies, still recognizes the necessity of preparation for any emergency? Yes. On whom are we to depend to man these fortifications and use these arms? On the militia, of course. Then the question arises what will prove the most economical and the best policy? To wait until the necessity overtakes us, and then rely upon the masses of patriotic men who will assemble readily enough, but whose very numbers would prove their destruction; or shall we reduce this harum-scarum institution to a systematic, economical and available organization, whose discipline will enable them, with one-half the number, to accomplish double the amount of service to that of the mob. Will any statesman who has examined this matter say that the maintenance of a limited but sufficient militia as the main defense and reliance of our country for protection against invasion, for enforcement of the laws and all ordinary purposes for which, in all countries, a greater or less number of troops are occasionally necessary, is not a measure of the highest importance to our security? And how much is the expedience of this policy enhanced when it is known that this militia, if properly organized, can, in times of peace, be engaged in doing a great good by diverting the attention of our young men from the popular, fashionable and pernicious means of amusement that now constitute almost their only recreation, and opening to them the means of physical exercise and social intercourse, which, surrounded by the proper safeguards, will result in the developement of a manly and independent spirit. While wishing that it might take a national character as a permanent and reliable institution, divested of all its objectionable features, we are compelled to acknowledge that our present system does no general good, and for its true purpose is valueless—a nonentity—and therefore useless. But we are told, that though this is undoubtedly true, yet it cannot well be remedied, it has been so for years, a dour people don't see the necessity of encouraging the militia, and it usually has a bad effect on those who join, and does them no permanent good, and, therefore, as there is no inducement for any one to devote their time to a general change, it will have to run on so. Now we have arrived at the issue precisely. With the first assertion I decidedly disagree. With the second I am compelled to coincide, and this is the reason why no evidence is shown by the mass of our staunch citizens in wanting a militia, not because they do not recognize the importance of it, but because it is diverted from its true purposes and does no good to the country or its individual members. Now I believe that the moment the military spirit is turned in the true direction and becomes a source of benefit to all who connect themselves with it, the public will be as one in their approval of it. I believe this can be done. I know we have abundance of spirit, and that militia organizations are susceptible of being made incalculably beneficial to the young men of the country; that the best class of citizens in the country would soon fill its ranks; that it may be raised to the dignity of a necessary and beneficial public institution; that a membership may become a guarantee of respectability, and command the guarantee of ability and consideration. Every man, according to the extent of his ability, owes it to his country to do all in his power to aid in the establishment and maintenance of its institutions and all the safeguards and supports which surround and uphold it. Some men have great abilities and splendid talents, and they devote themselves to the conduct of our government; others to the establishment of our literature; others the developement of the resources of the country; others, again, to our army. The importance of all these pursuits is recognized, and they give power, wealth and honor. But no one seems to feel encouraged to devote himself to the work of bringing about a change in this matter, partly because there seems no immediate prospect of reward, and because of the overwhelming difficulties which stand in the way—although all unite in saying that 'if these things can be done, it is worth the labor of any man.' Knowing this, yet believing that every step in the right direction will meet the public approval, and that it only requires a determined, persistent movement to awaken attention to the importance of the matter, and bring to its support men of greater and sufficient ability to assure a successful recognition and ultimate success, I think that I can best fulfill the measure of my duty by devoting myself to the extent of my ability to the work. Your people in New York, and others who appreciate this matter in Massachusetts and other States have labored very hard and accomplished a great deal; but the work must be commenced at the fountain head, in order that all the States may unite and be benefitted alike by it."

I inquired of Colonel Ellsworth what measures he thought would be calculated to effect the changes he suggests, and he showed drafts of laws, the manuscripts of half written books, and various memoranda, the result of five years' hard labor. From these I am permitted to abstract the following points in the proposed reconstruction of the volunteer militia of the United States:

First. An entire change in the present system, and the recognition of the real importance of the militia, and their true relation to the army.

Second. Measures which elevate the standing of the militia, by limiting the number in each State, by opening membership to only those who will comply with certain reasonable requirements, which guarantee the suppression of the present objectionable features of our military bodies.

Third. To make it an object for a good class of men to take hold, by a general adherence to these principles and by adding to the benefits of the exercise to be derived by the establishment of gymnasiums, reading rooms, libraries and lectures in connection with the organization, and an exemption from certain duties.

Fourth. To debar from officer and command all incompetent persons—in short, making membership equivalent to a guarantee of respectability, and command an evidence of ability, thus removing the only barrier that has existed between the officers of the army and militia, and leading the way to a cordial co-operation and unity of feeling.

Fifth. A change in the present system of appointment of cadets to the Military Academy, providing for the appointment of those who are selected from the cadet organizations (it is a part of his plan to introduce a systematic drill as an exercise into the schools) for their superior ability, and requiring these men, from the time of their entrance into the army until they attain the grade of captain, or are appointed to duty, to spend a certain portion of their time, say one or two months in each year, in the district from which they were appointed, in instructing the militia officers, thus disseminating the benefit of the Military Academy throughout the entire militia organization.

Sixth. Giving the militia the right of occupation and use for practice of all available United States fortifications.

Seventh. The introduction of a cheap, economical and serviceable uniform, and a uniform system of arming the militia, and the introduction of a uniform system of drill throughout the militia.

I asked how it was possible to bring about all these changes. And he replied, that it could be done by the establishment of a Department of Militia at the headquarters of the army, the officers of which should act in concert with the Adjutant Generals of the States, and should devote themselves to the accomplishment of these ends. The first step would be to publish and circulate from this department a complete set of works particularly adapted to the militia. This would lead to concert of action among the militia, and result in the passage, first, of the necessary laws by the general government, and then in a uniform system of laws throughout the States, which would make the project a success.

Although Col. Ellsworth had held these views, and been laboring to develope and perfect his plan for five years, yet his extreme youth made him hesitate about thrusting them forward. After he had matured his plans, about a year since, he laid out his programme to bring them into effect. The first step was to demonstrate the practicability of such of his ideas as could be demonstrated through the medium of a limited organization. Hence the organization of the Zouaves and their brilliant success. After their return to Chicago, having accomplished that portion of his programme, the next step was to bring about the establishment of the Military [Militia] Department in connection with the War Department, in order to bring about the other portions of his programme. To gain the necessary influence, he being on the wrong side of politics, it was necessary to gain position and bide his time. So, forming an organization for the Zouaves which opened the way for the study of battalion evolutions and the formation of a regiment at the proper time, officered exclusively by the Zouaves, he left them and came to Springfield and commenced the study of law.

Col. Ellsworth, in addition to his law studies, is now engaged in writing a book especially adapted to the use of the militia, giving all the details of military organization, for formation of military corps, selection of officers, necessary forms, &c.; choice of arms, uniforms, &c.; directions for the manufacture of uniforms and care of arms, forms of parades and everything connected therewith; instructions for camp duties, all matters connected with military affairs; also another book adapted for self-instruction, containing all the drill of the infantry and light infantry—skirmishing and bayonet drill, direction for instruction and use of the sword, a system of military gymnastics, directions for use of the arms—in fact, a complete compendium of everything pertaining to the militia that can be useful and available.

The Colonel showed me a lithographic pattern of a new uniform just completed. He has been experimenting until he thinks he has obtained a uniform that will meet general approbation. It is pronounced by all experienced officers who have seen it as superior for all purposes of economy, comfort and durability to any now in vogue in this country or Europe.

February 5, 1861

Springfield, 5 February 1861
[New York *Herald*, 16 February 1861]

No artist ever longed more ardently for a classical model than the HERALD's correspondent for an opportunity to add the philosopher of the *Tribune* [Horace Greeley] to the gallery of political portraiture collected by him since November for the benefit of your readers in this place. Ever since the once mighty, but alas! now fallen, chieftain of the Albany lobby [Thurlow Weed] excited the natives of this village nearly out of their wits by a visit to the President elect, I have devoutly, but vainly, scanned the hotel registers with diurnal regularity for the well known scrawl of the senior of the *Tribune.* Giddings, Weed, Covode, Reeder, Wilmot, Cameron, Baker, Chase and Corwin, and other republican eminences, had all been here. Why, then, should not Greeley likewise wend his way hither? It is true his advent would most naturally be looked for immediately after Weed had plied "Old Abe" with his cunning wag. But the *Tribune* man had probably learned from the HERALD's Springfield correspondence that Weed's compromise pills operated more *ad nauseum* than otherwise, and never thought the administering of an antidote necessary. Again, he knew that the great rail splitter was in the habit of relying on his own energies as equal to the job of Cabinet making without his assistance. Moreover, he doubtless took the broad hint conveyed by the writer at a very early date, that the President elect would not receive applications for subordinate offices until after the 4th of March, and hence was in no great haste to make tracks for this point.

However this may be, his hieroglyphics[12] among the latest arrivals at the St. Nicholas Hotel furnished conclusive evidence this morning that he had acted upon the maxim "better late than never," and at last made his long expected appearance.

It would be superfluous to state that the event created a great flurry among our political quidnuncs. To be sure, for the last ten days big posters had conveyed the intelligence in gigantic letters on all sides that the Hon. Horace

Greeley, of New York, was to lecture on "America west of the Mississippi" on the evening of the 5th last. But his old hat, his cowhide boots and general oddity of appearance, together with his political fame, will never fail to attract universal notice, no matter how well and long apprised a community may be of his coming. Besides, would any reader of the HERALD believe for a moment that Greeley came here for the sole purpose of delivering a lecture? Why, the idea of a purely accidental professional visit to the biding place of the powers that are about to be is simply absurd.

How did Horace take the news of his defeat at Albany? is probably the first question asked by your readers, on reading of his advent in this region. Well, your correspondent must confess that he has not conversed with the disappointed aspirant on this rather pertinent subject. But if the face is in reality the mirror of the soul, the smiling serenity of his countenance indicated most unmistakeably that he is a philosopher, not only by name, but also by virtue of the calm resignation he displayed under this fatal blow to his ambitious dreams. The only effect the failure of his hopes for the Senatorial toga appeared to have upon him was to make him more than usually reticent and retired. He stuck closely to his room all day, and admitted but few visiters to his presence.

But what of his relations to the President elect during his stay? Candor compels me to state that he stood on his dignity and awaited the approach of Mr. Lincoln, instead of approaching. This independent stroke of policy was somewhat hazardous, in view of the constant demands upon "Old Abe's" time by visiters, that gladly submit to the trouble of hunting him up, but proved successful in the end. During the entire morning and a portion of the afternoon, however, Horace sat in his room in patient expectation of seeing the gaunt form Presidential loom up in his door. Many a deceptive knock was heard and many an unwelcome visiter entered until his wishes were realized. It was, indeed, not until about four P.M. that Mr. Lincoln could rid himself of the importunities of the curious and expectant crowd that daily besieges him, and pay his respects to the man whose pen contributed as much, if not more than any other influence, to his elevation to the highest office in the land.

Mr. Lincoln was conducted to Mr. Greeley's room by Mr. G. B. Lincoln, the well known merchant of your city,[13] who has been sojourning here for the last two days. Quite a number of newsmongers were standing in the vestibule of the hotel when the two passed through it on their way up stairs, and it was truly wonderful to behold the inquiring stretch of necks, the widely opened mouths and the distended eyes.

What would not most of them have given for the privilege of being present at this interview between the most potential republican journalist and the coming guide of the destinies of this country? What a sight the meeting of these two awkward and homely, but remarkable personages, must have afforded. What a treat to have listened to their exchange of advice and opinion, unrestrained as that must have been, from their common, characteristic, frank bluntness. But, unfortunately, the privacy customary on such occasions was not deviated from, and hence I am unable, at the hour of this writing (seven P.M.), to give "full particulars," but trust to be able to do so in my next.

The interview lasted nearly three hours. Mr. G. B. Lincoln was present only during part of it.

Greeley will deliver his lecture this evening, and leave for St. Louis on the early morning train.

Springfield, 5 February 1861
[New York *Herald*, 6 February 1861]

Mr. Lincoln has restricted the time for receiving visitors to one and a half hours each day during the remainder of his stay. A last general reception will be given to-morrow evening at his private residence.

Horace Greeley returned from the West this morning. This afternoon he was called upon at his hotel by Mr. Lincoln. The interview lasted several hours. Mr. Greeley urged a strict adherence to an anti-compromise policy, and is said to have received gratifying assurances. His opinion as to the Cabinet and other appointments was solicited and given. He is known to be strongly opposed to Cameron, and very much interested in the appointment of Chase and Colfax. Colonel Fremont, he thinks, should have the mission to France. Although just defeated in Albany, he did not ask anything either for himself or friends. G. B. Lincoln, of New York, was present during part of the interview.

The "irrepressible conflict" is raging among the Republican organs of this State. The Chicago *Tribune* is severely attacked for denouncing Seward and Kellogg as untrue to the republican faith, and claiming to reflect Mr. Lincoln's views.

Governor Curtin has been invited to meet Mr. Lincoln at Philadelphia.

W. S. Wood, of New York, acts as *avant courier* to the President elect, making arrangements for special trains and appointments at hotels.

S. N. Pettis, of Pennsylvania,[14] is here, recommending himself for the Governorship of Nebraska.

Another Indiana delegation, consisting of J. L. Smith,[15] O. L. Clark,[16] and A. L. White, M. C.,[17] is in town to press Smith for the Cabinet. Their presence at this late hour of Mr. Lincoln's stay is altogether undesired.

The influx of politicians is so great that a large number are nightly obliged to seek shelter in sleeping cars.[18]

Springfield, 5 February 1861
[San Francisco *Bulletin,* 26 February 1861]

THE PRESIDENT ELECT AND THE
COMPROMISE PROPOSITIONS AGAIN

Since my last so many unfounded reports as to the position of Mr. Lincoln in reference to the Compromise question have again found their way into the leading journals, both East and West, that I feel warranted in referring once more to the views of the President elect upon the same subjects, lest your readers receive wrong impressions.

On Tuesday last [January 28], a despatch was sent out from Washington to the "associated press," stating in positive terms that Mr. Lincoln had written to his Congressional friends, recommending a conciliatory disposition towards the South, and expressing a readiness to acquiesce in an adjustment of the present difficulties on the basis of the Border State propositions. A rumor reached here at the same time, that Schuyler Colfax was one of the recipients of the alleged letters. So soon as the despatch and report had become known to the friends of Mr. Lincoln, a number of them at once interrogated him on the subject. Seeing their evident uneasiness, he did not hesitate a moment, but removed their apprehensions forthwith by denying in the most positive manner—first, that he had written any letters of the reputed tenor to any Congressman, and secondly, that he was prepared to acquiesce or to counsel the acquiescence of his friends in any measure suggested thus far for the settlement of the difficulties between the North and South. The Springfield [*Illinois State*] *Journal* of the following morning had an obviously authorized paragraph to this same effect at the head of its editorial columns. It pronounced the despatch in question a "canard of the first water," and wound up with this significant declaration: "The country may rest assured that in Abraham Lincoln they have a Republican President, one who will give them a Republican Administration. Mr. Lincoln is *not* committed to the Border State propositions, nor to any other. He stands immovably on the Chicago platform, and he will neither acquiesce in nor counsel his friends to acquiesce in any compromise that surrenders one iota of it."

Your correspondent himself had occasion, but a few days since, to learn Mr. Lincoln's opinion in this matter from his own lips. It was in the reception room, and during a conversation of the President elect with a prominent politician of this State. He then and there reiterated the assertion, given in my last, that of all the compromise measures proposed in both Houses of Congress, the Border State propositions alone would be worth considering, and acceptable only after embodying a provision prohibiting the acquisition of any more territory without the consent of two-thirds of the States.

In the course of the same conversation, Mr. Lincoln also gave it to be understood, that he scorned the idea of buying his right of way to Washington by showing an anxiety for compromise, and that he hoped his friends would not consent to anything of the kind until their Constitutional right of taking possession of the Federal Government, was recognized *without consideration*. On the other hand, however, he let it out that, his own opinions and predilections to the contrary notwithstanding, he would probably not withhold his sanction from any measure passed by Congress for the re-consolidation of the Union, provided he would be satisfied that it expressed the wishes of a majority of the nation. But he took no pains to conceal his conviction at the same time that nothing the North could offer could induce the cotton States to retrace their steps and return to their allegiance to the Federal Government, and have no other effect than to humiliate and demoralize the Republican party.

LINCOLN AND THE WASHINGTON CONVENTION OF COMMISSIONERS FROM THE BORDER SLAVE STATES

A good deal of agitation has been experienced in Presidential circles during the last week in connection with the proposition to appoint representatives of Illinois to the Convention of Border States Commissioners now holding in Washington. Both the Governor and the Legislature were at first utterly disinclined to respond to the Virginia invitation—not from any unreasonable hostility and spirit of retaliation towards the South, but simply because of their conviction that the Convention should have been held after, and not before the inauguration of the Republican Administration, and that the character of the Southern demands already announced to be made upon the Convention were such as to preclude in advance all possibility of arriving at an understanding. Mr. Lincoln was also known to be opposed to the appointment of Commissioners, a fact which doubtlessly did as much towards preventing it for the time as the reluctance of the executive and legislative authorities. But, on Thursday last [January 31], strong appeals were received from the Governors of New York, Pennsylvania, Ohio, Indiana and other Northern States, seconded by distinguished Republican leaders in Washington, in favor of the appointment, and although their effect was paralyzed to a great extent by the telegraphic remonstrances of radical Republicans from all parts of the country, the President elect, the Governor and the Legislature, after several days of constant consultation and deliberation, came to the conclusion at the eleventh hour that the sending of Commissioners was advisable, after all. Accordingly, the annexed joint resolutions were introduced on Friday last and passed by the Republican majorities in both Houses, after a most animated discussion. As they are known to have been proposed under the immediate supervision of Mr. Lincoln, and embody a reflection of his views in the premises, I subjoin them in full: [omitted—see above, entry for 1 February 1861]

In pursuance of these resolutions, the Governor appointed Judge Logan, ex-Gov. Wood, G. P. [Burton C.] Cook, Thomas J. Turner, and John M. Palmer, Commissioners. They are all decidedly anti-compromise Republicans, and go with the determination of not yielding anything. Judge Logan is the oldest and most intimate friend of Mr. Lincoln.

CABINET MATTERS

Within the past few days Mr. Lincoln has repeated his already expressed intention not to do anything further towards the construction of his Cabinet until after his arrival in Washington, to various visitors that came here to press the claims of different aspirants. He intimated also to the same parties, that being engaged in preparing the first draft of his Message, he desired as little allusion to Cabinet matters as possible. The only noteworthy facts developed in regard to this subject since my last, are a declaration made by him to Gen. Larimer, late a prominent citizen of Pittsburg[h], and now of Denver City, to the effect that, "if Pennsylvania was to be represented in the Cabinet at all, it would be by Senator Cameron and no one else["]; and an intimation conveyed to a California politician as to the prospect of a selection of a member from the Pacific coast. To this latter, reference is made below.

It is now known here that open charges of corruption were lodged against Cameron by Judge [Alexander K.] McClure and other antagonists, and that the improvement of his chances indicated in the foregoing is owing to a refutation of these accusations. To give your readers an idea of the intricacy of the Cameron imbroglio, I will state that over two hundred letters (some of them covering dozens of pages) bearing upon it have been received by Mr. Lincoln.

MR. LINCOLN VISITS HIS STEPMOTHER

On Wednesday morning last, Mr. Lincoln started upon a two days' visit to the vicinity of Charleston, the county seat of Coles county, in the Southern part of this State. The trip was undertaken in accordance with the wishes of his aged step-mother, who resides in that locality on a small farm—the old homestead of the Lincoln family. He reached Charleston on Wednesday morning, and, passing the night at the residence of his friend, State Senator

[Thomas A.] Marshal, who accompanied him from here, rode out into the country the next morning to his stepmother's. He remained until late in the afternoon and drove back into town, after visiting the grave of his father. In the evening he held a public reception in the courthouse. Hundreds of ladies and gentlemen attended. Being called on for a speech, he said that the time for a public definition of his policy was not yet come, and that he could but express his gratification at seeing so many of his friends, and give them a hearty greeting. Most of those in attendance then shook hands with him and disbursed, amidst enthusiastic cheering. On the following morning he set out upon his return trip, and arrived here at 11 A.M. While on the way, he met a Committee of Cincinnatians who were on the way to Springfield to tender him the hospitalities of Porkopolis on his journey to Washington. The invitation was at once accepted, and the visit fixed for the 13th instant.

A SAN FRANCISCAN IN SPRINGFIELD

On Thursday evening last [January 31] Joseph A. Nunes, of San Francisco, made his appearance here. He had arrived on the afternoon train direct from Washington city. The object of his visit was, of course, to make the personal acquaintance of the President elect, and hence his chagrin upon finding the Presidential bird temporarily flown. He waited patiently till his return. Having brought letters of introduction from prominent Republican leaders in Washington to Mr. Lincoln, he was at once afforded all the facilities for realizing the object of his mission. Mr. Nunes had a two hours' interview at Mr. Lincoln's private residence, on Saturday afternoon [February 2], where a very free exchange of views took place between them. Mr. Nunes expressed the loyalty of California to the Union, and urged the appointment of a member of the Cabinet from the Pacific coast, as a means of strengthening the ties that connected the Golden State [with the rest of the Union]. Mr. Lincoln stated in reply that the Cabinet was not yet made up; that the representation of the Pacific States among its members was still an open question, and by no means an impossibility. No names were mentioned, but strong hints given and taken of Mr. [Eugene] Sullivan, since Col. Fremont is now supposed to be unwilling to serve.

Mr. Nunes also became acquainted with Mrs. Lincoln and "Bob," the Harvard student, whose independent way of talking of the "old man" is often very amusing. In the evening, he addressed in an able manner a large audience, including the most prominent politicians of the State, in the House of Representatives, in response to an invitation, on the questions of the day.

No communication has passed between Mr. Lincoln and Col. Fremont since the latter's landing in New York city. A meeting is, however, expected to take place after Mr. Lincoln's arrival in the East.

In spite of the absence of the President elect during a portion of the week, a very large number of place-seekers have been here since my last. The most prominent among them were J. P. Usher of Indiana, who is after a U.S. Marshalship; Gen. Larimer of Denver city, who wants to be Governor of the proposed Territory of Idaho (Pike's Peak); S. N. Pettis of Pennsylvania, who is after the Governorship of Nebraska; and Mark W. Delahay of Kansas, who desired, but did not get Mr. Lincoln's endorsement of his aspirations to the U.S. Senatorship.

Governor Kirkwood of Iowa[19] has also been here. He is strongly anti-compromise.

Horace Greeley has just arrived. Full particulars of his visit in my next.

February 6, 1861

Springfield, 6 February 1861
[New York *Herald*, 16 February 1861]

Were it not for the frankness of the two participants in the memorable interview to which allusion was made in my last, nothing authentic would probably have ever been learned as to its results. But the unreservedness of speech for which both the philosopher of the *Tribune* and "Honest Old Abe" are distinguished has enabled their friends to ascertain pretty correctly what has passed between them. It is from this indirect source that I derive the following, not exactly authoritative, but nevertheless reliable statement.

Greeley in the first place told his friend Lincoln bluntly that the passage of any compromise measure by Congress would be tantamount to a disrupture of the republican party, and that its endorsement by his (Lincoln's) administration would force the radical republicans into a hostile attitude towards it. He urged that firm fidelity to the teachings of the Chicago platform was the only safety, not only of the party that made him Chief Magistrate of the country, but also of the nation at large. He insisted that no compromise or concession the North could make, without placing the destinies of the country forever at the mercy of the slaveholding aristocracy of the South, would satisfy the latter, and hence that all propaganda, both within and without Congress, for like measures, would but distract, demoralize and humiliate the republicans in the eyes of not only their political opponents, but also of themselves.

In accordance with these views, he farther contended that the incoming administration should not identify itself with any one who was ready to abandon republican principles in this hour of trial, and that simply because firmness and unity of sentiment and action were evidently the only means, in the face of the present internal difficulties, of avoiding an utter administrative wreck. Upon this ground he based a vigorous remonstrance against Cameron's appointment, a strong denunciation of Kellogg, and, it is said, even some reprehensive hints at Seward's want of stamina. Nor did he confine himself to these negative suggestions in reference to the composition of the Cabinet. Thaddeus Stevens,[20] Chase and Colfax were recommended by him with much warmth, and their appointment [was] represented as desired by the most trustworthy portion of the republicans throughout the country.

As to the part acted by Mr. Lincoln during the interview, I am informed that he managed to draw much more, in the way of opinion and suggestion, out of the impulsive senior of the *Tribune* than he himself gave. As to the compromise question, I have from as good authority as can be found at this latitude, that Greeley obtained gratifying assurances as to the line of policy in reference to the secession and slavery extension issue to be drawn in the inaugural message. As to the Cabinet, however, the President elect did not commit himself. He gladly noted down the preferences of the *Tribune* philosopher, but thought [it] best not to express any himself.

From remarks made by Greeley to other visiters, it is inferred that he would rather see Colonel Fremont appointed Minister to France than Secretary of War. He is reported to have said openly that the appointment of the first republican candidate for the Presidency to a first class position, either at home or abroad, was not a matter of choice, but of necessity, with Mr. Lincoln.

Other well informed parties pretend to know that Greeley's advice in reference to New York city and State appointments was freely solicited and given, and that he improved the opportunity to warn the President elect of attempts to exact a monopoly of the federal patronage likely to be made by the Regency during his impending visit to Albany and New York.[21]

A rumor was afloat last evening that Greeley had been asked for his own desires, in the way of place, and that he peremptorily and positively declared his declination to serve in any capacity. Not being able to trace the story to any responsible source, I give it for what your readers may consider it worth.

The utmost cordiality is known to have prevailed during the meeting. Abraham seemed to have entirely forgotten his old grudge against Horace on account of the latter's qualified Douglasism in 1858.[22]

The most interesting phenomenon on our political horizon at the present time is the internecine feud raging among the leading republican organs: The Chicago *Tribune*, like its New York namesake, has made the late partial recantations of Seward and Kellogg the occasion for a succession of those bitter, relentless personal onslaughts for which it is celebrated. The *Journal* of Chicago, and of this city, and other "defenders of the faith," are endeavoring to break the force of these attacks, but thus far only with limited success. That the *Tribune* reflects the opinions of the bulk of the republicans of this State in the premises is certain beyond all doubt. A rather amusing feature is the energy with which each side to the controversy insists upon reflecting correctly the views of Mr. Lincoln. As their several allegations in this respect vary most radically, it is evident that some of them will have to relinquish their titles to organship after the public definition of the policy of the republican administration on the 4th [of March] prox.

The result of the Senatorial canvass in your State is looked upon in Presidential circles as a repudiation of Seward, Weed & Co.[23]

Springfield, 6 February 1861[24]
[New York *Herald*, 7 February 1861]

The President elect and suite will leave Springfield at nine A.M. on the 13th inst. But few stoppages will be made on the way, and Indianapolis reached at four P.M.; Cincinnati will be made on the following afternoon. No further appointments are as yet made.

The Presidential party will consist of fifteen persons. A number of outsiders are impatiently exerting themselves to get invitations to accompany Mr. Lincoln to Washington, but all will be excluded with the exception of the reporters of the press.

The English Consul at Chicago [John Edward Wilkins] has paid a visit to Mr. Lincoln.

Fitz Henry Warren, of Iowa,[25] is in town. His name is familiarly mentioned in connection with the Postmaster Generalship.

The report of the election of a majority of Union men to the Virginia Convention was received with much gratification by Mr. Lincoln.[26]

Horace Greeley left this morning for St. Louis, after lecturing to a very large audience last night. The radical republicans derive a good deal of comfort from the invigorating influences his emphatic anti-compromise declarations are presumed to have upon the wavering members of the party. They are in high glee over the gratifying assurance he is claimed to have received of the intention of the President elect to adhere firmly to the doctrines embodied in the Chicago platform. He (Greeley) expressed a fear during his stay that a sufficient number of weak backed republican Congressmen could be mustered to secure the passage of a compromise measure before the 4th of March.

The soiree at the private residence of the President elect this evening is a brilliant affair. Seven hundred ladies and gentlemen, composing the political *elite* of this State and the beauty and fashion of this vicinity, are present. Mr. and Mrs. Lincoln are in their happiest mood, and do the honors with much dignity and affability.

> Springfield, 6 February 1861
> [Cincinnati *Commercial*, 7 February 1861]

The soiree at the private residence of the President elect, this evening, is a brilliant affair. Some two hundred ladies and gentlemen, comprising the political elite of this State and the beauty and fashion of this vicinity, are present. Mr. and Mrs. Lincoln are in their happiest mood, and do the honors with much dignity and affability.

The President elect and suite will leave Springfield at 9 A.M., on the 13th inst. But few stoppages will be made on the way, and Indianapolis reached at 4 P.M. Cincinnati will be made on the following afternoon. No further appointments are as yet made. The Presidential party will consist of fifteen persons. Quite a number of outsiders are imprudently exerting themselves to get invitations to accompany Mr. Lincoln.

All will be excluded with the exception of the representatives of the press.

The English Consul at Chicago, has paid a visit to Mr. Lincoln.

Fitz Henry Warren, of Iowa, is in town. His name is faintly mentioned in connection with the Postmaster Generalship.

The report of the election of a majority of Union men to the Virginia Convention, was received with much gratification by Mr. Lincoln.

February 7, 1861

> Springfield, 7 February 1861
> [New York *Herald*, 16 February 1861]

If any doubt existed as to the prevalence of apprehensions among the republicans of this region of vital dissensions in the ranks of their own party, it would have been speedily removed by the pre-eminent gratification manifested by the radicals or anti-compromisers at the invigorating influences of the visit of the *Tribune* philosopher [Horace Greeley] upon their faltering political associations. They evidently derived great comfort from the way he stiffened up the weak backs by his bold, defiant, threatening denunciation of anything and everything in the shape of either concession or compromise, and the ready anathema he hurled against all that have shown a disposition to abandon the republican standard in the hour of trial and of danger. "Would that they were all like him," have I heard escape many a time from many a lip since his departure. The greater firmness with which many republican members of the Legislature express themselves in reference to the position lately assumed by Seward, and more particularly by Kellogg, shows, indeed, most conclusively, that an infusion of backbone has been effected by Greeley. Even the [Springfield] *Daily [Illinois State] Journal*, the qualified organ of the President elect, seems to have been sympathetically moved by his presence. On the day before he arrived it published a communication upbraiding the Chicago *Tribune* most severely for attempting to read Seward and Kellogg out of the party. This morning, on the contrary, it contains a leading article pronouncing Kellogg's propositions a flagrant political heresy, that deserved the disapprobation and contempt of every true republican. The leader concludes as follows:

> Our despatches this morning state that Mr. Kellogg has received a message from a leading republican here, stating that his proposition is satisfactory. Such is not the case. We believe no republican of character has transmitted any such despatch. The Breckinridge platform will never be received by the people of Illinois as the basis of adjustment.

Verily, Horace is yet a power in the land. At no time during the preceding three months has the pressure of politicians been so great here as since Monday last [February 4]. The hotels are all literally crammed from roof to cellar, and yet every night numbers of legislative logrollers and expectants of federal offices can be found wandering through the streets in vain search of accommodations. This superabundance of visitors has induced a number of Chicagonians to charter a sleeping car, in which they nightly seek shelter and rest. The occupants of this movable hotel are a gay crowd. I venture to say, from what I saw of them, that the god of slumber is not the only one invoked of nights in their coach.

It is almost impossible to denounce in adequate terms the impudent obtrusiveness with which place hunters still crowd upon the President elect, in spite of the distinct and emphatic announcement of his desire to be let severely alone by them during the remainder of his stay in Springfield. Men came here this week that should have known better. Indiana and Pennsylvania lived up to their reputations of breeding the most corrupt and rapacious politicians, by sending additional squads of Cameron and Smith emissaries. All these gentlemen doubtless came to the conclusion, from their experience with Mr. Lincoln, that it would have been better for them to have stayed at home.

The farewell soiree given by Mr. and Mrs. Lincoln to their friends in this city last evening was the most brilliant affair of the kind witnessed here in many years. Hundreds of well dressed ladies and gentlemen gathered at the Presidential mansion to spend a last evening in company with their honored hosts. The occasion was a success in every respect, with the exception of a slight jam created by the limited dimensions of the building. Every room both on the first and second floor was densely packed with a fashionable multitude. The President and lady received their guests in the parlor on the first floor. They stood close to each other nearly all the evening, in order to facilitate presentations. Mrs. Lincoln's splendid toilette gave satisfactory evidence of extensive purchases during her late visit to New York.

I have just learned of a signal rebuke Mr. Lincoln gave to a classical snob who endeavored to impress him with a profound idea of his scholastic attainments during a call by extensive quotations in Latin. Mr. Lincoln allowed him to go on for a while, when at last a lengthy phrase, attributed to Julius Caesar, induced him to let off the cutting remark:

My friend, I regret to say that I have to refer your classics to these gentlemen (pointing to other visiters), who, I presume, are better versed in Latin lore than myself.

Abraham Kohn, the City Clerk of Chicago, has sent Mr. Lincoln a small flag (red, white and blue) inscribed with Scriptural citations in Hebrew.

A rumor has been afloat for some days that the rotund proportions of Warren Leland, of the Metropolitan,[27] had been seen in Mr. Lincoln's anteroom one day this week. Knowing that the volume of his corporation would render avoidance of reportorial notice all but impossible, I am inclined to consider the report the product of the imagination of some wanton sensation writer.

The reason of Mr. Lincoln's determination to stop at the Metropolitan during his sojourn in New York, as given to me by a waggish friend of his, is that it is the conservative hotel of the Empire City.

Mr. Wilkins, the British Consul at Chicago, has paid a brief visit to Mr. Lincoln.

Fitz Henry Warren, of Iowa, has loomed up at this eleventh hour. His name is very faintly mentioned in connection with the Postmaster Generalship.

Springfield, 7 February 1861
[New York *Herald*, 8 February 1861]

The Springfield [*Illinois State*] *Journal* of this morning has an evidently inspired leader, denouncing any of Mr. Kellogg's propositions, and their support by republicans [as] an impossibility. It also denies the statement that a prominent republican had sent a dispatch to Washington announcing the approbation of the propositions by members of the party here.

Mr. Lincoln's wishes will be met by dispensing with all established receptions in the different localities he proposed to visit on his way to Washington. Lengthy reception speeches will prove especially unwelcome. The probability of an infliction of the New York Alderman is greatly dreaded here.

Horace Greeley, just before starting for St. Louis, received information which induces him to forego his intention to lecture in that city, and change his course east. He wrote a letter to the [St. Louis] *Missouri Republican*, in which he states that leading republicans had advised him that he would probably be mobbed should he attempt to lecture.

H. B. Sargent,[28] bearer of resolutions of the Massachusetts Legislature, arrived here to-day. John Quackenbush of New York,[29] is visiting Mr. Lincoln. W. S. Wood, the avant courier of the President elect, has returned from the East, arrangements for the journey are now perfecting, and will be published in the course of a day or two. Mr. Lincoln pronounces the letter published in the Charleston *Mercury*, purporting to be addressed by him to Mr. Spencer, of Wheeling, a forgery.

Last Monday's despatches were garbled by a bungling operator east of Chicago. Mr. Lincoln's name was submitted in the despatches relating to Greeley's movements.

A Dayton committee, consisting of J. W. Lowe, E. A. Phillips, and W. H. Gillespie have to-day invited Mr. Lincoln to visit their city. The invitation was conditionally accepted.

February 8, 1861

Springfield, 8 February 1861
[New York *Herald*, 9 February 1861]

Mr. W. S. Wood furnishes by authority the following schedules, showing the arrivals and departures in and from the various localities the President elect and party will visit on their journey from here to New York:

Monday, Feb. 11—Leave Springfield at eight A.M., and arrive at Indianapolis at five P.M.

Tuesday, 12th—Leave Indianapolis at eleven A.M., and arrive at Cincinnati at three P.M.

Wednesday, 13th—Leave Cincinnati at nine A.M., and arrive at Columbus at twelve P.M.

Thursday, 14th—Leave Columbus at eight A.M., and arrive at Steubenville at two P.M., leave Steubenville at twenty minutes past two P.M., and arrive at Pittsburg[h] at five P.M.

Friday, 15th—Leave Pittsburg[h] at ten A.M., and arrive at Cleveland at four P.M.

Saturday, 16th—Leave Cleveland at nine A.M., and arrive at Buffalo at four P.M.

Sunday, 17th—Remain at Buffalo.

Monday, 18th—Leave Buffalo at six A.M., and arrive at Albany at three P.M.

Tuesday, 19th—Leave Albany at ten A.M., and arrive at New York at three P.M.

The following railroads will be travelled over: Great Western, Wabash Valley, Lafayette and Indianapolis, Indianapolis and Cincinnati, Dayton and Columbus, Columbus and Pittsburg[h], Pittsburg[h] and Cleveland, Cleveland and Erie, Buffalo and Erie, New York Central, Hudson River Railroad.

Mr. Wood has made such arrangements as will insure both the comfort and safety of those under his charge. He has provided special trains, to be preceded by pilot engines all the way through.

Cards of invitation will be issued by him to all participants on the journey from point to point, and only holders will be found on the train.

State and local authorities and prominent persons, without distinction of party, will be invited.

To avoid crowding and annoyance to Mr. Lincoln, representatives of the leading papers only will be admitted in the different stopping places.

The Presidential party will be under the charge of the local committees, and no party coloring being intended to be given to the trip, Wide Awake and other demonstrations of a partisan character, will prove objectionable.

Military escorts through the stopping places will be accepted, but none on the journey.

The invitation to visit Boston by the Executive and legislative authorities of Massachusetts, has been declined by Mr. Lincoln for want of time.

The Presidential family has broken up housekeeping, and is now sojourning at a hotel.

C. Rabe,[30] of San Francisco, is visiting Mr. Lincoln.

Springfield, 8 February 1861
[San Francisco *Bulletin*, 5 March 1861]

APPREHENSIONS OF A RUPTURE IN THE REPUBLICAN PARTY

Just three months ago the great Republican party of the North emerged victoriously from the desperate and protracted struggle for the Presidential succession. Its members were then flushed all over with victory—exultant at the prospect of the long-coveted control over the Federal Government— deriding their vanquished opponents in the North and defying and threatening the restive malcontents of the South. How all this has been changed within the short period of three weeks! The mettle of the victorious host seems to be broken. Solidity no longer distinguishes its ranks. Both leaders and followers waver. A unanimity of sentiment no more pervades them. Loud discussion is heard on all sides. In short, the nearer the fruits of victory are approached, the less the probability of a peaceful, undisturbed enjoyment appears to grow.

Grave apprehensions of an impending fatal rupture in the Republican party have been felt for some time in Presidential circles. A split upon the compromise and concession question is not only feared, but reluctantly believed in. The developments of the last fortnight have furnished ample ground for it. There are the bitter denunciations and attempts at ostracism leveled by the New York *Tribune* and its namesake at Chicago, the most influential Republican journal in the Northwest, against Senator Seward. There are the open recantations of Senator Cameron and Judge Kellogg, the Republican member from this State. There is the irreconcilable diversity of opinion on the various reports of the Committee of Thirty-three. There is the open wrangle between Greeley and Cassius M. Clay. In fine, stubborn facts, fraught with discord and disintegration, rise in rapid succession, and almost compel all reflecting men to grow familiar with the idea of seeing the victors of November disjoined into two rival factions—the Radicals and Conservatives—likely to engage in a violent struggle for the control of the incoming Administration.

The President elect, with his characteristic clear-sightedness, has well perceived the dangers threatening from these daily widening divergences of his present cares. The fear of the awakening influence of troubles among his friends, is not the least. Under his very eyes, among a large number of Western politicians now congregated here, the manifestations of a dissembling, quarrelsome spirit are of unmistakable portent. Nor does he find himself able to keep entirely aloof from their polemics. Both the pro and anti-Compromisers daily beset him with the unjust appeals either to yield or to stand firm, and much of his now so valuable time is lost by arguing with them, and endeavoring to make up their differences. As to his own position, he still adheres to the conviction that compromises or concessions are ill-timed in the face of the menacing, seditious attitude of the South, and cannot possibly have the desired effect, that is, reconsolidate the Union. But, as already stated in a former letter, he always accompanies the private definition of his views in the premises by a qualification to the effect, that he does not as yet speak as the President of the United States, and that he will not hesitate to subordinate his own opinions to the fairly-expressed will of the majority of the nation after having attained to the office of chief minister of the Federal Constitution and laws.

THE "IRREPRESSIBLE CONFLICT" AMONG THE "ORGANS"

About a week ago a quarrel sprung up between the Chicago *Tribune* and Chicago *Evening Journal*, the leading Republican papers in Illinois, about Kellogg's compromise propositions. The *Tribune* reads him out of the party, by virtue of the heretic doctrines embodied in them. The *Journal* endorses his position. Both claim to represent Mr. Lincoln's views, and charge each other with falsifying them. The *[Illinois State] Journal* of this place, looked upon by Republicans as the organ *par excellence*, joined issue with the *Tribune* in an elaborate editorial on the day before yesterday, and cudgeled Kellogg in the most approved style. Mr. Lincoln, of course, takes no active part in this newspaper fight, but is nevertheless sorely grieved at this pernicious family quarrel. He does not conceal, however, his disapprobation of Kellogg's scheme for the settlement of the difficulties.

VISIT OF HORACE GREELEY TO MR. LINCOLN

My last [dispatch] wound up with a brief notice of the advent of the *Tribune* philosopher [Horace Greeley] in this focus of Republican politicians. No artist ever was more anxious for a model than your correspondent for the addition of that journalistic eminence to the gallery of distinguished visitors to the President elect, collected during the last two months, in my correspondence to the *Bulletin*. Ever since the crafty lord of the Albany lobby [Thurlow Weed] plied honest Old Abe with his wily arts I expected my diurnal examinations of the hotel registers to reveal the well-known scrawl of the *Tribune* oddity to me. Week after week elapsed, but no Horace came. The conviction gradually settled upon my mind that the triumph of the Weed faction, in the appointment of Seward to the Secretaryship of State, had persuaded the old radical that there was no place for him in Abraham's bosom—still filled with rankling recollections of the *Tribune's* Douglasism in '58—hence, that a visit to Springfield would result in disappointment and humiliation rather than gratification and profit. Providence, however, willed it that Horace had various lecture engagements to fill during the last month, within from 100 to 300 miles of this point. Being so near the centre of Republican attraction, *centripetal* influences were so strongly experienced by him, that a *detour* to Springfield was resolved upon. Having no advance engagement in the Republican Mecca, a lecture under his own auspices was announced—for the sake of keeping up appearances, it is presumed—for the evening of the 6th inst. Accordingly, the Chicago morning train of that day discharged the philosopher at this point. His arrival being looked for, a crowd of determined quidnuncs had soon collected in the vestibule of his hotel. Your correspondent, too, went to greet his old acquaintance at the earliest possible moment. He found him with as cloudless a countenance and in as complacent a temper as ever, although he had received the news of the failure of his Senatorial aspirations at Albany only the evening before. He stood under a new edition of his wonted unique style of hats, a specimen of which, lost by him during his tour to the Rocky Mountains two years since, the writer rescued from the head of a dirty Arapahoe Indian, upon payment of a pound of sugar and two pounds of bacon, in the course of last summer. His boots were of the one-horned cow-hide material. In fine, the general rigging-up of the individual showed a stolid adherence to his old, loose, careless ways. Not the least interesting feature of his accoutrement were the identical red and blue blankets that accompanied him overland and through the Golden State.

But your readers want to know, not how Horace looked, but what he talked and did and what occurred between him and the President elect. Well, be it said to his credit, he acted like a man of real independence. He did not seek the company of politicians, but expressed himself frankly and boldly and consistently to the large number of those that called on him at his hotel, not only in regard to the Secession and Compromise questions, but also as to what he expected of the Republican President and Administration. He declared his implacable hostility to all compromises and concessions in the most emphatic terms—pronounced in favor of a rigid enforcement of the Federal laws in the rebellious States with the aid of the army and navy of the Confederacy—asserted in plain terms that fidelity to the teachings of the Chicago platform was the *conditio sine qua non* of the success of the incoming Administration—that its countenance of any Compromise measure would surely result in the break up of the party that elected it to power—that it should not identify itself with the backsliding propensities of any of its leaders by appointing them to influential stations, (allusion to

Seward, Cameron, Kellogg & Co.,) and that, as far as he knew Abraham Lincoln, he was confident that he would act in exact conformity with the line of policy defined by those that nominated and elected him to the Presidency.

In his intercourse with Mr. Lincoln, he likewise stood on his dignity. He awaited his approach instead of approaching him. This independent attitude involved the risk of not meeting the real object of his visit to Springfield, owing to the constant encroachments upon the time of the President elect by other visitors that cheerfully took the trouble of hunting him up. But Horace's calculations proved correct after all. Shortly after 4 P.M., while sitting alone in his room looking over the lecture he was about to deliver, he was interrupted by a loud knock at the door and the appearance, upon an inviting response, of the gaunt form of "Honest Old Abe," in company with G. B. Lincoln, a prominent merchant of New York city.

So far my information is positive. But not having been present at the interview, and not having impudence enough to state that I was, the particulars of the memorable meeting, as given below, will receive, of course, only such credit as *outside* reports are entitled to. The only evidence of their correctness I can offer is their exact coincidence with the statements made by both Greeley and his caller before and after the interview, relative to the same matters. It is claimed, then, that Greeley exhorted the President elect to remain firm and true to the principles upon which he was elected; that he warned him of a Compromise policy, which, he urged, would prove as fatal to him as "Lecompton" to his predecessor[31]; that he told him bluntly that the *Tribune* could not and would not support such, and that it would array the bulk of his party against him. Nor did he confine himself to this, according to report. He contended that Cameron had virtually detached himself from the Republican party by his indorsement of Bigler's propositions, and that in the face of this and his well-established elasticity of conscience as to the means of his political success, he should not go into the Cabinet. Again he expressed the decided partiality of himself for the appointment of Gov. Chase as Secretary of the Treasury; Schuyler Colfax for the Postmaster-Generalship, and some one from the Pacific Coast, (Eugene Sullivan is believed to be his favorite.) Col. Fremont he recommended for the mission to France, alleging that the old Republicans would like to see him in the Cabinet, were it not for his supposed disinclination to serve in that capacity; but would insist on the nomination for some first-class position of their first candidate for the Presidency.

To all these outspoken representations and remonstrances of the *Tribune*, the President elect is said to have replied with equal unreservedness. He is represented to have given satisfactory assurances of his soundness on the

Compromise question, and of his intention to inaugurate and conduct a Republican Administration; but, on the other hand, to have intimated, in reference to the Cabinet, that his selections would not be made without consulting the wishes of the several sections of the country that were properly entitled to a representative, and that he would not allow his own preferences to prevail over them. As to the representation of the Pacific coast, the same answer that Mr. Nunes obtained was given, viz: that it was still an open question, not likely to be settled before his (Lincoln's) arrival in Washington.

The interview lasted nearly three hours, and the cordiality that signalized the parting of the two in the portico of the hotel warrants the inference that it was gratifying to both participants. Mr. G. B. Lincoln was present only during a portion of it.

As a matter of special interest to your readers, I will state, that Greeley expressed himself decidedly adverse to the claims of Mr. Washburn, of the San Francisco *Times*,[32] to the Collectorship of your city [San Francisco], during his stay.

The radical, anti-compromise Republicans derive a good deal of comfort from Greeley's visit. They express confidence in a large infusion of backbone into shaky members of the party through his agency. Greeley intended to visit St. Louis from here for the purpose of delivering a public lecture, but having received information just before starting of the danger of his being mobbed, he forewent his intention and directed his course Eastward.

February 9, 1861

Springfield, 9 February 1861

[New York *Herald*, 16 February 1861]

The day fixed upon for the departure of the President elect to the federal capital is fast approaching. In three times twenty-four hours more the four years' absentation from this scene of the greatest part of his life will be entered upon. What events may not this quadrennial be fraught with! A more enviable, but at the same time more delicate, and hazardous lot than that accorded to Abraham Lincoln, never fell to any member of this nation. The path he is about walking may lead to success, glory, immortality, but also to failure, humiliation, and curses on his memory. He may steer clear of the rock of disunion and the shoals of dissension among those that elevated him to the office he is about to assume, and safely conduct the ship of State from amidst the turbulence of fanaticism and lawlessness to the port of peace and reunion. But he may, on the other hand, take his place at the helm of the craft only to sink with it. Why, then, should it be a matter of surprise that the countenance of the President elect has begun to wear a more sober, solemn expression than heretofore? Why [is it] that a certain sadness pervades his conversation and restrains the wonted outbursts of humor? Why [is it] that he loves to dwell on the cherished past in preference to the contemplation of the uncertain future? Whatever his other characteristics may be, no one that knows him so well as the writer will deny that he has a heart susceptible of all truly humane emotions, and hence is now grieving at the prospect of a speedy separation from the locality that for thirty years has witnessed his woes and joys; that he entered a poor, friendless youth, and is now about leaving as the Chief Magistrate of the nation; that contains nearly all that is dear to him—whose every man, woman and child will see him part with feelings of regret and good wishes for the success of his exalted mission.

Next to the President elect himself the parties that experience and manifest the most sorrow at his impending departure are our hotel, boarding house, billiard saloon and rumshop keepers. The climax of their prosperity is reached. The turning point of their fortunes is about being passed. As soon as "Old Abe" will have turned his back to Springfield, [the city will experience] an instantaneous relapse into the former profitless dullness. The quietness of a graveyard will prevail here after Monday next, and most of the aforementioned individuals might as well shut up their establishments and retire from the hopeless field with what they gouged out of the office seekers during the heyday of "Old Abe's" stay.

It is as yet uncertain whether the Presidential family will accompany its head on his circuitous journey to Washington. Mr. Lincoln himself is opposed to their starting with him, but desires to be joined by them in New York. Mrs. Lincoln, however, is anxious to go, and so are many of his and her friends, and I think it more than probable that the whole of the family will come along.

Mrs. Lincoln is engaged night and day in perfecting the details of the preparations for the removal of the family. She, too, is anything but rejoicing at the imminent parting with her many old, tried, faithful friends in this vicinity. Her impulsive nature will doubtless draw out many a tear before she will take a last glance at Springfield. "Bobby," on the contrary, and the two younger sons, are jubilant at the coming good time on the trip to and in Washington. To-night the Presidential mansion will be abandoned, and the whole party take quarters at the Henry [i.e., Chenery] House for the remainder of their stay.

A large number of presents have been received by Mr. Lincoln within the last few days. The more noteworthy among them are a complete suit, manufactured under the auspices of Titsworth & Brother, of Chicago, and to be worn by his Excellency on the 4th of March, and another two hundred dollar cane from California. The inauguration clothes, after being on exhibition for two days, will be first tried on this evening—a most momentous event, to be sure. The cane was expressed to Mr. Lincoln without any explanations as to the name of the donor, &c. The oddest of all gifts to the President elect came to hand, however, in the course of yesterday morning. It was no more nor less than a whistle made out of a pig's tail. There is no "sell" in this. Your correspondent has seen the tangible refutation of the time honored saying that no "whistle can be made out of a pig's tail" with his own eyes. The donor of the novel instrument is a prominent Ohio politician, residing at Columbus, and connected with the State government.[33] Mr. Lincoln enjoyed the joke hugely. After practising upon the masterpiece of human ingenuity for nearly an hour this morning, he jocosely remarked, that he had never suspected, up to this time, that "there was music in such a thing as that."

The Cincinnati *Gazette*, which is Mr. Chase's organ, says: "We have information from a most reliable source that the Hon. Salmon P. Chase has been tendered by Mr. Lincoln the position of Secretary of the Treasury, which offer he holds under advisement. We are further advised that Mr. Chase will probably accept."

In a letter from a distinguished lawyer at Chicago, the writer speaks as follows of the President elect: "He is the man for the times. He has as much backbone as any man in America. I know him well. A better man does not live. He is kind hearted, but a man of principle and a man of courage. Personally he has the strength of two ordinary men, being all bone and muscle, and his will is in proportion to his strength when he believes himself in the right."

Springfield, 9 February 1861
[New York *Herald*, 10 February 1861]

The President elect, having completed the first draft of his inaugural, is now busily engaged in arranging his domestic affairs. He attends to the minutest details of the preparations for the impending removal of himself and family with his characteristic dutifulness. The close approach of his departure has rendered him unusually grave and reflecting. The parting with this scene of his joys and sorrows during the last thirty years, and a large circle of old and faithful friends, apparently saddens him, and directs his thoughts to the cherished past rather than the uncertain future. His interviews with the more intimate of his friends are more frequent and affectionate, and visits of strangers are not encouraged; but, although more than ordinarily moved with tender feelings, he evidently fully realizes the solemnity of the mission on which he is about to enter, and is resolved to fulfil[l] it firmly, fearlessly and conscientiously.

The following gentlemen will compose the suite of the President elect: Col. Sumner, Major Hunter, R. T. Lincoln (Bob), J. G. Nicol[a]y, Private Secretary; J. Hay, Assistant Private Secretary; E. E. Ellsworth, of Zouave fame; Col. W. N. [H.] Lamon,[34] Gov. Yates, Aid-de-Camp; Judge [David] Davis, Hon. J. K. Dubois, Hon. O. H. Browning,[35] E. L. Baker, editor of the Springfield *Journal*[36]; G. C. Latham,[37] and R. Irwin.[38]

Mr. Baker will return here from Indianapolis to escort Mrs. Lincoln and family to New York. Miss [Julia Edwards] Baker will accompany Mrs. Lincoln and assist in doing the honors of the White House. Mrs. [Ninian] Edwards and Miss [Mary] Wallace will not be in Washington as heretofore reported.

Mrs. Lincoln will start for St. Louis Monday [February 11] evening, to make additional purchases for the White House.

Dr. Rabe, Jas. R. McDonald[39] and Thos. Fitch,[40] of San Francisco, are here urging the appointment of a California member of the Cabinet. Dr. Rabe is supposed to be willing to take either the Collectorship or Post Mastership of San Francisco.

A member of the Georgia Secession Convention called and had a long talk with Mr. Lincoln yesterday [after]noon. He tried to exact a positive committal on one of the compromise propositions from him, but was unsuccessful.

Some days since a box was expressed to Mr. Lincoln from Tennessee, no letter accompanying it. Some hesitation was first felt to open it. This morning, however, his private secretary overturned the box, when it was found to contain a stuffed figure representing an African.

February 10, 1861

Springfield, 10 February 1861
[San Francisco *Bulletin*, 7 March 1861]

PREPARATIONS FOR MR. LINCOLN'S DEPARTURE

The President elect, having completed the first draft of his Inaugural Message, with which he has been engaged during the last fortnight, devoted the two days preceding this exclusively to the arrangement of his domestic affairs, and the preparations for the impending removal of himself and family to the Federal Capital. The minutest details were attended to with his characteristic faithfulness, and at the present hour the perplexing task is completed. The Presidential household is broken up, and all the members of the family quartered at the Chenery House of this city, where they will remain until their several departures from [for] Washington.

The time of his four years' absence from this scene of the joys and sorrows of nearly thirty years having closely approached, Honest Old Abe is more than usually given to seriousness and meditation. It is evident that the immediate parting with the locality where he made his way from poverty and humbleness to the highest office in the land, where a large circle of old, faithful and valued friends surrounds [him], and where almost every man, woman and child knows and loves him, is exercising a saddening influence upon him. He contemplates the cherished past rather than the uncertain future. He seeks the company of a few intimate friends in preference to that of strangers, and good old Springfield apparently was never dearer to him than now, when he is about to leave it—perhaps forever.

DISPOSITION OF THE PRESIDENTIAL FAMILY

It is now definitely settled that only the head of the Presidential family and his oldest son, "Bob," the Harvard student, will embark for the East tomorrow morning, as the public ovations likely to be extended to the former would render the journey anything but pleasant to his lady and the remainder of the family. Mrs. Lincoln will start for St. Louis to-morrow, to make additional purchases for the White House. She will be accompanied by her niece, Mrs. E. L. Baker [née Julia Edwards], and both will be under the charge of Mr. Baker, the editor of the Springfield [*Illinois State*] *Journal.* She (Mrs. Lincoln) will return to this point during the present week, and leave for New York with her two youngest sons to meet the President elect on the 18th. Mr. and Mrs. Baker will escort her East. Mrs. Baker will assist in doing the honors of the White House. Neither Mrs. Edwards nor Miss Wallace will be in Washington, as previously reported.

PROGRAMME OF LINCOLN'S JOURNEY

W. S. Wood of New York city, who kindly volunteered his services as *avant-courier* to the President elect, returned from Washington last evening. He has completed his arrangements for the safe, speedy and comfortable transit of Mr. Lincoln and suite, and politely furnished me their details.

The following schedule shows the arrivals and departures from the various localities to be visited on the journey from here to New York:

> *Monday* 11th—Leave Springfield, 8 A.M.; arrive at Indianapolis,
> 5 A.[P.]M.
> *Tuesday* 12th—Leave Indianapolis, 11 A.M.; arrive at Cincinnati,
> 3 P.M.

Wednesday 13th—Leave Cincinnati, 9 A.M.; arrive at Columbus, 2 P.M.

Thursday 14th—Leave Columbus, 8 A.M.; arrive at Steubenville, 2 P.M. Leave Steubenville, 2:30 P.M.; arrive at Pittsburg[h], 5 P.M.

Friday 15th—Leave Pittsburg[h], 10 A.M.; arrive at Cleveland, 4 P.M.

Saturday 16th—[Leave] Cleveland, 9 A.M.; arrive at Buffalo, 4:30 P.M.

Sunday 17th—Remain at Buffalo

Monday 18th—Leave Buffalo, 6 A.M.; arrive at Albany, 3 P.M.

Tuesday 19th—Leave Albany, 10 A.M.; arrive at New York, 3 P.M.

The route from New York to Washington has not been definitely laid out, but will probably be by way of Trenton, N.J., Philadelphia, Harrisburg and Baltimore.

The following railroads will be traveled over: The Great Western and Wabash Valley; Lafayette and Indianapolis; Indianapolis and Cincinnati, (short route:) Cincinnati, Dayton and Columbus; Columbus, Steubenville and Pittsburg[h]; Pittsburg[h] and Cleveland; Cleveland and Erie; New York Central and Hudson River.

Special trains will be used all the way through. Pilot engines will precede them over all the roads.

Cards of invitation will be issued to all participants in the journey, and only holders will be allowed on the Presidential train. State and local authorities and prominent men, without distinction of party, will be invited. To avoid crowding and annoyance to Mr. Lincoln, representatives of the leading papers only will be admitted.

In the different stopping places the President and suite will be under the charge of the local committees. No party coloring being intended to be given to the trip, Wide-Awake and other demonstrations of a partisan character will prove objectionable. Military escorts through the stopping places will be accepted, but not on the journey.

WHO WILL ACCOMPANY MR. LINCOLN TO WASHINGTON

The following gentlemen will form the Presidential suite: R. T. Lincoln, (Bob), Robert Irwin, (prominent banker of this place, and old friend of Lincoln,) John G. Nicolay, (private secretary,) John Hay, (assistant private secretary,) Judge Davis, the Hon. O. H. Browning, the Hon. Jesse K. Dubois, Col. Sumner and Maj. Hunter, U. S. A., (to act as aid-de-camps, by order of Gen. Scott,) Col. W. H. Lamon, Gov. Yates, (aid-de-camp,) E. E. Ellsworth, (of Zouave fame,) Henry M. Smith (of the Chicago *Tribune*,) and the Correspondent of the *Bulletin* [i.e., Villard].

A great pressure was brought to bear upon Mr. Lincoln during the last week for invitations by individuals who desired to dead-head [i.e., ride for free] through to Washington, but the above list will be rigidly adhered to, and additions only made from time to time.

LAST PUBLIC RECEPTION OF MR. LINCOLN AT SPRINGFIELD

On Wednesday evening [February 6], a last public reception was held by Mr. and Mrs. Lincoln at their private residence. Several hundred ladies and gentlemen, comprising the political *elite* of the State, and the beauty and fashion of this vicinity, were present. Both the upper and lower floors of the building were crowded to suffocation. The host and hostess stood close to each other all the evening in a parlor on the lower floor, in order to facilitate introductions. They were in their happiest mood, and their affability made everybody feel at home.

The pressure of crinoline around "Bob," the heir apparent of the Great Rail-splitter, was tremendous. Bob is, like his father, not exactly an Apollo in appearance, but seems, nevertheless, to possess extraordinary attractions in the eyes of the damsels of Springfield.

CONTINUED INVASION OF OFFICE-SEEKERS— RABE, FITCH AND MCDONALD

"Better late than never," I exclaimed involuntarily, on Friday evening last, upon discovering on the register of the American Hotel of this place the name of Dr. William Rabe, of your city. What made this man come out here, to see Old Abe at this eleventh hour? Well, he says that it was purely his desire to see California represented in the Cabinet! Your correspondent, however, thinks that Rabe did not rush out here from Washington, stay a few hours and hurry back, at an expense of least $100, for any such disinterested purpose. I venture to say that the late visit to and favorable reception by the President elect of Mr. Nunes had something to do with this trip, and that at this moment his (Rabe's) name figures on Abraham's slate in connection with the Collector or Postmastership of San Francisco. By this I do not wish to say that the Doctor was entered on the list upon his request; he doubtless knows too much of the proprieties of life to be guilty of such indiscretion. But, on the other hand, it is not unfair to presume that he improved his opportunity to remind the coming dispenser of Federal patronage of his distinguished services to the cause during the Presidential campaign. The Doctor seems a pretty smart fellow, and would have doubtlessly impressed the President elect in his favor, were it not for the conviction of his own great importance, that seems to pervade everything he says and does. He came here early in the morning, had an hour's chat with Mr. Lincoln in the course of the day and started back for Washington in the evening.

Simultaneously, Thomas Fitch and James H. McDonald of your city and State were here in attendance on the President. Whatever the subject of their visit may have been, they selected a most unfortunate time for making their respective wants in the way of office known. Mr. Lincoln anxiously desired the strictest privacy during the last week of his residence here, and is not likely to conceive favorable impressions of office-seeking intruders.

ODD PRESENTS

Several noteworthy additions were made within the last few days to the collection of gifts gathered since November by the President elect. There was, in the first place, a complete broadcloth suit, manufactured by an enterprising firm of merchant-tailors, at Chicago and to be worn by the recipient on the 4th of March! Then there was a second gold-headed cane, expressed from California by some unknown admirers of the Great Rail-splitter. A box arrived furthermore some days since from Tennessee with the name of the Presidential consignee, but not of the consignor. Hence some hesitation to open it was at first felt by Mr. Lincoln's private secretary, and the box left untouched until yesterday morning, when, upon cautiously removing the lid, it was found to contain a stuffed figure, intended to represent a "nigger boy."

The oddest of presidential presents, however, came to hand night before last. It was nothing less than a *whistle made out of a pig's tail!* In the face of the old saying to the contrary, you may perhaps think this a joke; but I have seen the novel instrument with my own eyes, and heard the President elect practice upon it with my own ears, so that there can be no mistake about it. Mr. [Addison Peale] Russell, the Secretary of State of Ohio, is the person who heretofore owned and sent the whistle, which is well-known to politicians in Ohio. Mr. Lincoln, after trying it for some time, was heard to remark that he had not suspected, up to this time, that there was "music in such a thing as a pig's tail."

CONCLUSION

This letter concludes the *Bulletin's* Springfield correspondence. The only attraction of this otherwise intolerably dull town ever had being about removing, your correspondent's mission is ended. Future personal intelligence of President Lincoln will doubtless be furnished in ample measure by your regular Washington correspondent. *Adios.*

Springfield, 10 February 1861
[Cincinnati *Commercial*, 11 February 1861]

Invitations to accompany Mr. Lincoln to Washington, have been extended to the following parties. The list comprises prominent Republicans, Douglas and Breckinridge Democrats: Gov. Yates, Ex-Gov. Moore, Honorables O. M. Hatch, Wm. Butler, N. Bateman, E. Peck, J. Grimshaw,[41] W. R. Morrison,[42] L. W. Ross,[43] M[artin] H. Cassel, Wm. H. Underwood, Wm. H. Carlin,[44] J. A. Hough,[45] D. H. Gilmer,[46] and Col. Burgess.[47] Karl Schurz[48] was invited but was obliged to decline.

The President is spending this last day of his stay in Springfield quietly, in a select circle of friends. Edward Bates was invited to accompany Mr. Lincoln to Washington, but he telegraphed last night that he would be unable to go.

Karl Schurz arrived last evening. Mr. Lincoln showed him marked courtesy, and introduced him personally to a number of prominent men, as the great German orator.

Major Hunter and Col. Sumner have not yet arrived.

Springfield, 10 February 1861
[New York *Herald*, 12 February 1861]

The President is spending this last day of his stay in Springfield quietly in a select circle of friends. Edward Bates was invited to accompany Mr. Lincoln to Washington, but telegraphed last night that he would not be enabled to go.

Carl Schurz arrived last evening. Mr. Lincoln showed him marked courtesy, and introduced him personally to a number of prominent men as the great German orator. Major Hunter and Colonel Sumner have not yet arrived.

Invitations to accompany Mr. Lincoln to Washington have been extended to the following parties. The list comprises prominent republicans and Douglas and Breckinridge democrats: Governor Yates, Ex-Governor Moore, Honorables O. M. Hatch,[49] William Butler, N[ewton] Bateman[50] and E[benezer] Peck; J[ackson] Grimshaw, William R. Morrison, L. W. Ross, M. H. Cassel, William S. [H.] Underwood, William H. Carlin, J. A. Hough, D. H. Gilmer and Colonel Burgess. Carl Schurz was invited, but is obliged to decline.

February 11, 1861

Springfield, 11 February 1861
[New York *Herald*, 12 February 1861]

The President elect, accompanied by his lady and a number of friends, left his hotel at half-past seven A.M., and rode up to the Great Western depot. Over a thousand persons of all classes were assembled in the depot building and on each side of the festivity [festively] decorated special train to bid farewell to their honored townsmen.

The President elect took his station in the waiting room, and allowed his friends to pass by him and take his hand for the last time. His face was pale, and quivered with emotion so deep as to render him almost unable to utter a single word. At eight o'clock precisely he was conducted to the cars by Mr. [W. S.] Wood and Mr. [Edward] Baker, of the [*Illinois State*] *Journal*. After exchanging a parting salutation with his lady, he took his stand on the platform, removed his hat, and, asking silence, spoke as follows to the multitude that stood in respectful silence and with their heads uncovered:

> MY FRIENDS—No one not in my situation can appreciate my feelings of sadness at this parting. To this place and to the kindness of these people I owe everything: here I have been a quarter of a century, and have passed from a young man to an old man. Here my children have been born and one is buried. I now leave, not knowing when or whether I ever may return, with a task before me greater than that which rested upon Washington. Without the assistance of that Divine Being who ever attended him I cannot succeed. With this assistance I cannot fail. Trusting in Him who can go with me and remain with you and be everywhere for good, let us confidently hope that all will yet be well. In that same Almighty Being I place my reliance for support, and I hope you, my friends, will all pray that I may receive that Divine assistance without which I cannot succeed, but with which success is certain. To His care commending you, as I hope in your prayers you will commend me, I bid you an affectionate farewell.

Towards the conclusion of his remarks himself and audience were moved to tears. His exhortation to pray elicited choked exclamations of "We will do it; we will do it."

As he turned to enter the cars three cheers were given, and a few seconds afterwards the train moved slowly out of the sight of the silent gathering. The train left at precisely half-past eight o'clock.[51]

The following gentlemen compose the party: A. Lincoln, R. T. Lincoln, John G. Nicolay, John Hay, Secretary; N. B. Judd, O. H. Browning, J. H. [K.] Dubois, E. Peck, J. Grimshaw, R. Irwin, J. Hough, Martin Cassel, L. W. Ross, Geo. Latham, Hall Wilson,[52] E. T. Leonard, W[illiam] Jameson,[53] Wm. Carlin, D. H. Gilmer, Major Hunter, United States Army; Col. Ward H. Lamer [Lamon], aid to Gov. Yates, and Col. El[l]sworth, L. Tilton Hall,[54]

W. R. Morrison, Wm. H. Cassell, G. A. Hough, E. V. Sumner, Jr. and G. W. Gilpin,[55] constitute the military portion of the cortege.

Dr. W. H. Wallace[56] accompanies the party as the physician of the President. Col. Sumner did not reach Springfield in time, but will join the party at Indianapolis. Curious crowds are stationed all along the line, endeavoring to catch a glimpse of the President as the train rushes past them. J[ohn] J[ames] S[peed] Wilson,[57] Superintendent of the Union Telegraph Company, is on the train, with an assistant and an apparatus ready to form a connection at any point.

APPENDIX

NOTES

INDEX

━━━━━

VILLARD'S COVERAGE OF THE 1858 SENATORIAL CONTEST BETWEEN LINCOLN AND DOUGLAS

July 10, 1858

Chicago correspondence by V., 10 July 1858

[Philadelphia *Press*, 15 July 1858]

When ancient Rome had reached the height of its power, and was following a mighty but fatal career of conquest and subjugation, its great captains, were rewarded for their valor and skill in extending the sway of the *Urbs* and reducing independent nations into Roman servitude, by being accorded the highly esteemed privilege of triumphantly entering the Eternal City. Pompous and dazzling was the pageantry displayed on such occasions. The eagles were fluttering, as it were, with victory. The *triumphator*, gorgeously attired, and standing erect in a magnificent chariot, rode through the festively decorated thoroughfares. Before him were carried the "spoils," and after him the captive flower of the subdued nations dragged their chains. These sturdy legions, whose arms had won the glories of the day, brought up the rear; and everywhere the returning warriors were hailed by the welcoming shouts of a jubilant multitude.

Chicago—the metropolis of an empire not less vast, and more republican; more just and peaceable, in which Mercury, not Mars, reigns supremely—yesterday witnessed an equally grand and more gratifying spectacle. The most distinguished of her citizens, Stephen A. Douglas, was solemnly received by his fellow townsmen. He also returned a conqueror; but it was fraud, trickery, and faithlessness he had crushed to earth. He had also triumphed, but it was on the bloodless field of parliamentary debate. He also had to boast of spoils—everlasting fame—less perishable, indeed, than those of the Roman generals. He also triumphantly paraded. The streets were also clad in festive attire. He was also surrounded by cheering thousands; but they greeted in him the victor in the cause of truth and justice. They joyously saluted not an oppressor, but a deliverer; not an aggressor but a vindicator. Who was the truly honored man—the Roman general or the American Senator?

What a flood of thoughts must have pressed upon the latter's mind in view of this general and enthusiastic ovation! But four years ago, in this very same city, when Senator Douglas undertook, after his return from an excited Congressional campaign, to publicly render account of his doings in connection with the Kansas-Nebraska bill, a deluded populace dared to hurl a "traitor" in his face, heaped dishonor on themselves by even denying him the right of speech. And now, truly, one might exclaim:

"Tempora mutantur, et nos mutamur in illis." [The times change and we change with them.]

Truth, indeed, will ever prevail, and justice be rendered to its expanders.

But let us pass over from the speculative contemplation to the simple narrative of yesterday's events.

At one o'clock P.M. an extra train left the Illinois Central Depot with the committee of reception, and other citizens, anxious to welcome the great champion of "Popular Sovereignty." At Michigan City they met the Senator, in company of a large number of Indianans, who had escorted him to that place from Laporte, a distance of some ten miles. The Chicago committee, after having extended a hearty welcome to the subject of the demonstration, started upon the return trip in charge of him. In the meantime, the appearance of the thoroughfares in the neighborhood of the Central Depot presented a most lively appearance. Banners were flying in all directions; inscriptions, indicative of the event of the day, were visible everywhere. The windows, and even tops of the buildings, became densely packed with human faces, and a steadily swelling tide of spectators thronged the streets. At half-past seven the sonorous voice of the cannon announced the approach of the train, and shortly afterwards a rapturous outburst of enthusiasm within the walls of the depot gave thrilling evidence of the appearance of the "Little Giant" among his constituents. With the greatest difficulty the committee succeeded in pushing with the senator through the immense crowd to the open carriage drawn by four horses, in front of the depot, that was to carry him to the Tremont House. The procession, consisting of three brass bands, several militia companies, about two dozen carriages, and at least *ten thousand* individuals, was then formed, amid the all but frantic cheers of the multitude, the waving of handkerchiefs and hats, the roaring of the cannon, and the splendid strains of the music, moved towards the point of destination. There, whatever had the use of legs seemed to be congregated. From State to Dearborn, on Lake street, and from Lake to Randolph, on Dearborn street, almost every available inch was occupied by human beings, and the reinforcements from the ranks of the procession made the pressure of the masses still greater.

By the utmost exertions only, the drivers forced their vehicles through the throng to the north front of the Tremont House, where the Senator was then formally received and expected to treat the audience to one of his powerful extempore efforts. The hotel was splendidly illuminated and decorated with innumerable flags. Directly opposite there was a transparency bidding welcome to the favorite of Illinois, and a pyrotechnic structure revealing in the course of the evening the motto "Popular Sovereignty," in blazing letters. Judge Douglas having alighted and ascended the stairs of the hotel, tarried but a few moments in an anteroom before he re-appeared upon the balcony. The wild cheering which greeted him anew rendered it impossible to understand a solitary word of the reception address delivered by Charles Walker, Esq. But when Douglas showed signs of his being ready to commence his reply, order was restored, and the air was soon filled with the clear and forcible sounds issuing from the eloquent lips of the Senator.

He led off by expressing his unqualified gratitude for the hearty reception bestowed upon him. He construed it not into a personal compliment, but as a demonstration of devotion to the great principle he represented. (The features of the speaker at this passage evinced very strong emotion.) He then reviewed in general terms the Lecompton controversy, concluding his remarks on the subject by the emphatic declaration, that the Lecompton battle had been fought and *virtually won by the passage of the English compromise bill*, which measure, although obnoxious in its main points to himself, he considered as settling the question for the present. After this introduction he proceeded to define the position he was to occupy in the ensuing canvas. He did so in a sort of negative way, by taking up the tenets of the opposition as advanced in the speech of rival candidate for the Senatorship, A. Lincoln, delivered before the last Republican State Convention, and contrasting his own teachings with them. (Mr. Lincoln, who had been hurried from Springfield at the instance of his Republican leaders in this city, is already announced to speak this evening in reply to Mr. Douglas, occupied a seat directly behind the latter, assigned to the opponent at his special request.)

In the course of his remarks he made two principal points, defining them at the same time as involving a direct and distinct issue on his part with the Republicans of this State. They were the assertion of Lincoln "that the Government of this Union will and must be either free or slave (as he called it); that the free-labor element was absolutely incompatible with slave labor, and that one had to give way to the other"; and his proposition to make relentless war upon the decision of the Supreme Court of the United States in the Dred Scott case.

With regard to the first point at issue, he held that the doctrine advocated by Lincoln was tantamount to a declaration of war between the two sections of the Union. Extermination of one or the other would be the watch-cry, if it were to be incorporated in the policy of the Federal Government. He, for one, contended that it was neither desirable nor possible that there should be uniformity of local institutions of the United States. If he had any predilections at all in this respect, he would so modify them as to make them accord with the "principles of Popular Sovereignty." He urged that the people of each State and Territory ought to be left entirely free to solve all the questions relating to their domestic affairs in such a manner as suited their wants best. Furthermore, he held that this Republican doctrine would lead to a uniformity of our institutions that would be utterly destructive of State rights, and result in a dangerous centralization of power, (Federalism.)

In reference to the second proposition of Mr. Lincoln, he said, that he, as a law-abiding citizen, would stand by the adjudication of the highest tribunal of his country, *whether in conformity with his views or not*, till reversed by proper judicial authority; that *to preach violent opposition to its decrees* he considered it as undermining the foundation of our institutions—obedience to the laws. But not only for this reason did he take exceptions to Mr. Lincoln's proposition. He would further and unequivocally say, that the doctrine of negro equality was repulsive to him. He alluded to the dangers of amalgamation—the natural consequence of an equality of rights—as historically illustrated by the Spanish American states. He would civilly endow the negro to a full extent, but political rights, placing them on an equal footing with white man, he would deny to them.

He concluded by alluding to the action of the small band of Federal office-holders in this State that were making war upon him by bolting the regular Democratic nominees and setting up others in direct opposition to them. He charged these deserters with having allied with the Republicans to insure his defeat. He would always adhere to Democratic usages, and all such that violated them in so flagrant a manner he looked upon as being outside of the party.

His speech was forcible in its delivery, clear in its arguments, and bold in its general tone. The audience expected to hear him on other leading questions of the day, but the extreme fatigue of the Senator prevented him from extending his remarks.

Thus the campaign is fairly opened, the banner of Democracy unfurled, the watchword given, and soon the clamor of a most spirited warfare will be heard. As to the result, the scenes enacted last evening removed all doubts. Bands will play for everybody—if paid for; fireworks can always be had for money; but the good will of the people can never be bought! Spontaneous in its impulses, it awards its tribute to the deserving without solicitation. The devotion to a great truth, indeed, must be at the bottom of a like demonstration, countless in numbers, unbounded in enthusiasm; and this universal and fervent homage rendered to its proclaimer shows conclusively that its light fully pervades the popular mind.

The speech was frequently interrupted by vociferous applause, the band striking up patriotic airs simultaneously. An hour after the Senator had withdrawn from the balcony, the gathering still showed unwillingness to disperse, and kept up cheering to a very late moment.

Thus ended a glorious day—a day, the events of which will not soon fade away from the memory of the citizens of Chicago. It inaugurated a new era, the bright era of redemption from the intolerance of fanaticism.

July 14, 1858

Chicago, 14 July 1858

[*New Yorker Staats-Zeitung*, 19 July 1858]

The main details of Senator Douglas's reception have already been transmitted to your esteemed paper via telegraph and other means, so I think it therefore superfluous to repeat them for your readers. Some noteworthy circumstances accompanying the event, however, which have not yet been mentioned in the daily press, might prove of interest.

The splendid demonstration, whose significance cannot possibly be overstated, and which forms a milestone in the political history of Chicago in particular and Illinois in general, did not appear to be strictly partisan, for the audience was not composed exclusively of Democrats by any means; the position taken by the famous statesman, in whose honor the demonstration was mounted, during the struggle over the Lecompton constitution, caused men of all parties to freely express their admiration and approval. When the proposal for such a celebratory reception was first made, many representatives of various political stripes felt moved to take part, and in fact the reception committee was composed of heterogeneous elements. This showed clearly that the opponents of the gifted Senator from the Prairie State were finally ready to do justice to his motives and principles, and that the strength of the so-called Republicans in Chicago had passed its zenith and that the era of political regeneration has begun. The conservative members in the ranks of the opposition party are tired of the extreme rashness of their colleagues and will in the future doubtless support the efforts of the Democratic Party.

The number of people who heard the clear, candid, and powerful exposition of the principles which Senator Douglas plans to champion in this summer's campaign cannot be less than 20,000. I myself made a precise count of them, and I am convinced that the above-mentioned number is 5,000 too small rather than too large. In any event, Douglas's reception was the largest mass meeting that has ever taken place in Chicago.

Since the arrival of the Senator, Chicago has become a true Mecca and the Tremont House a constantly overcrowded temple toward which stream Douglas's political sympathizers from every part of the Northwest. His reception room is jammed from morning till night. The statement he made in his speech—that his feelings for his opponent Abraham Lincoln were most friendly, and that he firmly intends to completely avoid dealing in personalities during the campaign and only discuss political opinions—was greatly appreciated by his audience. What he said he would do was foreshadowed in practice, for he allowed his opponent, who had made a special trip to Chicago from Springfield in order to hear the declaration of war with his own ears, to take a seat in close proximity to him and to do Lincoln the courtesy of praising his personal character.

On the morning after Douglas's reception, large placards on every street corner alerted the Republicans of Chicago that Lincoln would reply to Senator Douglas's speech that very evening. The Republican commanders, to avoid what apparently was in all likelihood going to be a small turnout, wisely arranged matters so that immediately before the announced hour ward meetings would be held to nominate delegates to the county convention, and that those "intelligent" voters would march directly before the Tremont House. This maneuver seemed shrewd, but it betrayed a lack of confidence in a big turnout, so that little more than half as many people as heard Douglas would be expected to hear Lincoln.

A great many means designed to swell Lincoln's audience were used, including fireworks and brass bands. Nonetheless, the turnout in this city—which is still *par excellence* a Republican stronghold—could not be regarded as very large. Two-thirds of the crowd, I am embarrassed to say, were Germans. German Republicans had to be deployed to increase the turnout. German voices were necessary to allow large Republican ovations in the form of serenades, hurrahs, etc., to be made. The Germans have become not only vocal sheep but also show sheep. So—will the matadors among them be able to make it appear that Chicago's German Republicans present a pure image of independent convictions, of emancipation from the corrupt influence of the Anglo-American wire pullers, from concessions made to radicalism, as for example they appear in the columns of the *Illinois Staatszeitung?* On the contrary, must they not all dance to the tune of John Wentworth, the incarnation of political and social immorality? Must not the radicals openly acknowledge their willingness to go along with the puritanical Christian Sabbatarians? But not all men are so constituted, especially not the German Republicans of Chicago.

Lincoln is what the Anglo-Americans call a man of "good common sense." He also has a great deal of mother wit, whose expression, however, does not always take an elegant form. He "can crack a good joke," as the English expression goes; but he has no ability whatsoever to tell a refined joke that does not do more than tickle the funny bone. In his long career as a lawyer, he has developed a clever tongue. But in only one respect does he resemble Cicero and Demosthenes, to whom the Republican press likens him: fluency. Before long you conclude from Lincoln's talks that he is better suited for the role of stump speaker than statesmanlike orator. There is no refinement of speech, no noble flourish—on the contrary a characteristic clumsiness; no elevation of thought, but rather a degree of cheapness; no logical arguments; everything about him has the aura of national authority which is peculiar to almost all native-born Americans, but beyond that nothing more. He is no match for Douglas, who outclasses him in force, freshness, and polished style. As for his outward appearance, I must admit, I have seldom seen a more awkward man than A. Lincoln. His gait, his carriage, his overall manners paint an extremely primitive picture. This, of course, does not say anything against his worthiness. I mention it only because a sketch of this man, whose sudden emergence on the public stage results from his rivalry with Douglas, might interest your readers. Lincoln is already pretty far advanced in years; I judge him to be 60 [he was actually 49]. He is tall and thin; his features indicate intelligence and an active mind.

His attempt to reply to the speech of Douglas was hardly a rhetorical success. Douglas gave a clear, concise, bold presentation of his political faith. Lincoln, on the other hand, offered a mishmash of unrelated, vague opinions and views. To cite only one example, he asserted that the direction in which the country was headed made it seem that it would either become all slave or all free. Eventually one system must yield to the other. He did not, however, say just how this would come about, lest he approach the brink of abolitionism, which his assertions would inevitably threaten to do. For tactical reasons, he did not want his listeners to see that possibility. Fortunately, people today are no longer content with simple assertions, but rather want the reasons spelled out. The "why" and "wherefore" are always demanded. Not only theories, but the practical means by which they are to be realized is what people want to hear from public men.

August 3, 1858

Springfield, 3 August 1858
[*New Yorker Staats-Zeitung*, 8 August 1858]

The assumption I made in one of my earlier articles, that the election campaign this summer in Illinois would be one of the most interesting episodes in the political life of the Union, is being confirmed more and more. Daily the enthusiasm among the participating parties rises, the language of the leaders [grows] more heated, the position of the parties [is] harsher, and the maneuvering of the opposing sides [is] more complex. With bold mottos on their banners, the Democrats, who this time have to deal with twice as many opponents as usual, struggle confidently and bravely on. Until now the combined opposition, although it prides itself on fighting in a good cause—one worthy of victory—has adopted no public stance; rather it has limited its tactics to underhanded intrigue and an unscrupulous use of shameful means.

Every day evidence grows showing that an alliance has been struck between the Republicans and the so-called National or Administration Democrats to defeat the uncorrupted Democracy and oust its leader, Stephen A. Douglas. In Chicago the heads of both factions, whose close agreement makes cooperation easy to achieve, consult together.

On the one side the Republican newspapers overflow with puff pieces about the National Democratic matadors and laudatory depictions of the public meetings that they hold, shamelessly exaggerating the numbers who attend and the success of such efforts; on the other side, they overflow with lying distortions and perversions of all that the anti-Lecompton Democrats have done and are going to do.

Cook, the leading spirit in the Chicago post office, instructs the other nation-saving postmasters of Illinois, with a frankness that merits a kind of negative admiration, that "it is the duty of every true patriot to move heaven and earth in order to prevent the re-election to the Senate of the 'traitor and deserter' and that if no other alternative remains, then they must vote for Lincoln and not Douglas." (To the credit of the Illinois postmasters, it must be said that two thirds of them scornfully and contemptuously reject this unreasonable demand.)

Senator [John] Slidell,[1] the pro-Lecompton champion from Louisiana, arrived in Chicago a few days ago to act behind the scenes as the commander-in-chief of the anti-Douglas operations. He is surrounded by a general staff of Federal Government employees and Republican chieftains.

Pro-Lecompton papers throughout the State are being subsidized by contributions which the poor post office clerks in Chicago are forced to pay. In short, the extremes—Republicanism and Lecomptonism—have not only bestirred themselves, but have fully merged. Indeed, it is a splendid alliance, in every respect fitting and proper!

The number of Lecompton papers, which until a short time ago had dwindled to three, has in the past three weeks grown substantially, thanks to the forces mentioned above. The blessed "National Union" has found a follower in the Chicago *Herald.* Likewise, in Putnam County the dim light of a "National Democrat" paper has emerged. Here in Springfield two weeks ago there appeared a man sent from Chicago with a printing press and soon thereafter honored the local populace with an anti-Douglas paper. At the appearance of this luminary, the delight of the Republicans, who are the paper's only subscribers, knows no bounds.

St. Clair County, the home of [Gustave] Koerner and [Friedrich] Hecker, has rejoiced at the birth of a Republican paper. John Reynolds,[2] the great temperance and anti-Nebraska gasbag who now adorns the Lecomptonites' ticket as their candidate for superintendent of public schools, has his own press in Belleville and has hired a bankrupt merchant and politician named Jim Hughes, who each week for three months has showered him with frankincense and has puffed him for the government post he seeks. I greatly fear, however, that he who earlier was in political oblivion will have to blow his horn somewhere else.

Other than these newly planted journalistic flowers, whose every line is full of nothing but common grumbling about Douglas and his friends, two other papers will be launched this week, a daily in Quincy and a weekly in Danville, on the border of Indiana. "Fools and their money are soon parted" goes the English expression that will be proven true in this case.

Like the allegory of the Grim Reaper with the hourglass which fixes as the time of death the moment that the last grain of sand passes from the upper half to the lower half, so too will these papers cease to exist when the last dollar paid to the editors by the men of this coalition slips through their fingers.

The furious attacks on Douglas coming from the combined forces of the Bogus Democrats and the Republicans is not rooted in a difference of opinion regarding basic principles but rather is solely rooted in personal hatred. [Charles] Leib[3] and [Isaac] Cook,[4] the leaders of one wing of the alliance, can never forgive the Senator for the merciless—although well deserved—means that he employed against them in a Senate speech, and the leaders of the other wing hate Douglas as the man whose political influence alone has prevented them from attaining political power. Both sides have sworn to kill him politically. To all appearances, however, the grave dug for him will be occupied by his opponents.

Douglas is two weeks into his campaign tour. The author of these lines, who accompanied him to Monticello (Piatt County), rejoices to be able to report that the enthusiasm with which he is received everywhere grows ever greater, in fact it grows stronger the further he gets from Chicago. The southern part of the State is the Democratic stronghold, and the closer he draws to it, the more wanes the strength of the combined forces of Republicanism and Lecomptonism, and the more widespread grows the enthusiasm which surrounds him.

During the addresses that the Senator gave in Clinton [on July 29] and Monticello [on July 27], I had frequent opportunity to note his powerful speaking voice. To be able to talk for three hours, in intense heat and in the open air, without the slightest weakening of his voice, shows that he certainly has extraordinary vocal resources. But not just in the tone of his words but also in their content he shows an almost uncanny power. Truth—undeniable truth—is conveyed in those words, and their effects are always apparent.

Abe Lincoln, who up till now has been sticking to Douglas's heels with amazing tenacity, has finally found himself nolens volens [willy nilly] forced to stop attempting to impose his political wisdom on Democratic audiences—not from any sense of propriety but, on the contrary, from an absolute lack of success in his attempt to promote himself at Democratic meetings. To use such festive receptions, which took place exclusively to honor Douglas, in order to make political capital for himself, certainly shows no great discretion on his part. An awareness of how disreputable such conduct was did not lead to his change in behavior so much as the merciless scourging that his political creed received on every occasion from Douglas. In Monticello he made his final attempt to weaken the powerful effect made by Douglas's speech by repeatedly claiming the last word for himself.

At the close of his speech he announced that he would no longer follow Douglas, but rather would follow the suggestion that each man speak on the same day in the same congressional district, one after the other. Since both rivals have spoken in Chicago [and Springfield], it was not necessary to have a joint session there. These debates at eight [seven] different points in the State promise to be significant episodes in the campaign. Douglas like Lincoln will be followed by a horde of oratorical "die minovam genitam" who will speak in English and German. The verbal duels in any event will be unique.

The removal of Austin G. Brooks, the postmaster at Quincy,[5] has created a great sensation here in Springfield. It is taken as a direct approval of all the hostile measures that the Federal officials here in the State have taken against Douglas and his friends for dereliction of duty (in the opinion of the Buchanan administration).

Brooks, who is both publisher and editor of the Quincy *Herald*—(he is one of the most skillful and gifted journalists in Illinois)—had in his newspaper freely answered a question about his political views. He candidly replied that he had supported the Buchanan administration in all things save the Kansas question and was prepared to continue supporting it. But 1000 post offices and 1000 Presidents could not move him to withdraw his support of the regular Democratic ticket and Senator Douglas. For this open statement he now has to suffer an undeserved fate! The powers in Washington appear to be as ruthless as the angry God Jehovah. They persecute even officials of the second and third rank. Brooks the father [Samuel S. Brooks] as well as Brooks the son must be sacrificed. The former was the editor of [an] anti-Lecompton paper in Cairo [the Cairo *Gazette*] at the confluence of the Ohio and Mississippi Rivers, and at the same time the postmaster there. He too found himself fired, like all his colleagues in southern Illinois, for opposing the administration's Kansas policy. For this boldness he was brought under the knife. At the instigation of the notorious Doug Barry, the candidate for state treasurer on the bogus ticket, he was replaced by a truly mean and corrupt loafer and drunk. A Cairo paper provided proof that because of his attempts to abduct and sell blacks to New Orleans, his successor was recently banished from Louisiana forever, after his head was shaved and he received 200 lashes. Does the Postmaster General know more about the past of this appointee?

August 21, 1858

From Villard's *Memoirs:*

> The first joint debate (in the famous series of seven) between Douglas and Lincoln, which I attended, took place on the afternoon of August 21, 1858, at Ottawa, Illinois. It was the great event of the day, and attracted an immense concourse of people from all parts of the State. Douglas spoke first for an hour, followed by Lincoln for an hour and a half; upon which the former closed in another half hour. The Democratic spokesman commanded a strong, sonorous voice, a rapid, vigorous utterance, a telling play of countenance, impressive gestures, and all the other arts of the practised speaker. As far as all external conditions were concerned, there was nothing in favor of Lincoln. He had a lean, lank, indescribably gawky figure, an odd-featured, wrinkled, inexpressive, and altogether uncomely face. He used singularly awkward, almost absurd, up-and-down and sidewise movements of his body to give emphasis to his arguments. His voice was naturally good, but he frequently raised it to an unnatural pitch. Yet the unprejudiced mind felt at once that, while there was on the one side a skillful dialectician and debater arguing a wrong and weak cause, there was on the other a thoroughly earnest and truthful man, inspired by sound convictions in consonance with the true spirit of American institutions. There was nothing in all Douglas's powerful effort that appealed to the higher instincts of human nature, while Lincoln always touched sympathetic chords. Lincoln's speech excited and sustained the enthusiasm of his audience to the end. When he had finished, two stalwart young farmers rushed on the platform, and, in spite of his remonstrances, seized and put him on their shoulders and carried him in that uncomfortable posture for a considerable distance. It was really a ludicrous sight to see the grotesque figure holding frantically on to the heads of his supporters, with his legs dangling from their shoulders, and his pantaloons pulled up so as to expose his underwear almost to his knees. Douglas made dexterous use of this

incident in his next speech, expressing sincere regret that, against his wish, he had used up his old friend Lincoln so completely that he had to be carried off the stage. Lincoln retaliated by saying at the first opportunity that he had known Judge Douglas long and well, but there was nevertheless one thing he could not say of him, and that was that the Judge always told the truth.[6]

[*New Yorker Staats-Zeitung*, 27 August 1858]

DOUGLAS AND LINCOLN

The election campaign in Illinois, which both on account of the importance of its outcome for the shaking up of the political parties as well as the galaxy of men and talents engaged in it, is being followed with the keenest interest throughout the Union, has so far been a veritable march of triumph for Senator Douglas. Wherever the celebrated statesman made his appearance he found himself surrounded by cheering masses who listened eagerly to his words. His Republican opponent, Lincoln, followed at first in the trail of this triumphal march and tried to use the meetings arranged for Douglas's reception for his own purposes. But he discovered soon enough that the crowds, as soon as he started to harangue them, dispersed just as quickly as the popularity of Douglas's name had brought them together. Therefore, he decided to abandon the tactic of following Senator Douglas around in an effort to cash in on the meetings convoked in the latter's honor. Instead, as we have already reported, he invited his opponent to a series of joint meetings where both candidates should address the assembled citizens alternately.

The first of these interesting meetings was held last Saturday [August 21] in Ottawa and, as could hardly have been expected otherwise, ended with a shining victory for Douglas.

In accordance with the agreement reached, Douglas delivered the introductory address, which lasted one hour. Lincoln replied for an hour and a half, then Douglas concluded the meeting with a half-hour speech.

Space does not permit us to give even a sketch of each of the speakers' arguments. We must resign ourselves to quoting some individual passages that may serve to illustrate the two men's tactics, to describe the outcome of the meeting, and to shed some light upon the impression which the addresses left on the audience.

The policy of Douglas was mainly to extract from his opponent a profession of his principles, for Lincoln, like all Republicans, is always wont to use the elasticity of their platform and the ambiguity of their principles in order to deny what their own words only a minute before had led one to believe to be the goal of their endeavors. Therefore, Douglas, quoting from the proceedings of the meeting held in 1854 at which Lincoln and Trumbull had introduced Republicanism into Illinois, asked his opponent whether he still stood by the views contained in that meeting's resolutions. But Lincoln, who by an unequivocal answer would have deprived himself of the chance to deny it later on, in good Republican fashion, offered one part of his principles while giving an arbitrary interpretation to the rest, tried to extricate himself from the predicament by asserting that when the meeting was held in Springfield, in 1854, he was not present but had attended a court session in Tazewell [County]. He thought that thereby he could evade answering the question whether or not he still shared the ideas announced at the time when the Republican party was founded. However, in his anxiety poor Lincoln made a serious blunder. His memory seemed to desert him completely when he faced the trap Douglas had prepared for him, and he tried to save himself by a lie. But Douglas came down on him mercilessly and pointed out the pettiness of his subterfuge. Douglas indeed proved that on the very day of the meeting, and in the very hall in which it was held, Lincoln had delivered a speech to which Douglas had replied. After Lincoln had finished on that occasion, Codding[7] had stepped forth to ask the Republicans that, instead of listening to Douglas's reply, they should follow him to the Senate chamber to hold the Republican convention. During that convention the above-mentioned resolutions were reached.[8]

Thus Lincoln had been present, and was not, as he had asserted, away at Tazewell to attend court.[9] Poor Lincoln tried to cover up his embarrassment by a counter accusation: he alleged that the principles of popular sovereignty had not been recognized with sincerity in the Kansas Bill,[10] since its sponsors had voted down the Chase amendment[11] according to which the people within a territory would have been free to abolish slavery there. But even this maneuver availed Lincoln as little as had his alleged trip to Tazewell. Douglas therefore proved that the reason for his and his friends' votes against the Chase amendment was that its sponsor had refused to accept Chase's proposal of giving the people the right either to introduce or to exclude slavery. Only after Chase had rejected an unconditioned recognition of the people's sovereignty, as moved by the Democrats, was the amendment voted down.

After this short resume our readers will be inclined to believe that the following picture, which the Chicago "Times" gives of the unfortunate Lincoln's appearance after the meeting ended, and it must be very true:

> There he stood like a pillar, staring fiercely at the people who surrounded the triumphant Douglas. His mouth was wide open, and he could not find a single friend to speak a word of comfort to him in his misery. It was a ticklish business for the Republicans, who had witnessed his defeat and knew how deeply he felt it, to lift up his spirits and give him hope for better times to come. After Douglas had been led away in triumph, Lincoln tried to step down from the platform, but his limbs refused the service and he had to be carried, for which labor the Republican master of ceremonies commissioned six strong, stout fellows who put the dead lion on their shoulders and, his feet trailing on the ground, dragged him to his den.

August 27, 1858

[*New Yorker Staats-Zeitung*, 4 September 1858]

DOUGLAS AND LINCOLN: THE SECOND
DEBATE AT FREEPORT, ILLINOIS

When Mr. Lincoln made his first address at Springfield, in which he on his part opened this year's election campaign, he compared Mr. Douglas to a "dead lion" and himself to a "living dog." The "Republicans" considered this a "most appropriate parable," and thus they cannot take it amiss if we hold their acclaimed candidate to his word. In his own language we may state as regards the outcome of the debates at Ottawa and Freeport that the "living dog" was badly mauled by the "lion" who is far from being dead and still completely possesses his full mental powers. We have given a short resume of the Ottawa debate, and we do not wish to withhold from our readers an account of the second discussion which took place at Freeport, Ill., on Friday, August 27. Unfortunately space does not permit to give both speeches *in extenso*. (They fill no less than nine closely printed pages of the large-sized *Chicago Tribune*.) We therefore limit ourselves to giving a literal translation of the most noteworthy passages in both speeches. The reader can then decide for himself whether the self-styled "living dog" may not have every reason to avoid further encounters with the "lion."

About fifteen thousand persons attended the open air mass meeting. If one bears in mind that, although it was raining and stormy almost throughout the discussion, the audience nevertheless remained until the last word was spoken, one can form some idea of the profound interest the people of Illinois are taking in this campaign. As Mr. Douglas had made the opening address at Ottawa, this time it was Mr. Lincoln's turn to speak first. He started at two o'clock in the afternoon. Everybody expected of him a great address that would fell the Democratic party at one blow; his friends hoped that he would blow all arguments previously advanced by Douglas sky-high.

But all were disappointed. It was the same old wrangling with trite phrases that hardly deserved to be honored with the designation of an "address." The main part of it was a play of questions and answers, for Douglas had formulated seven questions at the Ottawa meeting and requested that his opponent answer them. These questions were based on the platform of the abolitionists who had first nominated Lincoln as candidate for U.S. Senator. Lincoln had not dared to answer these questions at once; but after he had one solid week to consult with the leaders of the "Republicans" he had written down his answers, reading them to the Freeport audience as follows: [omitted]

While Mr. Lincoln was reading these questions and his replies from the manuscript, a considerable agitation started in the "Republican" part of his audience. These listeners thought it quite likely that by his seven answers Lincoln had repudiated the whole "Republican" creed. They therefore began to be restive, to grumble and to otherwise express their displeasure in undertones. He felt obliged, therefore, to clarify his words after he had read off his answers. The task took up the major part of his allotted time, and consisted in nothing more than paraphrasing the short sentences in which he had opened his seven answers. These seven answers more or less may still give Mr. Lincoln much trouble, and we should not be surprised if the "Republicans" in northern Illinois might label them "Lincoln's seven deadly sins." These explanatory paraphrases of his "seven deadly sins," however, included several sentences that we should like to quote for their naïveté. Regarding the law on fugitive slaves, he said that he did not approve of the present law but that the slave states were entitled under the Constitution to ask Congress for a similar statute—he himself, however, even if elected to Congress, would offer no proposal to amend or improve that law. As to the admission of new slave states, if that be desired by the people, he opined that he would hate to be placed in a position where he would have to vote against the admission of such a state! If these explanations, on which he had had a whole week's time to ponder, do not show a high degree of helplessness and moral cowardice, then we must declare ourselves at a loss how to interpret his language.

After he had continued for almost an hour, with rather lame and dull arguments, to talk around Senator Douglas's questions, half answering and half evading them, he suddenly took courage when he remembered that he had in his pocket another piece of paper, with four questions on it which he had been asked to ask of Douglas as though they were his own. Lincoln was so heartily convinced of the profundity and great importance of these questions that he did not expect Mr. Douglas to answer them at once; after all he, the "living dog," the *Lumen mundi illinoisieni* [the light of the Illinois world], had asked for eight full days to formulate his replies to a few questions;—therefore he was kind and magnanimous enough to concede an equal number of days of grace to the "dead lion" fighting against him. But, as we shall see, Douglas did not accept Lincoln's generous offer, but replied to the four questions at once—and in a very different and much more straightforward way than Mr. Lincoln had to his (Douglas's). Mr. Lincoln, then, after he had pulled himself together, took the paper from his pocket and read out the following questions: [omitted]

Mr. Lincoln declared that he had only been able so far to compose these four questions. Eventually, however, he would try to formulate three more so that, should he succeed, he too might complete the figure seven.

Thereupon Lincoln took up the topic of the resolutions quoted by Mr. Douglas. On this we shall dwell at length in another column. Then he came to discuss the Chase amendment to the Nebraska bill; his remarks on this subject were but a rehash of all the stock phrases warmed up by the "Republican" yellow press ever since 1854. But here his time was up. He had talked for an hour and sat down.

In the preceding paragraph we have presented so truthful an outline of Lincoln's "address" as possible. Should the reader jump to the conclusion that it was an address unworthy of a candidate for the United States Senate or, in general, of a man who endeavors to become the successor of a Douglas in the councils of the nation,—then this would be Mr. Lincoln's own misfortune and not *our* doing.

After Mr. Lincoln had withdrawn, Senator Douglas took the floor, greeted by three enthusiastic hurrahs intermingled with some hisses. Anyone who knows that Freeport is in the northwestern corner of Illinois, that it is the center of the northern Illinois population impregnated with ultra-abolitionist views, will be astonished that there were several thousand present to pay tribute to Douglas and that so few took part in the hissing. This circumstance can only be explained by the very depressed mood in which Lincoln's pitiful "address" had left his "Republican" listeners. After a few introductory remarks, Mr. Douglas began his address by answering Lincoln's four questions without much ado. In the following our readers will find a literal translation of this part of Douglas's speech: [omitted]

Here Mr. Douglas went over to a discussion of the situation with regard to the Chase amendment. This part of his speech we shall publish later on, as we intend to make a few comments of our own. Today, for reasons of space, we wish to limit ourselves to Mr. Douglas's answers to Lincoln's four questions.

Mr. Douglas then continued: [omitted]

We believe that every reader will agree with us when we state that this was a candid and frank address. There was no involved paraphrasing, no willful evasion of the issue, no petty playing with words, but clear, daring, and manly language such as one may expect from a man like Senator Stephen A. Douglas.

But before concluding this excerpt from his speech we shall quote one more passage, namely, Douglas's reply to Lincoln's remark that he, Lincoln, would hate to be placed in a position that might force him to vote on the admission of new slave states. Mr. Douglas once more read the resolutions he had quoted during the Ottawa discussion, the same which Lincoln has vehemently repudiated ever since, both personally and through his mouthpiece, the [Chicago] *Press and Tribune*, as though they felt offended at Douglas's suggestion that they should profess *such* principles. A certain Tom Turner[12]—who presided over the Freeport meeting as the Republican among the two umpires—said, after Douglas had read the resolutions, that he himself had been their author.

After Mr. Douglas had ended,—or rather after his time of an hour and a half was up—Mr. Lincoln once more took the floor and talked for half an hour about the address which Douglas had delivered in the Senate against the [Washington, D.C. newspaper] "Union"; sought to prove that Mr. Douglas might have meant the President rather than merely [editor Cornelius] Wendell's reporting.

With these words we take leave for the present from this great debate. Douglas's address was undeniably one of the best and most brilliant of his life. It offers many an inspiration to those Democratic journalists who desire to contribute as much as possible to making the principles of the party known among the masses of the people.

APPENDIX

September 9, 1858

Illinois, 9 September 1858
[*New Yorker Staats-Zeitung*, 16 September 1858]

PROGRESS OF THE CAMPAIGN

Party excitement usually reaches a climax in rhythmic cycles of four years with each presidential election campaign. In Illinois, however, the symptoms of that fourth year which mark, so to speak, the boiling point of political passions, are being repeated already, after an interval of only two years, because of the impending elections this autumn.

The reasons for this fact are well known to the readers of the New York *Staats-Zeitung.* The two great parties, which during the last five years were busily engaged in a strenuous contest over all matters of local and national politics, have now crystallized, as it were, in the Illinois Democratic and Republican camps; they have, one might say, delegated their respective interests to the party organizations in the Prairie State, and the outcome of the present heated struggle will in all probability determine not only the political character of that state but also the character of the Union for years to come, perhaps forever. The Democrats in Illinois are entrenched in a sharply defined position. They stand for the Democratic creed as formulated by the national platform of 1856, but if I may use this expression, in a chemically pure form free of everything not above board. The Republican camp in Illinois, on the other hand, represents in a concentrated form all the political heresies, chimerae, contradictions, and rivalries which are so characteristic of the Republican Party in all the various states. [The] Democracy in Illinois represents the conservative principle intent upon safeguarding the Constitution. It stands for the equality of the rights and duties of the individual states; it favors progress and evolutionary improvement and opposes haste and the use of violent methods for the cure of political and social evils. The colorful mosaic of opinions which, like the wolf in sheep's clothing, disguise themselves under the well-sounding name of "Republicanism," have inscribed on their banner everything that is revolutionary, destructive, and subversive of all constitutional bounds. Should such doctrines triumph, it would ring in the beginning of an era of revolution and decay.

The rival protagonists of Democratic and Republican doctrines have placed the main burden of the recently opened campaign upon the shoulders of their most prominent representatives—like in Greek and Roman antiquity and during the fierce, rough and always bellicose Middle Ages when the two hostile camps selected their bravest warriors to let their duel decide upon the general cause. From the Democrats only one leading personality—who, however, is mightier than a thousand lesser fighters—has so far entered the arena, namely, Stephen A. Douglas. The Republicans, on the other hand, have deemed it necessary to throw against him the two strongest brains they could muster. This "flower of Republican

328

knighthood" blossoms in Messrs. Abraham Lincoln and Lyman Trumbull—the first a would-be, the latter an actual United States Senator (though not for much longer). Both cavaliers have an equally strong stake in the outcome of the present party contest, since the legislature to be elected in November will not only have to fill the term of office of Judge Douglas but will also have to decide upon a successor to Mr. Trumbull.[13]

Lyman Trumbull is the very embodiment of that Yankeedom which is known for its shrewdness and selfishness, always ready to pull all possible tricks, honorable or otherwise, in order to shuffle the cards to its own advantage. In practice he has proved his "smartness" by the way he out-tricked his own comrade-in-arms, Lincoln, a few years ago to cheat him out of a seat in the United States Senate.[14] In 1854, as we recall, he and Lincoln agreed upon a plan that was to fulfill the ardent longing of both—their election into the United States Senate. Trumbull had fallen into political obscurity when, back in the forties, he had endorsed certain thoroughly unpopular measures; but he lay in waiting, biding his time until he might regain the lost popular favor. To achieve this he set out to exploit the so-called anti-Nebraska excitement, which was then running high, in order to rebuild his depleted political capital. He got Lincoln, a rather influential member of the Whig party, to oblige—he was to do his utmost to dissolve his own party and blend it with the intended new anti-Nebraska party. Trumbull, on his part, undertook to lure a certain section of the Democrats into the camp of the new party with the then so popular tune of the anti-Nebraska slogan.[15]

The plan succeeded inasmuch as the majority of the legislature, which convened in that year, favored the repeal of the Kansas-Nebraska bill and therefore elected a member of the opposition to take the place of General Shields.[16] However, Shields' successor was not, as had been stipulated in the agreement between Lincoln and Trumbull, Lincoln (Trumbull himself was slated as Douglas's successor [in 1859]); rather did the cunning Yankee scheme so perfectly that he himself received the seat which he had promised to Lincoln! The duped Kentuckian had to go home with a long nose and seek comfort in the vain hope of succeeding in 1859—the very hope which he at present tries to realize. In 1854, in an address before the anti-Nebraska meeting, that maneuver was publicly branded as infamous by none other than a certain James H. Matheny, who is now serving as a Republican matador. It is easy to see from these facts that the brotherly love between Lincoln and Trumbull cannot be particularly deep and that, if not merely their lips but their hearts were to speak out, they would be heard to wish each other to hell rather then make for a common Republican heaven in friendly embrace.

Trumbull's hatred for Douglas is of long standing. He can never forgive and forget that Douglas in the early eighteen-forties denounced him vigorously for the shameless political football he had been playing with the repudiation of the public debt and thereby relegated him to temporary political oblivion.

All the malice, lying invention and shameless distortion of facts which Trumbull displayed ever since he mounted the stump against Douglas must be attributed to his long nurtured personal antipathy toward that man. However, the energy, promptness, and pitiless precision with which Douglas refuted Trumbull's false accusations against him and publicly unmasked the accuser as a liar, turned to his advantage what had been calculated as a blow to his cause. Already now the unprincipled, demoralizing demagogue Trumbull has earned the contempt of every honest-minded and truth-loving voter in Illinois.

In my last report, under a Springfield dateline, I observed that Lincoln finally realized the lack of tact and delicacy in his strategy of clinging to Douglas's heels and imposing himself upon Democratic mass meetings which had come together to hear not him but Douglas, and that he had indicated that henceforth he would desist from such an arrogant behavior. Meanwhile, however, experience has proved that Lincoln is still trying to exploit Douglas in an unfair way which, though less insolent, does still not betray a very manly attitude or too much faith in the justice of his own cause. In all the towns along the Illinois River where Douglas had spoken before thousands of enthusiastic listeners, Lincoln appeared on the following day to rattle off the endless Republican platitudes about slavery and nothing but slavery. Anyone who is familiar with the influence that public speakers of opposing political opinions exercise on the same audience must know the advantage accruing to him who can make the closing remarks. It is this advantage which Lincoln, conscious of his natural inferiority, would apparently like to monopolize.

Since his return from Washington, Senator Douglas has delivered no fewer than 20 public addresses in the various parts of the state. The powerful flow of his forensic talent carried him usually beyond the time limit suggested by consideration for his health. None of his addresses—except the one in the debate with Lincoln—took less than two hours, and the tenacity he develops both regarding his vocal means and his mental as well as physical constitution during these strenuous exertions is indeed marvelous. So far he has remained in full possession of his strength which, instead of diminishing, seems to become steeled, as it were, by its constant use and to increase in effectiveness and perseverance. The feeling of certainty that he will return triumphantly to the U.S. Senate—a certainty which has imposed itself upon him more irresistibly with every day of the campaign—contributes its share in keeping him in a jovial and confident mood. This conviction of victory is absolutely essential to him for the completion of the huge task he has set himself for the two months still separating us from election day.

The writer of these lines has already in previous years had the opportunity of ascertaining the firm and unshakable confidence which the Democratic camp in Illinois places in the "little giant."[17] But the thundering ovations he received on his triumphal procession through the state—which I witnessed with my own eyes—were such emphatic votes of confidence as hardly any other American statesman has ever received. Douglas, by his fearless demeanor based solely upon his confidence in the truth and justice of his cause, has struck a chord, the vibrations of which are harmoniously resounding in the hearts of the people and have made him the greatest man of our time.

The readers of your paper are well informed that seven different debates between Douglas and Lincoln are envisaged in seven different congressional districts before this campaign ends. Two of these—at Ottawa in Lasalle County, and at Freeport in Stephenson County—took place during the last two weeks. The deep interest of the masses in the present contest in Illinois was evidenced most strikingly by the presence of tens of thousands who had come to witness this memorable struggle not between physical forces but between forces of the spirit. I estimated the crowds in Ottawa at about 50,000,[18] those in Freeport at 20,000.

In accordance with the agreement made with his opponent, Douglas gave the opening address at Ottawa. Although with the initiative and spirit characteristic of him he took to the offensive in all of his addresses, forcing Lincoln to resign himself to the defensive, Douglas yet surprised friend and foe alike by the originality and immediate results of his strategy of attacking his opponent. He knew that he was talking in a county that, in 1856, had shown a majority of 1200 votes in favor of [Republican presidential candidate John C.] Fremont. Therefore, he did not choose the course of proving the ephemerity of Republican doctrines by putting them to the acid test of democratic principles; rather did he charge the foe with his own weapons, namely, the Republican platform of previous years, which were conspicuous for their advocacy of extremism and their unbridled, inflammatory language. These platforms had, among other things, rejected in unmistakable terms the admission of new slave states and advocated the repeal of the fugitive slave law, the abolition of slavery in the District of Columbia, and the restoration of the Missouri Compromise.

Lincoln as well as Trumbull, [Congressman Owen] Lovejoy, [Congressman John F.] Farnsworth and the other Republican champions all had a hand in the framing of these platforms. Now Douglas knew that the Republican section of the audience consisted partly of moderate elements (former Whigs), whose conservatism made the above-mentioned radical measures abhorrent to them; partly (and perhaps even a majority) of ultra-abolitionists, for whose taste the same measures did not go far enough. By questioning Lincoln as to whether or not his political convictions were still the same as those of the time when the above-mentioned resolutions were formulated, Douglas placed him in an awkward dilemma. If Lincoln answered in the affirmative, he risked alienating forever his former party comrades, the conservative Whigs, who in this part of the state hold the balance of power; if he answered negatively, he was bound to incur the dissatisfaction of the abolitionist majority of his listeners. Lincoln, going on the assumption that the abolitionists would willy-nilly swallow the bitter pill of a disavowal of their doctrines and vote for the Republican ticket anyhow, thought it best to avoid any direct and comprehensive, manly answer. He preferred to launch a short denial, which he uttered with manifest reluctance and which was in every way incomplete and insufficient. It was fascinating to watch how the faces of the abolitionists became longer and longer at this direct disavowal of their principles.

Senator Douglas had quoted that platform from an 1854 issue of the *Springfield Register*—the Democratic central organ—which presented it as adopted at Springfield by the Republican state convention. Relying on this information, Douglas quoted the platform as such in his address. Later, however, it became clear that the platform had been adopted not by the Republican state convention, but by the Republican convention of Kane County. Every unbiased judge not blinded by party furor must realize at first sight that the question posed was not one of geography but whether these resolutions represented the views and opinions of Lincoln. The Republican press, however, exaggerating the matter and insinuating wrong motives, seized upon this unintended error of Senator Douglas in order to make up for the advantage he had won by throwing a bone of contention into the ranks of their party; but the prompt exposition of the true cause of his mistake, which Douglas gave in his next address, frustrated this Republican maneuver completely.[19]

During the debate at Freeport, Lincoln was cornered so hopelessly that even his most fervent friends had to admit that his position was vague, wavering and untenable. They were forced to concede Douglas's mental superiority, and this despite the fact that this time Lincoln had had the advantage of opening and closing the debate. Lincoln began with the recital of elaborate answers to Douglas's questions which he had failed to produce at Ottawa. The whole performance made it quite plain that he had previously prepared these answers and learned them by heart. It is after all well known that Lincoln is under the intellectual tutelage of a committee which travels around with him and with whom he consults on every sentence, every thought, every argument in advance.[20] That at Ottawa he refused to show his colors must be attributed solely to that committee's strict injunction against discussing even a single important point without previous instructions. During the four [six] days between the debates at Ottawa and Freeport, Lincoln had undertaken, in conjunction with that committee, to formulate his answers that clearly showed the mark of evasive sophistry.

After steering laboriously around the rhetorical shoals that Douglas had placed in his way, Lincoln thought that he had an opportunity for a masterstroke. Forgetting that his opponent is known the world over for his quick mind and ready wit, and thinking that Douglas, too, would need four days to have an answer ready, he imagined he could catch him off guard by shooting a few questions at him in his turn. But they had hardly come from his lips when he was presented with clear, precise and forceful replies—veritable oratorical masterpieces, as friend and foe conceded; they were the climax of Douglas's performance as a speaker in this election campaign so far. These answers were remarkable not only for their perfect form and their wealth of ideas; what made them so important was the fact that they touched upon the core of the problems of the day. It is my opinion that this address cannot fail to cause a far reaching sensation in all parts of the Union, not merely in view of its oratorical merits but because it defines the present and future position of the speaker toward the most burning questions of national home policies.

The first question addressed to Douglas pertained to his attitude for the case that Kansas, despite the provisions of the English Bill,[21] should during the next session of Congress apply for admission into the Union with a constitution to be drafted in the meantime. Douglas replied most unequivocally that *in principle he would favor a general rule according to which no territory with the population of less than 93,000 should be granted statehood; however, as long as no such rule existed he should feel that if 35,000 inhabitants were enough to make Kansas a slave state, that same figure should also be considered sufficient to transform it into a free state!* This frank and sincere declaration was received with a storm of applause. With astounding adroitness the speaker at once forged his reply into a weapon with which he administered a powerful blow to his opponent. He gave Lincoln the sarcastic advice that he should rather cross-examine his own party colleague Trumbull on this particular point—the latter after all opposed the admission of the *free* state Oregon solely for alleged reason it did not have a large enough population for a seat in the House of Representatives.

Douglas's answer is of considerable interest insofar as out west people believe that Kansas will present itself with a new constitution before the next Congress and ask for admission into the Union, but that the [Buchanan] administration will oppose this as contrary to the provisions of the English Bill. This would create a new conflict with Douglas.

The second [actually the fourth] question challenged Douglas to reveal his views on a possible expansion of the territory of the United States, even should this mean an extension of the territory of the slaveholders. Douglas declared that in his opinion the Union had not yet pushed its frontiers to the furthest point in the woodland territories, that in all probability a further expansion would become necessary in due time and would therefore also certainly take place in the natural course of things. As to the political institutions of the newly acquired regions he would be guided only by the principle of popular sovereignty. In other words, he would always try to safeguard the rights of the people within the area to be acquired to determine their own social and political mode of life independent from all authority, with the exception, of course, of the Constitution and the laws of the United States.

The third [actually second] question related to the prerogative of the population within United States territories to introduce or exclude slavery according to their own judgment, even before they had changed from the "off age" [territorial] status to the full sovereignty of statehood. Douglas expressed his opinion on this matter as follows: "Even though the Dred Scott ruling and its juridical interpretation of the Constitution recognized the *abstract* right of the people of the Southern states to enter with their property such territories of the United States still in *common* possession of the people of all states and therefore submitted to their common use, i.e., territories not yet transformed into sovereign states, the population of the territories yet had the supreme power of deciding whether slavery within their respective territories should or should not be tolerated." [This is a paraphrase of Douglas's language rather than a direct quote.] Douglas's opinion on this question has frequently been misunderstood and misconstrued by Democrats as well as Republicans. It was said that Douglas claimed a right for the majority of the population of a territory to exclude or to introduce slavery unconditionally—in spite of the Dred Scott case! In this way higher authority would be granted to such a majority than to the United States Supreme Court. Thereby Douglas would have publicly conceded a dissenting opinion in regard to the Dred Scott ruling.[22]

However, only a superficial skimming of Douglas's sentences can lead to such a conclusion; a conscientious analysis of his words and the entire context of the address will furnish entirely different results. Douglas drew a distinction between right and power; he said that although the Supreme Court had affirmed the abstract right of slaveholders to move with their property (the slaves) into the territories, the people yet retained the power to make the exercise of this right either possible, or to make it impossible by abstaining from promulgating specific local laws without which slavery could not exist. Without the concrete recognition of the abstract right by specific acts of the territorial legislature guaranteeing the exercise of that right, such a right would always remain a dead letter.

I have it on the best authority, namely, from Senator Douglas himself, that it was this sound opinion, which avoids every conflict with the United States Supreme Court, that he really had in mind. Quite a few of the so-called government [i.e., pro-Buchanan] papers in the West and a number of Southern periodicals misrepresented Douglas's theories and are already making them the object of a flood of unbridled abuse. Hence it is of far-reaching importance that Douglas's correct views, which are implied in the controversial language, should become known throughout the country.

After Douglas had disappointed his catechizing foe by answering him in an unequivocal and comprehensive manner, he read a number of resolutions which had been introduced in 1855 in the state legislature by the well-known abolitionist Lovejoy but which the Democrats had succeeded in voting down. Of course these resolutions smacked of the ultra-abolitionist doctrines so popular at the time of the anti-Nebraska party. While Douglas was reading, the Republican part of the meeting ranged themselves with mad demonstrations of approval solidly behind the policy outlined by those resolutions. (Of course they deceived themselves completely as to the purpose behind Douglas's tactics.)

Douglas knew very well that Lincoln's adherents would heartily applaud these doctrines, but that Lincoln on the other hand would not dare to address them directly because of the impression this would make upon the people of the southern part of the state. What he had foreseen indeed happened. Lincoln was forced to disavow these extremist views despite all the shouts of approval. Douglas at once took advantage of this manifest difference of opinion between Lincoln and the Republican part of the audience to maneuver his opponent into a truly pathetic position by highlighting with trenchant sarcasm the extraordinary phenomenon of a party candidate disavowing of his party's principles.

Both the debates in Ottawa and in Freeport demonstrated conclusively Douglas's mental superiority over Lincoln. The latter's rhetoric showed that he lacked depth and thoroughness, seriousness of mind, creative methods, and sharp logical thinking—qualities which so eminently distinguish his rival. Just imagine a would-be statesman who adorns his speeches with the most appalling platitudes, who juggles worn-out clichés, and indulges in corny little puns—a man who sanctimoniously uses Bible quotations instead of arguments, and instead of appealing to the intelligence of his listeners merely tries to entertain them by making them laugh. It is indeed regrettable that Douglas and Lincoln are not appearing on the same platform in every single county of the state. The Republican fever would then be cured radically and within a short time.

On the evening after the Freeport debate I had the doubtful pleasure of listening to the most revolting soapbox oratory of the notorious Owen Lovejoy, Representative of the third congressional district and candidate for reelection. He spluttered his oratorical expectorations before a mob of political fanatics. The Hon. Owen Lovejoy had been a clergyman not so long ago, but the metamorphosis from unctuous preacher to a Republican activist has had little effect upon the bigotry of the transformed gentleman. The substance may be different, but the fanatical intensity with which it poured forth has remained the same. How the German radicals can stomach this narrow-minded, fanatic demagogue, who from his soutane has sneaked into a Republican coat, is beyond my understanding.

Recently there were again some interesting revelations about the alliance between the Republican standard-bearer and the so-called Administration Democrats. These two groups are meeting for joint consultation in Chicago. It is really an edifying spectacle to find [prominent Republicans like] Deacon Bross, N[orman] B. Judd, E[benezer] Peck, Captain [George] Schneider in a daily tête-à-tête with [pro-Buchanan Democrats like Graham] Fitch, [Richard B.] Carpenter, [Charles] Leib, [Isaac] Cook etc. The *Chicago Times* recently received documentary evidence that the Republican bigwigs from Chicago spirited $500 into the pocket of the above-mentioned Carpenter, who must make a stumping tour through the state, ostensibly for the Administration party but in reality for the Republican ticket. This noble man, when his price was paid, indeed launched a speech at Clinton, De Witt County, but then withdrew into the more comfortable regions of Saratoga to have a good time with the remainder of the $500, thumbing his nose at the Republicans.

The dismissal of James W. Davidson, United States Marshal for Northern Illinois, and the appointment of Mr. [Charles N.] Pine, editor of the pro-administration paper in Chicago (the *Chicago Herald*) has caused much ill-feeling in the state. These steps are interpreted as a direct endorsement on the part of the Administration of all the infamous lies and dirty invectives heaped upon Judge Douglas by that paper.

In a sort of counter-move, the Douglas Democrats of Chemung [County] and Adams County have nominated the dismissed postmaster of Chicago [William

Price] for the office of state senator and adopted strongly worded anti-administration resolutions.

Yesterday the so-called Administration Democrats staged a mass meeting at Springfield. I have never seen a more telling fiasco. Though for weeks the most intensive preparations had been going on in all parts of the state to attract the faithful, exactly 174 persons, all told, made their appearance. No fooling—I counted them myself.

September 12, 1858

St. Louis, 12 September 1858
[*New Yorker Staats-Zeitung*, 20 September 1858]

[The opening paragraphs of this dispatch are omitted, for they describe an agricultural fair in St. Louis and say nothing about the political campaign.]

The fair had attracted a considerable number of political bigwigs from all parts of the country. The most notable were ex-governor Jones (the well-known congressman) of Tennessee,[23] and Senator Douglas of Illinois. The first spoke enthusiastically for the re-election of the latter to the U.S. Senate and declared publicly that he intended to campaign for him in Illinois. (In fact he has already carried out this intention.) Douglas, who was on his way to Southern Illinois, received a hearty welcome from the Democratic Party in St. Louis. Last Thursday evening he and his wife were honored with a serenade, and Friday morning 500 Missourians escorted him to Belleville where he spoke in the afternoon.

Among the Germans in St. Louis a noticeable shift of political opinion has taken place recently. Many have reached the conclusion that the emancipation projects of their leaders are partly political chimeras which cannot be realized until a much later time, partly the counsels of a narrow and blatant selfishness, and partly popular, easily played-up slogans which ambitious politicians find handy to use in order to promote their own personal aims.

The shift in the policy of the Republicans for the purpose of amalgamation with the "red-blooded" Americans [i.e., nativists] *of the State of New York has caused a great sensation among the Germans in Missouri and Illinois and will, in the latter state, certainly produce many thousands of votes for the Democratic ticket.*[24]

September 21, 1858

Alton, 21 September 1858
[*New Yorker Staats-Zeitung*, 4 October 1858]

You are certainly aware that the "Giants" of the German Republican press, in the East and the West alike, have shown great imagination in coining high-sounding phrases about the principled attitude and proud independence of the German representatives of the party of "intelligence and decency," ever since the orthodox Republican gospel was revealed in the State of New York. Betrayed and sold out by their Anglo-American party comrades, and mercilessly kicked out of the party in the most insulting way, they are now trying to cover up their humiliation with the mantle of pride of principle and of an emancipation from all party obligations. Evidently the phantom of a "German" party, which for four years has been reposing in the grave of forgotten illusions, is to be conjured up again, and the world is to be offered another opportunity to shake their heads over the already once deceased force of so-called free Germanism and to marvel at the incorrigible niaiseries of our radical world reformers. Particularly the [St. Louis] *Anzeiger des Westens* and the [St. Louis] *Westliche Post* are swelled with pride and boast mightily about their recently declared political independence. However, the kind of response which this new tune is arousing in the hearts of their leaders in the part of Illinois bordering the Mississippi River is shown by a report received about the public appearance of the assembled opposition elements of Madison County last Saturday. Since I was present myself I can fully vouch for the truth of the reported facts.

For the sake of a better understanding I should mention that the majority of the native citizens of Madison County consist of so-called "Americans" who in 1856 had voted for [nativist candidate Millard] Fillmore. The Nativists in that year had about 2000, the Democrats 1600, and the Republicans 1100 votes. The first group therefore forms the "balance of power," while the other two parties must try in their struggle for supremacy to make inroads into the ranks of the Know-Nothings. The Democrats based their strategy on an appeal to principles, and in fact hundreds of Fillmore men have already recanted their errors and are now gathering around the Democratic banner. The Republicans, on the other hand, do not ask of the "Americans" to adopt their principles; rather do they offer to them, as will be shown in a moment, a monopoly on all public offices. Without the slightest feeling of shame or honesty they yield most submissively to everything that is demanded of them; they do not expect the slightest change of heart on the part of those whose favors and votes they are seeking. In short, there is nothing they find too humiliating or too mean if it will only lead to the desired results.

In all Republican county papers as well as the *Anzeiger des Westens*, advertisements of a mass meeting have been featured prominently for some time. That meeting was to be held on September 18 at Edwardsville, the county seat, and it was to bring together all those citizens of Madison County who were "opposed to Steven A. Douglas's reelection" to the United States Senate. However, in the organs of the Fillmore party one could simultaneously find the following appeal:

Place none but Americans on guard!

A convention of the American party will be held at the Court House in the town of Edwardsville on Saturday 18th day of September 1858 at 10 a.m., to nominate candidates to be voted for at the November election.

> Jacob B. Cox,
> Presd't Marion Council No. 337

The Republican papers, therefore, announced a meeting of *all* elements of the opposition; the Nativists, however, were instructed by the Republican wire pullers to appeal only to the "Americans" lest the latter might be frightened away by too close an association with the Republican Party.

Since I was curious to observe the beautiful romance of the two groups who were about to amalgamate, I decided to add my humble self to the "masses" of that meeting. I had thought that the above-mentioned advertisement had only been to lure as many people as possible to the meeting, but that afterwards they would constitute themselves as one convention. However, the story of that day revealed that an entirely different plan was in the back of the organizers' minds.

At eleven o'clock in the morning, after a two hour drive, I arrived and at once made for the Court House. Already from the carriage I had noticed a number of people in the upper floor, the courtroom. As I thought that the mass convention—"mass" in the sense of *lucus a non lucendo* [i.e., something of which the qualities are the opposite of what its name suggests]—had already come to order. Up there, however, I found the door guarded by two individuals. When I wanted to enter they stopped me and posed a number of mysterious questions in a sort of Free-Masonic jargon. Since I did not catch the meaning of it I was unable to answer them. The consequence of my inability to give a satisfactory reply was that I was refused entry and told to go back downstairs. After this involuntary retreat I tried to enlighten myself about the reasons of my mishap, asking one of my Republican acquaintances. With visible reluctance he admitted that the Know-Nothings on the upper floor were holding a "preliminary meeting" behind closed doors. "What!" I exclaimed involuntarily, "those fellows have the nerve to conduct their business in broad daylight!"

Upon my further question about what the "sole rulers of America" had to decide before joining the general convention, the self-assured, "independent" German Republican replied innocently: "Why, they are making the nominations to present them to the Republicans for ratification." So that was to be the "amalgamation"! Now I suddenly understood. First the Know-Nothings convened in secret conclave, then the Republicans would meet separately—and then this whole maneuver was to be presented to the world as the noisily proclaimed, highly praised, and enthusiastic union of all under the proud, all-encompassing banner of an alleged anti-slavery platform, a brave unity based on mutual concessions and the sacrifice of all "minor" differences of opinion! Could it be, I asked myself, that the star actors in the drama of this convention were the "Americans," while the Republicans were only extras? Was it really possible that the former could have the insolence of dictating the ticket and the latter the cowardly swallowing of all this without protest? The ensuing events made it clear that with the Republicans a thing like this is not impossible, any more than so many other things they have done or put up with. They are accustomed to stomach a lot that, to others, would be as indigestible as shoe nails, and they were even going to swallow this present outrage.

After two hours of deliberations, the doors on the upper floor opened and the noble sons of America—not very impressive numerically—swarmed into the rooms downstairs. Soon the rumor spread that they had really nominated a one hundred percent Nativist ticket composed of nothing but full-blooded, aggressive Nativists; this ticket they would present to the Republicans as a *conditio sine qua non* for amalgamation. Assuming that some individual German Republicans among those present would no doubt get up and protest against accepting a ticket thus imposed by the Know-Nothings, I expected a few scenes during the Republican convention, which started at three o'clock in the afternoon. But the German Republican Party coolies seemed too much accustomed to obey the commands of their Anglo-American directors. Not a single voice of disapproval was heard when the motion was introduced to accept the nominations just made by the Know-Nothing council.

Only one sly politician got up to suggest that it would be wiser to replace one of the Know-Nothing candidates by a certain Alwood, because only the latter would be able to get the Dutch votes in and around Highland. Thus, this one modification was proposed only for the purpose of catching the votes of the somewhat obstinate Dutchmen a little more easily! However, even this direct insult was lost on the thick-skinned German Republicans assembled there, and it remained unavenged. The motion was not followed up, and after a few frantic swallowings on the part of the assembly, the whole pretty dish cooked up by the Know-Nothings was happily crammed down their throats into the sturdy Republican Party stomach.

In order to appreciate the extent of the humiliation of the Germans involved in this solemn affair one must remember that around here the Know-Nothing party is still exactly what it was at the time of its founding. The representatives of Know-Nothingism still demand all the countless extreme and proscriptive measures which Nativism had written on its banner in 1854 with all the insolence of its greatest popularity. In the East, those people will at least make certain concessions to the Republicans, such as going back on the originally demanded substantial extension of the time required for naturalization. In this part of the country, however, they still maintain their intolerant and arrogant attitude towards all foreign born with unmitigated harshness. And yet, although the German Republicans had known nothing of the arrangement between Nativists and Republicans and were therefore shamelessly sold out by the latter to the former; and in spite of the fact that Joe Gillespie[25] and Sydney Hart,[26] the two most violent and aggressive nativists of this region abounding in nativist prejudices, were at the head of the list of nominations—in spite of all these facts not one of the Germans, who already by their presence degraded themselves, had the courage to stand up against this infamous horse trade. When they were forced to swallow the bitter pill, not a single one showed a sign of that moral revulsion which any German with even a spark of honor left will betray in such a case! Also a representative of the German press, the editor of the Republican organ of this city, was present. To his dishonor it must be said that he, too, drained the cup of shame without disgust.

Will also the *Anzeiger des Westens*, the *New Yorker Abendzeitung*, and so on, find only flattering words and an approving slap on the back for these remarkable representatives of "free, independent Germanism"?

_____

September 15, 1858

DOUGLAS AND LINCOLN: THE THIRD DEBATE AT
JONESBORO, ILLINOIS, SEPTEMBER 15, 1858

The third debate between the two champions of the parties contending for supremacy in Illinois, Douglas and Lincoln, took place at Jonesboro, in the southern part of the state, on Wednesday, September 15. The crowd that attended the meeting was not as large as it had been at other places, and the reason for this is said to have been that the State Agricultural Exposition opening the same day had drawn away thousands of farmers from the political arena. Still, there were about 5000 people present—a remarkably large number in view of the fact that southern Illinois is less densely populated than the northern part of the state. With a few exceptions all those present were personal or political friends of the "[Little] Giant from Illinois"—the "Republicans" having about 100 representatives and the postmasters' clique [i.e., supporters of the Buchanan wing of the Democratic party] not over 25. At the last debate at Freeport Lincoln had spoken first; at Jonesboro Douglas's address opened the meeting. He spoke for an hour, followed by Lincoln, who talked for an hour and a half, whereupon Douglas closed the discussion with a half-hour address. Douglas showed his well-known mastery in expounding the principles of the Democratic Party, whereas Lincoln was as usual lame in his argument and ambiguous in his whole presentation. But we will not anticipate the result and proceed to the addresses themselves.

Douglas began with reference to the earlier history of the country. He mentioned the period previous to 1854, before the two big parties, Democrats and Whigs, parted ways over great national issues—a time when each party upheld principles which in the South and North alike could be defended and attacked with the same arguments. He then proceeded to speak of the events in Illinois occasioned by the passage of the Nebraska Bill. Lincoln as a Whig and Trumbull as a Democrat were both ambitious to represent Illinois in the United States Senate. These two joined forces therefore and promised each other to break up their respective party organizations throughout the state and to replace them by black Republicans. But in order to achieve this it was necessary to cater to the sentiments of the people in various parts of the state. Hence while Lincoln, [Owen] Lovejoy, [John F.] Farnsworth and others in the northern part of Illinois started out to preach extreme abolitionism and treasonable doctrines of all kinds, their partners in the south contented themselves with declaring that the repeal of the Missouri Compromise line had been wrong and untimely. These were Messrs. [John] Reynolds of Belleville (now candidate of the postmasters clique for State

Treasurer), John Doherty of Union (now candidate of the same clique for State Commissioner for Public Education), Sidney Breese of Carlyle (he too a candidate of that clique for United States Senator), and Lyman Trumbull. The same double-dealing is now being repeated all over again. While in northern Illinois all conventions of the opposition are held under the banner of the black Republican party, the same opposition became considerably milder when it comes to the center of the state and convenes a meeting of "all opponents of the Administration," and in the south its voice sinks to a whisper and Mr. Trumbull convokes meetings under the slogan "Free Democracy." Douglas at this point read the text of a poster announcing that on September 13 a meeting of the "Free Democracy" was to be held at Waterloo. He said: [omitted]

Douglas went on to describe the abominable political deal between Lincoln and Trumbull in 1854 and how the former was cheated in the end. He quoted from an address of a certain James H. Matheny, then as now Lincoln's devoted political advisor. Matheny, incensed about Trumbull's election to the Senate, had aired his view of the matter in the most bitter language, and revealed the conditions of the agreement between the various factions of the opposition in 1854. According to Matheny these conditions were the following: "1) Trumbull was to be elected to Congress in order to assure his district to the opposition in the legislature. 2) when the legislature should convene, all offices such as the speakers, the clerks, the attendants etc. were to be filled by abolitionists, and 3) a Whig—Lincoln—should become United States Senator. In compliance with the good faith assumption that this program would be carried out completely, Trumbull was elected to Congress and the abolitionists received all the offices of the legislature. But in the most outrageous manner Trumbull's friends refused to elect Lincoln to the Senate, and that vulgar, creeping snake Trumbull, that excrement of the rotten bowels of the Democracy, succeeded in getting himself elected to the United States Senate by promising everything to everybody." Matheny is now a "Republican" candidate for Congress in the district of Springfield, running against [incumbent Congressman] Thomas L. Harris.

After a few well-chosen sarcastic remarks about this confession of a "Republican" about the extraordinary wickedness of another prominent "Republican," Douglas proceeded to another important point. He picked from Lincoln's address in the Springfield convention those passages where he had said that, divided into slave states and free states, this Union, like a house divided against itself, could not in the long run survive; either all would have to become slave states, or all free states; he, Lincoln, would work for the latter. With irrefutable arguments and masterful logic, Douglas proved that such a declaration was challenging the South to undertake a war of annihilation against the North, while inciting the North to make war on the South.

However, since we presented this whole argument to our readers when reporting on his Chicago address of July 9th, we limit ourselves now to a short sketch of Douglas's point of view. He holds that every state and every territory, without any interference from the outside, can claim the right to decide upon their home affairs according to the conditions of soil and climate. He also remarked that the Dred Scott decision of the Supreme Court had adopted this principle in all its implications, endowing it with legal force.

He also spoke against all those endeavors that would elevate the negro socially and politically to an equal status with the white. The negro belongs to an inferior race which, when living together with a superior race, should enjoy only such rights as are compatible with the general welfare of the society in which they live. Each state should be free to decide independently to what extent those rights should be given. The closing part of the address we do not wish to abbreviate. It well deserves to be adopted by every friend of his fatherland as the high-souled view of a true patriot. [omitted]

When Mr. Douglas withdrew, it seemed as if the applause and the hurrahs would never end. Finally, the apostle of the abolitionists, negro-amalgamationists, nativists, and all other "-ists" stepped forth to reply to his opponent. An enthusiastic friend of Lincoln asked for "three cheers," and five people followed suit. Lincoln recognized how ridiculous this effort was and exclaimed, "I hope that the few friends I have here will not be inconvenienced; that's all I am asking." After this introduction he began his "address." His first sentence was that there were many things in which he agreed with Douglas, that he too recognized the states' right of deciding on the slave question by themselves, and he complained that Douglas was trying to make it appear as if he had a different view. After this complaint, delivered with the mien of the hypocrite, he confirmed in the following sentences all the accusations which Douglas addressed against him; namely, he reiterated that this Union, if it remained divided between slave states and free states, could not exist much longer, and he intimated that the life of the United States as a federation could be made secure only if all its members became either slave states or free states. He then tried to show that the policy of the founding fathers would necessarily have led towards the establishment of free states only and towards the abolition of negro servitude. Douglas, he contended, has changed this policy, diverting it to a new course that would finally transform all members of the Union into slave states where negro servitude would be a matter of right. This was the gist of a long argument in which he referred to a few remarks made by Brooks of South Carolina. No man with a grain of common sense will be able to take Lincoln's argument at its face value. The "Republican" music boxes have played this same tune for years, but it has frightened only a few fanatics unable or unwilling to think for themselves, and a few old women. Besides, Lincoln's argument is based upon an historic forgery—something rather common among "Republicans"—for the policy of the founding fathers was, though not the opposite of, at least something very different from the picture Lincoln has painted. For instead of opposing negro servitude everywhere and initiating its abolition, Kentucky (in 1792) and Tennessee (in 1796) were admitted into the Union, both of them slave states. So much for the sake of historical accuracy.

Mr. Lincoln then proceeded to the revelations which Douglas had made about the unsavory agreement with Trumbull and the treachery of that gentleman. He flatly declared that they were untrue. He did not deny, though, that his bosom friend and advisor [James Matheny] in the first fit of rage had made those revelations, but he opined that Matheny had thereby committed an *"immoral thing"* (Lincoln's own words). Lincoln, Trumbull, and Matheny—*trio nobile fratrum*—may now thrash it out among themselves which of them perpetrated the "immoral thing."

The historic account given by Douglas at the beginning of his speech was declared by Lincoln to be correct and accurate. He talked of the sanctity of the Missouri Compromise, what a sin it had been ever to touch it; he said that he agreed with the compromise measures of 1850 (whereby for all practical purposes the Missouri Compromise had been repealed), and that he would uphold them. He then talked about slavery as a means of agitation and contended that the agitation for its abolition would last as long as slavery itself. As he realized that Douglas had hit him hard by forcing him to disavow and to reject the platform of the "Republican" party of Illinois, he conceived the ridiculous defense of passing the buck back—but his argument did not hold water. He pointed out that in 1850 also several Douglas Democrats in northern Illinois had professed extreme anti-slavery views and quoted a number of letters, newspaper articles and resolutions to bolster his accusation. However, he did not seem to know that Douglas had condemned those documents as anti-Democratic already in 1850 when they were first published, whereas Lincoln had endorsed the treasonable platforms of his own party drafted as late as 1854, 1855, and 1856, and even participated in formulating them. But in order to give our readers a full chance of judging Lincoln's oratory for themselves, we should quote a characteristic passage from his address *verbatim.* Lincoln, after quoting the above-mentioned letters and newspaper articles, wanted to tell his audience that he could not personally vouch for the correctness of the material he had introduced. He did this in the following classic manner: [omitted]

Then he started to discuss the four replies which Mr. Douglas had made in answer to Lincoln's Freeport questions. He opined that the answer regarding the admission of Kansas without consulting its population was unclear, but if Douglas did not object he would assume that he would vote to have that state admitted into the Union. Douglas's reply was that the people of the territory, despite the Dred Scott ruling, still retained the right to exclude negro servitude, simply by refusing to pass the necessary police measures for the protection of slave property, had swept Lincoln completely off his feet. Since he had to disprove this view of his opponent he, Lincoln, champion of abolitionism and extreme northern Yankeedom, suddenly adopted the extreme southern standpoint. He said, if the Dred Scott decision of the Supreme Court was binding (and which ruling of the Supreme Court was *not* binding?), each member of Congress, by virtue of his oath to uphold the Federal Constitution, was under an obligation to vote for a law giving protection to the slaveholders in all territories; if he acted otherwise, he would be guilty of perjury! Also any member of a territorial legislature refusing to vote for similar laws commits perjury. It was for this very reason, namely, in order not to perjure himself, that he, Lincoln, had despite his hatred for slavery given his assent to the fugitive slave law. The South had a claim under the Constitution to insist that such a law be passed. At the end of his argument, which sounded very strange in the mouth of an abolitionist, he asked Douglas whether he would vote in Congress for a law for the protection of slaveholders in the territories. The reader will find Douglas's short and precise reply in the closing passages of his address.

Lincoln then complained about a number of remarks which Douglas had made about him in his Joliet address. There Douglas had said that Lincoln had been so upset by the seven questions he had put to him at Ottawa that he had to be carried down from the speakers' platform and that it took him seven full days to formulate his answers. These sarcastic and biting remarks had infuriated Lincoln so much that in an outburst of rage he called Douglas a fool, and altogether indulged very generously in handing out similar titles at the end of his address. He closed with the assertion that he was more familiar with the people of southern Illinois than Douglas, for while he had been born and brought up in this neighborhood, Douglas was a complete stranger among them, coming as he did from a Yankee state, Vermont, high up in the North. However, Lincoln seems to be unlucky with his parables and figures of speech. Once he compared himself to a "living dog" fighting with a "dead lion"—in Jonesboro he ventured to use another metaphor, calling himself in the last phrase of his speech "a poor, destitute mouse" (eine verkomene Maus.) *Ipse dixit* [i.e., he himself said it], hence it must be true!

Lincoln closed his address before his time—an hour and a half—was up. He could have continued for 10 more minutes, and if he were a man of intelligence, of talent and political wit, he could have pressed a masterful speech into these 10 minutes—he could have reviewed the whole field of politics! But he had reached the end of the rope and since he could not think of anything else to say (all his ideas having been spent and exhausted), he simply stopped and sat down,—under the circumstances certainly the best he could do. An eyewitness says, however, that the hundred "Republicans" present, who had been brought together from the four corners of the earth within a radius of 60 miles, made very long faces at such a closing. They had expected much, very much of a man who dared to challenge Douglas to a debate, and so to their acute sorrow now saw with their own eyes and heard with their own ears how pigmy-like the "living dog," the "poor destitute mouse," was [when] confronted with the giant of the West. Many are said to have exclaimed: "This is not the Lincoln that we would like to see—this man is not a match for the Little Giant," and so on.

When Douglas stepped forth to make his closing remarks, he was greeted by stormy applause, a proof that Lincoln had wasted his efforts on his listeners. Douglas expressed his thanks for these enthusiastic demonstrations of loyalty but asked not to be interrupted by applause as this would deprive him of valuable speaking time. He then took up Lincoln's jeremiads on "being carried down the platform," and the "seven days it had taken him to answer seven questions," and so forth, and showed that Lincoln had taken everything literally that he, Douglas, had said jokingly at Joliet. But as a matter of fact, Lincoln had indeed been carried down from the platform at Ottawa, and this was what had caused him to make those remarks. Then Douglas discussed his seven questions and Lincoln's seven answers. He reiterated that his questions were based on the resolutions of county "Republican" conventions, and that he felt perfectly justified in asking whether or not Lincoln approved of the principles set forth in the platform of his party. And what was Lincoln's answer to the question whether he would vote for the admission of a slave state should the population of the state decide in favor of slavery? He had replied that "he would dislike greatly to have himself placed in a position that would force him to vote on such a question." But should he become Senator he will have to make a decision on that question, and therefore it follows that he would not like to see himself put in the position of United States Senator. "I hope the people of Illinois will save him that embarrassment by not placing him into that position." (Thousands of voices: there is no danger,—he won't get in, etc.)

Douglas then analyzed Lincoln's afterthought to his reply and showed that its involved language was undoubtedly phrased so as to deceive the people about the true intentions of Lincoln and the abolitionists. Lincoln did not want to show his colors, or give a straight answer without "ifs" or "buts;" he wanted a free hand to preach one principle to one part of the people and another principle to another part, and in the end he would dupe and cheat all of them. As to the contemptible horse-trading between Lincoln and Trumbull in 1854 which Lincoln had denied, Douglas quoted the events of that day which indicated the existence of such a deal, such an "immoral thing." Apart from the already mentioned testimony of Matheny, who acted as one of the go-betweens in the deal and could therefore speak with full knowledge of all its phases, Douglas mentioned that he had still another witness who also had first-hand knowledge of all the circumstances connected with the "immoral thing." But he was not yet authorized, Douglas said, to give the name of that witness.

"Lincoln," so the speaker pointed out, "does not wish to be responsible for the principles of his party, and in order to defend himself against any endeavors to hold him responsible for them he quotes out of context from letters and speeches of some Democrats tending toward abolitionism." Douglas then declared that the Democratic Party as such had always opposed such views. He proved that [Democratic Congressman] John Wentworth was the originator of those resolutions, while he, Douglas, had strongly disapproved of them as soon as he had heard about them. Things were totally different regarding the platforms of the Republican Party which Lincoln represented. The whole party, particularly in northern Illinois, had accepted the principle that no further slave states should be admitted into the Union, and Lincoln had accepted this policy. But neither he himself nor his party dared to profess that same policy in southern Illinois;

there they shed their fanaticism and presented themselves as moderates. They thereby gave the spectacle of a house divided against itself, and Douglas could pass back Lincoln's Bible quotation that a house divided could not stand. That saying applied with greater justification to the "Republican" party, he said, which in northern Illinois stood for blackest abolitionism while in the southern part of the state it rejected that abolitionism with expressions of contempt. Such a party was a house divided. It could not and would not last, and indeed it must not, for it was an attempt to hide its true opinions by fraudulent means and to solicit votes from the American people under false pretenses.

Douglas also mentioned Lincoln's assertion that, since he had been born in Vermont while Lincoln came from the neighborhood of southern Illinois, the latter should be better qualified to judge popular opinion in Illinois!

Douglas paid warm tribute to his home state and mentioned that when he was on a visit in the land of his birth he had been honored with the title of doctor of law. At that occasion he had made a short address thanking the Vermonters for their kindness and adding: "My friends, Vermont is the most beautiful place on earth to be born in, provided one emigrates at an early age!" He did not want to boast about the land of his birth but rather to expound his own philosophy of life; he wanted to be judged not by the place of his birth, but by the great public institutions and constitutional principles upon which rest the peace, the welfare and the continued existence of this republic.

Douglas's reply to Lincoln's latest question followed next: [omitted]

Douglas then repeated his earlier answer regarding the admission of Kansas into the Union in the clearest and most unequivocal way, so that Lincoln will find no further opportunity to accuse his opponent of duplicity as he has done in a perfidious manner. Then Douglas examined Lincoln's strangest argument— strange because it comes from the lips of an abolitionist and yet is the argument of the most fire-eating fire-eaters from the deepest South. Douglas said: [omitted]

Douglas added a patriotic, warm and deeply felt appeal to the people. In a country like ours, he said, the citizens must abide by the decisions of the courts upon which peace, order, and security of man and property are based; it was only through the maintenance of the state rights that the harmony and unity of the Union could be safeguarded. Then Douglas closed this third debate with his opponent.

The fourth debate took place three days later at Charleston on September 18. As soon as the addresses will be available to us we shall once more bring out their significant parts so that our readers may keep posted on this election campaign.

NOTES

INTRODUCTION

1. J. Cutler Andrews, *The North Reports the Civil War* (Pittsburgh: University of Pittsburgh Press, 1955), 77.

2. Henry Villard, *Lincoln on the Eve of '61: A Journalist's Story*, ed. Harold G. and Oswald Garrison Villard (New York: A. A. Knopf, 1941).

3. Even the most detailed monographs on Lincoln as president-elect make no use of Villard's dispatches in the San Francisco *Bulletin* or Cincinnati *Commercial*. William E. Baringer, *A House Dividing: Lincoln as President-Elect* (Springfield, IL: Abraham Lincoln Association, 1945); Harold Holzer, *Lincoln President-Elect: Abraham Lincoln and the Great Secession Winter, 1860–1861* (New York: Simon and Schuster, 2008).

4. Alexandra Villard de Borchgrave and John Cullen, *Villard: The Life and Times of an American Titan* (New York: Doubleday, 2001), 108.

5. Among the papers that employed him were the New York *Tribune*, the New York *Neue Zeit*, and the German edition of *Frank Leslie's Illustrated Newspaper*. In addition, he briefly edited a German-language newspaper in Racine, Wisconsin.

6. Henry Villard, *Memoirs of Henry Villard, Journalist and Financier, 1835–1900*, 2 vols. (Boston, New York: Houghton, Mifflin, 1904), 1:89–91.

7. A letter by "Veritas," n.d., published in a Quincy newspaper, 3 September 1858, copied in the *Belleviller Zeitung*, 23 September 1858, identified "Villardt" as an agent for John Wien Forney's *Press*. That he played such a role is confirmed in a footnote, evidently by Villard's son, Oswald Garrison Villard. Villard, *Memoirs*, 1:91n.

8. Villard, *Memoirs*, 1:96–97. Villard added: "I had it from Lincoln's own lips that the United States Senatorship was the greatest political height he at the time expected to climb. He was full of doubt, too, of his ability to secure the majority of the Legislature against Douglas" (Ibid., 1:96). Lincoln spoke at a rally in Petersburg on October 29.

9. H. Villardt to Douglas, Chicago, 24 August 1858. I am indebted to Professor Allen C. Guelzo for providing me with a partial transcript of this document.

10. Chicago *Weekly Times*, 5 August 1858; Bloomington *Pantagraph*, 20 August 1858.

11. Joliet correspondence, 17 August, Chicago *Times*, n.d., copied in the Jacksonville *Sentinel*, 27 August 1858.

12. A letter by "Veritas," n.d., published in a Quincy newspaper, 3 September 1858, copied in the *Belleviller Zeitung*, 23 September 1858; Quincy *Herald*, 1, 2 September 1858.

13. Villardt to the editor of the Quincy *Herald*, Alton, 21 September 1858, Quincy *Herald*, 24 September 1858.

14. H. Villardt to Douglas, Chicago, 24 August 1858. I am indebted to Allen Guelzo for providing me with a partial transcript of this letter.

15. Alton *Weekly Courier*, 28 October 1858. The Alton *Beobachter* was established in June 1856 to champion Douglas Democrats. Seven years later it became a Republican organ. In 1866, a fire destroyed the paper's office and its back issues.

16. Villard, *Memoirs*, 1:94, 95.

17. San Francisco *Bulletin*, 14 August 1888; St. Joseph correspondence, 25 November, Philadelphia *Press*, 5 December 1859.

18. Villard, *Memoirs*, 1:134–35.

19. On Hudson, see Louis M. Starr, *Bohemian Brigade: Civil War Newsmen in Action* (New York: A. A. Knopf, 1954), 21–25.

20. "Henry Villard a Man of Ability, Who Succeeds in All He Undertakes as a Newspaper Correspondent," Cincinnati *Commercial Tribune*, 20 August 1883; Eugene Virgil Smalley, *History of the Northern Pacific Railroad* (New York: G. P. Putnam's Sons, 1883), 248–9.

21. Villard, *Memoirs*, 1:141.

22. Springfield *Illinois State Register*, 24 April 1890. Edward F. Leonard (1837–1915) was a Massachusetts-born lawyer who settled in Springfield in 1857 and spent most of his life there. In February 1861, he was a passenger on the special train that conveyed Lincoln from Springfield to Washington. Reminiscences of Leonard in Walter B. Stevens, *A Reporter's Lincoln*, ed. Michael Burlingame (1916; Lincoln: University of Nebraska Press, 1998), 178. Before becoming the president of the Toledo, Peoria and Western Railroad, Leonard served as private secretary to Illinois governor and later senator Shelby Cullom. Springfield *Illinois State Journal*, 6 April 1915; Springfield, Massachusetts, *Republican*, 8 April 1915. On November 27, 1860, the Springfield *Illinois State Journal* reported that the "Nashville (Ill.) Herald says a new bank starts there December 1st, called Montau's Bank, owned by Edward F. Leonard, of Sangamon; capital $500,000, divided into 5,000 shares of $100 each; charter expires 1883."

23. Villard, *Memoirs*, 1:141.

24. New York *Herald*, 22 November 1860.

25. Villard, *Memoirs*, 1:162.

26. Springfield correspondence, 28 December 1860, New York *Herald*, 3 January 1861.

27. Springfield correspondence, 29 January, New York *Herald*, 4 February 1861.

28. Michael Burlingame, ed., *Lincoln's Journalist: John Hay's Anonymous Writings for the Press, 1860–1864* (Carbondale: Southern Illinois University Press, 1998); Michael Burlingame, ed., *With Lincoln in the White House: Letters, Memoranda, and Other Writings of John G. Nicolay, 1860–1865* (Carbondale: Southern Illinois University Press, 2000).

29. Villard, *Memoirs*, 1:143. Villard added that Lincoln

never refused to talk with me about secession, but generally evaded answers to specific interrogatories, and confined himself to generalizations. I was present at a number of conversations which he had with leading public men upon the same subject, when he showed the same reserve. He did not hesitate to say that the Union ought to, and in his opinion would, be preserved, and to go into long arguments in support of the proposition, based upon the history of the republic, the homogeneity of the population, the natural features of the country, such as the common coast, the rivers and mountains, that compelled political and commercial unity. But he could not be got to say what he would do in the face of Southern secession, except that as President he should be sworn to maintain the Constitution of the United States, and that he was therefore bound to fulfil that duty. He met in the same general way the frequent questions whether he should consider it his duty to resort to coercion by force of arms against the States engaged in attempts to secede. In connection therewith I understood him, however, several times to express doubts as to the practicability of holding the Slave States in the Union by main force, if they were all determined to break it up. He was often embarrassed by efforts of radical antislavery men to get something out of him in encouragement of their hopes that the crisis would result in the abolition of slavery. He did not respond as they wished, and made it clear that he did not desire to be considered an "abolitionist," and that he still held the opinion that property in slaves was entitled to protection under the Constitution, and that its owners could not be deprived of it without due compensation. Consciously or unconsciously, he, like everybody else, must have been influenced in his views by current events.

Ibid., 1:145–46.

30. Springfield correspondence, 12 January, New York *Herald*, 17 January 1861.

31. Springfield correspondence, 21 January, Cincinnati *Commercial*, 25 January 1861.

32. Villard, *Memoirs*, 1:97.

33. Ibid., 1:138.

34. Springfield correspondence, 10 January, Cincinnati *Commercial*, 11 January 1861.

35. Springfield correspondence, 20 November, Cincinnati *Commercial*, 21 November 1860.

36. San Francisco *Bulletin*, 14 August 1888.

37. Villard left the train in New York City and was replaced by Stephen R. Fiske.

1. NOVEMBER 1860

1. In his memoirs, Villard described the onslaught of office seekers:

The Jacksonian "doctrine" that to the "victors belong the spoils," was still so universally the creed of all politicians that it was taken for granted there would be a change not only in all the principal, but also in all the minor, Federal offices. It was also expected that the other time-honored party practice of a division of executive patronage among the several States would be carried out. Accordingly, there appeared deputations from all the Northern and Border States at Springfield to put in their respective claims for recognition. Some of them came not only once, but several times. From a number of States several delegations turned up, representing rival factions in the Republican ranks, each pretending to be the rightful claimant. Almost every State presented candidates for the Cabinet and for the principal diplomatic and departmental offices. The hotel was the principal haunt of the place-hunters. The tricks, the intrigues, and the maneuvres that were practised by them in pursuit of their aims, came nearly all within the range of my observation, as it was my duty to furnish the earliest possible news of their success or failure. As a rule, the various sets of spoilsmen were very willing to take me into their confidence, but it was not always easy to distinguish what was true in their communications from what they wished me to say to the press purely in furtherance of their interests.

Villard, *Memoirs*, 1:146–47.

2. Stephen T. Logan (1800–80) was Lincoln's second law partner (1841–43), good friend, and political ally. Lincoln called him "almost a father to me" and felt for him a reverent affection that he never felt for his biological father. Lincoln's endorsement, dated 26 March 1862, on a letter by Logan, Springfield, 13 January 1862, Gilder-Lehrman Collection, New-York Historical Society.

3. Jeremiah Black (1810–83) served as U.S. attorney general (1857–60) and as U.S. secretary of state (1860–61).

4. Henry Winter Davis (1817–65) represented Baltimore in the U.S. House (1855–61, 1863–65), where he became a vehement critic of Lincoln.

5. William Pennington (1796–1862) represented a New Jersey district in the U.S. House (1859–1861) and was chosen speaker of that body in 1860 after a two-month battle pitting northerners, who favored John Sherman of Ohio, against southerners, who opposed Sherman because he was considered too hostile to slavery.

6. William Henry Seward (1801–72), after serving as governor of New York (1839–49), represented that state in the U.S. Senate (1849–61). He later served as U.S. secretary of state (1861–69). In 1860, he was Lincoln's chief rival for the Republican presidential nomination.

7. In his memoirs, Villard told a different story: Lincoln "gave me to understand early, by indirection, that, as everybody expected, William H. Seward and S. P. Chase, his competitors for the Presidential nomination, would be among his constitutional advisers. It was hardly possible for him not to recognize them, and he steadily turned a deaf ear to the remonstrances that were made against them as 'extreme men' by leading politicians from the Border States, particularly from Kentucky and Missouri." Villard, *Memoirs*, 1:145.

8. Thurlow Weed (1797–1882), editor of the Albany *Evening Journal*, was William Henry Seward's close friend and advisor as well as a powerful kingmaker. Villard had met him in 1857 when the journalist needed help procuring transportation from New York to Minnesota. In Villard's memoirs, he described that occasion:

> His exterior was the index of a remarkable man. His tall form, beardless face, set in a frame of gray, bushy hair, heavy eyebrows, and a large mouth made a strong combination of features. His kindly eyes and pleasant smile were in contrast to the rest of his face. He gave me a friendly welcome and listened to my request. After questioning me as to the object of my Western trip, he said promptly, "I think I can help you," sat down, and wrote a letter of introduction for me to a local railroad official, requesting him to obtain passes for me as far westward in the direction of St. Paul as possible. The thanks that I expressed were sincere, for I certainly had no claim upon him.

Villard, *Memoirs*, 1:74.

9. John McLean (1785–1861), associate justice of the U.S. Supreme Court (1829–61), was a perennial aspirant for the presidency.

10. New Jersey attorney general William L. Dayton (1807–64) served as minister to France (1861–64).

11. Iowan Fitz Henry Warren (1816–78) of the New York *Tribune* had served as first assistant postmaster general (1849–50) and would become a general during the Civil War.

12. Journalist-lawyer-politician Cassius Marcellus Clay (1810–1903) championed the antislavery cause in Kentucky and served as minister to Russia (1861–62, 1863–69).

13. Henry Emerson Etheridge (1819–1902) represented a Tennessee district in the U.S. House (1853–57, 1859–61) and became clerk of that body in 1863.

14. Galusha Aaron Grow (1822–1907) represented a Pennsylvania district in the U.S. House (1851–63), where he served as Speaker (1861–63).

15. Nathaniel P. Banks (1816–94) had represented a Massachusetts district in the U.S. House (1853–57) and served as governor of that state (1858–61). He belonged to the moderate wing of the Republican Party and was widely regarded as a trimmer.

16. The pictures appeared in the November 24 issue of *Frank Leslie's Illustrated Newspaper.*

17. In 1841, Horace Greeley (1811–72) founded what became one of the nation's most influential newspapers, the New York *Tribune*, which he edited until his death in 1872.

18. Henry Wilson (1812–75) represented Massachusetts in the U.S. Senate (1855–73). Like several other eastern Republicans, he wished to see Douglas reelected and the rupture within the Democratic Party continue.

19. This day John G. Nicolay recorded that Lincoln had told two men who inquired about the secession crisis that "this government possesses both the

authority and the power to maintain its own integrity" but that the "ugly point is the necessity of keeping the government together by force, as ours should be a government of fraternity." Burlingame, *With Lincoln in the White House*, 10.

20. Chicago Mayor John Wentworth (1815–88), who had served in the U.S. House of Representatives (1843–51, 1853–55), was editor of the Chicago *Democrat*, which was publishing radical antislavery editorials at the time.

21. He later reduced these hours significantly, agreeing to see visitors only from 3:30 to 5 P.M. Springfield correspondence, 4 February, Chicago *Tribune*, 5 February 1861.

22. As time passed, Villard came to take a dimmer view of Mrs. Lincoln. In his memoirs, he wrote that during the period between November 1860 and February 1861, Lincoln grew ever more careworn. Villard offered a partial explanation:

> Not a little was added to his trials by the early manifestation of the inordinate greed, coupled with an utter lack of sense of propriety, on the part of Mrs. Lincoln, whose local reputation had repressed in me all desire to know her. I could not, however, avoid making her acquaintance towards the end of my stay in Springfield, and subsequently saw much of her in Washington. How the politicians found out Mrs. Lincoln's weakness, I do not know, but it is a sorry fact that she allowed herself to be persuaded, at an early date, to accept presents for the use of her influence with her husband in support of the aspirations of office-seekers.

Later, during the Civil War, she

> again added not least to his worries. She meddled not only with the distribution of minor offices, but even with the assignment of places in the Cabinet. Moreover, she allowed herself to be approached and continuously surrounded by a common set of men and women, who, through her susceptibility to even the most barefaced flattery, easily gained a controlling influence over her. Among the persons who thus won access to her graces was the so-called "Chevalier" Wikoff, whose name figured as much as any other in the press in those days, who made pretension to the role of a sort of cosmopolitan knight-errant, and had the entree of society, but was, in fact, only a salaried social spy or informer of the New York Herald. Wikoff was of middle age, an accomplished man of the world, a fine linguist, with graceful presence, elegant manners, and a conscious, condescending way altogether, just such a man as would be looked upon as a superior being by a woman accustomed only to Western society. Wikoff showed the utmost assurance in his appeals to the vanity of the mistress of the White House. I myself heard him compliment her upon her looks and dress in so fulsome a way that she ought to have blushed and banished the impertinent fellow from her presence. She accepted Wikoff as a majordomo in general and in special, as a guide in matters of social etiquette, domestic arrangements, and personal requirements, including her toilette, and as always welcome company for visitors in her salon and on her drives.

Villard, *Memoirs*, 1:147–48, 156–57. Cf. Michael Burlingame, "Mary Lincoln's Unethical Conduct as First Lady," in Burlingame, ed., *At Lincoln's Side: John Hay's Civil War Correspondence and Selected Writings* (Carbondale: Southern Illinois University Press, 2000), 185–203.

23. Elizabeth Todd Edwards (1813–88) was the eldest sister of Mary Todd Lincoln.

24. Mary Wallace (1842–1911) was the daughter of Mary Todd's sister Frances and her husband, William Wallace, the Lincoln family's physician. Evidently Mary Wallace found her stay in Washington disagreeable, for when Mrs. Lincoln appealed to have her return to help comfort her after the death of the Lincolns' son Willie in 1862, the young lady refused. She married John Pope Baker, brother of Edward L. Baker, editor of the Springfield *Illinois State Journal.*

25. On November 7, a journalist writing from St. Louis reported that a

gentleman of this city, who is on terms of personal and political familiarity with him [Lincoln], paid him a visit a day or two ago at Springfield. He called Lincoln's attention to the paragraph in the Boston *Courier* . . . to the effect that he had been in correspondence with Southern conservatives, not of his own party, with a view of having them take places in his Cabinet. Lincoln, he says, disavowed the statement *in toto*, and heard that that and all similar statements were roorbacks, got up by the northern fusionists to damage him with the ultra members of his own party. He had made no pledges, and had in no instance foreshadowed the policy he would pursue if elected. This alleged letter, then, of Mr. Corwin to Hodges, is evidently of that class of statements Lincoln has disposed of with a wholesale denial. My informant learned, however, in the course of conversation, that he would put three Southern men into his cabinet; but Lincoln did not tell him, nor did my informant ask, whom he had in view. It is a very reasonable supposition that Edward Bates of this city will be one of the three, provided he accepts an appointment of the kind, which is doubtful. Henry Winter Davis of Maryland and Cassius M. Clay of Kentucky are looked upon by some as probable members of the Lincoln cabinet.

Whether appointees of Lincoln will be allowed peaceably to hold office under the commissions from him in some of the disturbed districts of the south, is a question yet to be solved. There are people, however, It seems, who are willing to take the chances. Lincoln's neighbors and visitors learn the fact that he has already had applications for office from almost every quarter of the South. A New Orleans paper states that on the day the intelligence was received in that city of Republican victories in Ohio, Indiana and Pennsylvania, no less than 47 letters were put in the post office addressed to "His Excellency, Abraham Lincoln."

Saint Louis correspondence, 7 November, San Francisco *Bulletin*, 19 November 1860.

26. William Henry Herndon (1818–91) was Lincoln's third law partner (1844–61) and eventually his biographer.

27. In 1860, vice president John C. Breckinridge (1821–75) of Kentucky was the presidential nominee of the Southern Democrats.

28. George Peter Alexander Healy (1813–94) was an American artist whose portrait of Lincoln was admired by Mrs. Lincoln, though she "remarked that it gave Mr. Lincoln a graver expression than he usually wore." In his memoirs, Healy described a session with Lincoln:

> During one of the sittings, as he was glancing at his letters, he burst into a hearty laugh, and exclaimed: "As a painter, Mr. Healy, you shall be a judge between this unknown correspondent and me. She complains of my ugliness. It is allowed to be ugly in this world, but not as ugly as I am. She wishes me to put on false whiskers, to hide my horrible lantern jaws. Will you paint me with false whiskers? No? I thought not. I tell you what I shall do: give permission to this lover of the beautiful to set up a barber's shop at the White House!" And he laughed again with perfect delight.

George Peter Alexander Healy, *Reminiscences of a Portrait Painter* (Chicago: A. C. McClurg, 1894), 69–70.

29. John George Nicolay (1832–1901) was a German-born journalist who served as Lincoln's private secretary (1860–65).

30. Connecticut-born Lyman Trumbull (1813–96) represented Illinois in the U.S. Senate (1855–73).

31. One of the Border State visitors alluded to may have been Judge Daniel Breck (1788–1871) of Richmond, Kentucky, who had a long conversation with Lincoln that morning. Nicolay described it at length in a memorandum dated November 16. Burlingame, *With Lincoln in the White House*, 10–11.

32. Congressman John Covode (1808–71) represented a western Pennsylvania district in the U.S. House (1855–63, 1867–71).

33. In 1861, Lincoln appointed Ohio representative Thomas Corwin (1794–1865) minister to Mexico, a post he held until 1864. He had previously served as secretary of the treasury (1850–53) and would soon chair the House Committee of Thirty-three, which was tasked with finding a compromise to relieve the tension between the North and the South that eventually caused the Civil War.

34. Moses Grinnell (1803–77) was a successful New York merchant and generous philanthropist. He did not hold public office during Lincoln's administration, but later became collector of the port of New York (1869–70).

35. Zachariah Chandler (1813–79) represented Michigan in the U.S. Senate (1857–75, 1876–79).

36. Schuyler Colfax (1823–85) represented an Indiana district in the U.S. House (1855–69).

37. Cassius Marcellus Clay (1810–1903), known as the "Lion of White Hall,"

edited an antislavery newspaper in Kentucky and helped establish the Republican Party there.

38. Francis Preston Blair Jr. (1821–75) represented a Missouri district in the U.S. House (1857–64).

39. Attorney Edward Bates (1793–1869), a leading Whig, then Know-Nothing, and then Republican in Missouri, served as Lincoln's attorney general (1861–64).

40. John Bell denied that Lincoln had offered him a cabinet post.

41. In an open letter to anxious merchants in New Orleans, Douglas rather contemptuously said of Lincoln: "What good or harm can he do to anybody, except to humble the pride and wound the sensibilities of a large portion of the American people by occupying the chair once filled by Washington, Jefferson, Madison and Jackson?" Letter dated New Orleans, 13 November 1860, New York *Times*, 20 November 1860.

42. Covode urged Lincoln not to appoint Simon Cameron to a cabinet post.

43. James Watson Webb (1802–84), editor of the New York *Courier and Enquirer*, was a perennial office seeker who served as U.S. minister to Brazil (1861–69).

44. Founder and editor of the New York *Times*, Henry Jarvis Raymond (1820–69) had served as lieutenant governor of New York (1855–56) and speaker of the New York State Assembly (1852–53). In 1864 he became chairman of the Republican National Committee.

45. Preston King (1806–65) represented New York in the U.S. Senate (1857–63).

46. Simeon Draper (1804–66) was a shady political operator who served as chairman of the New York State Republican Party (1860–62) and collector of the port of New York (1864–66).

47. James Warren Nye (1815–76) was a leading New York Republican whom Lincoln appointed as governor of the Nevada Territory.

48. Attorney William Maxwell Evarts (1818–1901) had been chairman of the New York delegation to the 1860 Republican National Convention.

49. On May 24, Weed had met with Lincoln, who reported that his guest "asked nothing of me, at all. He merely seemed to desire a chance of looking at me, keeping up a show of talk while he was at it. I believe he went away satisfied." Weed "showed no signs whatever of the intriguer" and "said N.Y. is safe, without condition." Lincoln to David Davis, Springfield, 26 May 1860, Roy P. Basler and Christian O. Basler, eds., *Collected Works of Abraham Lincoln, Second Supplement, 1848–1865* (New Brunswick, NJ: Rutgers University Press, 1990), 20; Lincoln to Trumbull, Springfield, 5 June 1860, Roy P. Basler et al., eds., *Collected Works of Abraham Lincoln* (8 vols. plus index; New Brunswick, NJ: Rutgers University Press, 1953–55), 4:71.

50. Lincoln carried New York by fifty thousand votes.

51. In the winter of 1859–60, Ohio Congressman John Sherman (1823–1900) lost a bid for the speakership of the U.S. House because he had allowed his name to be added to a list of Republican leaders endorsing a book attacking slavery: *The Impending Crisis of the South*, by Hinton Rowan Helper.

52. Lincoln actually took several steps to enhance his candidacy.

53. It was in the third debate (at Jonesboro), not the second debate (at Freeport), that Lincoln declared, apropos of one of Douglas's more outrageous comments: "Now, I say, there is no charitable way to look at that statement, except to conclude that he is actually crazy." Basler, *Collected Works of Lincoln*, 3:134.

54. In 1861, Willard Brigham Farwell (1829–1903), editor-in-chief of the San Francisco *Alta California*, was appointed naval officer in the custom house of San Francisco, a post he held until 1865.

55. Lincoln's running mate, Hannibal Hamlin (1809–91), represented Maine in the U.S. Senate (1848–61) and served as vice president (1861–65).

56. Donn Piatt (1819–91), a prominent attorney and judge in Ohio who served as secretary of the American legation in Paris (1853–60), stumped throughout southern Illinois on behalf of Lincoln in 1860. While in Springfield he spoke at a Republican rally, consulted with Lincoln about cabinet appointments, and angled for a government job.

57. Richard Yates (1815–73) represented Lincoln's district in the U.S. House (1851–55) and served as governor of Illinois (1861–65).

58. Dedicated on August 4, 1860, the Wigwam in Springfield was modeled on the Chicago Wigwam, where Lincoln was nominated in May. Much smaller than the Chicago structure, this circular frame building, ninety feet in diameter, could accommodate three thousand people.

59. Wealthy businessman Joel Aldrich Matteson (1808–73) served as governor of Illinois (1853–57).

60. Democrat John A. McClernand (1812–1900) represented an Illinois district in the U.S. House (1843–1850, 1859–1862).

61. Edward D. Baker (1811–61), an intimate friend of Lincoln, represented Oregon in the U.S. Senate (1860–61). In October 1861, he was killed while leading his regiment at the Battle of Ball's Bluff, Virginia.

62. Democrat John Calhoun (1806–59), who had befriended Lincoln in the 1830s, achieved notoriety as the surveyor general of the Kansas Territory when he participated in electoral fraud involving ballots secreted in a candle box.

63. Democrat Peter Cartwright (1785–1872), a noted Methodist revivalist minister in Illinois, lost to Lincoln in the congressional election of 1846.

64. Democrat Albert Taylor Bledsoe (1809–77), a professor of mathematics at the University of Virginia, had been a good friend and political ally of Lincoln in the 1840s.

65. In the late 1830s and early 1840s, while awaiting completion of the capitol building, the legislature met in Springfield's Second Presbyterian Church.

66. Evidently an allusion to Christ's parable of the sower, found in the Gospel according to Luke, 8:5: "A sower went out to sow his seed: and as he sowed, some fell by the way side; and it was trodden down, and the fowls of the air devoured it."

67. On November 18, Nicolay told his fiancée: "The letters still keep rushing along to Mr. Lincoln—the last two days have brought an installment of about

seventy each. Fortunately they do not need much answering. They fall very naturally into two classes—those merely congratulatory, and those asking for office, neither of which I answer. The majority of letters I have sent off for a week past have been those concerning Mr. Lincoln's autograph. . . . Just think of my probably having to read 80 and perhaps 100 letters a day for the next three months!" Burlingame, *With Lincoln in the White House*, 11–12.

68. Peter Cooper (1791–1883) of New York, a wealthy industrialist, inventor, and philanthropist, dressed in unfashionable, out-of-date clothes.

69. Covode chaired the Select Committee to Investigate Alleged Corruptions in Government, appointed by the U.S. House of Representatives in 1860. It issued a report highly critical of the Buchanan administration.

70. Lincoln told a friend that he never used tobacco because "he knew that he must be made sick by it before he could enjoy it, and did not want to get sick." Letter by an unidentified "professional gentleman" to a Boston gentleman, n.d., Springfield, n.d., Boston *Journal*, n.d., copied in the New York *Times*, 10 November 1860.

71. The day after the election, Lincoln had tentatively chosen a cabinet, but six weeks later he complained that "the making of a cabinet, now that he had it to do, was by no means as easy as he had supposed." He believed "that while the population of the country had immensely increased, really great men were scarcer than they used to be." Gideon Welles, "Recollections in regard to the Formation of Mr. Lincoln's Cabinet," undated manuscript, Abraham Lincoln Collection, Beinecke Library, Yale University; Thurlow Weed Barnes, *Life of Thurlow Weed including His Autobiography and a Memoir* (2 vols.; Boston: Houghton Mifflin, 1884), 1:605–6.

72. Wide Awakes were young Republican men who wore quasi-military attire and marched in demonstrations carrying torches.

73. Lincoln wrote the following part of this speech:

I have labored in, and for, the Republican organization with entire confidence that whenever it shall be in power, each and all of the States will be left in as complete control of their own affairs respectively, and at as perfect liberty to choose, and employ, their own means of protecting property, and preserving peace and order within their respective limits, as they have ever been under any administration. Those who have voted for Mr. Lincoln, have expected, and still expect this; and they would not have voted for him had they expected otherwise. I regard it as extremely fortunate for the peace of the whole country, that this point, upon which the Republicans have been so long, and so persistently misrepresented, is now to be brought to a practical test, and placed beyond the possibility of doubt. Disunionists *per se*, are now in hot haste to get out of the Union, precisely because they perceive they can not, much longer, maintain apprehension among the Southern people that their homes, and firesides, and lives, are to be endangered by the action of the Federal Government. With such *"Now, or never"* is the maxim. I am rather glad of this military preparation in the South. It will enable the people the more easily to suppress any uprisings there, which their misrepresentations of purposes may have encouraged."

Basler, *Collected Works of Lincoln*, 4:141–42. It was intended as a trial balloon to see if secessionists might be placated by its moderate tone. They were not.

74. In 1866, William O. Stoddard, who served in Lincoln's White House as an assistant to the two principal presidential secretaries—John G. Nicolay and John Hay—wrote that during his presidency Lincoln on average received one death threat a day: "Most of them were manifestly merely intended to harass and provoke the President, while others but too evidently breathed a spirit that only needed courage and an opportunity to have anticipated [John] Wilkes Booth. It was impossible to secure the attention of Mr. Lincoln to any of these, except as a matter for contemptuous ridicule." Stoddard, "White House Sketches, Number 4," New York *Citizen*, 8 September 1866, in William O. Stoddard, *Inside the White House in War Times: Memoirs and Reports of Lincoln's Secretary*, ed. Michael Burlingame (1890; Lincoln: University of Nebraska Press, 2000), 158.

75. John Wood (1798–1880), a banker from Quincy, had been elected lieutenant governor in 1856 and became governor in 1860 upon the death of the incumbent, William Bissell. During the Civil War he served as the state's Quartermaster General.

76. In his memoirs, Villard painted a more favorable picture of the capital:

Springfield was then a small but attractive town of some nine thousand in-habitants. The business part centred in the square in which stood the State-house, with the offices of the Governor and of the heads of departments and the legislative chambers. The residence streets extended at right angles from the square. None of the streets were paved, and in wet weather, of which a good deal prevailed during that winter, they were simply impassable. There was but one decent hotel, where I put up, and this became the principal stopping-place of thousands of visitors, who, from curiosity or for political consultation and place-hunting, made a pilgrimage to this transient Mecca during the succeeding months.

Villard, *Memoirs*, 1:141.

77. In his memoirs, Villard described Lincoln's receptions more fully:

I was present almost daily for more or less time during his morning recep-tions. I generally remained a silent listener, as I could get at him at other hours when I was in need of information. It was a most interesting study to watch the manner of his intercourse with callers. As a rule, he showed remarkable tact in dealing with each of them, whether they were rough-looking Sangamon County farmers still addressing him familiarly as "Abe," sleek and pert com-mercial travellers, staid merchants, sharp politicians, or preachers, lawyers, or other professional men. He showed a very quick and shrewd perception of and adaptation to individual characteristics and peculiarities. He never evaded a proper question, or failed to give a fit answer. He was ever ready for an argument, which always had an original flavor, and, as a rule, he got the better in the discussion. . . . The most remarkable and attractive feature of those daily "levees," however, was his constant indulgence of his story-telling propensity. Of course, all the visitors had heard of it and were eager for the privilege of listening to a practical illustration of his pre-eminence in that line. He knew this, and took special delight in meeting their wishes. He never was at a loss for a story or an anecdote to explain a meaning or enforce a point, the aptness of which was always perfect. His supply was apparently inexhaustible, and the stories sounded so real that it was hard to determine whether he repeated what he had heard from others, or had invented himself.

None of his hearers enjoyed the wit—and wit was an unfailing ingredient of his stories—half as much as he did himself. It was a joy indeed to see the effect upon him. A high-pitched laughter lighted up his otherwise melancholy countenance with thorough merriment. His body shook all over with gleeful emotion, and when he felt particularly good over his performance, he followed his habit of drawing his knees, with his arms around them, up to his very face, as I had seen him do in 1858.

Villard, *Memoirs*, 1:142–43.

78. In his memoirs, Villard offered a slightly different account of Lincoln's routine:

Mr. Lincoln soon found, after his election, that his modest two-story frame dwelling was altogether inadequate for the throng of local callers and of visitors from a distance, and, accordingly, he gladly availed himself of the offer of the use of the Governor's room in the Capitol building. On my arrival, he had already commenced spending a good part of each day in it. He appeared daily, except Sundays, between nine and ten o'clock, and held a reception till noon, to which all comers were admitted, without even the formality of first sending in cards. Whoever chose to call, received the same hearty greeting. At noon, he went home to dinner and reappeared at about two. Then his correspondence was given proper attention, and visitors of distinction were seen by special appointment at either the State-house or the hotel. Occasionally, but very rarely, he passed some time in his law office. In the evening, old friends called at his home for the exchange of news and political views. At times, when important news was expected, he would go to the telegraph or newspaper offices after supper, and stay there till late. Altogether, probably no other President-elect was as approachable for everybody, at least during the first weeks of my stay. But he found in the end, as was to be expected, that this popular practice involved a good deal of fatigue, and that he needed more time for himself; and the hours he gave up to the public were gradually restricted.

Villard, *Memoirs*, 1:142.

79. A term describing office-seekers and others who strive to be associated with the rich, the powerful, and those perceived to be celebrities.

80. In his memoirs, Villard stated that he spent "only a few days early in January 1859 in Springfield," where he was covering the session of the General Assembly for the Cincinnati *Commercial.* He does not mention this conversation with Lincoln. The visit to Lincoln took place on December 5, the day the legislature reelected Douglas.

81. In 1861, Lincoln appointed Alexander H. Connor (1832–91) postmaster of Indianapolis.

82. In 1861, Lincoln appointed William Frederick Milton Arny (1813–81) secretary of the New Mexico Territory. The Kansas Relief Committee, also known as the National Kansas Committee, with headquarters in Chicago, sent arms, supplies, and recruits to help antislavery settlers in the Kansas Territory.

83. James Montgomery (1814–71), a fervent abolitionist, led militant antislavery forces, known as Jayhawkers, in raids against proslavery Kansans.

84. After the execution of John Brown in December 1859, James Montgomery announced that he and his Jayhawker guerillas would drive all proslavery settlers from Kansas. His raids were widely criticized.

85. Massachusetts-born B. W. Hathaway (1803–67) of San Francisco was a member of the California state senate.

86. In California, Lincoln received 38,733 votes (32.32 percent of the total) to Douglas's 37,999 (31.71 percent) to Breckinridge's 33,969 (28.35 percent), to Bell's 9,111 (7.60 percent).

87. In 1860, Democrat Joseph Lane (1801–81), who served in the U.S. Senate from 1859 to 1861, was the vice-presidential running mate of Kentuckian John C. Breckinridge. Douglas and his supporters deeply resented the Democrats (primarily in the South) who bolted his nomination to support Breckinridge and Lane.

88. Lincoln visited a Sunday school in a poor area of Chicago and told the children: "With close attention to your teachers and hard work to put into practice what you learn from them, some one of you may also become president of the United States in due time, like myself, as you have had better opportunities than I had." John Villiers Farwell, *Early Recollections of Dwight L. Moody* (Chicago: Winona, 1907), 9.

89. Nicolay clerked in the office of Ozias M. Hatch, secretary of state.

90. On November 14, Stephens delivered a speech to the Georgia state legislature in which he argued that since the Democrats would control Congress, Lincoln could do little harm; that his mere election was no justification for rash action; and that secession should not be undertaken unless the federal government committed an aggressive act. Lincoln commented that "Mr. Stephens is a great man—he's a man that can get up a blaze whenever he's a mind to—his speech has got up a great blaze in Georgia—I never could get up a blaze more than once or twice in my life."

91. In 1861, Lincoln appointed George Gilman Fogg (1813–81) minister resident to Switzerland. He urged Lincoln not to name William Henry Seward to a cabinet post.

92. This also appears in the New York *Tribune* of the same date.

93. Hugh White (1798–1870) represented a New York district in the U.S. House (1845–51). He and Lincoln became friends during Lincoln's term in Congress (1847–49). He is not to be confused with Hugh Lawson White, the Tennessee politician and presidential candidate for whom Lincoln voted in 1836.

2. DECEMBER 1860

1. Weed published a series of conciliatory editorials in late November.

2. Gyges was a king of ancient Lydia who attained his position with the help of a magic ring that rendered him invisible.

3. Weed's newspaper ran editorials calling for the extension of the Missouri Compromise line to California, thus throwing open to slavery the Mexican cession territory south of latitude 36° 30´. In addition, the paper called for the repeal of personal liberty laws in the North. Albany *Evening Journal*, 19, 24 November 1860.

4. In 1858, Seward gave a speech in which he stated that there was an "irrepressible conflict" between slavery and freedom. Widely (and mistakenly) interpreted as a call for war between the North and South, it made Seward seem like an antislavery radical. During the 1860 Republican National Convention in Chicago, Lincoln told his campaign operatives: "I agree with Seward in his 'Irrepressible Conflict,' but I do not endorse his 'Higher Law' doctrine."

5. The text of the interview was copied in the Richmond *Daily Dispatch*, 27 November 1860:

This planter desired to purchase an additional supply of negroes to pick his present crop of cotton, but feared to do so on account of the great depreciation in their value, and the alarming excitement which pervaded the South. In order to ascertain, from his own lips, Lincoln's policy, he visited him at his residence in Springfield, Illinois. Mr. Lincoln informed him that he was opposed to any interference with slavery in the States, or with the inter-State slave trade; that he was opposed to abolishing or interfering with slavery in the District of Columbia; and that he was only opposed to its extension in the Territories, but added, "that was only an opinion of his." He was then asked what would he do in the event that South Carolina seceded from the Union? He replied that he would let her go, if Congress did not pass a "Force Bill." He stated that if no one would accept office in that State, of course they could receive no benefits from the Government, and the whole expense for the distribution of the mails would devolve on her own citizens. He concluded by advising the Mississippian to purchase as many negroes as he needed, and expressed the opinion that in twelve months slave property would be worth more than it ever had been. Upon these assurances, the gentleman was, on Saturday, making his way to Virginia to purchase more negroes.

6. John C. Heenan (1834–73) was an American prizefighter known as the "Benicia Boy" as well as the "Hero of Farnborough."

7. Perhaps Hugh White of New York, who spoke with Lincoln on November 30.

8. Senators Charles Sumner and Henry Wilson of Massachusetts were among the most outspoken opponents of slavery in Congress.

9. An eminent antislavery politician, Joshua Reed Giddings (1795–1864) had represented an Ohio district in the U.S. House (1843–59). Lincoln, who had befriended him during his term in Congress (1847–49), appointed him consul general in Canada.

10. Daniel W. Corwin (1811–86) was a merchant in Cincinnati.

11. Frederick Guiterman was a clothier in Cincinnati.

12. In the final weeks of the 1858 campaign, Colfax delivered several speeches in Illinois endorsing Republican principles but not Lincoln specifically. O. J. Hollister, *Life of Schuyler Colfax* (New York: Funk & Wagnalls, 1886), 132–33.

13. Actually, Douglas did heroic work to help save the Union once war broke out.

14. Attorney Thomas Ewing (1789–1871) served as the nation's first secretary of the interior (1849–50) and later represented Ohio in the U.S. Senate for a brief time.

15. In 1860, attorney Henry Smith Lane (1811–81) won election as governor of Indiana, a post he quickly relinquished in order to take a seat in the U.S. Senate.

16. In 1861, John Dougherty Defrees (1810–82), editor of the Indianapolis *Atlas*, was appointed public printer of the United States.

17. Richard Wigginton Thompson (1809–1900), who served in Congress with Lincoln (1847–49), was a prominent conservative Whig and later Republican.

18. As a member of the Republican National Committee, Chicago attorney Norman B. Judd (1815–78) helped to secure the Republican Convention for his city and to win the presidential nomination for Lincoln, who appointed him minister to Prussia (1861).

19. William B. Ogden (1805–77), the first mayor of Chicago (1837–38), was a prominent railroad and canal promoter.

20. Joseph Gillespie (1809–85) of Edwardsville was a close friend and political ally of Lincoln's from the time they served together in the Illinois General Assembly.

21. Lincoln appointed attorney Ebenezer Peck (1805–81), a close friend and political ally, to a seat on the U.S. Court of Claims.

22. James Rood Doolittle (1815–97) represented Wisconsin in the U.S. Senate (1857–69).

23. Alexander Williams Randall (1819–72) served as governor of Wisconsin (1858–62).

24. German-born Carl Schurz (1829–1906) was a prominent Republican orator whom Lincoln appointed U.S. minister to Spain in 1861.

25. Francis Preston Blair Jr. (1821–75) represented a Missouri district in the U.S. House (1859–64).

26. In 1861, Lincoln appointed his friend, attorney Mark W. Delahay (1828–79), surveyor general of Kansas; two years thereafter he appointed Delahay a member of the U.S. District Court for Kansas. A decade later Delahay's alcoholism prompted the U.S. House to impeach him.

27. In 1861, Thomas Ewing Jr. (1829–96) was elected chief justice of the supreme court of Kansas.

28. Marcus Junius Parrot (1828–79) served in Congress (1857–61) as a delegate from Kansas.

29. Businessman Abel Carter Wilder (1828–75) was a delegate to the 1860 Republican National Convention. He represented Kansas in the U.S. House (1863–65).

30. Saunders W. Johnston (1820–1905) of Ohio served as associate justice of the supreme court of the Kansas Territory (1854–55).

31. Judge Robert Eden Scott (1808–62), a prominent Virginia Unionist, was recommended for a cabinet post by William Henry Seward.

32. Former Congressman John Minor Botts (1802–69) was a leading Virginia Unionist.

33. Jesse K. Dubois (1811–76) was a neighbor as well as a good friend and political ally of Lincoln's. Villard worked in his office.

34. In 1861, George Schneider (1823–1905), editor of the Chicago *Illinois Staats-Zeitung*, was appointed consul general to Elsinore, Denmark.

35. In 1861, Heinrich Börnstein (1805–92), publisher of the St. Louis *Anzeiger des Westens*, was appointed consul general to Bremen, Germany.

36. During the Civil War, Bernard Domschke (1827–69) served as a captain in a Wisconsin regiment.

37. John Lutz Mansfield, born Johann B. Lutz in Germany in 1803, served in the Indiana state legislature and organized the Indiana Legion in the Civil War.

38. In 1861, Friedrich Hassaurek (1831–85), editor of the Cincinnati *Hochwachter*, was appointed minister to Ecuador.

39. In 1862, Gustav Philipp Koerner (1809–96), a political ally of Lincoln's, was appointed minister to Spain.

40. In 1862, schoolteacher Nicholas J. Rusch (1822–64) was appointed a captain in the army's commissary department. He served as lieutenant governor of Iowa from 1860 to 1862.

41. Sigismund Kaufmann (1825–89) of Brooklyn was a lawyer and ardent Republican.

42. Koerner served as U.S. minister to Spain (1862–64), not Prussia.

43. Buchanan had said: "The late Presidential election . . . has been held in strict conformity with its express provisions. How, then, can the result justify a revolution to destroy this very Constitution? Reason, justice, a regard for the Constitution, all require that we shall wait for some overt and dangerous act on the part of the President elect before resorting to such a remedy. It is said, however, that the antecedents of the President-elect have been sufficient to justify the fears of the South that he will attempt to invade their constitutional rights."

James Daniel Richardson, ed., *A Compilation of the Messages and Papers of the Presidents* (20 vols.; New York: Bureau of National Literature, 1917), 7:3159.

44. Leonard Swett (1825–99), an attorney based in Bloomington, was a close personal friend and political ally of Lincoln's.

45. Attorney John McAuley Palmer (1817–1900), a former Democrat who helped found the Illinois Republican Party, became a corps commander in the Civil War.

46. Allen Curtis Fuller (1822–1901) of Belvidere served as adjutant general of Illinois (1861–65).

47. William B. Plato (1810–73) of Geneva served in the Illinois General Assembly (1848–1855, 1859–1861).

48. In 1861, Lawrence Weldon (1829–1905) of Clinton, who had practiced law with Lincoln on the eighth judicial circuit, was appointed district attorney for southern Illinois.

49. In 1861, William Pitt Kellogg (1830–1918) of Canton was appointed chief justice of the supreme court of the Nebraska Territory.

50. Merchant James Stark (b. 1817) of Augusta had served in the Illinois General Assembly (1846–47).

51. Springfield attorney James C. Conkling (1816–99), a close friend of Lincoln, served in the Illinois General Assembly (1850–52, 1866–68).

52. Attorney Henry Pelham Holmes Bromwell (1823–1903) of Charleston was a leader of Freemasonry in Illinois.

53. Attorney Thomas G. Allen of Chester served as the colonel of the 80th Illinois Infantry during the Civil War.

54. During the Civil War, attorney John Olney (1822–1900) of Shawneetown served as quartermaster of the 18th Illinois Infantry.

55. Democrat Isaac Newton Morris (1812–79) of Quincy served in the U.S. House of Representatives (1857–61). His resolution, which was adopted, read:

> That we properly estimate the immense value of our National Union to our collective and individual happiness; that we cherish a cordial, habitual, and immovable attachment to it; that we will speak of it as the palladium of our political safety and prosperity; that we will watch its preservation with jealous anxiety; that we will discountenance whatever may suggest even a suspicion that it can, in any event, be abandoned, and indignantly frown upon the first dawning of every attempt to alienate any portion of our Country from the rest, or enfeeble the sacred ties which now link together the various parts; that we regard it as a main pillar in the edifice of our real independence, the support of tranquility at home, our peace abroad, our safety, our prosperity, and that very liberty which we so highly prize; that we have seen nothing in the past, nor do we see anything in the present, either in the election of Abraham Lincoln to the Presidency of the United States, or from any other existing cause, to justify its dissolution; that we regard its perpetuity as of

more value than the temporary triumph of any Party or any man; that whatever evils or abuses exist under it ought to be corrected within the Union, in a peaceful and Constitutional way; that we believe it has sufficient power to redress every wrong and enforce every right growing out of its organization, or pertaining to its proper functions; and that it is a patriotic duty to stand by it as our hope in Peace and our defense in War.

56. Attorney Andrew H. Reeder (1807–64) of Easton, Pennsylvania, served as the first governor of the Kansas Territory (1854–55).

57. James Sheahan edited the Chicago *Times* and wrote a campaign biography of Douglas in 1860.

58. Charles Lanphier (b. 1820) was publisher of the Springfield *Illinois State Register*, a leading Democratic newspaper.

59. As he was about to leave office in 1856, Matteson fraudulently redeemed $388,528 worth of twenty-year-old canal scrip for new state bonds. The scrip had already been redeemed once but had not been cancelled; Matteson knowingly enriched himself at the expense of the general public.

60. James Shields (ca. 1806–79) served as a U.S. senator from Illinois (1849–55) and Minnesota (1858–59).

61. President Buchanan sent an advance copy of his annual message to the newly installed governor of South Carolina, Francis W. Pickens.

62. Chicago attorney Isaac Newton Arnold (1815–84) represented an Illinois district in the U.S. House (1861–64).

63. On December 3, Virginia congressman Alexander Boteler (1815–92) introduced a resolution calling for the appointment of a special House committee to deal with the problems that President Buchanan alluded to in his annual message concerning the "present perilous condition of the country."

64. In his memoirs, Villard deplored Lincoln's vulgar sense of humor. Villard, *Memoirs*, 1:93–94, 144.

65. According to Nicolay's memorandum of December 11, Lincoln also spoke that day with Solomon Meredith and William T. Otto, both of Indiana, about cabinet appointments. Burlingame, *With Lincoln in the White House*, 15.

66. Murat Halstead of the Cincinnati *Commercial* had been urging Lincoln to name some Southerners to the cabinet. When Villard showed Halstead's editorials to Lincoln, the president-elect wrote this brief response, in pencil on three separate sheets, which he gave to Villard, who sent them along to Halstead. Murat Halstead, "Some Reminiscences of Mr. Villard," *American Review of Reviews* 23 (1901): 62. On January 3, 1861, Halstead sent Villard one of his editorials from the Cincinnati *Commercial*. Villard gave it to Lincoln. Halstead to Villard, Cincinnati, 3 January 1861, Lincoln Papers, Library of Congress.

67. On December 6, Bell wrote a public letter in which he condemned the Republicans for "pursuing a policy which is in violation of the spirit, if not of the letter, of the Constitution, and revolutionary in its tendency."

68. That day Nicolay penned a memorandum describing Blair's conversation with Lincoln. Burlingame, *With Lincoln in the White House*, 16.

69. Democrat John Alexander McClernand (1812–1900) represented Lincoln's district in the U.S. House (1859–61).

70. Emerson Etheridge (1819–1902) represented a Tennessee district in the U.S. House (1853–57, 1859–61) and served as clerk of that body (1861–63).

71. John Adams Gilmer (1805–68) represented a North Carolina district in the U.S. House (1857–61).

72. James Guthrie (1792–1869) served as U.S. secretary of the treasury (1853–57).

73. According to Wentworth's biographer,

> If Wentworth's radical pronouncements were in fact a deliberate attempt to embarrass the Republican cause, his main target was probably Lyman Trumbull rather than Lincoln. The inevitable suspicion that Long John had his eye upon Trumbull's seat in the Senate was strengthened by his unusual conduct during September. Republican leaders of Cook County had generally agreed upon William B. Ogden as the successor to Judd in the upper house of the state legislature, but soon the word spread through Chicago that Wentworth was himself a candidate for the position. And although he was conducting a vigorous editorial crusade for the reform of county governments, it seemed obvious that he really wanted to become a state senator in order to lead the fight against Trumbull's reelection.

Don E. Fehrenbacher, *Chicago Giant: A Biography of "Long John" Wentworth* (Madison, Wisconsin: American History Research Center, 1957), 182.

74. In fact, Lincoln had written letters—and was still doing so—to Republican congressmen urging them to resist any compromise measure allowing slavery to expand.

75. Democrat Milton Latham (1827–82) represented California in the U.S. Senate (1860–63).

76. Chicago correspondence, 14 December, Philadelphia *Evening Bulletin*, n.d., copied in the New York *Times*, 20 December 1860.

77. On December 14, a mass meeting in Philadelphia adopted nine resolves calling for concessions to Southerners' demands for the protection of slavery, the rigorous enforcement of the 1850 Fugitive Slave Act, and the cessation of all criticism of slavery and slaveholders.

78. Republican Andrew Gregg Curtin (1817–94) served as governor of Pennsylvania (1861–67).

79. Ozias Mather Hatch (1814–93), a friend of Lincoln's who served as Illinois secretary of state (1856–64), married Julia R. Enos, daughter of Pascal P. Enos, another friend of Lincoln's.

80. The cover of the December 15 issue of *Frank Leslie's Illustrated Newspaper* featured an accurate woodcut version of a photo of Mrs. Lincoln and her sons Willie and Tad, taken by Springfield photographer Preston Butler.

81. In fact, Lincoln offered him the post of attorney general, which he accepted.

82. This conversation is described at length in a memorandum of this date by Nicolay and also in Bates's diary. Burlingame, *With Lincoln in the White House*, 17–20; Howard K. Beale, ed., *The Diary of Edward Bates, 1859–1866* (Annual Report of the American Historical Association for 1930, vol. 4; Washington, D.C.: U.S. Government Printing Office, 1933), 164 (entry for 16 December 1860).

83. Villard was mistaken.

84. John Charles Frémont (1813–90), famous for his exploration of the western territories, had been the Republican Party's nominee for president in 1856. During the Civil War he served as a general in the Union army.

85. On November 27, John Minor Botts of Virginia wrote a long letter, widely reprinted in the press, heatedly denouncing secession. He declared that "one of the inconceivable and irreconcilable things of this world to my mind, is that an idea, of such unmixed and unmitigated nonsense and absurdity as that of the right of a State to secede at pleasure, should ever have obtained a place in the mind of any man, who was not an absolute lunatic." New York *Times*, 11 December 1860.

86. Secretary of State Lewis Cass (1782–1866) resigned his post in protest against President Buchanan's timid response to the Southern threats of secession.

87. On December 22, Lincoln said apropos of rumors that Buchanan had ordered the surrender of the Charleston garrison: "If that is true they ought to hang him." Burlingame, *With Lincoln in the White House*, 21.

88. Several Northern states passed "personal liberty laws" providing legal protection to blacks accused of being runaway slaves.

89. On December 17, Weed's newspaper, the Albany *Evening Journal*, reiterated its support for the extension of the Missouri Compromise line and declared that it was "*almost* prepared to say, that Territories may be safely left to take care of themselves; and that, when they contain a Population which . . . entitles them to a Representative in Congress, they may come into the Union with State Governments of their own framing."

90. D. D. Dana was the treasurer of the Douglas Axe Manufacturing Company of Boston.

91. William Lewis Sharkey (1798–1873), a strong opponent of secession, had served as a justice of the Mississippi state supreme court (1832–50).

92. This episode is described at length in a letter from Nicolay to his fiancée, Therena Bates, dated 19 December 1860. Burlingame, *With Lincoln in the White House*, 20.

93. On December 20, delegates to South Carolina's secession convention, meeting in Charleston, voted unanimously to withdraw their state from the Union.

94. A term denoting kingmaker, named after the English nobleman, Richard Neville, 16th Earl of Warwick (1428–71), who was known as "Warwick the Kingmaker."

95. In his autobiography, Weed described this interview at length. Thurlow Weed Barnes, *Life of Thurlow Weed including His Autobiography and a Memoir* (2 vols.; Boston: Houghton Mifflin, 1884), 1:605–6.

96. Lincoln gave Weed the following resolutions to pass along to Seward for submission to Congress:

> That the fugitive slave clause of the Constitution ought to be enforced by a law of Congress, with efficient provisions for that object, not obliging private persons to assist in it's execution, but punishing all who resist it, and with the usual safeguards to liberty, securing free men against being surrendered as slaves—
> That all state laws, if there be such, really, or apparently, in conflict with such law of Congress, ought to be repealed; and no opposition to the execution of such law of Congress ought to be made—
> That the Federal Union must be preserved.

97. In a letter to the New York *Times*, Judge John Slosson (1806–72) of the New York Superior Court denied that he had visited Springfield. New York *Times*, 22 December 1860.

98. James H. Van Alen (1819–86) was a wealthy New York merchant who was bringing a letter from Gen. Winfield Scott to Lincoln urging support of the Crittenden Compromise.

99. On December 6, U.S. secretary of the treasury Howell Cobb (1815–68) of Georgia wrote a public letter to the people of his state in which he denounced Lincoln as a rank abolitionist: "Mr. Lincoln has covered the entire abolition platform—hatred of slavery, disregard of judicial decisions, negro equality, and, as a matter of course, the ultimate extinction of slavery." Milledgeville, Georgia, *Daily Federal Union*, 16 December 1860.

100. The editorial, reproduced verbatim below, was summarized in the New York *Herald*, 21 December 1860.

101. It is unclear why this passage was enclosed in quotation marks.

102. Lincoln asked Hannibal Hamlin to deliver the letter offering Seward the state department portfolio.

103. Benjamin F. Wade (1800–78), who represented Ohio in the U.S. Senate (1851–69), delivered a speech in which he denounced any retreat from the Republican platform adopted in Chicago.

104. Edward Lewis Baker (1829–97), editor and co-owner of *Illinois State Journal*, was married to Julia Cook Edwards, daughter of Mary Todd Lincoln's eldest sister, Elizabeth Todd Edwards (Mrs. Ninian Edwards).

105. On December 17, the New York *Tribune* ran an editorial declaring that "if ever 'seven or eight States' send agents to Washington to say 'We want to get out of the Union,' we shall feel constrained by our devotion to Human Liberty to say, Let them go! And we do not see how we could take the other side without coming in direct conflict with those Rights of Man which we hold paramount to all political arrangements, however convenient and advantageous."

106. This statement allegedly appeared in a letter by Clay to Daniel Ullman and other New Yorkers, 3 October 1851, Louisville correspondence, 10 November

1860, New York *Times*, 15 November 1860. Lincoln may have gotten it from the *Times* account.

107. This passage appears in Calvin Colton, ed., *Works of Henry Clay, Comprising His Life, Correspondence, and Speeches* (New York: Henry Clay Pub. Co., 1897), 390–91. It was allegedly uttered by Clay in July 1850.

108. David Wilmot (1814–68) represented a Pennsylvania district in the U.S. House (1845–51) and served briefly in the U.S. Senate (1861–63). In 1846, he became famous as the author of a legislative proviso stipulating that slavery was to be excluded from all territory acquired as a result of the Mexican War.

109. There is no such hostelry listed in the Springfield city directory for 1860. This is probably a misprint for "Chenery House."

110. On December 24, Weed's newspaper (the Albany *Evening Journal*) praised Lincoln as "capable in the largest sense of the term. He has read much and thought much, of Government, 'inwardly digesting' its theory and principles. His mind is at once philosophical and practical. He sees all who go there, hears all they have to say, talks freely with everybody, reads whatever is written to him; but thinks and acts by himself and for himself. Our only regret is, that Mr. Lincoln could not have taken the helm of State, as successor to Mr. Buchanan, on the first Monday in December."

111. Attorney Thomas A. Marshall (1817–73) of Charleston was elected to the Illinois state senate in 1856 and reelected in 1860.

112. Davis was not a law partner of Lincoln but a judge of the Illinois Eighth Judicial Circuit, where Lincoln practiced.

113. In 1862, Lincoln appointed Davis to the U.S. Supreme Court.

114. On March 22, 1862, Lincoln wrote to Gen. John C. Frémont: "This will introduce my friend, Col. Thomas W. Sweeney, of Philadelphia, who has already done some service with volunteers, and is a gentleman of great intelligence and good principles." In 1863, Sweeney was appointed a federal revenue assessor for Pennsylvania. He befriended Tad Lincoln and the First Lady.

115. In 1860, Lincoln won 56 percent of the vote in Pennsylvania.

116. In 1861, the wealthy merchant George Opdyke (1805–80) was elected mayor of New York.

117. Charles Francis Adams was named minister to Great Britain.

118. Poet William Cullen Bryant (1794–1878) edited the New York *Evening Post* for many years. George Perkins Marsh of Vermont was named minister to Italy.

119. Norman B. Judd was named minister to Prussia.

120. Gustav Koerner (1809–96) served as lieutenant governor of Illinois (1853–57) and U.S. minister to Spain (1862–64).

121. Perhaps Franklin Metcalf, a Boston photographer in the firm of [John A.] Welldon and Metcalf.

122. J. V. Fletcher (1812–99) was a Boston banker and a selectman of the town of Belmont (1859–61).

123. Abijah Fletcher (1806–62) was a farmer.

124. James F. Sherron (b. 1822) was listed as a salesman in an 1868 Philadelphia city directory.

125. In 1849, Lincoln helped Turner R. King win the post of register of the Springfield land office.

126. Charles H. Noyes (1834–81) was a merchant in New York.

127. Perhaps Maj. Chauncey Bush (ca. 1805–65), who was a businessman involved in mining.

128. John C. Henshaw (1815–77) of New York, a major in the U.S. Army, had met Lincoln in Clinton, Illinois. He had been court-martialed for refusing to help pursue fugitive slaves. When he asked for reinstatement as a paymaster, Lincoln endorsed his appeal. In 1864, Henshaw became a judge advocate.

129. Chester Ward Kingsley (b. 1824) was a Boston businessman and philanthropist.

130. Rufus F. Andrews served as surveyor of the port of New York (1861–64).

131. Richard C. Parsons (1826–99), speaker of the Ohio House of Representatives (1860–61), was appointed consul to Rio de Janeiro in 1862.

132. In 1858, Isaac Smith Kalloch (1832–87) was dismissed from his pulpit in Boston for sexual impropriety. In 1865, he founded Ottawa University in Kansas and eventually served as mayor of San Francisco (1879–81).

133. Attorney and politician Daniel Ullman (1810–92), a nativist leader in New York, was an opponent of the Seward faction of the Republican Party. In February 1861, Lincoln received from Ullman "an exquisite medallion portrait of Henry Clay." Springfield correspondence, 1 February, Chicago *Tribune*, 2 February 1861.

134. In 1857, attorney James Osborne Putnam (1818–1903), postmaster at Buffalo and a close friend of former president Millard Fillmore, had run unsuccessfully for secretary of state of New York on the American Party (Know-Nothing) ticket. In 1860, he was a presidential elector for Lincoln and Hamlin.

135. Journalist Erastus Brooks (1815–86) supported the Constitutional Union party in 1860.

136. President Buchanan dismissed Secretary of the Interior John Floyd for having embezzled $870,000 worth of Indian trust bonds.

137. Benjamin Franklin Harding (1823–99) served as speaker of the Oregon House of Representatives (1860–61) and replaced Lincoln's friend Edward D. Baker in the U.S. Senate after Baker was killed in October 1861.

138. Sculptor Thomas Dow Jones (1811–81) executed a bust of Lincoln.

139. Duff Green (1791–1875) of Kentucky was a prominent Democrat who had served in Jackson's kitchen cabinet and whose wife was distantly related to Mrs. Lincoln. On December 28, Green and Lincoln conversed at length; the president-elect said of the Crittenden compromise resolutions

that he believed that the adoption of the [Missouri Compromise] line proposed would quiet *for the present* the agitation of the Slavery question, but believed it would be renewed by the seizure and attempted annexation of

Mexico.—He said that the real question at issue between the North & the South, was Slavery "propagandism" and that upon that issue the republican party was opposed to the South and that he was with his own party; that he had been elected by that party and intended to sustain his party in good faith, but added that the question of the Amendments to the Constitution and the questions submitted by Mr. Crittenden, belonged to the people & States in legislatures or Conventions & that he would be inclined not only to acquiesce, but give full force and effect to their will thus expressed.

Green to James Buchanan, Springfield, 28 December 1860, Buchanan Papers, Historical Society of Pennsylvania.

140. Samuel P. Oyler (1819–98) was a prominent attorney.

141. Attorney Nathaniel P. Usher (1827–73) of Vincennes served as a justice of the New Mexico Supreme Court (1864–65) and as U.S. attorney for the northern district of Florida (1865–69).

142. In 1861, attorney Caleb Blood Smith (1808–64), a prominent Indiana Republican who had served in the U.S. House of Representatives with Lincoln during the 1840s, became secretary of the interior. He stepped down the following year.

143. Pennsylvania journalist and politician John Phillip Sanderson (1818–64) was a confidential advisor to Simon Cameron.

144. On December 29, Lincoln stopped receiving guests at the capitol. He took rooms at the nearby Johnson's Building, where his secretary, John G. Nicolay, spent his workdays and where Lincoln tended to correspondence and worked on his inaugural address.

3. JANUARY 1861

1. Journalist-politician Alexander K. McClure (1828–1909) of Chambersburg was chairman of the Pennsylvania State Republican Committee.

2. Lincoln did telegraph McClure, who had sent the president-elect a lengthy indictment of Cameron, inviting him to Springfield to consult about cabinet selections. On January 3, the two men conferred for four hours.

3. A Latin term that means trespass with "force and arms" causing injury to someone's person or property or both.

4. The brief dispatch, dated December 31, indicated that Cameron had been offered the treasury department portfolio and had accepted it.

5. A fold in the microfilmed newspaper file has obscured these words, but their substance can be gleaned from the January 1 dispatch Villard sent to the New York *Herald*, reprinted in this volume.

6. Amos Tuck (1810–79) served with Lincoln in Congress in the 1840s and hosted Robert Lincoln when he was a student at Phillips Exeter Academy (1859–60). In 1861, Lincoln named Tuck naval officer of the port of Boston.

7. Nathaniel Prentice Banks (1816–94) was a Republican who represented a Massachusetts district in the U.S. House (1853–57) and served as speaker of that legislative body (1856–57). He also served as governor of the Bay State (1858–61).

8. On January 10, Mrs. Lincoln left for New York, accompanied by Amos Tuck.

9. On December 20, Maryland congressman Henry Winter Davis proposed finessing the vexed question of slavery expansion by admitting into the Union the New Mexico Territory, which had adopted a slave code in 1859, thus sanctioning slavery in territories south of 36° 30′. The residents could, under Davis's plan, adopt a constitution outlawing slavery. In 1860, there were no slaves in the territory.

10. B. C. Webster was a director of the North River Bank in New York.

11. Benjamin Ward Dix (1835–98) was a Boston merchant.

12. They urged Lincoln not to appoint Cameron to a cabinet post, but the president-elect said he did not see a politically viable alternative. Thomas J. Mc-Cormack, ed., *Memoirs of Gustave Koerner, 1809–1896* (2 vols.; Cedar Rapids, Iowa: Torch Press, 1909), 2:114.

13. Attorney David Dudley Field (1805–94) championed legal reform in New York and opposed Seward's nomination at the 1860 Republican National Convention.

14. In 1858, Greeley had urged Illinois Republicans to nominate no one to oppose the reelection of Senator Stephen A. Douglas.

15. Democrat Samuel Scott Marshall (1821–90) of McLeansboro represented an Illinois district in the U.S. House (1857–59, 1865–75).

16. On December 25, Major Robert Anderson, in command of the small army garrison in Charleston, South Carolina, moved his men from the vulnerable Fort Moultrie to the more defensible Fort Sumter. As they left Fort Moultrie, the soldiers spiked its cannons.

17. Attorney Andrew Gregg Curtin (1817–94) served as governor of Pennsylvania (1861–67).

18. John Hay reported that after Lincoln entered the Hall of Representatives in the state capitol, he "cordially saluted the Supreme Judges and quietly took his seat near them. He glanced up at the crowded galleries" and "soon dived into his capacious coat pocket, and bringing up a handful of letters began to look over them. He reads letters constantly—at home—in the street—among his friends. I believe he is strongly tempted in church." After Trumbull's reelection was announced, Lincoln "rose from his chair, and was straightway overwhelmed. He began to shake hands. . . . All Lincoln's old time friends were gathered around him." Springfield correspondence, 7 January, St. Louis *Missouri Democrat*, 9 January 1861, in Burlingame, *Lincoln's Journalist*, 17–18.

19. The Radical Republican George W. Julian (1817–99) represented an Indiana district in the U.S. House (1849–51, 1861–71).

20. In January 1861, *The Star of the West*, a civilian steamship, was hired by the U.S. government to convey reinforcements and supplies to Fort Sumter in Charleston Harbor. When fired upon as it neared its destination, it turned back.

21. Democrat William Bigler (1814–80) represented Pennsylvania in the U.S. Senate (1855–61).

22. U.S. Senator John J. Crittenden of Kentucky introduced a package of constitutional amendments designed to solve the secession crisis. The most important one provided for the extension of the Missouri Compromise line across the
Mexican Cession to the California border, a line below which slavery would be
allowed and above which it would be prohibited.

23. New York assemblyman and future governor Lucius Robinson (1810–91)
introduced into the legislature a compromise proposal which included the admission of all territories, including Kansas, as two states divided by the 36° 30′
line, below which slavery could extend. It was supported by Thurlow Weed and
other prominent political and business leaders in New York, but congressional
Republicans rejected it.

24. Around this time, Lincoln told a group of eight or ten men, some from
Free States and some from Slave States, that (according to one who was present)
"he had no objection" to restoring the Missouri Compromise line "if that would
preserve the Union and restore harmony." He added

> that some provision ought to be made in regard to territory which may be
> hereafter acquired. It was suggested that we ought not to acquire any more
> territory. To this Mr. L. replied that such a compact could not be safely made;
> for circumstances might arise in which it would become necessary for us
> to accept it. It was then suggested by a gentleman present, "Let there be a
> provision inserted into the Constitution requiring a vote of *all the States* to
> the confirmation of any such acquisition." To this, Mr. Lincoln replied that
> he thought a vote of two-thirds of the States ought to admit it.

In making these comments, Lincoln spoke on the assumption "that it would not
be expected by the North, [that] the line 36° 30′ being restored and extended, and
proper assurances given in respect to the other matters referred to [like personal
liberty laws], that the South would insist upon having slavery expressly recognized
South of 36° 30′; or that it should be fastened in advance upon the territory we
may hereafter acquire there." Undated communication by R. S. H. to the editors
of the *Missouri Democrat, Missouri Democrat* (St. Louis), 18 January 1861.

25. William A. Graham (1804–75) of North Carolina had served his state as
governor (1845–49) and U.S. senator (1840–43). He also was secretary of the navy
(1850–52).

26. Scott wrote a letter to the editors of the Richmond *Enquirer* in which he
called for Virginians to elect a secession convention but opposed any form of secession that would "leave a diminishing number of slaveholding States exposed,
defenceless, to the Federal power" as well "as any form of secession which would
leave the present Federal Government installed at Washington." Augusta, Georgia,
Chronicle, 16 January 1861.

27. John Moore (1793–1863) had served as lieutenant governor of Illinois (1842–
46).

28. Charles Henry Ray (1821–70) was part owner and an editor of the leading Republican newspaper in the Midwest, the Chicago *Tribune.*

29. In 1861, Lincoln appointed the proprietor of the Chicago *Daily Journal,* Charles L. Wilson (d. 1878), secretary of the American legation in London, a post he held until 1864.

30. Among visitors that day was Hawkins Taylor of Iowa, who showed Lincoln a letter endorsing Cameron for a cabinet post.

31. Perhaps Whitfield D. Bunting, the coproprietor of a coal shipment business (Bunting and Hills) in Cleveland.

32. Edgar Cowan (1815–85) represented Pennsylvania in the U.S. Senate (1861–67).

33. Attorney James Churchman (1808–69) helped found the Republican Party in California. Before moving there, he lived in Illinois, where he had befriended Lincoln.

34. Samuel Gamage (1828–91) was a metals dealer in California.

35. The same day, John Hay described the gift as "an exquisitely executed cane, the staff made of South American wood, and the carved head of solid gold, a perfectly polished specimen of the Nevada quartz being set in the massive metal. It is of great cost and unimpeachable taste. It is the gift of a California mechanic, who did not even care to have his name connected with the princely present." Springfield correspondence, 12 January, St. Louis *Missouri Democrat,* 14 January 1861, in Burlingame, *Lincoln's Journalist,* 18.

36. William Jones, a prosperous merchant in Gentryville, Indiana, had employed young Lincoln in his store and served as a friendly, encouraging mentor to him.

37. German-born Francis Hoffmann (1822–1903) of Chicago served as lieutenant governor of Illinois from 1861 to 1865.

38. Ozias Mather Hatch (1814–93), a good friend of Lincoln's, served as secretary of state from 1856 to 1864.

39. Jesse K. Dubois (1811–76), a neighbor of Lincoln's, served as state auditor (1857-64).

40. William Butler (1797–1876), a good friend and benefactor of Lincoln's, served as state treasurer from 1859 to 1862.

41. Newton Bateman (1822–97) served as Illinois superintendent of public instruction from 1859 to 1863.

42. In his memoirs, Villard was less euphemistic:

I must mention a remarkable occurrence in Springfield, of which I was myself an eye-witness. Early in January, the State Legislature met, and, according to custom, the newly elected Republican Governor was to read the inaugural message to that body in person. The lawmakers assembled in the Lower Chamber at the appointed hour, but the Governor failed to appear. Search was made for him, and, after a delay of half an hour, the doorkeeper formally announced him, and he was escorted through the middle aisle to the Speaker's chair. He seemed hardly able to walk. His attempt to read the first sentences of the message disclosed the nature of the trouble. He was too drunk to stand or to read. He fell back into his chair, and the Clerk of the House read the message in his place. Of course, the scandal was great in the Legislature, in the town, and throughout the State.

Villard, *Memoirs*, 1:148.

43. The "pocket" was the southwestern corner of Indiana, where Lincoln had lived from 1816 to 1830.

44. Attorney Hiram Barney (1811–95) served as collector of the port of New York (1861–64).

45. Henry Hogeboom (1809–72) served as a justice on the New York state supreme court (1858–72).

46. "General Cameron's Nose Out of Joint," New York *Herald*, 12 January 1861.

47. John Dean Caton (1812–95) served on the Illinois State Supreme Court (1842–64), acting as chief justice (1855, 1857–64).

48. Democrat George Ellis Pugh (1822–76) represented Ohio in the U.S. Senate (1855–61).

49. Democrat William Alexander Richardson (1811–75) narrowly lost the 1856 Illinois gubernatorial election. In 1863, he took the U.S. Senate seat that had been occupied by Stephen A. Douglas, who died in June 1861, and was subsequently held by Lincoln's friend Orville Hickman Browning.

50. Samuel Hubbel Treat Jr. (1811–87) served as a judge on the U.S. District Court for the Southern District of Illinois (1855–87).

51. Zadok Casey (1796–1862) served as lieutenant governor of Illinois (1830–33)

52. Belleville attorney James Lowery Donaldson "Don" Morrison (1816–88) represented an Illinois district in the U.S. House (1856–57).

53. Charleston attorney Orlando B. Ficklin (1808–86), a friend of Lincoln's, represented an Illinois district in the U.S. House (1843–49, 1851–53).

54. Lawrenceville attorney Aaron Shaw (1811–87) represented an Illinois district in the U.S. House (1857–59).

55. Democrat Sidney Breese (1800–78) served in the U.S. Senate (1843–49).

56. William French served as a delegate to the 1858 Illinois Democratic state convention.

57. Democrat Henry Satterlee Fitch (1834–71) served as U.S. district attorney for the northern district of Illinois (1858–61).

58. Benjamin Eggleston (1816–88), a Cincinnati merchant and Republican leader, would represent his district in the U.S. House (1865–69).

59. Lincoln nominated David K. Cartter (1812–87), who had represented an Ohio district in the U.S. House (1849–53), as minister to Bolivia, in which capacity he served from 1861 to 1862. In 1863, the president nominated him to be chief justice of the supreme court of Washington, D.C., a tribunal over which he presided until his death in 1887. He cast the decisive votes at the Chicago convention that put Lincoln over the top.

60. In fact, Eggleston did submit letters favoring Cartter for a cabinet post. Eggleston to Lincoln, Cincinnati, 24 January 1861, Lincoln Papers, Library of Congress.

61. In fact, Eggleston urged Lincoln to include Caleb B. Smith as well as Cartter in his cabinet. Ibid.

62. George W. Gage and his brother David were co-proprietors of the Tremont House, one of Chicago's most famous hotels. Lincoln named John Locke Scripps of the Chicago *Tribune* postmaster of Chicago.

63. State Senator Austin Brooks (d. 1870), editor of the Quincy *Herald*, was a fiercely partisan Democrat who was reelected to his seat on January 29.

64. On January 11, the New York State Assembly passed the following antisecession resolutions:

> *Whereas*, The insurgent State of South Carolina, after seizing the Post-offices, Custom-House, moneys and fortifications of the Federal Government, has, by firing into a vessel ordered by the Government to convey troops and provisions to Fort Sumter, virtually declared war; and
>
> *Whereas*, The forts and property of the United States Government in Georgia, Alabama, and Louisiana have been unlawfully seized, with hostile intentions; and
>
> *Whereas*, Their Senators in Congress avow and maintain their treasonable acts; therefore,
>
> *Resolved*, (if the Senate concur,) That the Legislature of New York is profoundly impressed with the value of the Union, and determined to preserve it unimpaired; that it greets with joy the recent firm, dignified and patriotic Special Message of the President of the United States, and that we tender to him through the Chief Magistrate of our own State, whatever aid in men and money may be required to enable him to enforce the laws and uphold the authority of the Federal Government; and that, in the defence of the Union, which has conferred prosperity and happiness upon the American people, renewing the pledge given and redeemed by our fathers, we are ready to devote our fortunes, our lives, and our sacred honor.
>
> *Resolved*, (if the Senate concur,) That the Union-loving citizens and representatives of Delaware, Maryland, Virginia, North Carolina, Kentucky, Missouri, and Tennessee, who labor with devoted courage and patriotism to withhold their States from the vortex of secession, are entitled to the gratitude and admiration of the whole people.
>
> *Resolved*, (if the Senate concur,) That the Government be respectfully requested to forward, forthwith, copies of the foregoing resolutions to the President of the Nation, and the Governors of all the States of the Union.

New York *Times*, 12 January 1861.

65. In a major speech on January 12, Seward urged immediate concessions to keep the Upper South from seceding and offered a long-range proposal to settle

the differences between the sections. After extolling the advantages of the Union for all sections, including the South, the senator in conciliatory tones endorsed the creation of two huge new states, one slave and one free, out of the existing western territories; a constitutional amendment guaranteeing slavery where it already existed; a modification of the Fugitive Slave Act exempting bystanders from any role in the pursuit of runaways; and a law forbidding invasions of one state by residents of another. He also recommended a cooling-off period of two or three years, to be followed by a national constitutional convention.

66. In 1849, attorney Eugene L. Sullivan (1820–85) moved from New York to California, where he was soon elected to the state senate. Later he became collector of the port of San Francisco, a city in which he loomed large in social and political circles. He achieved fame for his handsome bet ($25,000 to $5,000), early in the presidential campaign of 1860, that Lincoln would win.

67. Augustus Schell (1812–84), collector of the port of New York during Buchanan's presidency, became chairman of the Democratic National Committee in the 1870s.

68. Attorney R. P. L. Baber (1823–85) of Columbus was a nephew of Noah Swayne, whom Lincoln appointed a justice of U.S. Supreme Court in 1862.

69. Probably William G. Coffin of Parke County, Indiana, whom Lincoln appointed in May 1861 superintendent of Indian affairs in the southern superintendency. Coffin had been an Indiana state senator in the 1840s, had run unsuccessfully for Congress in 1860, and was endorsed by Lincoln's good friend, David Davis.

70. In 1861, Lincoln appointed William T. Otto (1816–1905) of Indiana assistant secretary of the interior.

71. Lawrence Weldon (1829–1905), an attorney in Clinton, Illinois, practiced law on the eighth circuit with Lincoln, who appointed him district attorney for southern Illinois.

72. Attorney Stephen Augustus Hurlbut (1815–82) of Belvidere, Illinois, was a member of the Illinois House of Representatives. A good friend of Lincoln's, he became a major general in the Civil War.

73. In 1861, Lincoln appointed businessman Joseph Russell Jones (1823–1909) U.S. marshal for the northern district of Illinois.

74. During the winter of 1860–61, William Kellogg (1814–72), who represented an Illinois district in the U.S. House (1857–63), served on the House committee appointed to find some compromise measures to smooth over differences between the North and South.

75. Actually Lincoln did work to secure the presidential nomination by giving speeches in many states and working with friends who represented him at the Chicago convention.

76. William S. Wood, a one-time jeweler and hotel manager, came to Springfield in January 1861 at the suggestion of Seward, Weed, and their friend Erastus Corning, a railroad manager, leading New York Democrat, and relative of Wood, who was to take charge of the train journey from Springfield to Washington.

Seward "stated that Mr. Wood had had great experience in railroad transportation, and especially in organizing excursion trips over long distances" and "was well acquainted with railroad officials." In his memoirs, Villard called Wood "a man of comely appearance, greatly impressed with the importance of his mission and inclined to assume airs of consequence and condescension."

77. In 1858, Republican Leander Holmes (b. 1820) of Clackamus had run unsuccessfully for secretary of state of Oregon. Two years later he was elected as a delegate to the 1860 Republican convention in Chicago but could not attend, so assigned his proxy to Horace Greeley. In 1862 he was appointed district attorney for the Washington Territory.

78. J. W. Donohue was part owner of the Cincinnati and Indianapolis Junction Railroad.

79. James Kennedy Moorhead (1806–84) represented a Pennsylvania district in the U.S. House (1859–69).

80. William Tully Bascom (1812–77) edited the Columbus *Ohio State Journal* and other Ohio newspapers.

81. John Franklin Farnsworth (1820–97) represented an Illinois district in the U.S. House (1857–61).

82. In late December and early January, representatives and senators from the border slave states formed a "Committee of Fourteen" that proposed a scheme similar to the Crittenden Compromise; both allowed slavery to expand south of the Missouri Compromise line but, unlike the Crittenden plan, the border state proposal did not apply to territory that might be acquired in the future. Moreover, any new territory could be acquired only if two-thirds of both houses of Congress approved or two-thirds of the Senate approved, if the territory was acquired by treaty.

83. William J. Robinson, Jr., was the first mayor of Allegheny City.

84. In 1880, Moorhead described those conversations to John G. Nicolay. Michael Burlingame, ed. *An Oral History of Abraham Lincoln: John G. Nicolay's Interviews and Essays* (Carbondale: Southern Illinois University Press, 2006), 41. Lincoln told the congressman: "All through the campaign my friends have been calling me 'Honest Old Abe,' and now I have been elected mainly on that cry. What will be thought now if the first thing I do is appoint C[ameron], whose very name stinks in the nostrils of the people for his corruption?"

85. In 1859, Matias Romero (1837–98) became Mexico's chargé d'affaires in Washington, where he lived for nearly two decades.

86. Martin H. Cassell was a member of the Illinois Republican State Central Committee.

87. In 1860, the New York *World* was established as a penny newspaper emphasizing religious matters. It favored the Republican Party until 1862, when it was sold to Democrats who transformed it into a powerful voice for their party under the editorship of Manton Marble.

88. Francisco Ocampo to Matias Romero, Vera Cruz, 22 December 1860, Lincoln Papers, Library of Congress.

89. Matias Romero to Francisco Ocampo, 23 January 1861, in Charles Segal, ed., *Conversations with Lincoln* (New York: G. P. Putnam's Sons, 1961), 65–67. See also William Moss Wilson, "Lincoln's Mexican Visitor," New York *Times*, 17 January 2011, and Ernest G. Hildner Jr., "The Mexican Envoy Visits Lincoln," *Abraham Lincoln Quarterly* 6, no. 3 (1950): 184–89.

90. Blanton Duncan (1827–1902) was a wealthy planter and an active political organizer.

91. In 1860, James W. Sheahan (1824–83), sold the Chicago *Times*. That year he published a campaign biography of Stephen A. Douglas. From 1861 to 1865 he edited the Chicago *Post*.

92. Robert Alexander Cameron (1828–94), who served as a delegate to the 1860 Republican National Convention, edited the Valparaiso, Indiana, *Republican*.

93. David C. Branham (1812–77) of North Madison was a member of the Indiana House of Representatives (1855–67, 1873).

94. State senator Walter March (1814–83) was an attorney and judge in Muncie.

95. Elihu Washburne (1816-87) of Galena, Illinois, represented his district in the U. S. House (1853-69).

96. W. W. Gitt was a delegate from Montgomery County Court House, Christiansburg, Virginia.

97. Democrat James Stephen Green (1817–70) represented Missouri in the U.S. Senate (1857–61).

98. Democrat Trusten Polk (1811–76) represented Missouri in the U.S. Senate from 1857 until 1862, when he was expelled for supporting the rebellion.

99. Democrat Claiborne F. Jackson (1806–62) served briefly as governor of Missouri in 1861. He fled the state to join the rebellion.

100. Cincinnati *Commercial*, 26 January 1861.

101. Businessman O. H. P. Parker was a member of the Select Council of Philadelphia.

102. A Philadelphia newspaper ran the following account of this interview: Dr. SMITH, Chairman of the Committee, stated to Mr. LINCOLN the purpose of the resolutions intrusted to the care of the Committee, and had reached the point where it was stated that Pennsylvania desired to have in the Cabinet one who had ever been true to her interests, when Mr. LINCOLN interrupted him by saying: "Yes, I know who you allude to—Gen. CAMERON. This subject has already engaged a large share of my attention, and I have every reason to hope that your wishes will be gratified. I feel a strong desire to do something for your big State, and I am determined she shall be satisfied, if I can do it."

The resolutions were read to him, when he continued, nearly in this language:

"Gentlemen, in the formation of my Cabinet, I shall aim as nearly as possible at perfection. Any man whom I may appoint to such a position, must be, as far as possible, like Caesar's wife, pure and above suspicion, of unblemished reputation, and undoubted integrity. I have already appointed Senator

SEWARD and Mr. BATES, of Missouri, and they are men whose characters I think the breath of calumny cannot impeach. In regard to Gen. CAMERON, I have received assurances without limit from gentlemen whose word is entitled to credit, that he is eminently fitted for the position which his friends desire him to fill, and that his appointment would give great satisfaction to Pennsylvania. I have a great desire to appoint Gen. CAMERON, for the reason that he was formerly a Democrat, and I wish to give that element a fair representation in the distribution of the offices. Both Mr. SEWARD and Mr. BATES were formerly old line Whigs, and, for this reason, I feel a disposition to appoint Gen. CAMERON. But on the other hand, there is a strong opposition to him; not from his own State, it is true, for the opposition to him there is so slight that it is scarcely worth mentioning. The feeling against him appears to come from Ohio, and one or two of the other Western States. His opponents charge him with corruption in obtaining contracts, and contend that if he is appointed he will use the patronage of his office for his own private gain. I have no knowledge of the acts charged against him, but I intend to make an investigation of the whole matter, by allowing his opponents to submit their proof, and I shall give him an opportunity of explaining any part he may have had in the transactions alleged against him. For my own part, I can see no impropriety in his taking contracts, or making money out of them, as that is a mere matter of business. There is nothing wrong in this, unless some unfairness or dishonesty is shown, which supposition I have no doubt Gen. CAMERON will be able to disprove. I shall deal fairly with him, but I say to you, gentlemen, frankly, that if the charges against him are proven, he cannot have a seat in my Cabinet, as I will not have any man associated with me whose character is impeached. I will say further, that if he vindicates himself, I have the strongest desire to place him in the position you wish him to fill, and which you think the interests of your State demand. If, after he has been appointed, I should be deceived by subsequent transactions of a disreputable character, the *responsibility will rest upon you gentlemen of Pennsylvania who have so strongly presented his claims to my consideration.* But this is supposing a state of things which may never occur."

Philadelphia *Mercury*, n.d., copied in the New York *Times*, 7 February 1861, in Basler, *Collected Works of Lincoln*, 4:179–81.

103. Democratic senator William Bigler of Pennsylvania proposed an extension of the Missouri Compromise line (36° 30′), with slavery allowed south of it and prohibited above it; no abolition of slavery in the District of Columbia so long as the peculiar institution remained in Maryland and Virginia; and a prohibition on future amendments regarding slavery.

104. Christopher Oscanyan, known as "The Oriental Lecturer," was the consul general of the Ottoman government at the port of New York City.

105. On January 12, Seward gave a widely anticipated speech in the Senate during which he struck a conciliatory note that alienated many Republicans.

106. In 1860, army captain George W. Hazzard (1825–62) of Indiana wrote Lincoln about political and military affairs; the following year he accompanied the president-elect on the train trip to Washington as part of the military guard.

107. Abandoning his panacea of popular sovereignty, Douglas initially supported the Crittenden Compromise, then proposed a complicated package of adjustments, then, when compromise hopes faded, supported a plan of "reconstruction" whereby the seceding states would be allowed to withdraw from the Union, but the newly formed nation would be closely allied with the United States.

108. In mid-January, Ohio representative Thomas Corwin, chairman of the U.S. House Committee of Thirty-three, presented the report of his committee, recommending a constitutional amendment guaranteeing slavery where it already existed, repeal of personal liberty laws, and jury trials for those accused of being fugitive slaves.

109. Abolitionist John Parker Hale (1806–73) represented New Hampshire in the U.S. Senate (1847–53, 1855–65).

110. Shortly before election day in 1860, Virginia congressman Roger A. Pryor (1828–1919), a leading secessionist, reportedly said: "The first anti-slavery President will be assassinated, and if no other hand can be found to perform that duty, I will be the Brutus to plant a dagger in his heart."

111. Army general Winfield Scott ordered Edwin Vose Sumner (1797–1863) to accompany Lincoln on his train journey from Springfield to Washington.

112. David Hunter (1802–86), who had written Lincoln expressing strong antislavery views, accompanied Lincoln on the train journey from Springfield to Washington.

113. In January, the Virginia state legislature called for a peace conference of the states to deal with the secession crisis. On February 4, it convened in Washington, where delegates from twenty-one of the nation's thirty-four states discussed various measures to settle sectional differences. It was informally known as the Washington Peace Conference.

114. Jesse L. Williams to Lincoln, Fort Wayne, 10 October 1860, Lincoln Papers, Library of Congress.

115. William Mitchell (1807–65) represented an Indiana district in the U.S. House (1861–62).

116. Perhaps attorney Lyman W. Potter (1824–66) of New Lisbon, who served as an Ohio delegate to the 1864 Republican National Convention and two years later was appointed by President Andrew Johnson as the revenue collector for the 17th district of Ohio.

117. "He brings letters to Mr. Lincoln, and is to have an interview to-morrow morning. The declared object of his mission is to represent the state of public sentiment in Tennessee, and to pledge it to the Union, which he does with emphatic terseness. The supposition is that he plans to suggest the name of some one of the patriots of that State for a Cabinet appointment." Springfield correspondence, 28 January, Chicago *Tribune*, 29 January 1861. John Hay reported on January 29 that

Mr. Rodgers, a prominent conservative politician of Nashville, Tennessee, has been here for a few days, bearing with him letters from the leading conservatives of that State. His interviews with the President were strictly private, but those who have enjoyed his confidence inform me that he will return to his home with the assurance that Mr. Lincoln is earnestly devoted to the preservation of the Union with all its constitutional guaranties, and that everything consistent with honor and with principle will be done by him to keep them intact. He appreciates also the dignified reticence which Mr. Lincoln preserves, as concessions at this time would be a confession that the minority may at any election rebel against the constitutionally expressed decision of the majority.

Springfield correspondence, 29 January, St. Louis *Missouri Democrat*, 30 January 1861, in Burlingame, *Lincoln's Journalist*, 22. Attorney John B. Rodgers (1799–1873) was a Whig politician who attended the 1860 Republican National Convention and stumped Tennessee for Lincoln that year.

On January 29 John Todd Edgar (d. 1882) arrived in Springfield bearing letters to Lincoln from John Bell. Edgar allegedly was "not as confident of the triumph of the union men of Tennessee as Gen. Rodgers." Springfield correspondence, 30 January, Chicago *Tribune*, 31 January 1861. Edgar headed a girls' school in Tennessee, but left the state when war broke out. In 1861, Lincoln appointed him consul general at St. Thomas in the West Indies.

118. William J. "Deacon" Bross (1813–90), an editor of the Chicago *Tribune*, was elected lieutenant governor of Illinois in 1865.

119. John Pettit (1807–77) served as chief justice of the United States courts in the Kansas Territory (1859–61). Previously he had represented Indiana in the U.S. House (1843–49) and Senate (1853–55).

120. In 1861 Mark W. Delahay (1828–79), a distant relative of Lincoln and editor of the Leavenworth *Territorial Register*, was appointed surveyor general of Kansas and Nebraska.

121. William Larimer Jr. (1809–75) founded Denver City, Kansas Territory, in 1858. Colorado was not an official territory until February 1861, when it was carved out of the Kansas Territory.

122. Indiana attorney general John Palmer Usher (1816–89) arrived at noon this day. In 1862 Lincoln appointed him assistant secretary of the interior. The following year Usher replaced Caleb B. Smith as secretary of the interior.

123. George Frederick Wright (1828–81), who worked primarily in Connecticut and Illinois, painted a portrait of Lincoln that now hangs in the library of the University of Chicago.

124. Joseph A. Nunes (1818–1904), attorney and author, wanted to discuss appointments to federal office in California.

125. Lincoln appointed Larimer as a U.S. commissioner and judge of probate in Colorado's first judicial district. William Gilpin of Missouri became the first governor of the Colorado Territory.

4. FEBRUARY 1861

1. Andrew McAlpin Jr. (1793–1863) was a civic-minded Cincinnati businessman.

2. Attorney William Henry Underwood (1818–75) of Belleville served in the Illinois state senate (1856–64).

3. Col. Edwin Vose Sumner (1897–1863) was detailed by Scott to head the military escort accompanying Lincoln on his train journey from Springfield to Washington.

4. Burton C. Cook (1819–94) of Ottawa served in the Illinois state senate (1852–60) and later represented his district in the U.S. House (1865–71).

5. Attorney Thomas Johnston Turner (1815–74), who had represented an Illinois district in the U.S. House (1847–49), was a leading citizen of Freeport.

6. Attorney William Harrow (1822–72) had practiced on the Illinois Eighth Circuit with Lincoln before moving to Mt. Vernon, Indiana, in the late 1850s. He became a controversial general in the Civil War.

7. John George Bowman (1827–1905) served as a colonel in the corps of engineers during the Civil War.

8. On February 5, the New York legislature rejected Greeley's bid for a U.S. Senate seat.

9. Israel Washburn Jr. (1813–83) represented a Maine district in the U.S. House (1853–61) and served as governor of Maine (1861–63).

10. Isaac Newton (1800–67) of Delaware County, Pennsylvania, was reportedly in Springfield to support Cameron's bid for a cabinet post. He left on the morning of February 4. Springfield correspondence, 4 February, Chicago *Tribune*, 5 February 1861. Just when he spoke with Lincoln, if he did, is unclear. In 1861, Lincoln appointed him superintendent of the agricultural division of the U.S. patent office and the following year commissioner of the newly established U.S. department of agriculture. He had earlier written Lincoln endorsing Cameron for the cabinet. Newton to Lincoln, Springfield, Delaware County, Pennsylvania, 14 January 1861, Lincoln Papers, Library of Congress.

11. Elmer Ephraim Ellsworth (1837–61) was a law clerk in Lincoln's office and colonel of Chicago's National Guard Cadets, who dressed in exotic uniforms modeled on those worn by French Zouaves (colonial troops in Algeria).

12. Greeley's handwriting is notoriously illegible.

13. In May 1861, Lincoln appointed George Burt Lincoln (1817–90) postmaster of Brooklyn, a post he held until 1867. In 1874 he described a meeting he had with Lincoln:

> Early in January 1861 I visited my friend at Springfield. Spending an evening at his house by invitation, in the course of conversation the President remarked that he had tendered to Mr Bates a seat in his Cabinet and asked me what I thought of it. I told him that I thought it a proper appointment in all respects—and especially a compliment to a class with whom Mr Bates had acted politically and who had come in with us. I then said, "Mr President,

pardon me if I tell you what else I would do"—and then I said "were I in your place I would say to Mr Seward [']Sir!—what have I at my command that you will accept? You can be my Secretary of State or if you prefer—the court of St James is at your service["]—At this Mrs Lincoln rallied with "Never! Never! Seward in the Cabinet! Never! If things should go on all right—the credit would go to Seward—if they went wrong—the blame would fall upon my husband. Seward in the Cabinet! Never!" I then stated to Madam that she had not waited to hear the remainder of what I had to say—which was this "That will be your part. I hope Mr Seward will have the sense of propriety and delicacy to say in reply—'Sir! I am a Senator and just now I desire nothing more.' I do not desire to see Mr Seward in the Cabinet." Mr. Lincoln performed his part—but the sense of delicacy, & as it seemed then to me propriety was lacking upon the other side.

George B. Lincoln to Gideon Welles, Rivervale, NJ, 25 April 1874, in Mark E. Neely Jr., "New Light on the Seward-Welles-Lincoln Controversy?" *Lincoln Lore, Bulletin of the Louis A. Warren Lincoln Library and Museum,* No. 1718 (April 1981).

While in Springfield, George B. Lincoln also presented to his host a handsome silk hat, a gift from a New York hatter. The president elect then turned to Mrs. Lincoln, saying: "Well, wife, if nothing else comes out of this scrape, we are going to have some new clothes, are we not?" "Reminiscences of George B. Lincoln," *The Caledonian* (St. Johnsbury, Vermont), 13 November 1890.

14. In 1861, Lincoln named Solomon Newton Pettis (1827–1900) of Meadville justice of the territorial court of Colorado.

15. The Rev. Mr. John L. Smith of Otter Creek, Indiana, was a presiding elder in the Methodist Church.

16. Dr. O. L. Clark was a pioneering physician in Lafayette, Indiana.

17. Albert Smith White (1803–64) represented an Indiana district in the U.S. House (1837–39, 1861–63).

18. Among the politicians in town was former congressman William Cumback (1829–1905), who was arguing vociferously against the appointment of Caleb B. Smith to a cabinet post. Springfield correspondence, 6 February, Cincinnati *Enquirer,* 8 February 1861.

19. Samuel J. Kirkwood (1813–94) served as governor of Iowa (1860–64, 1876–77).

20. Radical Republican Thaddeus Stevens (1792–1868) represented a Pennsylvania district in the U.S. House (1849–53, 1859–68), where he wielded great power.

21. On February 6, the New York *Tribune* ran a dispatch, probably by Greeley:

Horace Greeley returned from the West this morning. This afternoon he was called upon at his hotel by Mr. Lincoln. The interview lasted several hours. Greeley urged a strict adherence to an anti-compromise policy, and is said to have received gratifying assurances. His opinion as to the Cabinet and other appointments was freely solicited and given. He is known to be strongly opposed to Cameron, and very much interested in the appointment of Chase and Colfax. Colonel Fremont, he thinks, should have the mission to France. Although just defeated in Albany, he did not ask anything either for himself or friends.

The same day, Greeley gave Lincoln the following note about patronage in New York, endorsing three friends for patronage positions:

I want to be heard by you with reference to our local troubles in New York for the first, and I hope for the last time. And I ask you to lay this note aside, to be considered when the matter comes up in due course. You know that I want nothing for myself, and will judge what I have to say candidly.

That it will be very difficult for you to do justice to the anti Weed Republicans of our state, in view of Mr. Seward's position in the cabinet, I fully comprehend; and yet the endurance of the Republican party depends on it: so I think it will be done. Allow me to suggest a way.

Let a list be made of the offices local to New York and of such share of the Foreign and Washington appointments as may fairly be apportioned to our State, and from among these do you indicate such appointments as you choose to make of your own volition. Those being so made, let Gov. Seward or whoever may be chosen to represent that side select one office and name the person whom he recommends to fill it; then let the other side select an office from the list and name a person to fill it; and so on alternating till the list is completed—each name of course subject to your approval or rejection. Thus you may dispose of New York at a single sitting and avoid the bitter heart burnings which are likely to follow any presumption that one side or the other has the dispensing of Federal patronage in our State. I believe this will save you from collisions else inevitable and restore the unity of the party, now so sadly [jarred?]. Of course, details may be varied, but the essential matter is that those who favored your nomination shall not *for that reason* be proscribed and turned over to the tender mercies of those they by that act made their implacable enemies. I think, should you think favorably of this proposition, even Gov. Seward would not demur to its essential fairness and justice.

P.S. Without boring you with reasons or entreaties, let me say that I feel a personal interest in the application of Rufus F. Andrews to be District Attorney and Benj. F. Camp to be Surveyor of the Port, and that I know Mr. Thomas B. Carroll of Albany who aspires to be Government Printer to be thoroughly worthy and qualified. All these are secondary places, and I do not ask you to appoint any of the above if you think the public service can better be provided for otherwise. Nobody who is fit for an office really needs one, or will whine because some other good man is preferred, *provided* we are not sacrificed because we took the course which led to your nomination. I believe that John C. Fremont ought to be Minister to France, not so much for his own sake as because the Republicans of '56 will feel that *they* are slighted if he is

385

not recognized by the new Administration. I pray you to consider this. Col. F. never intimated to me that he desired or would take any office whatever; but whether he will or will not accept, it is due to the Fremonters of '56 that he be offered a position of dignity and honor.

Greeley to Lincoln, Springfield, 6 February 1861, Lincoln Papers, Library of Congress.

22. Greeley had urged Illinois Republicans not to oppose Stephen A. Douglas's reelection in 1858.

23. On February 5, the New York state legislature elected Ira Harris to serve as U.S. senator.

24. This item also ran in the New York *Tribune.*

25. Fitz Henry Warren (1816–78) was an editorial writer for the New York *Tribune.*

26. The convention was called by the Virginia legislature to consider whether the state should secede from the Union.

27. Warren F. Leland of the Metropolitan Hotel in New York was the brother of Horace Leland, who in 1866 established the Leland Hotel in Springfield. Lincoln referred him to W. S. Wood, who was in charge of arrangements for the upcoming train journey. Springfield correspondence, 4 February, Chicago *Tribune,* 5 February 1861. Some other New York hoteliers were in Springfield vying for the privilege of hosting Lincoln on his visit to their city.

28. Horace B. Sargeant served as a colonel in the First Massachusetts Cavalry during the Civil War.

29. John Adam Quackenbush (1828–1908), town supervisor of Schaghticoke, New York, was also chairman of the Rensselaer County board of supervisors.

30. In 1861, Lincoln appointed Dr. William Rabe, a San Francisco druggist, marshal for the northern district of California. Rabe was associated with the Leland Stanford faction of California Republicans.

31. By supporting the unrepresentative Lecompton constitution of Kansas, President Buchanan split the Democratic Party badly in 1857–58.

32. Charles Ames Washburn (1822–89), a brother of Lincoln's good friend Elihu B. Washburne, edited the San Francisco *Daily Times.* In 1861, Lincoln appointed him commissioner to Paraguay.

33. The donor, Addison Peale Russell (1826–1912), was Ohio's secretary of state (1858–62).

34. Attorney Ward Hill Lamon (1828–93) was a close friend of Lincoln, for whom he was to serve as a kind of informal bodyguard.

35. Quincy attorney Orville Hickman Browning (1806–81) was a close friend and political ally of Lincoln. That night at the Chenery House, Browning and Lincoln discussed compromise proposals. Theodore Calvin Pease and James G. Randall, eds., *The Diary of Orville Hickman Browning* (2 vols.; Springfield: Illinois State Historical Library, 1925–33), 1:453 (entry for 9 February 1861).

36. Edward L. Baker (1855–74), editor and co-owner of the *Illinois State Journal*, was married to Mrs. Lincoln's niece, Julia Edwards.

37. At Phillips Exeter Academy in New Hampshire, George Clayton Latham (b. 1842) was a classmate and close friend of Robert Todd Lincoln.

38. Robert Irwin (1808–65) was Lincoln's friend and banker.

39. Born in Scotland, James Roderick McDonald (1828–1902) settled in central Illinois in the 1840s. In 1850 he moved to California, where he took active part in Republican politics, serving as a delegate to the 1860 Chicago convention.

40. Thomas Fitch (1838–1923) was a journalist, attorney, and Republican activist. An obituarist called him one of "the three great orators who kept California loyal to the Union during the Civil War."

41. Attorney Joseph Jackson Grimshaw (1822–75) of Quincy, Illinois, was a friend and political ally of Lincoln, who appointed him a collector of internal revenue.

42. Democrat William Ralls Morrison (1824–1909) of Waterloo, Illinois, had been the speaker of the Illinois state house of representatives (1859–60) and later represented his district in the U.S. House (1863–65).

43. Democrat Lewis Winans Ross (1812–95) of Lewistown, who had served with Lincoln in the Illinois legislature, ran unsuccessfully for lieutenant governor of Illinois in 1860.

44. Democrat William H. Carlin of Quincy was a state senator from Adams County. He had opposed Douglas's reelection in 1858.

45. Jackson A. Hough (d. 1879) was a Springfield furniture dealer.

46. Attorney Daniel H. Gilmer (d. 1863) was a leading Republican in Pittsfield, Illinois, and a friend of Lincoln.

47. Wisconsin Governor Alexander Randall sent James M. Burgess (b. 1811), colonel of the 9th Regiment of the Wisconsin State Militia, to Springfield to help protect Lincoln on the journey to Washington. In March 1861, he was appointed postmaster of his hometown, Janesville, Wisconsin.

48. Carl Schurz (1829–1906) of Wisconsin was a leading German-American Republican orator.

49. Lincoln's friend Ozias Mather Hatch (1814–93) served as the secretary of state of Illinois (1856–64).

50. Newton Bateman (1822–97) served as the Illinois superintendent of public instruction (1859–63).

51. In his memoirs, Villard gave the following somewhat different account:

The start on the memorable journey was made shortly after eight o'clock on the morning of Monday, February 11. It was a clear, crisp winter day. Only about one hundred people, mostly personal friends, were assembled at the station to shake hands for the last time with their distinguished townsman. It was not strange that he yielded to the sad feelings which must have moved him at the thought of what lay behind and what was before him, and gave them utterance in a pathetic formal farewell to the gathering crowd, as follows:

"My Friends: No one not in my position can appreciate the sadness I feel at this parting. To this people I owe all that I am. Here I have lived more than a quarter of a century; here my children were born, and here one of them lies buried. I know not how soon I shall see you again. A duty devolves upon me which is, perhaps, greater than that which has devolved upon any other man since the days of Washington. He never would have succeeded except for the aid of Divine Providence, upon which he at all times relied. I feel that I cannot succeed without the same Divine aid which sustained him, and in the same Almighty Being I place my reliance for support; and I hope you, my friends, will all pray that I may receive that Divine assistance, without which I cannot succeed, but with which success is certain. Again I bid you all an affectionate farewell." I reproduce this here, as but for me it would not have been preserved in the exact form in which it was delivered. It was entirely extemporized, and, knowing this, I prevailed on Mr. Lincoln, immediately after starting, to write it out for me on a "pad." I sent it over the wires from the first telegraph station. I kept the pencil manuscript for some time, but, unfortunately, lost it in my wanderings in the course of the Civil War.

Villard, *Memoirs*, 1:149.

52. This may be a misprint for J. J. S. Hall. See note below.

53. This may be a misprint for William Johnson (d. 1864), a black servant in the Lincoln home who accompanied the president-elect to Washington and acted as his barber and valet.

54. Lucien Tilton (1811–77) of Springfield, a railroad engineer who helped build the Chicago, Burlington, and Quincy line, was in charge of the train. Before his departure for Washington, Lincoln rented him the family house at Eighth and Jackson Streets.

55. Col. G. W. Gilpin of Missouri was slated to travel with the party only to Indianapolis. Janesville (Wisconsin) *Daily Gazette*, 13 February 1861. Captain G. W. Hazzard of Indiana was also a member of the military escort.

56. William S. Wallace (1802–67), husband of Mrs. Lincoln's sister Frances, was the Lincoln family physician.

57. J. J. S. Wilson was superintendent of the eastern division of the Illinois and Mississippi Telegraph Line, headquartered in Springfield.

APPENDIX: VILLARD'S COVERAGE OF THE 1858 SENATORIAL
CONTEST BETWEEN LINCOLN AND DOUGLAS

1. John Slidell (1793–1871) represented Louisiana in the U.S. Senate (1853–61).

2. John Reynolds (1788–1865) was governor of Illinois (1830–34).

3. Charles Leib (1826?–1865), who in 1856 had edited a pro-Buchanan paper (the Chicago *Democratic Bugle*), was supporting the pro-Buchanan forces opposed to Douglas in 1858. His official position was special postal inspector. Rodney O. Davis, "Dr. Charles Leib: Lincoln's Mole?" *Journal of the Abraham Lincoln Association* 24 (2003): 20–35.

4. At Douglas's instigation, Isaac Cook (1813–86) had been fired as postmaster of Chicago, but Buchanan reinstated him in 1858 to undermine Douglas's reelection bid.

5. Austin Brooks (d. 1870) was the pro-Douglas editor of the Quincy *Herald*.

6. Villard, *Memoirs*, 1:92–93.

7. Congregational minister Ichabod Codding (1810–66) was a leading abolitionist in central Illinois. At Springfield in October 1854, he helped convene a meeting of anti-slavery forces which elected Lincoln, who did not attend, to the organization's central committee.

8. Douglas falsely alleged that some radical anti-slavery resolutions passed by militant abolitionists in northern Illinois had been adopted by more moderate Republicans in central Illinois.

9. Lincoln spoke in Springfield on October 4, 1854. The next day he left for court in Tazewell County before Codding and his allies held their meeting.

10. In 1854, Douglas had introduced the Kansas-Nebraska Bill, which threw open to slavery millions of acres of land that in 1820 had been set aside for freedom as part of the 1820 Missouri Compromise.

11. Ohio Senator Salmon P. Chase had proposed an amendment to Douglas's Kansas-Nebraska Bill explicitly providing that settlers who moved to Kansas had the power to exclude slavery from the territory if they so wished.

12. Attorney Thomas J. Turner (1815–74) served as the first mayor of Freeport (1855), as a member of the U.S. House (1847–49), and as speaker of the Illinois House of Representatives (1854).

13. In fact, Trumbull's term ran through 1860, not 1858.

14. In 1855, the Illinois state legislature chose Trumbull over Lincoln to serve in the U.S. Senate. Lincoln came very close to winning, but five Democrats who opposed slavery expansion refused to vote for a former Whig like Lincoln, and so the former Democrat, Trumbull, won even though he began the balloting with only a handful of votes.

15. The contention that Lincoln and Trumbull colluded to destroy their parties, a staple of Douglas's campaign rhetoric, was false.

16. James Shields (1810–79) represented Illinois in the U.S. Senate (1849–55).

17. Villard had not been observing the political scene in Illinois for years.

18. Approximately 10,000 people attended the Ottawa debate.

19. When Robert R. Hitt, the Republican shorthand reporter working for the Chicago *Press and Tribune*, transcribed Douglas's remarks at Ottawa, he discovered that the Little Giant was quoting a radical platform adopted in 1854 at Aurora, in far northern Illinois, not the more moderate one endorsed at Springfield, in central Illinois. Douglas later claimed that he had relied on an 1856 speech by Democratic Congressman Thomas L. Harris, who cited a resolution adopted by what he termed the "first State convention of the Black Republican party in Illinois." (The day before the Ottawa debate, this resolution appeared in the *Illinois State Register*, which mistakenly alleged that it had been written by a committee

on which Lincoln had served.) In mid-August, Douglas had asked Harris where and when that convention was held. Charles H. Lanphier, editor of the *Illinois State Register*, replied for the indisposed Harris, saying that it had occurred in Springfield in October 1854. Lanphier also provided an article from the *Illinois State Register* containing the Aurora platform, which was misidentified as the Springfield platform. Republicans at the time pointed out the *Register's* gaffe, and some leading party newspapers, like the Chicago *Journal* and *Democrat*, had opposed those Aurora resolutions. When the Chicago *Press and Tribune* revealed Douglas's error, he recounted this tale and asked rhetorically at Galena on August 25, "Had I not abundant reason for supposing they *were* the Republican State platform of 1854?" This was a lame argument, for Douglas in 1856 had made the same mistake in a speech on the U.S. Senate floor, where Trumbull set him straight. In October, Douglas repeated his explanation and scornfully declared, "It will not do for him [Lincoln] to charge forgery on Charles H. Lanphier or Thomas L. Harris. No man on earth who knows these men or Lincoln could believe Lincoln on oath against either of them. . . . Any man who attempts to make such charges as Mr. Lincoln has indulged in against them, only proclaims himself a slanderer." The Chicago *Press and Tribune* scoffed at Douglas's "evasion of responsibility of his own act," which it called "mean and pitiful to the last degree, second only to the pusillanimity of trying to fasten it upon an absent friend." Clearly Douglas had not made an honest error, his protestations to the contrary notwithstanding.

20. Lincoln did have friends who offered advice and encouragement, but he was hardly their puppet.

21. In 1858, Democratic Congressman William Hayden English (1822–96) of Indiana submitted a bill offering the settlers in the Kansas Territory expedited admission to the Union and a large land grant if they would agree to approve the fraudulent, unrepresentative Lecompton Constitution of 1857. The bill passed, but the voters of the Kansas Territory rejected the offer.

22. This reply became known as the Freeport Doctrine and badly injured Douglas's standing with Southerners, who had been led to believe that the senator's "popular sovereignty" formula benefited the Slave States more than the Free States.

23. James C. Jones (1809–59) served as governor of Tennessee (1841–45) and U.S. Senator from that state (1851–57).

24. In New York, the American party proposed to fuse with the Republicans, but the attempted merger failed when the Republican state convention rejected the idea.

25. Attorney Joseph Gillespie (1809–85) of Edwardsville had served with his good friend Lincoln in the Illinois House of Representatives (1840–42) and later was a member of the Illinois State Senate (1846–58).

26. At this convention Sidney Hart was nominated for sheriff of Madison County.

INDEX

abolitionists, 340–42, 345–46

abolition of slavery, 85–87, 342–43;
Lincoln's D.C. bill, 85–87

Adams, Charles, 233–34, 261

Albany, NY, 241, 243–44, 262, 273–74,
294, 304

Albany *Evening Journal*, 63, 70, 108,
131, 176, 182, 225, 361n3, 369n110

alcoholic beverages, 78–80, 173

Allen, Cyrus M., 223–24, 231

Allen, Thomas G., 80, 364n53

American Party, 148–49, 336–39,
390n24

Anderson, Robert, 172, 195, 241, 260,
372n16

Andrews, Rufus F., 147, 370n130,
384–86n21

anti-disunion resolutions, 163, 205,
376n64

Arnold, Isaac N., 95, 365n62

Arny, William F. M., 51, 360n82

Associated Press, 197, 248, 283

attorney general: Bates as, 144–45,
159–60, 221, 223–24, 227–28; proposed candidates for, 12–13, 19, 25,
69, 89, 114, 144

Baber, R. P. L., 208–9, 211, 216, 226,
377n68

Baker, Edward D., 27–28, 57, 83, 89–
90, 92, 96, 112, 138–40, 142–43, 146,
149, 280, 356n61, 367n81; reception
for, 146; speeches by, 146–47

Baker, Edward Lewis, 118, 127, 130,
134, 302–3, 308, 368n104, 387n36

Baker, Julia Edwards, 302–3

Baltimore, MD, 241, 244, 263, 304

banking, 118; crisis in, 24, 27, 39, 42

banking laws, amendment of, 170, 179,
181, 212

Banks, Nathaniel P., 13, 159–60, 174,
351n15, 371n7

Barney, Hiram, 192–94, 197, 205,
207–9, 230, 375n44

Bascom, William T., 216, 218, 221–22,
224, 378n80

Bateman, Newton, 190, 307, 374n41,
387n50

Bates, Edward, 72, 114, 116, 121, 253,
307, 355n39; as attorney general
nominee, 144–45, 159–60, 221,
223–24, 227–28; and cabinet post,
19, 52–54, 69, 96, 114, 116, 119,
121, 137, 141, 144, 167, 181, 353n25,
355n39; speech by, 255–58; supporters of, 235; visit to Lincoln by, 108,
113–14, 116, 121, 137, 141, 151–54, 157,
159, 171–72, 254

Bell, John, 19, 44, 97, 101, 103, 105–7,
114, 119, 150, 355n40, 360n86,
365n67; letter by, 101, 103, 105–6,
365n67

Bigler, William, 178, 200, 234, 236,
238, 372n21, 380n103; compromise
plan of, 234, 236, 238–39, 261, 298

Black, Jeremiah, 12, 222, 350n3

Blair, Francis P., Jr. (Frank), 18, 72,
102, 108, 114, 116, 121, 150, 224,
229–30, 232, 355n38, 362n25

Blair, Montgomery, 224, 229

391

slave states, admission of new, 326–27, 331, 342, 345

Slidell, John, 319, 388n1

Slosson, John, 126–27, 131, 139, 368n97

Smith, Caleb B., 96, 151, 159, 212, 228, 371n142; opposition to, 151, 170, 174–75, 177, 183, 221, 224, 226–27, 231–32, 384n18; as interior secretary candidate, 159–60, 184, 187, 192–93, 211–12, 214–15, 218–20, 224, 226–27; supporters of, 159, 211–14, 218–20, 224, 226–27, 231, 246, 282, 292

Smith, H. Gale, 233–34, 261, 379–80n102

Smith, John L., 282, 384n15

South, taunting of, 103–4, 109

South Carolina, 82, 93; and disunion, 36, 64, 109, 124, 128, 361n5; and firing on Star of the West, 175–77; nullification threatened by, 134, 136; secession of, 125–28, 130, 134–35, 180, 367n93; threats to Lincoln from, 215–16

Southern: honor, 82; mob violence against Northerners, 102; unionism, 69, 73

Southerners: as cause of national upheaval, 258; rebellion by, 259; rejection of Northern compromise efforts by, 77; unacceptable demands by, 265, 284

Springfield, IL, 1, 7–8, 14–16, 43, 45, 85, 243, 358n76; illustrations of, discussed, 13, 351n16; negative comments about, 43, 45, 54, 98, 300, 306

Stark, James, 80, 364n50

Star of the West (ship), 175–77, 372n20

State House (Springfield, IL), 15, 20–21, 28, 31, 33, 40, 46, 79, 154, 359n78

State Normal School (Bloomington, IL), opening of, 231

state rights, 34–35, 267, 315, 346

Stephens, Alexander H., 61–62, 69, 360n90

Stevens, Thaddeus, 288, 384n20

St. Louis Missouri Democrat, 10, 54, 144

St. Louis Missouri Republican, 6, 17, 150, 293

St. Nicholas Hotel (Springfield, IL), 137, 141–42, 197, 280

stock market, 63, 73

stocks, decline of, 24, 27, 42

Street, H. Z., 238, 252

Sullivan, Eugene L., 207, 228, 271, 286, 298, 377n66

Sumner, Charles, 67, 191, 362n8

Sumner, Edwin V., 243, 245, 252, 262, 266, 268, 302, 304, 307, 309, 381n111, 383n3

Sumner, Edwin V., Jr., 309

Sunday School, 58, 360n88

Sweeney, Thomas W., 141, 369n114

Swett, Leonard, 79–81, 83, 140, 171, 214–15, 218–19, 227, 364n44

tariff: opponents of protective, 208, 229; protective, 230

telegrams, 56, 78, 248, 309

telegraph office, 43, 359n78

Tennessee, 381–82n117

territories, 219, 221, 223–24, 239, 259, 284; popular sovereignty for, 132–33, 140, 324, 333–34, 389nn10–11; slavery in, 117–18, 126–27, 129–30, 132, 138, 142, 161–62, 180, 288, 324, 326, 333–34, 367n89, 372n9, 389nn11–12, 390n22

Thanksgiving Day, 60, 62

Thompson, Richard W., 72, 362n17

Tilton, Lucien, 308, 388n54

MICHAEL BURLINGAME, holder of the Chancellor Naomi B. Lynn Distinguished Chair in Lincoln Studies at the University of Illinois Springfield, is the author of *Abraham Lincoln: A Life*; *The Inner World of Abraham Lincoln*; and *Lincoln and the Civil War*, as well as the editor of many collections of Lincoln primary source materials, including several that have been published by Southern Illinois University Press (*Inside Lincoln's White House: The Complete Civil War Diary of John Hay*, coedited with John R. Turner Ettlinger; *Lincoln's Journalist: John Hay's Anonymous Writings for the Press, 1860–1864*; *With Lincoln in the White House: Letters, Memoranda, and Other Writings of John G. Nicolay, 1860–1865*; *At Lincoln's Side: John Hay's Civil War Correspondence and Selected Writings*; and *Abraham Lincoln: The Observations of John G. Nicolay and John Hay*). A graduate of Princeton University and Johns Hopkins University, he taught at Connecticut College in New London for many years before joining the faculty at the University of Illinois Springfield in 2009.